Arsenic

in Assinippi

The Trial of Jennie May Eaton for the Murder of Her Husband, Rear Admiral Joseph Eaton

John F. Gallagher

Riverhaven Books

www.RiverhavenBooks.com

Arsenic in Assinippi is a historical work; all materials referenced may be found in the Bibliography and Notes sections at the end of this book.

Copyright© 2014 by John F. Gallagher

First printing.

Published in the United States by Riverhaven Books
www.RiverhavenBooks.com

ISBN: 978-1-937588-38-0

Printed in the United States of America
by Country Press, Lakeville, Massachusetts

Edited by Bob Haskell
Formatted by Stephanie Lynn Blackman
Whitman, MA

Acknowledgements

The author thanks the following individuals and organizations:

Deborah Springhetti and the late Marian Frame Hurley, Rockland, MA; Ann Marie Linnabery, Niagara County Historical Society, Lockport, NY; Olga Tsapina and Brian Moeller, Huntington Library, San Marino, CA; Robyn Christensen, Worcester Historical Museum, Worcester, MA; Jack Eckert, Francis A. Countway Library of Medicine, Boston, MA; Nancy Dooley and Lois Arnold, Norwell, MA; Melisa Seval, Washington State Library, Olympia, WA; Arlene Balkansky, Reference Specialist, Library of Congress, Washington, DC; Sheriff Joseph D. McDonald Jr. and John Birtwell, Director of Public Information and IT, Plymouth County Sheriff's Office, Plymouth, MA; Mrs. John Pendergast, Tyngsborough, MA; Sean D. Visintainer, Curator, Special Collections Librarian, Herman T. Pott National Inland Waterways Library, St. Louis Mercantile Library, University of Missouri, St. Louis, MO; Patrick Labadie, Historian, Thunder Bay National Marine Sanctuary, Alpena, MI; Marlo Broad, Special Collections, Alpena County George N. Fletcher Public Library, Alpena, MI; William Slattery, Norwell Historical Society, Norwell, MA; Robert Cowherd, Ph.D., President, New England Society of Architectural Historians, Boston, MA; Maryalice Perrin-Mohr, Archivist, New England Conservatory of Music, Boston, MA; Elizabeth M. Foster, Town Archivist, Scituate, MA; David Ball and the late John Carr, Scituate, MA; David D. Paquin, Harvey Gagnon, and Norma Taplin, Dracut Historical Society, Dracut, MA; Laura L. Schaefer, Plymouth Redevelopment Authority, Plymouth, MA; Gertrude Daneau and Lynne Rose, Norwell Cemetery Committee, Norwell, MA; Aaron Schmidt, Print Department, Boston Public Library, Boston, MA; Sean Giere, Pickering Educational Resources Library, Boston University, Boston, MA; Laura Russo, Howard Gotlieb Archival Research Center, Boston University, Boston, MA; Elizabeth Bouvier, Massachusetts Supreme Judicial Court Archives, Boston, MA; Massachusetts Archives, Boston, MA; Boston Public Library, Boston, MA; Brockton Public Library, Brockton, MA; Plymouth Public Library, Plymouth, MA; Rockland Memorial Library, Rockland, MA; Hanover Historical Society,

Hanover, MA; Abington Historical Society, Dyer Memorial Library, Abington, MA; John Harrison, Project Director, Harrison DNA Project; New England Historic Genealogical Society, Boston, MA; Massachusetts Bureau of Vital Records and Statistics, Boston, MA; Linda Derry, Site Director, Old Cahawba, Alabama Historical Commission, Selma, AL; New York Historical Society, New York, NY; U. S. Department of Veterans Affairs, Baltimore, MD; Carnegie Library of Pittsburgh, Pittsburgh, PA; McNamara-Sparrell Funeral Home, Norwell, MA; Nancy Martucci, Town Clerk, Madison, CT; Adam Baler, Assistant Clerk Magistrate, Plymouth Superior Criminal Court, Plymouth, MA; James J. Landers Jr., Milton, MA; Alan Rogers, Professor of History, Boston College; Dawn Richards.

The author thanks Stephanie Blackman of Riverhaven Books; F. Joseph Geogan II, Esq., Rockland, who generously shared his grandfather's scrapbook and photographs; Mary Jo Curtis, Holyoke, MA, and Bob Haskell, Falmouth, MA, for their assistance in editing this book; and Robert P. Harrington, who provided technical expertise on trial procedure. The author also extends his gratitude to his father, John F. Gallagher Sr., his brothers, Dan and Jim Gallagher, and his sister-in-law, Regina Lawson, who reviewed the manuscript and made valuable suggestions and corrections. He especially thanks his wife, Jeanne, for her encouragement and support.

For my wife, Jeanne

Principal Characters

Victim:
Rear Admiral Joseph Giles Eaton, U. S. Navy (retired) (1847-1913)

Accused:
Jennie May Eaton (1872-1959)

Family:
Virginia Harrison, Jennie's mother (1835-1918)
June (Ainsworth) Keyes, Jennie's daughter (1892-
Dorothy Ainsworth, Jennie's daughter (1898-1957)
Joseph Giles Eaton Jr., Jennie and Admiral Eaton's adopted son (1909-1909)
Eleanor Ainsworth Keyes, June's illegitimate child (1912-1983)
Ralph Preble Keyes, June's husband (1879-1938)
Daniel Henry Ainsworth, Jennie's first husband (1864-1937)
Mary Anne (Varnum) Eaton, Admiral Eaton's first wife (1848-1906)
Isabel Varnum Eaton, Admiral Eaton's daughter (1874-1888)
Woodrow Wilson Keyes, June's illegitimate child; abandoned in Brookline (1917-1917)

Judges:
Chief Justice John A. Aiken, trial judge, Plymouth County Superior Court (1850-1927)
Associate Justice Hugo Dubuque (superior court arraignment) (1854-1928)
Associate Justice Edward B. Pratt (inquest and district court arraignment) (1866-1934)
Judge John Gibbons, Cook County Circuit Court, Chicago (Ainsworth divorce) (1848-1917)

Prosecution:
Albert F. Barker, district attorney, Southeastern District of Massachusetts, Plymouth and Norfolk Counties (1859-1933)
Frederick G. Katzmann, assistant district attorney, Southeastern District of Massachusetts, Plymouth and Norfolk Counties (1875-1953)
George E. Adams, assistant district attorney, Southeastern District of Massachusetts, Plymouth and Norfolk Counties (1877-

Defense:
William A. Morse, former Massachusetts state senator (1863-1925)
Francis Joseph Geogan, Rockland attorney (1884-1952)
George W. Kelley, Plymouth County judge and Eaton family attorney (1851-1926)

Jury:
James A. Thomas, foreman, Middleboro (1849-1933)
J. Ellsworth Dunham, Abington (1842-1930)
Henry C. Chandler, Duxbury (1862-1934)
Charles S. Tinkham, Middleboro (1862-1942)
George E. Swift, Plymouth (1861-1934)
Seneca T. Weston, Middleboro (1856-1923)
Alfred H. Henshaw, Wareham (1885-1952)
Daniel P. Murphy, Brockton (1854-1934)
Robert W. Holmes, Carver (1885-1956)
John G. Milner, Marshfield (1881-1950)
Harry W. Bell, Whitman (1877-1937)
Eugene L. Dunham, Middleboro (1881-1931)

Investigators:
Detective John H. Scott, Massachusetts District Police (1850 -1932)
Deputy Sheriff John T. Condon, Plymouth County Sheriff's Office (1861-1935)

Physicians
Dr. Gilman J. Osgood, medical examiner, Southeastern District of Massachusetts (1863-1934)
Dr. Joseph Frame, Eaton family physician (1866-1941)
Dr. Frank G. Wheatley, associate medical examiner, Eaton autopsy (1851-1926)

Dr. William F. Whitney, pathologist, Harvard Medical School (1850-1921)

Dr. Alfred William Balch, chemist, Harvard Medical School (1873-1929)

Dr. Harry Cleverly, attending physician, Joseph Eaton Jr. death (1878-1940)

Dr. Charles H. Colgate, Eaton family physician (1874-1933)

Dr. John Winthrop Spooner, medical examiner, Joseph Eaton Jr. autopsy (1845-1910)

Dr. Frank Fremont-Smith, attending physician at Mary Anne (Varnum) Eaton's death, defense witness (1856-1922)

Dr. Jacob Wales Brown, convict doctor, defense witness (1830-1915)

Dr. Benjamin S. Blanchard, Eaton family physician in Brookline, defense witness (1856-1921)

Dr. A. Everett Austin, poison expert, defense rebuttal witness (1861-1938)

Dr. Thomas F. Carroll, expert on syphilis, prosecution witness (1873-1941)

Undertakers
Ernest H. Sparrell (1871-1946)
Joseph L. Wadsworth (1892-1966)

Court and County Jail:
Plymouth County Sheriff Henry Porter (1852-1919)
Mrs. Henry (Laura) Porter, sheriff's wife and a matron at the jail (1851-1935)
Deputy Sheriff Joseph T. Collingwood (1867-1931)
Deputy Sheriff Earl P. Blake (1873-1928)
Deputy Sheriff James W. Hurley (1848-1935)
Deputy Sheriff John H. Geary (1858-1917)
Deputy Sheriff Herman W. Tower (1871-1947)
Deputy Sheriff George Hersey (1850-1928)
Deputy Sheriff George A. Wheeler (1842-1923)
Deputy Sheriff George W. Conant (1846-1935)

Local Police
Norwell Police Chief Walter T. Osborn (1869-1925)
Norwell Constable Lloyd Frank Hammond (1860-1938)

Illustrations

Preface

Vivid silk floral arrangements adorn the façade of an imposing building located at 427 Washington Street on the outskirts of Assinippi Village in modern-day Norwell, Massachusetts. The echoes of times gone by lend charm to the location. Today, the building serves the needs of a retail business specializing in home décor, but for many years it was home to generations of families.

A century ago, the house and its occupants became the focus of national attention when authorities found retired Rear Admiral Joseph Giles Eaton dead in an upstairs bedroom, the victim of arsenic poisoning. His wife, Jennie May, fell under suspicion and, following a brief inquest, police arrested her for his murder. She stood trial at Plymouth County Superior Court where a jury of twelve men decided her fate. In a unique twist, the prosecution, not the defense, petitioned jurors to consider a verdict of not guilty by reason of insanity.

The Eaton "murder" stunned the peaceful, bucolic community. The prominence of the admiral in military and social circles, the sensational nature of the charges, and the rare indictment of a woman for a capital crime generated extensive press coverage. Boston newspapers, all in competition for increased circulation, captivated readers with dramatic headlines, photographs, diagrams and sketches, lurid details of the investigation, and trial testimony.

This book is an account of the events leading up to Admiral Eaton's death, the ensuing investigation and trial, and the tragic aftermath. Contemporary newspapers, court records, town histories, census returns, vital records, genealogical records, military records, archival manuscripts, and other documentary evidence are among the sources used to recreate this dramatic chapter in the nation's history.

Chapter 1

Just before dawn on Saturday, March 8, 1913, Dr. Joseph Frame steered his horse and carriage along Union Street, the main thoroughfare of Rockland, Massachusetts. His thick wool clothing and heavy carriage robe shielded him from the bitter cold as he made his way home from a house call.

Against a chilly gust, he gathered the collar of his overcoat and turned the corner onto Webster Street. When he reached his home at No. 39, his horse instinctively turned and proceeded up the short driveway to the barn. Frame alighted from the carriage and led the horse inside where he unhitched it, led it to a stall, covered it with a blanket, and rewarded it with fresh water and hay. A smile crossed his lips as he retrieved his medical bag from the buggy, closed the barn door, and walked the few steps to the house. He looked forward to the warmth of his hearth and a quiet breakfast with his family.

Entering the house, Frame carried his medical bag into his office and glanced at the clock on his desk. It was 5:50 a.m. At that moment, the telephone rang. When he picked up the receiver, he recognized the voice of Jennie May Eaton.

Jennie, calling from the home of her next door neighbor, Mrs. Herbert Simmons, stunned him with the news that her sixty-six-year-old husband, retired U.S. Navy Rear Admiral Joseph Eaton, was dead. Frame had examined the admiral at the Eaton home in Assinippi just the day before and prescribed medication to remedy what he had diagnosed as acute gastroenteritis. There was no indication that the admiral's condition was life-threatening.

Jennie insisted he come to her house right away. It was impossible at the present time, Dr. Frame told her, and there was little he could do for the admiral now. He said he would call on her later. When he asked her for the exact time of her husband's death, Jennie hesitated. Frame thought this odd. Given her husband's discomfort, he felt she would have been more attentive. When he pressed her for an answer, she disclosed that the admiral had died about fifty minutes earlier.

When the conversation ended, Frame telephoned Dr. Gilman Osgood of Rockland, the Plymouth County medical examiner, and told him about his visit to the Eaton home the previous day and his concern about the unexpected death. Osgood agreed to meet Frame at the Eaton house at 10:45 a.m. to examine the body.

Before she left the Simmons' house, Jennie telephoned Norwell undertaker Ernest Sparrell. At about 7:00 a.m., Sparrell and his assistant, Joseph Wadsworth, arrived at the Eaton home. Jennie met the two men at the door and escorted them upstairs to the admiral's bedroom.

Dr. Joseph Frame (*Courtesy of Deborah Springhetti and Marion Frame Hurley*)

Moments later, Mrs. Simmons came to the Eaton house with a message from Dr. Frame, asking that Sparrell call him from the Assinippi post office. Sparrell summoned Wadsworth and both, puzzled by Frame's request, immediately walked the short distance to the post office. Just as they arrived, Frame called and asked for Sparrell. When Sparrell took the phone, the doctor briefly explained his concerns about the circumstances of Admiral Eaton's death. Frame instructed Sparrell to leave the corpse untouched until Dr. Osgood could examine it and asked him to keep the matter confidential.

~

Assinippi Village lies at the crossroads of Webster and Washington streets between the towns of Norwell and Hanover, nearly twenty miles south of Boston. It acquired its name from an ancient spring in the area used by the Wampanoag Indians who called it "*Hassen Ippi*," meaning "rocky water."

Poultry farms dominated the Assinippi landscape in 1913. Poultry and egg production supplied the Boston markets and households throughout the South Shore. Dairy farms in the area produced milk, butter, and cheese, while other farms provided fruits and vegetables.

The village proper, typical of its time, contained a general store, a butcher shop, a wheelwright and blacksmith shop, a cigar shop, and a pool hall. Deliverymen rolled along the village's unpaved roads carrying their wares of dry goods, flour, sugar, and milk, and specialties like meats, fish, and clams.

Residents of both Norwell and Hanover worshipped at the Universalist Church, located on a hillock with a commanding view of the village. In Union Hall, villagers held minstrel shows, political rallies, business meetings, and an annual harvest festival that drew people from miles around.

The Brockton Street Railway operated a trolley line on Webster Street from the village to Mann's Corner in North Hanover where passengers could continue to neighboring Rockland for connections by rail or trolley to Boston or Plymouth. At Mann's Corner, passengers could also board a trolley for busy Queen Anne's Corner in Hingham and for Nantasket Beach, a popular summer resort in Hull.

The Eatons' yellow, two-and-one-half story, ten-room home stood back about a hundred feet from Washington Street on twelve acres of land in Norwell, a half mile north of the village center. The admiral and his wife purchased it from Ella Dunham in July 1907. Built in a Folk Victorian style by Franklin Jacobs in the 1860s, the first floor included a dining room, a sitting room, and a living room with an adjoining library, each with a fieldstone fireplace. Off the dining room was a large kitchen with an ample pantry. Stairways front and back led to four bedrooms and a maid's quarters on the second floor and a spacious attic above. The rooms were well appointed with "rare and handsome furniture, tasteful carpets, valuable curios from all over the world, and books in abundance, exquisite china, delicate bric-a-brac, and rare pottery from various climes," the *Boston American* reported.

Adjacent to the house was a large barn that also served as a carriage house. Behind it were the outbuildings typical of a poultry farm – chicken coops, brooder and incubator houses, a packinghouse, and a duck pond.

The inhabitants of this idyllic setting in 1913 were living a less-than-idyllic life. In their newfound grief, they were surely unaware that their

3

private, domestic squabbles were about to become a public spectacle.

Eaton home, circa 1913 (*Courtesy of Norwell Historical Society*)

Dr. Frame first visited the Eaton home in February 1911 when he treated Jennie's ailing mother, Virginia Harrison, who lived in the house with the Eaton family. Several weeks later, he returned to see Jennie who was bed-ridden with the grippe (influenza). He recommended rest, an analgesic, and a tonic that he sent to her the same afternoon. When he spoke to her the next day, he was glad to hear she was slightly improved but surprised that she had not taken the prescribed medicine because, she said, it had passed through her husband's hands and she feared he had poisoned it.

Surely she didn't mean this, Frame thought. Such an idea was preposterous, and he told her so. She was startled by his abruptness. In defense of her claim, she said the admiral was capable of such an act and, furthermore, that he was insane and belonged in an institution.

Frame dismissed her claims. His colleague, Dr. Charles Colgate of Rockland, had counseled him earlier about Jennie's irrational behavior. Colgate had been the Eatons' attending physician from 1907 until 1909 when he withdrew his medical services following the tragic death of a child the Eatons had adopted.

Jennie had publicly accused her husband of poisoning the child, and the couple had separated for a brief time. Later, when analysis confirmed that the child had died of natural causes, Jennie returned home. The couple never fully reconciled, and Jennie continued to blame her husband for the child's death. Her persistent accusations, complaints to Colgate about the admiral's mental instability, and demands for his institutionalization led the doctor to sever his relationship with the family.

One afternoon in August 1912, Frame went to the Eaton house to treat Admiral Eaton for a stomach complaint. He found the admiral sitting in a wicker chair on the front porch. As the two men conversed, Jennie emerged from the house and declared that her husband's excessive drug use had caused his illness and had affected his mind. The admiral calmly denied his wife's assertion.

Frame saw no evidence in his examination to refute the admiral's contention, nor did Eaton say or do anything to suggest a mental disorder. The doctor prescribed a remedy to quell the admiral's discomfort and told him to call if the condition persisted.

Several weeks later, Jennie appeared unannounced at Frame's office. Determined to convince the doctor that her claims about the admiral's instability were valid, she repeated the concerns she had expressed during the doctor's earlier visit to her home. She pleaded with the doctor to reexamine Admiral Eaton and have him committed, but Frame refused. He said he had seen nothing during his interaction with the admiral to suggest that he was an addict or in need of institutional care. Frame reiterated his belief that her fears were unfounded. Jennie stormed from the office in exasperation. Why could this doctor not see what was so patently obvious to her?

~

On Saturday, March 1, 1913, Frame went to Assinippi again to see Mrs. Harrison who was complaining of general weakness. He wrote her a prescription and recommended fluids and rest. As he prepared to leave, he assured Mrs. Harrison of a prompt recovery and said he saw no need to return. Admiral Eaton, however, expressed concern about his mother-in-law's frail health and implored the doctor to look in on her the next week. Frame agreed to do so.

At 8:30 a.m. on the following Friday, Frame called as promised to check on Mrs. Harrison's progress. He knocked at the side door and, after a brief wait, Jennie answered.

"How fortunate you came, Dr. Frame," she said. "The admiral has been sick all night."

Frame followed Jennie to the second floor and found Eaton lying in bed, complaining of excruciating abdominal pain. The admiral told the doctor he had been purging all night after dining on roast pork. He had become sick almost immediately after eating.

"No more roast pork for Joseph," the admiral woefully remarked to the physician.

The doctor felt that Eaton's symptoms were consistent with gastroenteritis. He gave the admiral subgalate of bismuth tablets and instructed him to continue with the bismuth and take limewater or saleratus (sodium bicarbonate) as he improved.

Frame left the admiral and went to Mrs. Harrison's room. She was still in bed, but her condition had noticeably improved. He advised her to stay in bed and continue with the medicine he had prescribed, then he departed for his office.

~

Frame arrived at the Eaton home some five hours after Jennie had called him to report the admiral's death. He met Jennie at the front door and went with her to the admiral's bedroom where he found the undertakers Sparrell and Wadsworth and Jennie's daughter, Dorothy, conversing quietly. Frame saw the admiral's corpse lying in a supine position at the edge of the bed. He noted moist vomit on the sheet in the center of the mattress.

Jennie told Frame that her husband had continued to purge throughout the night. His retching had prevented him from retaining the medicine the doctor had prescribed. She had done her best to make him comfortable and, after he had fallen asleep, she had retired to Dorothy's bedroom.

At about two thirty in the morning, Jennie's mother had roused her and Dorothy to tell them the admiral had fallen. They had gone to his room and found him sitting on the floor against the bed. They had helped him to a chair, changed his nightclothes and his bed linens, and assisted him back to bed. Jennie had then sent Dorothy back to her room, had laid down next to the admiral and quickly fallen asleep. She had awoken just before dawn and found him cold to the touch.

After hearing Jennie's report, Frame left the admiral's room and went down the hall to see Mrs. Harrison. She was still indisposed and appeared visibly shaken by the admiral's death. She told the doctor how she had heard the admiral fall from his bed during the night and how perplexed and saddened she was by his astonishing demise.

The doctor briefly examined her. Satisfied with her progress, he told her to continue with fluids and rest and started out of the room. At the threshold, he stopped abruptly, turned to Mrs. Harrison, and said, "There's something behind all this." She lay in stunned silence, bewildered by his remark. A sense of foreboding engulfed her and, as she watched the doctor depart, the frail, frightened woman wept.

Chapter 2

At ten forty-five on the morning of her husband's death, Jennie May Eaton opened the door to Dr. Gilman Osgood. He introduced himself as he stepped into the foyer, offered his condolences, and explained the purpose of his visit. After relating her husband's medical history and the events leading up to his death, Jennie led the Plymouth County medical examiner up the stairs to the admiral's bedroom.

Osgood entered the room, acknowledged Dr. Frame, Dorothy, and the two undertakers, and then approached the corpse. He pulled back the sheet covering the admiral's face and lifted his eyelids, noting the absence of a corneal reflex. He gently depressed Eaton's jaw and slowly extended his neck, confirming that rigor mortis was present but waning. After inspecting the body further, Osgood estimated that death had occurred between 3:00 and 4:00 a.m. Based on his examination and his earlier conversation with Frame, Osgood agreed that an autopsy was essential to determine how the admiral had died so unexpectedly.

He returned to his Rockland office to call an associate, Dr. Frank Wheatley of Abington, and ask if he'd assist with the procedure. Wheatley agreed and Osgood scheduled the autopsy for that afternoon at the Eaton home.

Jennie May Eaton
(*Courtesy of F. Joseph Geogan II,*

Wheatley appeared as promised at about 3:00 p.m. Jennie led him up to the admiral's chamber where Osgood and Frame and the undertakers, Sparrell and Wadsworth, were assembled. Two flickering kerosene lamps cast eerie shadows across the white sheet covering the admiral's body. A portable "cooling board," a table perforated with holes under which the undertaker placed a block of ice to slow decomposition, stood adjacent to the deathbed.

Osgood removed the sheet and noted the condition of the admiral's nightclothes. He then inspected the rest of the room, starting with the bed. He observed the admiral's false teeth and a small blue bottle on a nightstand next to the bed. He noted a bottle containing Bromo-Seltzer, a jar of arnica (skin balm), and a bottle of whiskey on a mahogany bureau. Several small boxes and envelopes contained pills, headache powders, and saleratus.

He found another bottle on a commode in the room. He asked Jennie what it contained. She rather glibly said it was poison. Osgood excused Jennie from the room.

Sparrell opened the drapes for light. Osgood removed the admiral's nightclothes and, with Frame and Wheatley, lifted the body from the bed and laid it on the cooling board in a supine position. The three doctors carefully inspected the body for evidence of exterior trauma but found none.

Osgood took a scalpel and scored the trunk of the body from shoulder to shoulder above the sternum, then from the upper margin of the sternum along the midline to the umbilicus, exposing the abdominal cavity. He bisected the sternum with a saw and separated the rib cage. He noticed the stomach was visibly inflamed and distended. He observed similar inflammation in the membranes supporting the intestines. He ran his fingers along the length of the intestines, feeling for masses.

He next made an incision from ear to ear at the back of the cadaver's skull and pulled back the scalp. He made two cuts in an elliptical pattern with a saw and removed a piece of the skull to expose the brain. He detected a slight swelling of that organ, a finding consistent with poisoning.

One by one, taking the utmost care to prevent contamination, Osgood removed the brain, heart, lungs, liver, and kidneys. He weighed the organs on a sterile scale and placed them individually in sanitized jars that he sealed and marked.

To preserve the stomach's contents, Osgood tied it off high at the esophagus and low at the duodenum, incised the connecting tissue, cut both ends, and removed it. He placed the entire unopened organ in a separate glass jar.

He collected swabs of vomit he had detected on the admiral's body and sealed the samples in a vial. He gathered the admiral's vomit-stained nightclothes and bed linens and placed them individually in paper bags.

Osgood completed the postmortem examination after three exhausting hours and surmised, preliminarily, that gastroenteritis had caused the admiral's death. He gathered his jars, vial, and paper bags containing evidence, and the bottles, pills, powders, and other evidence he found about the room, and took it all to his automobile. He would personally deliver the items to Dr. William F. Whitney, a Harvard Medical School professor and noted pathologist, later in the evening.

When he had the results of Whitney's analysis, Osgood would render a final decision on the cause of death. In the meantime, he saw no need to delay interment of the body and authorized its release to Ernest Sparrell.

After securing their surgical implements and other effects, Frame, Osgood, and Wheatley descended the stairs to the first-floor hallway where Jennie was waiting for them.

"I don't know anything about poison. I have no knowledge of poison," she exclaimed. The three doctors were taken aback by this unsolicited utterance since no one had mentioned poison in her presence.

When Jennie asked how the admiral had died, Osgood told her he had found indications of gastroenteritis but was uncertain if that was the cause. She asked if they had found any evidence of "homicidal mania" in the admiral's brain and was told such a condition would be impossible to determine through an autopsy.

Osgood, who had served as a physician for two years at Kings County Lunatic Asylum in Brooklyn, New York – an experience that afforded him a deep understanding of mental disorders – considered Jennie's words and behavior. Like Frame, he was aware of Jennie's allegations against the admiral following the much-publicized death of the couple's six-month-old child in 1909. Here was a woman who had incessantly pleaded with doctors to examine her husband for evidence of insanity. Osgood wondered if it was she, not the admiral, who was unsound.

Later the same evening, Osgood contacted Albert F. Barker, district attorney for the Southeastern District of Norfolk and Plymouth counties. A shrewd, meticulous prosecutor with a keen sense of justice and a reputation for integrity, Barker heard Osgood's report and opened a formal investigation into the death of Rear Admiral Joseph G. Eaton.

He immediately assigned Detective John H. Scott of the Massachusetts District Police (later the Massachusetts State Police) and Plymouth County Deputy Sheriff John T. Condon of Rockland to the case. Both officers appeared at the Eaton household on Sunday, March 9, to begin their probe.

Within three days, *The Boston Daily Globe* published a front-page story headlined "Secret Inquiry on Eaton Death." An accompanying article revealed that the district attorney, the medical examiner, and a member of the district police were quietly investigating the suspicious death of Admiral Eaton. The article disclosed that police had questioned Jennie Eaton, Virginia Harrison, and the admiral's stepdaughter, Dorothy Ainsworth, and conveyed rumors that the police were focused on foul play.

Officials stymied newspapermen by refusing to provide further information. One reporter, however, managed to coax a brief statement from Frame: "The whole story will come out in time. It is rather peculiar to me that the neighbors near the Eaton home, who undoubtedly know or have heard things, didn't let this come out before. I did not sign the certificate giving the cause of death; that was up to the medical examiner. It is his case. I saw the admiral last Friday. They say he died Saturday, but I've got nothing to say. I know a lot about the case, but I'm only going to say what I can reasonably say on a witness stand, if I have to. That's all I care to say."

Osgood, after repeated requests for details, told a *Globe* reporter, "I would tell you as much as I would tell anybody, and here it is. Admiral Eaton died Saturday of gastroenteritis; an autopsy was performed. As to anything else you may ask, I must refer you to District Attorney Albert F. Barker of Brockton."

The investigation into Admiral Eaton's death, in the context of his rank, his distinguished naval career, and his social status in Washington and Boston, drew national media attention. It was the era of sensationalism when newspapers published eight-column headlines above lurid, detailed stories about crimes and scandals, rich with sketches and photographs, to drive up circulation and profits.

Throngs of reporters from Boston's Newspaper Row, including the so-called "wrecking crew" of Edwin A. Grozier's *Boston Post*, the Hearst newspapers, and the Taylor family's *Boston Daily Globe*, converged on the Eaton home and the Brockton office of District Attorney Albert Barker at Plymouth County Superior Court. Wire service dispatches were copied and relayed to newspapers across the country. The Eaton case would remain front-page news for months to come.

Chapter 3

Rear Admiral Joseph Giles Eaton was born into a family of prestige and privilege. His father and mother were refined, affectionate people who instilled in their son the liberal values of their upbringing. They had high expectations for "Jodie," as they lovingly called him, and they stressed upon him, beginning at an early age, the importance of education, achievement, and public service.

Joseph's parents were from prominent New England families. His father, William, born in Plainfield, Connecticut, in 1817, was a graduate of Yale University and Harvard Law. He practiced law for several years but later abandoned the profession to devote himself to teaching. Joseph's mother, Sarah (Brazer) Eaton, was born in Groton, Massachusetts, in 1810 and graduated from Groton Academy, a school cofounded by her grandfather, James Brazer, in 1793.

Joseph Giles Eaton (*Courtesy of the Dracut Historical Society-Pauline Varnum Collection*)

The couple met at a private academy in Lowndesboro, Alabama, in 1845, and married the same year in nearby Benton. Shortly after their marriage, the couple moved fifty miles south to Greenville, Alabama, where Joseph was born on January 29, 1847.

In the fall of 1849, William and Sarah Eaton left Greenville for Cahaba, Alabama, to accept teaching positions at the Cahaba Male and Female Academy. When school recessed for the summer of 1850, William was hired to head a newly proposed academy in Cross Keys, Alabama. William and Sarah resigned from their positions at Cahaba and journeyed with Jodie ninety miles by steamboat and stagecoach to the obscure little village in Macon County.

Once settled, William's sense of optimism quickly turned to disappointment when potential benefactors hedged on their financial support for the school's construction due to "differences growing out of sectarian influence."

In December 1850, with the Cross Keys project stalled, William received an offer from Dr. Harwood Perry to oversee the administration of a new school in Harrison County, Texas. Doubtful of his future in Cross Keys and buoyed by Perry's optimism, William agreed to the proposal. He and Sarah again packed up their belongings and set off for Texas with Jodie.

The heat and humidity, a yellow fever epidemic, and an offer of employment from the Lockport Board of Education in western New York induced William and Sarah to return north in July 1854. In October, the board installed William as principal of Lockport's Union School and appointed Sarah as "preceptress." The couple enrolled seven-year-old Jodie as a pupil.

William and Sarah were charmed by Lockport's quaintness and beauty. Niagara Falls was only twenty miles to the west. They immersed themselves in the community's social, civic, and church affairs. That contentment ended abruptly when William contracted bilious pneumonia and died at age forty on March 17, 1857.

William's sudden and unexpected death left a void in ten-year-old Jodie's life. The boy was heartbroken and deeply mourned his father's passing. After the funeral in Lockport, Sarah and Jodie accompanied William's remains on a somber journey by rail to his hometown in Plainfield, Connecticut. Friends and relatives met them when they arrived and escorted William's body to the Plainfield Cemetery where they buried him in the Eaton family plot. Shortly thereafter, Sarah and Jodie departed for Lowell, Massachusetts, and the bosom of Sarah's family.

Jodie entered the Highland Military Academy in Worcester, Massachusetts, in the fall of 1857. The academy instructed students in the arts and sciences and later added military drill "to afford amusement, promote health, improve the figure and personal carriage, and make the good citizen."

Jodie excelled in his studies of United States and ancient history, philosophy, geography, oratory, reading, spelling, penmanship, composition, bookkeeping, arithmetic, algebra, Latin, and French. He placed first in his geometry class. In addition to drill, Jodie and his fellow cadets participated in "mimic warfare" on the parade grounds.

Young Mr. Eaton and his classmates had entered Highland on the eve of America's Civil War. By the time they graduated in 1862, they were eager to join the Union cause. Some went on to West Point and Annapolis. Others went directly to the front lines. Many would achieve distinction for their leadership and heroic actions. Many more would give "the last full measure of devotion" in the service of their nation.

Midshipman Joseph G. Eaton (*Courtesy of Dracut Historical Society-Pauline Varnum Collection*)

Joseph Giles Eaton was among those Highland cadets who sought the glory of battle. In 1863, due in part to his family's political influence, he won a coveted appointment to the United States Naval Academy. He was about to embark upon a long career of distinguished service, rising through the ranks until his retirement.

~

Established in 1845 at Annapolis, Maryland, the Naval School was reorganized as the United States Naval Academy in 1850. In May 1861, at the onset of war, the navy temporarily transferred the academy's staff, students, and resources from Annapolis north to Fort Adams in Newport, Rhode Island, to avoid attack and prevent the capture of the training ship USS *Constitution* by Confederate forces. (The Naval Academy returned to Annapolis after the war ended in 1865.)

Joseph G. Eaton reported to Newport on September 24, 1863, when he was sixteen, to commence a long and varied career with the U.S. Navy. The frequency and length of his assignments were typical for naval officers during his period of service. Following classroom instruction, practical training aboard the USS *Santee*, and two training cruises, Midshipman Eaton graduated from the academy on June 8, 1867. The slender but solid five-foot-nine junior officer with piercing blue eyes was assigned to sea duty until 1870 when the navy detailed him to the Darien Expedition, a geological survey in Panama commissioned to plot a route between the Atlantic and Pacific Oceans. He received promotions to ensign and master during the expedition.

He was promoted to lieutenant in March 1871 while assigned to the Boston Navy Yard. He married Mary Anne "Annie" Varnum of Dracut, Massachusetts, on July 31.

Isabel Varnum Eaton (*Courtesy of Dracut Historical Society-Pauline Varnum Collection*)

The honeymoon was short-lived. Lieutenant Eaton returned to the Darien Expedition in December 1872. That assignment lasted until August 1873 when the navy detailed him once again to the Boston Navy Yard and then to the Brooklyn Navy Yard. A return to sea duty followed his New York assignment, and he returned to Panama in December 1874.

The couple managed to find some time together between assignments. Annie gave birth to the couple's first and only child, a daughter, Isabel Varnum Eaton, in Dracut, Massachusetts, on July 8, 1874.

Eaton again shipped out in November 1875, serving aboard the *Marion*, the *Wabash*, and the *Alaska*. At the end of his tour, he served as an instructor at the Naval Academy from June 1881 to June 1884. An assignment aboard the *Nantucket* followed and, three months later, the navy transferred him to the *Ranger* as executive officer. Between October 1887 and March 1891, he served as inspector of steel for navy procurement in Pittsburgh and South Bethlehem, Pennsylvania, and Nashua, New Hampshire.

He was promoted to lieutenant commander during that assignment, but his celebration was tempered by the sudden death of his daughter on June 17, 1888. Isabel reportedly died of cerebral meningitis while living in Pittsburgh. She was buried three days later in Oakland Cemetery in Dracut, Massachusetts.

Still grieving, Lieutenant Commander Eaton reported to the USS *Monongahela* as executive officer in March 1891. He served in that capacity until June 1893 when he was appointed a member of the navy's Steel Inspection Board in Washington, DC. Two and a half years later, he received orders to command the school ship *Enterprise* at Boston. The navy promoted him to full commander on November 10, 1896.

The United States declared war on Spain on April 25, 1898, following the sinking of the battleship *Maine* in Havana Harbor on February 15. The navy placed Commander Eaton in command of the transport *Resolute,* assigned to patrol the waters between St. Nicholas Mole, Haiti, and Santiago de Cuba in search of the Spanish squadron under Admiral Pascual Cervera. *Resolute* participated in the Battle of Santiago on July 3, 1898, and, five days later, transported Spanish prisoners to the United States. Eaton's ship returned to the war zone later that month, taking part in the bombardment of Manzanillo, Cuba, on August 12.

Commander Joseph G. Eaton
(Courtesy of Dracut Historical Society-Pauline Varnum Collection)

The Treaty of Paris, signed on December 10, 1898, ended the Spanish-American War. *Resolute* performed postwar transport missions between Havana and Key West, Florida, until March 1899. From May to September of that year, the navy deployed *Resolute* as a marker vessel for the new battleship *Kearsarge's* steam trials off Portsmouth, New Hampshire.

The navy detached Eaton from *Resolute* in September 1899 to await orders. About five weeks later, he was again sent to the Boston Navy Yard where he carried out duties as the yard's ordnance officer and commanded the USS *Chesapeake.*

The navy promoted Eaton to captain in the fall of 1901, and he received orders to command the *Oregon*, in repair at Navy Yard, Puget

17

Sound, the following January. He was detached on August 29. He reported three months later to Washington where he served as a temporary member of the Naval Examining and Retiring Boards.

Captain Eaton completed his assignment with the boards on May 5, 1903, and was given command of the *Massachusetts.* He was

Rear Admiral Joseph G. Eaton, USN, with "Prince" (*Courtesy of Dracut Historical Society-Pauline Varnum Collection*)

reassigned to the Boston Navy Yard on March 2, 1905, pending his retirement on June 28.

In accordance with the Naval Personnel Act of March 3, 1899, Eaton retired as a rear admiral, the next higher grade to that held while on active duty.

Contrary to newspaper reports at the time of his death, Rear Admiral Eaton did not receive the Medal of Honor. He did, however, receive the Civil War Campaign Medal, the Spanish Campaign Medal, and the Sampson Medal with a bronze bar for his actions as commander of the *Resolute* at Santiago and Manzanillo.

Chapter 4

Less than a year after Admiral Eaton had retired from the navy, his wife, Annie, collapsed at home in Washington, DC. The admiral summoned the family physician, Dr. Frank Fremont-Smith, who found the fifty-seven-year-old woman unconscious in bed and determined that she had suffered an apoplectic stroke. In his estimation, she would not survive.

Fremont-Smith shared his prognosis with Eaton and suggested that he hire a nurse for his wife's care and comfort. The admiral recognized that necessity and asked the doctor to make arrangements.

Fremont-Smith contacted Mary Struble, director of nurse training at George Washington University Hospital, who recommended Jennie May Ainsworth. Although Ainsworth was not a registered nurse, the doctor determined that she had received sufficient training and was a competent caregiver. The day after Annie's stroke, Ainsworth accompanied Fremont-Smith to the admiral's home.

Annie's condition quickly worsened. Fremont-Smith brought in a specialist for a second opinion, but he could do little more. On February 6, 1906, six days after her collapse, Annie Eaton died. Fremont-Smith certified her official cause of death as arterial sclerosis and cerebral apoplexy.

On the same day, the admiral telegraphed the news of his wife's death to family, friends, and colleagues:

Mary Anne (Varnum) Eaton
(*Courtesy of Dracut Historical Society-
Pauline Varnum Collection*)

Annie, my wife, died just before 2 o'clock on the morning of February 6th after a stroke of cerebral apoplexy. There was no particular suffering and her end came as peaceful as a child's. She simply sighed her life out with her last breaths. I am content that I can tell you that there was no suffering during the last week of her life and that she left this world as quietly and peacefully as even her dearest friends could wish. The usual funeral services will take place in Washington at her residence at 2:00 P.M. on February 7th and she will be later interred at the family cemetery in West Dracut, Mass.

Always faithfully yours,
Admiral J. G. Eaton.

The Rev. Dr. Roland C. Smith of St. John's Episcopal Church officiated at funeral services in the Eaton home, after which Annie's body was temporarily interred at Glenwood Cemetery in Washington.

On May 11, 1906, a week after receiving permission to disinter her body, the admiral accompanied his wife's remains home to Massachusetts. Undertaker J. B. Currier met them at the train station in Lowell. A second funeral service was conducted for family and friends on May 23 at St. Anne's Episcopal Church in Lowell. Annie's remains were laid to rest at Oakland Cemetery in Dracut, next to the grave of her daughter Isabel.

In her will, dated July 1, 1889, and probated in Middlesex County Probate Court in Cambridge on April 10, 1906, Annie appointed her husband as executor of her estate but left him nothing. After setting aside funds for a monument in her memory and perpetual care for her burial lot, she bequeathed a portion of her assets, including money, silver, china, jewelry, and furniture to her dearest friends from Lowell and the navy. She bequeathed the remainder of her estate to her brother, William P. Varnum of Dracut.

~

The woman who came to care for Annie Eaton during her last days remained in the admiral's life after Annie's death. Jennie May (Harrison) Ainsworth was born on Prince Street in Alexandria, Virginia, on May 18, 1874, to George and Virginia (Smith) Harrison. Her father, a prosperous Alexandria fish merchant, was said to be warmhearted, impulsive, quick to pick a quarrel, and as quick to forgive. Her mother was described as one of the most beautiful women in Alexandria.

George Harrison suffered financial setbacks after the Civil War. He sold his business and the family home on Prince Street in 1877 and moved his family to Washington, DC, where he purchased and operated a boarding house and a small fish market. In 1879, when the house and market failed to generate the income he had anticipated, Harrison sold them, packed up his family and property, and headed north to the village of Crawford's Quarry on Presque Isle in Michigan. There, he and his wife ran a hotel that catered to sportsmen.

On September 24, 1881, Jennie's father and her oldest sister, fourteen-year-old Georgia, were crossing Lake Huron's Thunder Bay in a small skiff with two hotel guests. All four drowned when a sudden squall overturned the boat. George Harrison's body and the bodies of the two patrons were never found. Georgia's body, badly decomposed, was recovered later and was identified solely on the basis of personal items found with her remains.

After the tragedy, Jennie's mother was unable to support her family and manage the business on the lake. She returned with her children to Washington and boarded with close relatives until she secured a government job that paid wages sufficient to rent a place of her own.

In 1890, Jennie found employment as a stenographer in the government's General Land Office. There she met Daniel Henry "Harry" Ainsworth, a clerk at the nearby offices of the Interstate Commerce Commission. They courted for a short time and were married in July 1891. Jennie gave birth to Lucia June, later called June Louise, the following summer. The Ainsworths welcomed their second daughter, Dorothy Virginia, in 1897.

To Jennie's dismay, it soon became apparent that Harry was an alcoholic. His intemperance cost him successive government positions and placed great strain on the couple's marriage. Evicted from place after place for failing to pay their rent, they found themselves living day-to-day in a second-rate room at the Lincoln Hotel on 10th Street NW.

Anxious for a fresh start, Harry accepted a position as a clerk at a federal land office in Guthrie, Oklahoma, the territorial capital, at an annual salary of $1,000. He arrived in Guthrie on August 13, 1897, and sent for Jennie to join him three weeks later. When she arrived with her children in Oklahoma, Jennie found little had changed. Her husband had already accumulated more than $1,200 in debts from gambling and drinking. With the help of his father, Harry paid off his debts, resigned from his position, and returned with Jennie and his children to Washington.

Harry found work as an itinerant salesman for several publishing companies based in the Midwest. The family drifted from city to city – Minneapolis, Chicago, and St. Louis – living in cheap hotel rooms and disreputable lodging houses as Harry was summarily dismissed from one company after another. Struggling to make ends meet, the couple's woes multiplied when infantile paralysis (polio) left Dorothy partially crippled.

Frustrated with her husband and desperate to provide for her family, Jennie took up bookselling in St. Louis. Her earnings allowed her to save enough money to return to Washington and purchase a home. Harry secured and lost one more position with the government. "Deciding at last that patience was no longer a virtue," Jennie left him in 1905. She placed her two girls in a convent school in Frederick, Maryland, and enrolled at George Washington Hospital and Nurse's Home to study nursing. The hospital assigned her to care for Annie Eaton shortly thereafter.

~

When Admiral Eaton returned to Washington from Dracut, he contacted Jennie, who had been reassigned to a family in the city's Columbia Heights section, and asked her to give up her position and become his fulltime private nurse. She agreed to do so and immediately moved into his Washington home with her two daughters.

A month later, Eaton decided to leave Washington for Boston and asked Jennie to accompany him. She hesitated, telling him that she had become increasingly concerned about their living arrangements; that people would gossip. The admiral offered a solution. If she consented, they would be married with his promise to support Jennie and her children. Jennie promptly accepted the admiral's proposal.

After their marriage at Boston's Park Street Church in July 1906, they rented a cottage in Hull, a seaside community south of the city. At summer's end, they moved to Brookline, just outside Boston, where they rented a fourteen-room Georgian Revival home.

Problems developed soon after they moved to Brookline. Jennie was unhappy about the admiral's excessive drinking and his socializing at Boston's Algonquin and Army and Navy clubs. She accused him of flirting with the maids she employed in the household and discharged six of them because she believed they had encouraged his errant behavior.

When her daughter June told her that the admiral had made an inappropriate advance toward her, Jennie had heard enough. She believed the only way she could curtail the admiral's drinking was to remove him from the adverse influence of city life. She thought a farm in the country might preoccupy him and improve his mental and physical health. She contacted a realtor and, within days, made an offer on the house in Assinippi.

Chapter 5

On Monday evening, March 10, 1913, Deputy Sheriff John Condon and District Police Detective John Scott visited the Eaton home. When Jennie answered the door, Scott informed her that he and Condon were there to investigate the admiral's sudden death. She expressed surprise at their presence. She couldn't understand what it was they had to investigate. Dr. Osgood had attributed the admiral's death to natural causes.

When the officers assured her that their inquiry was strictly routine, she invited them into the sitting room. They asked Jennie to recount in detail the events of the past few days. She repeated the story she had given to Drs. Frame and Osgood and spoke of the admiral's addiction to drugs and alcohol.

When the interview concluded, Scott asked to see the admiral's bedroom. Jennie led them up to the second floor. Her mother, Virginia Harrison, met them at the top of the stairs.

State Detective John H. Scott (*Boston Traveler and Evening Herald*)

When Jennie opened the bedroom door, the two investigators were jolted by the distinctive odor of embalming fluid. Once inside, they encountered the covered body of Admiral Eaton on a stretcher in the middle of the room.

As Scott and Condon searched the drawers of a mahogany dresser, Jennie turned to speak with them and collided with the stretcher, nearly knocking it over. She seemed anxious and talked incessantly, so much so that her mother cautioned her to remain silent. Jennie ignored her mother's warning and said to Scott and Condon, "She thinks if I talk too much they will put me in Taunton (psychiatric hospital). I hope they won't. I'd rather go to jail than to an asylum with the monkeys hopping round the bars."

Satisfied that they had thoroughly searched the bedroom, the two officers thanked Jennie, bade her good night, and left for Brockton to confer with the district attorney.

On Tuesday morning, undertakers Ernest Sparrell and Joseph Wadsworth arrived to make final preparations for the viewing at the Eaton home. That afternoon, friends and neighbors paid their final respects to Rear Admiral Joseph Eaton whose body was laid out in the living room in a casket with crepe lining bearing the seal of the United States Navy.

Early on Wednesday, Sparrell pulled up to the Eaton house in a hearse followed by Wadsworth in an automobile. In the sitting room, they briefly discussed with Jennie their intended route to the cemetery in Dracut. Sparrell assured her that he had made all of the necessary arrangements for the journey. He and Wadsworth then returned to the hearse.

Jennie went back to the kitchen to finish her breakfast with her mother and daughter. As she sat at the table, her mother showed her a newspaper account about the investigation into the admiral's death. Jennie turned pale. "Oh, my God," she groaned, "I have been afraid of this. For two years I have been afraid that if anything happened to Joe they would blame me for it, and now they probably will. The admiral has been in poor health for two years. The idea of their insinuating anything is wrong."

Outside, Wadsworth and Sparrell unloaded a pine box from the hearse and carried it into the house. They placed the admiral's casket inside it, secured a lid on top, and loaded it back into the hearse. They returned to the house, gathered the many floral tributes displayed throughout the room, and placed them in the hearse next to the casket. Jennie and Dorothy came out of the house and got into the automobile with Wadsworth.

The small procession rode to the Hingham depot and waited for the northbound train to Boston's South Station. When the train arrived at 9:30 a.m., Sparrell and Wadsworth placed the pine box in the baggage car, returned to the station waiting area, and escorted Jennie and

Dorothy to the train.

Undertaker Frederick D. Carder of Lewis Jones and Son met the two women as they alighted from their car at South Station an hour later. Carder was not alone. A phalanx of photographers and reporters, informed by colleagues of the train's departure from Hingham, rushed toward mother and daughter, startling them with their cameras and a flurry of questions. Carder called to several trainmen standing on the platform for assistance. They cleared a path through the chaos and accompanied Jennie and her daughter along the platform to the station's concourse.

Once inside the cavernous, crowded station, a trainman took Carder and the two women through a door to the stationmaster's office where they found refuge. Carder gave widow and daughter a few moments to collect themselves. He then explained he had brought a hearse to carry the admiral's body to the Boston and Lowell Railroad Terminal on Causeway Street but regretted he had no transportation for them. He suggested they take the elevated cars to North Station where he would meet them. He left them while, with an assistant, he retrieved the admiral's casket and floral arrangements from the train and placed them in his horse-drawn hearse.

When Carder departed South Station, Jennie and Dorothy exited the terminal and headed for the stairs to the Boston Elevated Railway. The press followed, snapping photos and barking questions over the din of trains passing above as the women, shielding their faces, made their way to the stairway. Dorothy struggled to keep up with her mother as she hurried along Atlantic Avenue in the cold shadows of the pale green steel structures supporting the tracks. Shrieking brakes pierced the air and sparks showered down from above as the bright red and gray trains rumbled to and from the station.

Within minutes after they reached the top of the stairs, a shuttle approached from North Station and pulled to a stop beside the station platform. As passengers disembarked from the rear of the wooden, open-platform gate car, Jennie and Dorothy boarded in the front. The newsmen got on behind them and walked to the rear of the car as the train made its way along the waterfront to North Station.

The two women exited their car at North Station and descended the stairs to the station concourse with the press close behind. On the concourse, they met Jennie's other daughter, June, who had arrived earlier aboard a trolley from Dorchester. The newsmen temporarily kept their distance as the three women ate a light lunch on a station bench.

June Ainsworth had married Ralph Preble Keyes, a bank clerk, on November 26, 1912. Their wedding had been an elaborate affair with services at the Hotel Vendome in Boston's Back Bay and a reception at the Algonquin Club on Commonwealth Avenue. June and Ralph had lived briefly with his family in Somerville but later took an apartment in Dorchester.

During lunch, June complained to her mother of a bad cold and told her she didn't feel well enough to make the trip to Dracut. Although she wanted June to accompany them, Jennie didn't insist.

Carder procured a freight cart, loaded the casket and flowers on it, and wheeled it onto the baggage car of the Lowell-bound train. He returned to the concourse where Jennie and Dorothy were parting company with June and escorted them to the station platform where they boarded the train. Several newsmen hustled aboard seconds before the local departed the station at 11:30 a.m.

June Ainsworth
(Courtesy of F. Joseph Geogan II, Esq.,)

When the train pulled into the Merrimack Street depot in Lowell, local undertaker W. F. Saunders and several of his assistants were waiting. Carder conferred with Saunders and directed him to the baggage car where Saunders' men retrieved the casket and flowers and placed them in another horse-drawn hearse. Carder, Jennie, and Dorothy boarded a curtained carriage that Saunders had supplied and, after everyone was comfortably seated, the cortege departed for Oakland Cemetery in Dracut for the interment. The press followed the somber group in hired hacks.

It was a clear, beautiful day as the procession made the five-mile journey along Merrimack Street, across the Pawtucketville Bridge to

Mammoth Road, and into Dracut and the old cemetery. As the party approached the lane leading to the cemetery, a caretaker met them and directed them to the graveyard's northeast corner.

Just inside a wrought iron gate set into a stone wall were the four closely-set graves of Admiral Eaton's first wife, Annie; his daughter, Isabel; and Annie's parents, William and Mary Varnum. A fifth grave now lay open, ready for the admiral's remains. Joseph Varnum, the admiral's nephew, waited solemnly at the gravesite.

The absence of a military contingent was conspicuous. Reporters thought this odd given the admiral's rank and distinguished service record. Even more peculiar was the absence of an American flag over the admiral's casket.

A *Lowell Sun* reporter later contacted Captain DeWitt Coffman, commandant of the Boston Navy Yard, and asked why the navy had neglected to send an honor guard. The captain explained that, although it was customary for the navy to provide military honors at an officer's burial, it was not obligatory.

"If a request had been made, I should have sent a detail of men to the funeral of Admiral Eaton," Coffman responded. "But I received no such request. Although we have very much less than our usual complement of Marines and bluejackets here at the navy yard now, I think I could have got together a small detail for the purpose. Lowell is quite far away, you know, and we would not send any men such a distance unless we received a special request."

Undertaker Saunders alighted from the hearse and, with the assistance of Carder and two newspapermen, removed the pine box and proceeded toward the burial site. As they approached, the undertaker realized the cemetery caretaker had not supplied the straps needed to lower the casket into the grave. The men lowered the box onto the grass while Saunders returned to the hearse. He removed the reins from his horses to substitute for the missing straps and placed them alongside the coffin.

Returning to the hearse, he retrieved the floral displays, carefully placing them on black broadcloth spread out on the opposite side of the grave. Saunders then pried open the top of the pine box, opened the lid of the casket, and exposed the face of the dead naval officer in the sunlight.

Carder assisted Jennie and Dorothy from their carriage and escorted them to the graveside. Jennie remained stoic, much as she had been during the journey from the Lowell station to the cemetery. Dorothy, however, wept openly. The two women gazed upon the admiral's face for the last time. Barely a word was spoken – not a prayer, an anecdote, or a tribute – before Saunders closed the casket's lid and the pallbearers unceremoniously lowered the admiral's remains into the grave.

Joseph Varnum approached Jennie, whom he had never met, as she made her way back to the undertaker's carriage.

"His death was rather sudden, wasn't it?" he asked the widow.

"Well," said Jennie, "he had been ailing ever since we moved to Norwell a few years ago. He ate some pork that didn't agree with him."

"Don't say anything about that here," Dorothy abruptly admonished her mother out of respect for her stepfather.

Varnum accompanied mother and daughter to the carriage. Just before the two women got on, a tearful Dorothy approached Carder and pleaded with him to allow her to take a lock of hair from the admiral's head. Carder acquiesced. He, Varnum, and several others raised the casket to the surface, and Carder opened the lid.

"It didn't seem just the right thing to do," Varnum later said, "but we were obliged to use a pocket knife to cut the locks which the daughter so much wanted. This done, the body was again lowered into the grave."

Dorothy, remembrance in hand, boarded the carriage and, with her mother, returned to the Lowell depot for the train ride back to Boston. The reporters who had accompanied them to the cemetery were on board and tried once again to elicit a statement from Jennie. She was terse with them. "I cannot talk about the subject. I am burying my husband, and I think you ought to let me alone."

Another throng of reporters confronted the two women when they alighted from their car at North Station. Jennie took Dorothy by the hand, elbowing her way through them, and boarded the elevated train to South Station where they caught the 4:29 p.m. train to Hingham. Still hounded by newsmen, mother and daughter briefly shopped in a dry goods store in Hingham. They then took the trolley back to Assinippi.

Chapter 6

Earl MacQuarrie Heartz was born at the Talitha Cumi Home, a hospital and shelter for unwed mothers in Boston's South End. On March 22, 1909, Joseph and Jennie Eaton filed a petition at Suffolk County Probate Court to adopt the seven-week-old boy. After a hearing at probate court on April 2, Judge Elijah George granted their petition and authorized a name change from Earl MacQuarrie Heartz to Joseph Giles Eaton Jr.

The Eatons were anxious to keep the boy's origins confidential. Concealing the child's adoption, they told friends and neighbors that Jennie had conceived and borne the child, delivering on March 25. The couple formally announced the child's birth in a notice published in the weekly *Rockland Standard and Plymouth County Advertiser* on April 16, 1909: "In Assinippi, March 25, to Admiral and Mrs. J. G. Eaton, a son." These developments struck villagers as odd because there had been no apparent change in Jennie's physical condition nor had the Eatons mentioned they were expecting.

That summer, the Eatons rented Isis, an oceanfront cottage in the Sand Hills section of Scituate. The admiral, Jennie, June, and Dorothy looked forward to a summer of fun and sunshine at the beach with the newest addition to the family.

During the hot and humid afternoon of August 21, six-month-old Joseph fell ill. At half past two, Jennie sent June to Dr. Harry Cleverly's office in Scituate Harbor village, about three-quarters of a mile from the cottage. After hearing the description of the symptoms, Dr. Cleverly gave June a tonic to settle the child's stomach. At 3:45 p.m., June returned to the doctor saying she had dropped the first bottle and spilled all of its contents. Cleverly gave June another bottle and cautioned her to take greater care.

Admiral and Jennie Eaton arrived at Cleverly's office with Joseph fifteen minutes later. The physician examined him and diagnosed cholera infantum, an acute and potentially fatal intestinal disturbance common in infants and young children during the summer months. He advised the couple to forego the tonic he had given June and gave them another prescription.

After stopping at the pharmacy, the admiral and his wife returned with Joseph to Isis where they administered the prescribed medication and did what they could to make him comfortable. The family kept a vigil at his bedside throughout the afternoon and into the evening, but Joseph's condition never improved. By nine o'clock, he was dead.

Jennie frantically summoned Cleverly, who arrived at the cottage at 9:30 p.m. He was barely through the door when Jennie declared that the admiral had poisoned the child and demanded an autopsy to confirm her accusation. Cleverly, stunned by her comments, tried to calm her, but she would have none of it.

The astonished doctor quickly contacted the medical examiner, Dr. John Winthrop Spooner of Hingham, and asked him to come to the cottage. When the medical examiner arrived, Cleverly advised him of his earlier diagnosis as well as Jennie's allegations. Cleverly did not immediately suspect foul play, nor did Spooner. But because of Jennie's repeated, strident demands, the two doctors deemed it prudent to proceed with a postmortem examination.

The doctors completed the autopsy that evening, finding nothing to indicate the child had died from unnatural causes. However, they withheld final certification of the cause of death pending forensic examination of the child's stomach and its contents. Spooner delivered the organ to Dr. Whitney at Harvard Medical School the next day for analysis.

An agonizing atmosphere of tension and hostility pervaded the Isis cottage after Cleverly and Spooner left with Joseph's body. Jennie refused to speak to her husband. He pleaded with her to return with him to Assinippi and allow them time to resolve their differences. At first his wife refused to go, but she relented when Eaton persisted. They packed up a few things and, with Dorothy and June, drove back to Assinippi in icy silence. The next morning, with nothing resolved, Jennie and her two daughters returned to Isis cottage without the admiral.

Jennie's private accusations against her husband soon became public. An anonymous source told the newspapers about the questionable death, and reporters raced to both the Assinippi home and the cottage at Sand Hills to cover the story.

Jennie gave them an earful at the cottage. "The admiral has been very good to me, and I have been good to him. He loves me, I know, but I never really knew him until the last year. Six months ago I determined to have Dr. Colgate of Rockland examine him, but the admiral's estate was so tangled and the doctor so busy that I kept putting it off. No matter what the result of the autopsy, I will have him examined. I would not dare now to live with him. I am positive that the baby was poisoned.

"I believed so from the outset, and that is why I was so insistent with Dr. Spooner when I asked him to perform the autopsy, which resulted in the infant's stomach being forwarded to Harvard medical experts for analysis."

She implied that the admiral, on other occasions, had tried to poison her and her daughter June.

"This is not the first chapter," she continued. "A cup of tea that was brought me was accidentally tipped over before I tasted it; in the bottom there were three lozenges. My daughter found her perfumery filled with foreign liquid. She has found tooth powder tampered with. Now the baby has suddenly died."

In hopes of soliciting a comment from the admiral about his wife's allegations, reporters went to the Assinippi farm where they found the retired sailor in isolated grief. When reporters told him what his wife was alleging, Eaton said, "My wife and the girl, June, have accused me of attempting to poison them so many times that the accusation after a while lost its weight and became merely a joke – and then the joke became a tragedy. Her [Jennie's] latest accusations are cruel, but they have lost their power to hurt. As for June, the little girl believes she has reasons. I think she believed that reasons existed for all the charges she has made against me during the last three years. So many times has she charged me with attempting to take her life that after a time little Dorothy began to joke with me about it. 'Look,' she would cry, running up to me and crooking her little finger when June would meet with some trifling mishap, 'June has been poisoned.' "

The admiral related how one day he, his wife, and the two girls had spent a day at Nantasket Beach in Hull. After returning home, June had accused him again of trying to poison her.

"As for June, I have tried to care for her as if she was my own daughter. That has angered her. She is an imaginative child and a great reader of romantic fiction. Not very long ago we all went to Nantasket, and my wife asked me to buy some sodas. While they sat at a table, I went to the fountain. I went over and brought four glasses, two at a time. After we got home, June declared that I had put poison in the soda. I asked her why she thought so. She told me that her head ached. That made Dorothy laugh. As a matter of fact, June had eaten ice cream and soda and candy and had gone in bathing. That would make almost anyone's head ache.

"June was always a harum-scarum sort of girl," Eaton continued. "She was full of life and animation. Once it became necessary for me to enjoin a sixty-year-old man from paying her attentions. She did not like me for that. One day it was necessary to send her to her room to avoid the keeping of an appointment. She made an excuse to go into another room and there took a dose of wood alcohol. We discovered her in time and administered emetics, and soon she was all right."

The admiral vehemently denied any involvement in the child's death and deemed preposterous any suggestion that he had poisoned him.

"The little boy is dead, and I had hoped that he would live," he lamented. "I had hoped to see him enter the navy, and I had wanted many other things. But if my baby has been poisoned, there is a thought that comes to me – so horrible that I dare not speak of it – not in connection with any of my household – but if I thought such people lived…"

In response to Jennie's accusation that he had tried to poison her tea, the admiral said, "My wife declares that she one time found poison tablets in her tea. I remember the incident well. She had been complaining of a sore throat, and I gave her several chlorate of potash tablets. A little later she accused me of having tried to poison her. I insisted on calling in a physician. When he came, I told him of the circumstances and asked Jennie to show him the tablets. She would not do so but continued to repeat that an effort had been made to poison her, that she knew the tablets were poison. Then the physician interrupted. 'Mrs. Eaton,' he said, 'that is ridiculous. You do not know what the tablets contain. Let me examine them, and I will tell you.' But she refused. Why, she must have believed that I carried in my pockets a perfect arsenal of East Indian drugs. It is absurd. One may read of such things, but one never witnesses them in real life.

"We have lived in Scituate for two years," Eaton went on. "During that time I have not purchased a drop of medicine, not to speak of poison. Does the charge that I attempted to poison her and June by means of poisoned perfumery or tooth powder sound sensible? It is absurd. As for the boy, he was my own child, my only son. For days at a time little Dorothy and I have taken care of him during the absence of his mother and June. Once they were away for fourteen days, and Dorothy and I washed him and fed him and dressed him."

Speaking with another reporter who had asked about Jennie's charges of poisoning, the admiral stated, "The story is ridiculous. Mrs. Eaton is highly nervous, and for some time past has been possessed of an idea that someone was trying to poison her. She is wrought up to a highly nervous state. I believe my son died a natural death from cholera infantum. I believe, also, that I felt his death far more keenly than did other members of the family. The boy is buried in the local cemetery. His mother did not even wait for the funeral but went back to Scituate on Sunday (to attend a social affair), and I had to bear the grief alone when the little body was lowered to its final resting place yesterday afternoon. My grief over the loss of my son is intensified by the action of my wife. Her accusations will probably result in an action for divorce, for I feel that I cannot peacefully live with her again after what she has said."

Reporters had questions regarding the child's natural parentage. Rumors swirled among neighbors in Assinippi Village about the boy being adopted by the Eatons. Reporters went to the cottage at Sand Hills on Thursday evening, August 26, after discovering records at Suffolk County Probate Court that confirmed their suspicions that the Eatons had adopted the child. A *Boston Daily Globe* reporter confronted Jennie with a copy of the adoption papers and pushed her to explain why she and the admiral had pretended the child was their own.

As soon as she saw the court documents, Jennie realized she could no longer guard the secret of the boy's adoption.

"Although we had two daughters at home, June, age sixteen [sic], and Dorothy, age twelve, the latter devotedly attached to the admiral," she said, "I believed that by bringing an infant child into the house, it would tend to restore the admiral to his former condition, for you must understand he had been giving evidence of having a disordered mind on at least one subject. I know there has been a suspicion created by the utterances of the admiral, but both June and myself know that we have undeniable proof which will show that the child came into this household as I have stated, and the proof is easily obtainable. It was only natural that we pretended that the child was the son of the admiral, and that fact appeared to give him unbounded satisfaction.

"I did not adopt the child," she continued, "until we had made a series of investigations regarding the paternity of the infant, in which we were told by Miss Marshall, in charge of Dr. Plummer's institution (Talitha Cumi Home) at 204 Brookline Street, Boston, that the mother was an educated woman of refined manners and that the father was from a sturdy family, both hailing from Nova Scotia. The introduction to the mother and the gentle, well-bred manner she exhibited during the interviews convinced me that the child, with proper training, could be brought up to be a credit to the admiral and myself, and for that reason I concealed the story of the child's birth and gave it out to the world that he was the admiral's son in fact."

During the interview, Jennie again brought up her displeasure with the admiral's transgressions and her suspicions about his involvement in the baby's death. Young Dorothy, who was present in the room, contradicted her mother's statements and defended the admiral. Jennie eventually silenced her and sent her from the room. After Dorothy left, Jennie turned to the reporter and said, "Dorothy knows nothing of the world and sees the admiral through a good child's eyes, and for that reason there is no reasoning with her. As far as living with the admiral again, that is entirely out of the question, as I would be afraid."

The next day, Friday, August 27, reporters sought out Admiral Eaton at the Assinippi farm for a statement about his child's adoption.

"It is true that the boy was our adopted son," he said. "I loved him dearly. I wanted him to grow up fine and strong and become a naval officer. Now it is all over. It is pitiful, pitiful."

Asked about Jennie's accusation against him, he added, "One night after twelve o'clock, the child was brought to our house here by a nurse, and such secrecy was maintained that everyone thought it was our child. It was just previous to the adoption of the child that I think

35

Mrs. Eaton, while lying sick in bed, allowed her daughter June, whom she idolized, to put thoughts into her head which led to her charging me with poisoning the baby. It was about that time that June's mind seemed to dwell upon poison all of the time."

Many questions flooded the reporters' minds. Who initiated the adoption? Were the admiral's wife and his stepdaughter June concerned about the child inheriting the admiral's possessions upon his death? Did Jennie, at thirty-seven years old and with two daughters, who were seventeen and twelve, really want to start another family?

As the admiral elaborated further about the circumstances of the adoption, it became clear that it was he who had most wanted the child.

"I only wanted a son; I never had one. My only child, a daughter by my first wife, died twenty years ago. My heart longed for a boy, whom I could train from infancy to manhood."

The admiral told the reporters that he and his wife had mutually agreed to the adoption and had purposely deceived not only friends and neighbors but those living in their own household about the child's origins.

"The thought that was paramount in my mind," Eaton continued, "was that no one except those legally in the secret service (adoption agency) should ever know the son was mine only by adoption. I am passionately fond of children, my heart was lonely, and I was prepared to welcome the adopted child as if he were really my own. Neither the neighbors, nor the children with whom he would grow up, nor my stepdaughters, nor the boy himself should ever know he was not my own flesh and blood. He was to be my son and heir, dear to my heart, and the secret of his birth was to lie buried in the court records."

The retired naval officer explained how he and his wife had found the child and legally adopted him. He offered the natural mother's name and described how he and his wife had gone to great lengths to determine the mother's background and whether she had been from a "good, healthy family."

When they received final legal approval for the adoption, the couple arranged to have the child brought to their home under the cover of darkness. On the night of March 25, 1909, two women from the Talitha Cumi Home brought the infant boy by train from Boston to the Hingham depot. The admiral had arranged to have a closed carriage meet them and transport the child to Assinippi. The baby was quietly brought into the house and was soon presented to June and Dorothy as their stepbrother. As part of the deception, Jennie remained in her bedroom for ten to twelve days, as if recovering from the birth. The Eatons introduced the boy to neighbors later on and placed the announcement of his birth in the local newspaper.

The admiral told reporters he and his wife had deceived everyone – except for Dorothy, who was suspicious.

"Many times she questioned me," Eaton related, "but I laughed and 'tacked,' as a sailor says; still her doubts remained, but she kept her own counsel."

His fondness for his stepdaughter became even more apparent when he said, "Dorothy, my girl and my chum, grew fond of the child and 'mothered' it in a way that was sweet to me. Dorothy and I used to talk over my plans for the baby's future. She never showed the slightest sign of jealousy. We built beautiful castles in the air. Dorothy is mature beyond her years and could enter into my hopes and plans for the boy with full sympathy."

The admiral's glow as he spoke of Dorothy quickly faded as he turned once again to his grief.

"Well, the dream is ended now," he said. "Over a little grave in the cemetery at Assinippi is written 'Finish' to my fond hopes." Now estranged from his wife and stepdaughters, he sadly reflected, "I am here all alone in my old age. There isn't another human being in the house. My heart, too, is as empty as my hearth is."

Dorothy Ainsworth
(*Courtesy of*
F. Joseph Geogan II, Esq.)

Later that evening, Jennie, June, and Dorothy drove from Sand Hills to their home in Assinippi and rang the doorbell. But the admiral, who was inside with a reporter, would not answer. Jennie called to him at several windows, but he ignored her. Finally, she gave up, returned to her car, and drove back to Sand Hills.

"If it was not for little Dorothy, if it was not for the love that I bear this child, all would have been ended between Mrs. Eaton and myself long ago,"

Eaton told the reporter. He said he had done everything possible to save the marriage, but given his wife's latest accusation he felt he had no choice but to separate from her and consult legal counsel to institute divorce proceedings against her.

When he first met Jennie, the admiral mistakenly believed she was a widow. It was not until he met her in Chicago during her divorce proceedings that he realized her husband, Daniel Ainsworth, was still alive and that the couple was still legally married.

"Throughout my entire acquaintance with her, until just before my marriage to her, I believed she was a widow, and that her husband had been dead for some time," he explained. "At that time, however, she was not actually divorced from her husband. It was not until just before my marriage that I learned she had a husband. Then she told me that her husband was alive, and that she had just obtained a divorce from him on the grounds of drunkenness and desertion. During the time that I paid attention to her, knowing her straitened circumstances, though thinking that her husband was dead, I helped toward the support of herself and children, giving her money, though at the time I did not know for what purpose she was using it. Later, after the marriage, I learned inadvertently that I had been paying for the divorce proceedings which she had instituted against her husband. I married her because I had said I would and was too much of a gentleman to withdraw my promise."

Jennie later addressed the admiral's remarks about the circumstances preceding their marriage. She said the admiral did know she was married and that he had accompanied her to Chicago to finalize her divorce. She also denied that the admiral had financed the legal costs of the divorce.

"He also knew and met my children, and, after knowing all about me, lived in the house where I nursed him as well as his wife," Jennie countered. "The admiral at this time was under the influence of liquor all the time and was quite as much care as his dear wife. I cured all that and, after getting him back to health and free from intoxication, he went with me and got my divorce, which was procured for me by my family, and then and not until then were we married. So the admiral is off when he states he met me in Chicago and thought me a widow."

Jennie secured counsel to represent her after learning of the admiral's threat to sue for divorce. She was overheard saying she intended to have her husband examined for insanity, regardless of the results of Dr. Whitney's examination of the child's remains.

Chapter 7

Dr. Charles Colgate of Rockland met Jennie for the first time in September 1908 when she came to his office seeking medical advice about her husband. She visited him again in February 1909 and asked for his help in having her husband committed to a hospital for the insane. After listening to Mrs. Eaton's complaint, the doctor agreed to examine the admiral and went to the Eaton home where, after analysis, he found no evidence of mental instability in Joseph Eaton.

Jennie was piqued when Colgate told her of his findings. Surely the doctor had overlooked something that would confirm her own observations. But the doctor insisted the admiral was sane. She later wrote an angry letter to Colgate, admonishing him for his obvious indifference:

I came to you for advice, for it is the brain of a world-renowned man who is going. We do not have family rows or quarrels. My husband loves his children and me as much as a poor diseased brain can. I gave up an elegant home in Brookline and three house maids' society to bring this poor deluded man out into the country to regain his health, which I thought was caused by drinking to excess and too much money and social obligations, etc. After hard, long, earnest, conscientious work, I proved to myself the trouble is of deeper origin than whiskey and wear and tear of city life – and its follies – and I am from a fine old family and a lady accustomed to the best class of society all my life. A woman who has been entertained and entertained the aristocratic people of the United States, and have [sic] always had the reputation of being a Christian woman and a lady by all that the word 'lady' implies, to be treated in the very uncalled-for manner of this afternoon to me is unpardonable.

Respectfully,
Mrs. Joseph G. Eaton

In a postscript she wrote:

> *Dear Dr. Colgate – Please remember in all this very dreadful affair, which is at times a nightmare to me in all its horribleness, that I am a woman now at the best time of my life, and by proving this to be the truth I practically beggar myself and lose hundreds, if not thousands, and I will have to face the world alone and without money or friends (for without money we have few), and possibly lots of talk, and three children. So you must see it is to my financial interests to live with him if it is possible.*

After the baby died, Jennie wrote another letter to Colgate and chided him for not heeding her warnings about the admiral.

> *I hold you morally responsible for the death of my boy. Had you examined the admiral for his sanity, it would have saved the life of my dear little boy.*

~

When the rental term for the Sand Hills cottage ended on September 1, Jennie and her two daughters returned home to Assinippi. Within days, a reporter came to the door and asked the admiral if Mrs. Eaton's return meant that they had reconciled.

The admiral was reluctant to answer. The child's death and the revelation about his adoption, his wife's public charges, and his own statements to the press had disrupted and embarrassed his family. He was determined to bring the entire matter to an end, and he asked the reporter to give him and his wife time to settle their dispute in privacy. He declined to make any further statement because, "too much about their family differences had already been said."

Inside the home, dissension and acrimony continued unabated. Jennie still firmly believed the admiral had poisoned their child and fully expected Dr. Whitney's examination to prove the presence of poison in the child's organs. On August 29, three days before she returned to Assinippi from Scituate, she delivered to Dr. Spooner the medicine that had been given to her child before his death and several jars of baby food, the contents of which, she believed, the admiral had tainted with poison. She asked Spooner to analyze the food and medicine and insisted he'd find the toxin used to kill her child. Spooner forwarded the items to Whitney for evaluation.

Impatient with Whitney and anxious for validation, Jennie wrote to him from Assinippi on September 11, 1909. She pleaded with the pathologist for a prompt report on his analysis and again accused her "dangerous, insane" husband of poisoning the child and trying to poison her.

Professor Whitney:

My Dear Sir – Will you kindly inform me how much longer it will be before you can state exactly what my dear, little, healthy, strong child died from? I am here alone in this isolated place with my husband, Admiral J. G. Eaton, whom I know to be a dangerous, insane man. His position in life seems to make it impossible for me to be treated like mere civilians would be treated, and my heart and pity go out to this man (who is so clever that he fools the world at large), but not me. He speaks at times to me in a rambling sort of way and inferred that the back bowels would contain the poison 'if any.' Now please search for foreign poisons, as he has talked to me freely about foreign poisons, and he has all the cleverness of a maniac and cunning enough to use one that would be hard to detect. He has been planning 'my death' all day today, and yet I am powerless, and I trust on the finding of poison to have him examined for insanity and taken care of. I don't want his money (salary); he has no money, but I do want the State to take charge of that dear little life and him, for he is mad. Please let me hear from you at an early date, and search for a cholera subtle poison.

Respectfully,
Mrs. J. M. Eaton.

In a postscript, Jennie insisted on a "thorough examination" of the food and medicine she had submitted to Spooner and asked him to send his response to her at the Rockland post office, *As I fear [the] letter would not reach me if it came here to Assinippi...*

Whitney sent his analysis to Spooner on September 25, 1909. Whitney confirmed that the Eaton child had died not from poisoning but from natural causes. When Spooner informed the Eatons of Whitney's finding, the admiral was not surprised, but Jennie remained unconvinced. She still believed the pathologist would find poison in the medicine and baby food she had submitted. Whitney's analysis of these items later proved negative for the presence of poison and, on October 4, 1909, Spooner certified the child's cause of death as acute gastritis.

There was much talk in the Assinippi neighborhood about the mystery surrounding the adopted child's death. Most people were appalled at Jennie's accusations against the admiral and the public spectacle that had ensued. When newspapers reported the admiral's son had died of natural causes, many of the villagers spurned her. For her to think that her husband was capable of murdering his own son was outrageous in the minds of those who knew and respected the old sailor.

Adding fuel to the fire was the sudden appearance of Jennie's former husband, Harry Ainsworth, during her estrangement from the admiral. Newspapers reported that Ainsworth had visited the Isis cottage in Scituate and the farm at Assinippi during the investigation into the baby's death. When confronted by reporters as to why he was present, Ainsworth stated he was there on the advice of his attorney to protect June and Dorothy.

~

Dissatisfied with Whitney's conclusion, Jennie provided a sample of the medicine given to the child on the day of his death to Dr. Henry Spaulding, a noted Hingham physician. She expected to challenge Whitney's findings and Spooner's certification with Spaulding's results which she was sure would prove to all that her suspicions had been correct. When Spaulding's analysis later corroborated Whitney's findings, Jennie suspected a conspiracy among the medical men to protect the reputation and stature of the admiral. She would always believe he had poisoned the child.

A *Washington Herald* correspondent sought a comment on the scandal from Jennie's mother at her home on G Street NW in Washington. Mrs. Harrison had just returned from a two-week stay in Atlantic City where she had first learned about her daughter's

43

accusations in the newspapers. She immediately rushed to the admiral's defense.

"Personally, I believe Admiral Eaton to be blameless," she said. "I know he is as kind and noble a man as ever lived. He has always been like a brother to me, and if he had been a brother, I could not have cared for him more than I do. He is incapable of administering poison to a child."

Mrs. Harrison recognized her daughter's unstable behavior. She had first noticed Jennie's mood swings when she had moved to Brookline to live with the admiral and her daughter. She believed the change in Jennie's temperament was the direct result of her first husband's abusive treatment. After her divorce from Ainsworth, Jennie had developed "an extreme nervousness" and exhibited erratic behavior. She believed her daughter was "momentarily unstrung" when she made the poisoning charges against the admiral, and Mrs. Harrison explained to the reporter how she had written to Admiral Eaton from Atlantic City, "asking him to do what he could to quiet his wife."

Mrs. Harrison was stunned when she read about the adoption of the now-deceased child. Jennie had given her every reason to believe the child was her own. "The manner in which she deceived even me regarding the adoption of the child," she said, "shows me that she is inclined to erratic spells."

The reporter asked Mrs. Harrison if she would testify in support of Admiral Eaton if the case resulted in court action.

"If I could aid him, I would," she replied, "for he is as much to me as any of my blood relatives. I know he is suffering a terrible injustice. The publicity given this affair and the claims of his wife have hurt him more than anyone knows, and, withal, he is as innocent as you or I."

Sometime after her interview with the *Herald* reporter, Mrs. Harrison left Washington to join her daughter's family in Assinippi. Her attempts to mediate reconciliation between her daughter and the admiral failed. Jennie refused to believe the admiral was not responsible for the baby's death, and so did June.

In September, June entered the New England Conservatory of Music in Boston to study voice and piano. During her first year, she commuted to school by train from East Braintree where she boarded at a home on Brookside Road.

June later left Braintree and joined her mother in Weymouth Landing where Jennie had taken a room at the home of Mrs. Frank Floyd.

The New York Times asked Mrs. Floyd in 1913 to comment on her impressions of the two women during their stay.

"June Ainsworth advertised for a room, and I answered the advertisement," Floyd recalled. "My husband did not want to take the girl in, but I did so. I did not see a great deal of her, but when I did sit with them (June and her mother) in the parlor, I invariably left the room because Mrs. Eaton insisted on talking about her husband. She often told me about her first husband and the fine time she had in Washington with him, and complained bitterly of the admiral's smallness regarding money matters. I gave June notice to leave my house because the manner in which she practiced her vocal lesson made me nervous."

When asked if she had ever met Admiral Eaton, Floyd replied, "My husband visited at Assinippi and went fishing with the admiral. He found him to be a most delightful companion. I have not seen either of the women since they left my house, except on one occasion, when I saw June."

Young Dorothy and Mrs. Harrison had remained with the admiral after June and her mother had left. Neither one believed he had anything to do with the baby's demise. Nor did they believe he had ever placed Jennie or June in peril.

~

By the summer of 1912, Jennie had had enough of the gossip and snubs. She was well aware that the entire village disliked her and criticized her behind her back. Word got back to her that a neighbor, Mrs. Annie (Farrar) Simmons, had been very vocal in her opinions of who was to blame for the adopted child's death.

On July 28, Jennie composed a lengthy typewritten letter defending her actions against the admiral regarding the baby's death and denouncing the women of Assinippi for treating her unfairly. Addressed to Annie's mother, Mrs. Alfred Farrar, she wrote (in part):

My Dear Mrs. Farrar,

I trust that you will not take what I am going to write you as an insult to you and your family, but I feel that I owe something to myself in only common justice to what occurred two years ago [sic] and so, after debating all these months if I should not write you or should not at least yield and write you what I know to be the truth as only fair to me and my girls. I am doing this simply because of the attitude of your daughter and all of the women of Assinippi towards me. I refer to the scandal in the newspapers of which I was the innocent center of talk.

Now I believe the general opinion around here is that I am a fool and an adventuress or something worse. I can realize that for a woman to compromise her husband and raise any talk against him is not often done by wise women, and had it not been under great provocation it would not have happened, and because I was foolish enough to yield to my anger and outraged sense of all that was moral and right and forget that it was my husband and only saw the crime of the thing as excuse for my talk.

But in justice to myself I will say that any woman of high instincts and refinement, and who loved a child as I did that boy, would be to a great extent excusable for crying out had she thought her baby to be the victim of a man whom she believed not to be himself mentally, and it appears to me that it would be only the hardened criminal, or woman of little mercy of pity or human love in her heart, who could know what had happened as truly as I did and not cry out. She must be a woman who is familiar with all that is terrible in life to have kept silent, knowing as clearly as I did what had really happened.

Now, it was the horror of leaving a happy, healthy, laughing baby, rosy with health, lying asleep while we all went for a swim, and coming back and finding that same boy in the last agony of death. It was the shock and horror of the terribleness and wickedness of it that made me forget husband or anything save a great wrong had been done by a man (who was and at times is not mentally himself.)

Do you think you could leave your baby asleep and happy and run back to find him dying under peculiar circumstances and in less than an hour dead, and know that a member of your family had a tumor on the brain and was only morally right half the time?

Would you not be apt to cry out through your love for the child, or would your wisdom of what the world would think keep you quiet? Or would your moral nature say this is a terrible thing; this person acts guilty, and I must find out if I am right, to save any more lives around him? Which is what you would probably do if you cared for the other members of your family.

Now, I have tried to give you a glimpse into my mind at the time of this unfortunate affair, and I hope I have made my position clear. Please bear in mind that I had taken another woman's child to raise so that I could have a son – something to live for when I grew to be an old woman.

Also bear in mind that I was crippled with debts, bills owed by my husband for years, and that I was going to wash and scrub for this other woman's child, and that I had no help, could not afford them and meet the losses he had met, and was doing it for my love of children and my desire to help an unfortunate woman.

Hoping that you may stay down here in Assinippi, which must be dear to you, and that you will call upon my mother, who is a lovable old lady, and that you will take the pains to study me and read my character as I am and know me before you decide for or against me, I am, respectfully yours.

An immense sense of relief and self-satisfaction came over Jennie as she brought her message to a close. But as she prepared to sign it, she hesitated. She knew her rebuke would not sit well with Mrs. Farrar, who was sure to share it with her daughter and other neighbors. She couldn't care less about their feelings, but she didn't want Dorothy and June to suffer the consequences of her actions. She carefully folded the letter and tucked it beneath the clothing in her dresser drawer. She'd sleep on it, and in the morning she would decide how to proceed.

Chapter 8

Detective Scott and Deputy Sheriff Condon returned to the Eaton house early on Thursday morning, March 13, to interview Jennie once more. She met the two officers at the side door and invited them inside. Dressed in nightclothes and a robe, Jennie told the two investigators she was not feeling well and only agreed to answer their questions if they promised to be brief.

As they were about to begin, Judge George W. Kelley of Rockland arrived at the house and joined the group in the kitchen. The judge, a spunky, slightly-built man who knew both officers, informed them that he was legal counsel for Jennie and her family and would represent her during the interview. He admonished them to not question any of the Eatons in the future unless he or other legal counsel was present. Scott and Condon acknowledged his directive and resumed the interview.

After nearly four hours at Jennie's kitchen table, the two investigators concluded their inquiry and emerged from the house at about 1:30 p.m. They proceeded to District Attorney Barker's office at Barristers' Hall in Brockton to brief him on their meeting with Mrs. Eaton and Judge Kelley.

During their discussion, Barker happened to glance out the window of his second-floor office to the street below and noticed a crowd of newspapermen milling about. Scott and Condon told him the newsmen had pursued them nonstop throughout the day, making it impossible for them to investigate the Eaton case discreetly. The district attorney was not surprised. The admiral's stature and notoriety, and the mystery surrounding his death, had all the makings of a high-profile case.

Barker left Scott and Condon in his office, walked down the hallway, and descended the stairs to the front entrance. He would give the reporters an interview, but he had no intention of disclosing any facet of the investigation publicly.

When he stepped outside the building, he encountered a mob of photographers and raucous correspondents. When a reporter asked him about possible suspects, Barker answered his question with a question.

"You fellows seem to have your minds full of suspects. Who told you there were any suspects?"

Another writer inquired, "Will you say that the police, under your orders, have been working for five days in consequence of something the medical examiner reported to you, if you do not suspect that a crime has been committed – and haven't found yet any reason for arresting anybody?"

Barker chuckled and refused to answer.

The newsmen were not amused. They needed facts, and the district attorney was stonewalling.

"If anything breaks tonight, at what hour will it break?" queried still another.

"I don't expect to roll over violently enough in my bed to break anything," retorted Barker with a smile. "If you do, I can't say at what hour you will do it."

After several more skillful evasions and denials, the district attorney excused himself and went back to his conference with Scott and Condon. His message to the press was clear. He would not issue a public statement until such time as he deemed it appropriate and necessary.

~

At about two thirty on the rainy Friday afternoon of March 14, reporters at the busy intersection of Washington and Webster Streets watched as the trolley from Rockland pulled up near Killam's general store. It came to a full stop, and June Keyes alighted. When reporters realized it was Jennie Eaton's daughter, they ran to her. She responded calmly to their questions.

She emphatically denied that authorities investigating the admiral's death had summoned her to Assinippi. She said she had come to call on her mother for two reasons. First, with the exception of a brief meeting at Boston's North Station two days before, she hadn't seen her mother since March 5 when she had visited her at her home in Medford. Second, and most importantly, June said, "I felt that at a time like this my place was at her side."

June openly discussed the family dynamics within the Eaton home and her feelings toward the admiral. "I believe that my mother loved the admiral," she said, "and I believe that he loved her, when they were married. We all respected his attainments and admired his achievements but some of his characteristics made him difficult to live with and my mother remained in his home simply to keep the peace."

She expounded on these characteristics, but her comments and opinions offended at least one newspaperman, a *Globe* reporter, who refused to reveal them publicly. He wrote in his article the next day, "…Some of her expressions of opinion [about the admiral] were such they are not to be repeated in print."

The New York Times, however, had no qualms about publishing these opinions. "If there was anyone crazy in our family, it was the admiral," the *Times* quoted June. "I was in constant fear of him. No one knows what my mother and I had to put up with. I was in constant fear that he would poison me.

"Once I was ill, and he brought me food," she continued. "After I stopped eating the things he brought me, I got well at once. I think my mother was right when she accused the admiral of poisoning the little boy. To the outside world the admiral presented a polished exterior. He was a mystery we watched with care and fear."

As to the admiral's death, she said, "I fully believe that he died from natural causes. For years he has had stomach trouble; morning after morning I have known him to have hemorrhages from the stomach, and though he knew his stomach was in bad shape, he took no care of himself. He was a huge eater and ate what and when he pleased. If he had liquor in the house – my mother tried to keep him from bringing it in, but he sometimes smuggled a bottle in – he would take a drink before breakfast. And he always smoked before breakfast."

June told reporters that she and her mother had always known the admiral used drugs, but they had never found any in their home. She said the admiral had enthusiastically studied anatomy, physiology, and biology, and she thought he had tried "experiments in these branches on members of the family."

Before June could go any further, Andrew Jacobs, a neighbor and friend of the Eatons, rushed up to her and told her a letter was waiting for her at the post office across the street. He took her by the arm and they went into the tiny building. Reporters followed and watched as

June opened the letter, which was from her mother, and began to read. Her eyes welled up and tears ran down her cheeks. Jacobs, still at her side, told her he would take her home. He advised June not to answer any more questions and escorted her to the Eaton farm.

Reporters found June's sudden appearance and her accusatory statements intriguing in light of information that led them to believe that the police considered her a suspect and wanted to question her about a man she and her mother had once known. This man's visits with Jennie and June had allegedly so angered the admiral that he had warned him to stay away. Police were anxious to identify and locate this man for questioning. An aggressive interrogation might make him a suspect or accomplice in the admiral's death.

~

By now, Jennie had just about had it. The district attorney, the medical examiner, and the police were refusing to answer any of her questions about the investigation and where it was headed. She felt the authorities were persecuting her and her family, and she wanted it to stop.

She was weary of the newspaper headlines, the scurrilous gossip, the whispers, and the stares. What frustrated her the most was the district attorney's order prohibiting her from speaking with the press. She wanted desperately to defend herself publicly and clear her name. She confided to a close friend, "Unless the authorities take some decided action on Saturday, I shall make a strong protest at their attitude."

On Friday evening, Judge Kelley met with District Attorney Barker at Barristers' Hall to convey Jennie's concerns and determine how the prosecutor intended to proceed. Kelley was stunned when Barker said he planned to open an inquest into the admiral's death the following afternoon before Associate Justice Edward B. Pratt at a session of the Second Plymouth District Court in Hingham. Barker also apprised the judge that Deputy Sheriff Condon was in the process of serving subpoenas upon Dr. Frame, June Keyes, and Dorothy Ainsworth, all of whom would testify during Saturday's session.

Jennie's demand for "decided action" was about to be realized.

Chapter 9

Plymouth County District Attorney Albert Barker left his Brockton office at one o'clock Saturday afternoon, March 15, and drove his Thomas automobile to the Hingham courtroom that was located on the second floor of the Hingham Water Company building on South Street. A court officer, posted at the door to prohibit press access, ushered the prosecutor inside.

Detective John Scott, Deputy Sheriff John Condon, Dr. Joseph

District Attorney Albert F. Barker (*Courtesy of F. Joseph Geogan II, Esq.*)

Frame, Dorothy Ainsworth, and June Keyes arrived at the courthouse at about two o'clock. The inquest convened shortly after their arrival and went on until seven that evening.

Barker came out of the courtroom and gave a brief statement to the press moments after the proceedings were halted. He declined to tell reporters how many witnesses he intended to call and would not predict how long the inquest would continue. He would only tell them that he planned to resume at 10:00 a.m. on Monday, March 17.

Detective Scott and Deputy Condon drove June and Dorothy back to Assinippi. Both officers realized the inquest would likely generate increased media attention and curiosity seekers, so they met with Norwell Police Chief Walter T. Osborn and asked him to provide security. Osborn himself went to the Eaton home the next morning and stood guard on the front lawn.

Meanwhile, reporters continued to interview anyone in the area with information about the Eaton family. They tracked down a former Eaton housekeeper, Hannah Barnes of Rockland, whom Jennie had employed intermittently during the previous two years. Barnes recalled a time when she was left in charge of the household while Jennie visited

Washington and the admiral remained at home.

"The admiral was without money," Barnes said. "I have known him to be obliged to borrow even his carfare to Rockland. He seldom bought himself new clothing, and sometimes got actually shabby. He was not a heavy drinker, in spite of what has been said. I never saw him intoxicated, nor under the influence of drugs in the slightest degree."

While Jennie was in Washington, she wrote a letter to Barnes and warned her not to allow a particular neighbor inside the house. Jennie said the admiral was paying undue attention to this woman who, Jennie feared, was after his money. Barnes showed Eaton his wife's letter, and he made a joking comment about it. When Jennie returned from Washington, she asked Barnes if she thought the admiral was crazy.

"Why, no," Barnes had responded, wondering why Mrs. Eaton would even ask such a question.

Reporters asked the housekeeper if she had seen any poison in the house. She told them she had seen a bottle of poison but wasn't sure what kind of poison it was. She only knew it bore a red label.

"When I heard of the death of the admiral, I said to myself that there should be an investigation, days before I heard that there actually was to be an investigation," she added.

~

In another development, newsmen heard that police were searching for Harry Ainsworth. One reporter tracked Ainsworth to a book publisher on High Street in Boston, but when he went there to interview him the reporter learned that Ainsworth had been dismissed. Police had previously confirmed that information and had also learned that Jennie had met secretly with her ex-husband on three occasions at Norwell's Ridge Hill Grove to give him money. Police knew that the admiral was aware of these liaisons with Ainsworth. According to witnesses, Eaton had confronted Jennie at the grove on one occasion and had openly chastised her for her duplicity.

~

When the inquest into Admiral Eaton's death resumed in Hingham

53

Court at 10:00 a.m. on Monday, March 17, Judge Pratt, District Attorney Barker, Officers Scott and Condon, Dr. Frame, Dr. C. H. Colgate, Dr. Osgood, and June's husband, Ralph Keyes, were present. Colgate, Osgood, and Keyes testified during the morning session.

After a lunch break, Pratt, his clerk, a stenographer, two court officers, Barker, and Scott and Condon proceeded, at Barker's request, to the Eaton home in Assinippi where the inquest continued. Jennie's mother, Virginia Harrison, was the only person examined.

Barker later acknowledged he had requested the unusual shift of location out of consideration for Mrs. Harrison and her condition. A reporter had told the district attorney that he heard Mrs. Harrison was on her deathbed.

"It is not true," Barker said. "Mrs. Harrison is an aged woman and is, of course, feeble; but she is not in bed. She was up and dressed and, I believe, could have taken the journey to Hingham to testify in the courtroom there. I did not ask her to do so, because I deemed it unwise to take any chances of prejudicing her health. She was, of course, a little nervous at seeing all these officers come in; but she was perfectly able to answer the questions put to her."

As to how many witnesses he intended to bring before the inquest, Barker would only say, "Every person who may have any knowledge of the death or cause of death of Admiral Eaton will be called before this matter is finished."

The same evening, *The Boston Daily Globe* received information from an anonymous source connected to the Eaton investigation. The *Globe* quoted the source as saying, "Because of things plainly apparent at the bedside of Admiral Eaton, the authorities have come to the conclusion that he did not reach death through natural causes."

When asked if he believed murder had been committed, the source replied, "There is a possibility that the admiral committed suicide, and we are considering that possibility. I cannot at this time say anything more. I will not indicate whether the investigation has led us toward suicide or murder."

Reporters questioned Barker about this information. He refused to comment. There was obviously a leak in his office or in his investigative team. He was not pleased.

Judge George Kelley's position as a justice in the Abington District

Court presented a conflict and precluded his appearance as counsel before the district court in Hingham. Kelley asked twenty-eight-year-old attorney Francis J. Geogan of Rockland to represent the Eaton family in the case. Kelley knew Geogan personally and considered him a competent lawyer.

Admitted to the Massachusetts bar in 1906, Geogan practiced both civil and criminal law. He had recently acted as co-counsel in a capital case with attorney William A. Morse.

Geogan had been present during the inquest at the Eaton home the day before. He had consulted with the entire family before court officials arrived to take Mrs. Harrison's testimony. When asked later if he would act as the family attorney during the investigation, Geogan said he wasn't sure.

"I do not know how far I shall go in the case," he said. Reporters were quick to infer that the change of counsel, plus Geogan's experience in criminal trials, signaled an impending arrest.

~

The inquest resumed for the third day at Hingham District Court on March 18 under the ever-present eyes of reporters stationed outside the water company building's entrance. They watched as Norwell undertaker Ernest Sparrell, Detective Scott, Deputy Sheriff Condon, Deputy Sheriff George W. Conant, and other officers involved in the case went into the building.

Four other witnesses appeared to offer testimony: Hannah Barnes, the Eatons' part-time maid who had given reporters a lengthy interview the previous Sunday; Earl Forsman, a clerk at Killam's store in Assinippi Village; an unidentified woman who reporters believed had worked in the Eaton household; and Dr. Gilman Osgood, the medical examiner.

Reporters pressed the witnesses for comments as they left the building. They all refused, maintaining the secrecy required of inquests. At the conclusion of the day's testimony, DA Barker advised Judge Pratt that the Government was not prepared to proceed the next day. The judge granted Barker's request for a continuance and suspended inquest proceedings until Thursday, March 20.

By chance, a *Globe* reporter happened upon Dorothy Ainsworth that evening at Mann's Corner in North Hanover where she was waiting for a trolley to take her home. The reporter asked her to comment on the admiral's cause of death and explain why an air of secrecy surrounded it.

"There is no mystery in the cause of daddy's death," she said. "I know just what it is. It is not murder, and it is not suicide."

She stopped abruptly and stayed silent until the reporter asked, "It was an accident?"

"I cannot say any more," Dorothy replied. "I can only say this; there is no mystery about it. The officials know what the cause is. I wish I could say more, but I cannot. I have been told not to talk."

Dorothy wouldn't say anything else about the circumstances surrounding the admiral's death, but she felt obliged to comment about false statements reported by the press and her astonishment that Ralph Keyes had testified during the inquest.

"I want to contradict the statement that our household is under arrest, as some of the papers have stated, and also that members of the family are under surveillance," she said. "The officers on duty at the house came there at the request of my mother; she wanted protection against intruders. I was surprised to learn that Mr. Keyes, my sister's husband, testified at the inquest. I don't think June knew he was to be called. My mother has been placed in a false position before the public. She is a good mother, and I know she loved the admiral dearly."

Dorothy's comment about her brother-in-law, Ralph Keyes, intrigued reporters. In the time since June's arrival at the Eaton home on March 14, they had not seen Keyes visit the house, nor had they seen June leave to visit him at their home in Medford. According to Dorothy, both she and June did not know that he was to testify during the inquest. Whether June did or did not know her husband was going to testify was open to conjecture. But one thing seemed certain. The Keyes' marriage was in jeopardy.

Chapter 10

Reporters covering the Eaton case were frustrated. No one connected with the case had been willing to speak to them because of the gag order issued by the district attorney. DA Barker's refusal to reveal any facet of the investigation had forced the press to rely on confidential sources and witnesses on the periphery of the case. The reporters needed facts. The use of anonymous, unofficial sources and persons unable to provide details would invite skepticism from the reading public. Uncorroborated facts and statements posed a risk to press credibility and, worse, exposed it to the possibility of libel.

The newspapers merely wanted an official source to confirm or deny information they had gathered from hearsay. Specifically, they wanted to know if the inquest had determined if the admiral was poisoned. Assuming he was poisoned, were prosecutors inclined to consider murder, suicide, or an accidental cause of death? If he had been murdered, had the evidence and testimony of witnesses identified possible suspects?

The district attorney faced mounting pressure to reveal the investigation's status, but he, too, was cautious. Issuing a public statement specifying a cause of death before completing a thorough autopsy and scientific examination would be political suicide. Implicating a person suspected of a criminal act without solid evidence and probable cause to arrest would cause his reputation and livelihood serious harm. He had no intention of placing himself in harm's way to satisfy the demands of the press. So the contentious relationship between the press and the prosecutor continued.

On Thursday, March 20, *The Boston Daily Globe* printed an article in which a source claiming close ties to officials conducting the inquest was quoted as saying the inquest's focus was no longer on suicide. However, the source said, the evidence necessary to secure a murder indictment was lacking at this point in the investigation.

"The suicide theory has been eliminated," he said.

"What is left then – murder?" asked the reporter.

"Something very serious," the source said, "but the Government is having a hard time getting the evidence. What the district attorney has learned, however, is enough to point very closely to one person."

"Who is that person?" another reporter asked.

"I could not say who that person is. Something must have happened. That something also warrants the district attorney in going the limit in the investigation. They have only heard seven or eight witnesses, and these have not taken them very far, but it is hoped that more will be brought out when all are heard."

Another anonymous source willing to speak with the press called the district attorney's inquest a "fishing expedition." The source, allegedly a confidant of Barker, said, "The district attorney has a perfectly good reason for remaining silent at present, and it is none of those which have been guessed – that a suspect might escape, that a case might be disclosed to a possible defense, that a libel might be committed. There is another reason yet, but nobody has guessed it. This is a fishing expedition of the authorities."

State Detective Scott and Deputy Sheriff Condon met with the district attorney in his office on Wednesday morning, March 19. After leaving the conference, the two policemen spent the day serving summonses to some of the Eaton neighbors in Assinippi.

Many of those served were alarmed when officers knocked on their doors to tell them they were required to appear at the inquest in Hingham. Scott and Condon served eighty-eight-year-old James Prouty, who lived almost directly across Washington Street from the Eaton house.

Prouty's friends and neighbors could not believe the district attorney would require a man of Prouty's age and condition to travel to Hingham, especially since his testimony could have been taken during the inquest at the Eaton home several days before. Why hadn't the district attorney questioned all of the neighbors at that time?

Reporters interviewed Prouty after Scott and Condon left his home, determined to find out what the investigators had asked him. Prouty said the policemen asked if he kept poison anywhere on his premises. He showed them a mixture of Paris green and plaster of Paris he had kept under lock and key in a shed for more than two years, and he told them the poison belonged to Admiral Eaton.

Eaton, he explained, had used some of the mixture to exterminate potato bugs in his garden. Unfortunately, a calf had gotten into the potato patch, ingested some of the poison, and died. Eaton didn't want another mishap with the poison, so he asked Prouty if he'd store it on his property. Prouty said the policemen took a sample of the powder with them. The reporters smiled. This was the first indication that if authorities had found poison in the admiral's body, it was arsenical.

A second lead developed by newsmen added another twist to the case. A district police detective had been visiting drugstores in Somerville during the past three days to examine records related to sales of poison. The significance of this lead was illustrated by a *Boston Daily Globe* reporter whose story cast suspicion on the admiral's stepdaughter, June Keyes. The story revealed that she and her husband, Ralph Keyes, had lived with Ralph's parents on Adams Street in the Winter Hill district of Somerville just after their marriage. Although Ralph and June had moved from Somerville to Dorchester and then Medford in January 1913, the insinuation still stirred debate about June's involvement in the admiral's death.

As activity furiously ensued – subpoenas issued, witnesses testifying, reporters relentlessly pursuing leads, the Eaton family being hounded at every turn – Chaplain Freeman A. Langley of the Kearsarge Association of Naval Veterans quietly went to the offices of the *Lowell Courier-Citizen.* He carried a blue flag adorned with white stars and the initials of the association as well as a metal association marker affixed to a steel post. The association, organized in 1887 by Civil War veterans who had served aboard the *Kearsarge*, was founded to commemorate all deceased United States Navy officers and sailors.

Kearsarge marker at Eaton grave
(Furnished by the author)

Langley expressed the deep regret shared by members of the association about the absence of a naval ceremony at Admiral Eaton's burial.

"The Kearsarge Veterans keenly feel the slight that the admiral received," Langley said, "and they have voted to send this flag to the grave, where it will indicate in a measure that there is some appreciation in America of work well done in the public service.

"As an organization, we knew nothing of the admiral's funeral arrangements," Langley continued. "From the family came no word and we little thought that representatives of the navy would not be present at the cemetery. The Kearsarge Veterans have their flags flying over the graves of several admirals, and others who have merited recognition by their service in the navy. We think it regrettable that no honors were paid Admiral Eaton as his body was borne from Norwell to its last resting place in Oakland cemetery, and in this modest way, we are endeavoring to show that the Kearsarge Veterans are not blind to good service and do not soon forget the work done by United States naval officers."

Langley left the flag and marker at the newspaper office. A *Courier-Citizen* reporter telephoned Joseph Varnum, Admiral Eaton's nephew, to tell him of the Kearsarge Association's effort to honor his uncle. Varnum met the reporter the next day and the two men went to the cemetery in Dracut. The admiral's grave was still covered with floral tributes left on the day of burial. After placing the *Kearsarge* flag and metal marker at the head of the grave, Varnum expressed his deep gratitude to the association for the mark of respect it had paid to his uncle. He later placed a marble stone at the site. It was inscribed: "Admiral Jos. G. Eaton, U.S. Navy."

Eaton headstone, Oakland Cemetery
(Furnished by the author)

Chapter 11

Boston Daily Globe reporter Frank Sibley got to the Eaton house early on Thursday morning, March 20. The sun, piercing through dark clouds, cast muted shadows as Sibley got out of his car and walked up the Eaton driveway unchallenged. No one from the Norwell police force had reported as yet, leaving the Eaton house and its occupants unguarded. He found Mrs. Eaton in the yard doing chores in a blue housedress. She seemed startled as Sibley approached and quickly explained who he was and why he was there. Jennie agreed to an interview and invited him into the house.

Sibley told Jennie he believed the district attorney was focusing on her as the primary suspect in her husband's death. She blanched.

"The idea of accusing me of poisoning is ridiculous," Jennie retorted. "They have absolutely nothing to base such an accusation upon. My whole income and sustenance depended absolutely upon the admiral's living and has ceased with his death. The most I can ever hope to get is not more than fifty dollars a month as a widow's pension; it probably won't be more than thirty dollars."

"There is a story," said Sibley, "that you used part of the admiral's income for the benefit of your former husband."

She laughed. "Are you going to bring him in? Wait till they see him – they'll wonder how I ever lived with him."

Then she abruptly told Sibley she had nothing more to say and showed him the door. Outside, a heavy rain had begun to fall. Sibley tucked his notebook inside his coat and scampered to his car.

Shortly after Sibley's departure, Detective Scott and Deputy Condon arrived at the Eaton house after a meeting with District Attorney Barker in his Brockton office. The officers went to the side entrance where Jennie greeted them.

Scott explained that he and Condon had come to take her to the inquest in Hingham. When she asked why, Scott told her he didn't know – that he was only following the district attorney's instructions. Jennie asked for some time to dress and told Scott and Condon to wait for her in the barn outside.

She came out of the house at just after nine thirty wearing a black dress, which she had worn at her husband's funeral, under a full-length black coat. On her head she wore a black crepe turban hat with a veil. Scott and Condon hurriedly ushered her to the waiting car. Once she was secure in her seat, Scott and Condon got in and proceeded toward Hingham. They arrived at the court twenty minutes later. Newspapermen and curious onlookers stood by under a sea of bobbing and bumping umbrellas. The two policemen carefully assisted Jennie from the car and, one on each side, rushed her into the water company building and up to the judge's office on the second floor to await DA Barker.

Barker arrived within moments followed by attorney Francis Geogan. Barker and Geogan conferred in the empty courtroom. When the conference ended, Geogan went to the judge's office to speak with his client.

Geogan asked for privacy. Scott and Condon left the room. Geogan forewarned Jennie that the police intended to arrest her for murder. The color drained from her face, and tears welled up in her eyes.

Geogan explained that the police would bring her before Judge Pratt

Attorney Francis J. Geogan
(Courtesy of F. Joseph Geogan II, Esq.)

for arraignment immediately after her arrest. He cautioned her not to say a word to anyone in the courthouse, then he called Scott and Condon back into the room.

Scott informed Jennie she was under arrest and read the complaint against her: "That on March 7, at Norwell, you willfully, maliciously, feloniously, and with malice aforethought, did poison by arsenic Joseph G. Eaton of said Norwell, and that you did kill and murder the aforesaid Joseph G. Eaton against the peace of the Commonwealth."

Barker stepped from the building into the pouring rain at eleven thirty, and the newsmen pressed forward.

"I will not go through the formalities by which we have arrived at our result," he said. "I make this statement now because I promised to do so. Mrs. Eaton is not in the inquest; she has not been in and will not go in. Mrs. Eaton is now under arrest, charged with the murder of her husband, Rear Admiral Joseph Giles Eaton. He did not die a natural death, but died from arsenical poisoning."

Barker stated he had received a preliminary verbal report on March 10 from Dr. Whitney of Harvard Medical School confirming the existence of poison in the admiral's organs. He added that Whitney had found no evidence of poison in any of the pills, bottles, and powders collected by Dr. Osgood. Barker justified his previous reluctance to release Whitney's analysis by saying, "Some peculiar features involved have prevented the communication of the facts to the public. We have been unable thus far to ascertain where the poison was procured."

When Barker completed his statement and went back into the court, sheriff's deputies allowed reporters, but not photographers, access to the building. The newsmen, after exhorting their photographers to find the nearest telephone to call their editors with this exciting development, sprinted to the second-floor courtroom in anticipation of Mrs. Eaton's arraignment.

Shortly after the press claimed their seats, Clerk of Court Herbert Pratt entered and sat down at his desk in front of the judge's bench. Barker and Geogan took their respective places inside the bar as Scott and Condon escorted Jennie to a seat in the front row of benches. Reporters later described her as "tall and matronly" and "in her somber gown ... of striking appearance." As for her demeanor, most thought her "composed" and "perfectly at ease," but some claimed they saw tears in her eyes.

Judge Pratt entered the room and took his seat at the bench. Clerk Pratt instructed Jennie to stand and began to read the charge against her. Geogan immediately interjected and asked for a waiver of the reading, which Judge Pratt allowed. Geogan entered a plea of not guilty on Jennie's behalf, and the judge continued the case until Friday morning, March 28.

Jennie left the courthouse at about 1:00 p.m. with Scott, Condon, and her attorney. All four got into a waiting car driven by Herbert Pratt, the clerk of court. He sped out of the area and began the journey through intermittent rain and fog to the Plymouth County Jail at Obery Heights with two carloads of reporters and photographers on his tail.

Plymouth County Jail *(Furnished by the author)*

At 2:50 p.m., Pratt pulled up to the jail where he and his passengers were met by the reporters who had passed them along the route. Condon and Scott exited the vehicle first, and Geogan assisted Jennie from the car and up the steps, shielding her from the rain and "at least one of the battery of picture machines" with his umbrella.

Deputy Sheriff Herman Tower met the quartet when they stepped into the jail's lobby and escorted them through a steel-grated doorway into the guardroom where Laura Porter, wife of the county sheriff and matron of the women's ward, was waiting. Mrs. Porter took Jennie into custody, led her up an iron staircase to the second floor on the south side of the building, and confined her to the ward used exclusively for female prisoners.

When Scott and Condon exited the jail, reporters asked them to outline the evidence against Eaton. Scott deferred to the district attorney, explaining, "I would rather he would explain the facts." He did admit that he first found out the admiral had died of poisoning when officials received Dr. Whitney's analysis on March 10. Asked if he knew how much arsenic was found in the admiral's system, Scott said, "There was considerable." Scott also verified that the investigation up to that point had failed to determine where the poison used to kill the admiral had been procured.

"We do not know where, when, nor by whom the poison was

bought," he said. "When we do find out, of course, a second arrest may be possible."

Scott's reference to a second arrest prompted reporters to discuss suspects among themselves. Was it Jennie's first husband, Daniel H. Ainsworth? What about members of the household? Was it possible that June or Dorothy or both had acted in concert with their mother? Was June or Dorothy individually responsible for the admiral's death? Was Jennie shielding one or both of her daughters?

Barker later put at least a temporary end to speculation about a second arrest when he told a reporter, "We have no reason to suppose that anyone besides Mrs. Eaton was concerned in this affair. Although we have not found where the poison was bought, no suspicion exists that anyone else bought it or had anything to do with it. I wish to set at rest unjust suspicions that may have arisen against another person."

Reporters were stymied in identifying a motive for the crime. If all the information they had obtained to date was true, the admiral was a man in considerable debt whose only source of income was his $4,700 annual pension. Why would his wife, whose sole support depended on a pension that ceased at the admiral's death, want to squander this income? The press surmised that the district attorney intended to prove a very different motive. They were determined to find out what it was.

The newsmen tried to get an answer about motive out of Scott and Condon. Both refused to answer. Condon simply "tapped his forehead, as if to signify that he doubted whether Mrs. Eaton was mentally sound, assuming that she were guilty of poisoning."

~

The district attorney was anxious to expedite Jennie Eaton's indictment, but the Plymouth County grand jury was not scheduled to sit until June. Barker met in Boston with John A. Aiken, chief justice of the Superior Court of Massachusetts. At Barker's request, Aiken authorized a special sitting of the grand jury on March 24.

Rumors about a second arrest resurfaced several days before the grand jury convened. Newspapers quoted an unofficial, unnamed source involved in the investigation. The source disclosed that police did not yet have enough evidence to establish probable cause for either an arrest or an indictment but had gathered enough evidence to raise reasonable suspicion that another person, whom he inadvertently identified as a woman, was involved in Eaton's murder.

"We have no positive evidence against her yet," the source said, "but men are hunting the drugstores and all places in which any form of arsenic can be purchased, and they are looking for records of a sale of poison to her. It is possible the grand jury may not take any action against her, but we have some very important evidence, and she will not be eliminated from the case, no matter what the grand jury does. We have had many talks with her, all of them unsatisfactory, and of course, she has positively denied any knowledge of the cause of the rear admiral's death."

~

As police continued their investigation, the press delved deeper into Jennie Eaton's background. A *Boston Daily Globe* reporter contacted the Cook County Circuit Court for details concerning her divorce from Daniel Ainsworth.

Jennie May Ainsworth, through her attorney, Marshall Gallion, had presented a bill of complaint to the Cook County Circuit Court on April 6, 1906, alleging that during the past two years her husband, Daniel H. Ainsworth, in a state of habitual drunkenness, had failed to sustain steady employment and provide support for his wife and two children. The complaint also contended that Ainsworth, while intoxicated, was quarrelsome and used abusive language. Jennie petitioned the court to grant her a divorce and sole custody of their two children.

Subsequently, on May 9, 1906, the Cook County court issued a summons for Ainsworth, ordering him to appear before the court on May 21. A deputy sheriff left the summons at Ainsworth's last known address on Dearborn Street in Chicago after all attempts to deliver it by hand had failed.

When Ainsworth failed to respond by July 10, Judge John Gibbons proceeded with Mrs. Ainsworth's suit for divorce without him. Questioned by Gallion, Mrs. Ainsworth described her husband as a habitual drunkard and drug addict who abused absinthe and morphine. She testified that he had threatened her and her children and, on one particular evening during dinner, had overturned their dining room table in a drunken rage.

Gallion asked Jennie if her husband contributed anything to the support for her and her children. She told the court that Ainsworth had been unable to provide any means of support for the last several years because his persistent drinking prevented him from maintaining steady employment.

Nine days after the hearing, the circuit court granted Mrs. Ainsworth the divorce and sole custody of their two children. Gibbons ordered her "released from all obligations of her marriage and restored to all and singular the rights and privileges of an unmarried woman, except that both parties are restrained from remarrying within the time limited by law." Gibbons further decreed that Jennie May Ainsworth "have the care, custody, control, and education of the said children, [Lucia] June Ainsworth and Dorothy H. Ainsworth, without any interference on the part of the defendant."

Globe reporter Frank Sibley contacted Gallion on March 21, 1913, and arranged to interview him about Jennie's 1906 divorce from Daniel Ainsworth. During their conversation, Gallion revealed the contents of a letter he had received from Jennie nearly five years after her divorce. The *Globe* and *The New York Times* exposed the letter the following day. Writing at Assinippi on March 15, 1911, Jennie had expressed her fears of living with Rear Admiral Eaton and the threat he posed to her and her family.

The condition of this poor man is dreadful, she wrote. *He is so much worse, and I fear to stay here this winter. My leaving him alone with my mother while I was in Chicago made him violent. If I had a doubt of his insanity, which I never had, it would be removed quickly, as he is so much worse, and what am I to do?*

Jennie was convinced the admiral intended to kill her and her daughter.

He is a sick, helpless, and sad, old man, and it goes to my heart, she continued. *He relies on me entirely. I am his eyes, brain, and life, and still how can I stay here alone and let him kill me and poor, little, innocent Dorothy, and he will do it and then wonder where we are. He is the most dangerous, subtle maniac, and still I have no way of escape.*

She felt alone and frustrated in her efforts to have him committed.

She believed the admiral's public persona was a lie, that he concealed his evil nature and deceived those who regarded him as a gentleman and a polished man of the world.

Public opinion, his rank, his age, and the Navy are all against me, she wrote. *All doctors are too diplomatic and afraid to attempt to deal with him as he should be dealt with, and it will cost me hundreds of dollars to get evidence and take a year at least to get it in shape, and then I probably will be outwitted by sentiment and pity. He is the most dangerous man you could meet any place.*

She asked Gallion for help in finding a reputable woman with psychological training who could live with her in her home to observe and document the admiral's demented behavior.

If he is as dangerous as I believe, I must protect my life, so find out whether you can get me a woman who is a Sherlock Holmes in criminal insanity and of highest moral character and of highest standing with doctors and alienists (psychiatrists), *one whose word would go. If she said he was insane, they would do the rest. Please see what you can do for me, and advise me.*

Sibley asked Gallion to comment on the letter, but Gallion declined. He did, however, tell Sibley of a strange visit Jennie made to his office in Chicago after her marriage to the admiral. Her story of the admiral's fascination with poison and his alleged stalking of her struck Gallion as paranoiac.

"Mrs. Eaton said that while in the South Seas in the navy, the admiral had learned a lot of poison lore from the savages," Gallion recounted. "She said he boasted of a poison he had brought from the South Sea Islands with him, an extract of the venom of a snake, and told her of a trick of carrying a tiny but deadly dose of it under the nail of his little finger. This, she said, he declared he could drop into a glass of water without detection. He told her, she said, that he had poisons hidden about the rafters of the house at Assinippi and about the barn. Mrs. Eaton said that he often followed her about silent and cat-like, and that sometimes when she was in town shopping or out on errands she would feel that he was about, and turning, would find the admiral leering at her."

The more that people heard and read about her allegations of insanity against the admiral, the more her own mental stability came

68

into question. Her statements and correspondence seemed filled with the rantings of a deluded, irrational mind. The general public, unaware of evidence and testimony gathered during the investigation, believed the district attorney's case against her was "more an accusation of insanity than of murder, for it is beyond the comprehension of most men that a sane person should kill the one person on whom she was dependent for support."

Chapter 12

On Good Friday, March 21, Detective Scott and Deputy Condon inspected the Eaton home, barn, outbuildings, and grounds for six hours in search of poison but found nothing. District Attorney Barker assigned additional investigators and enlisted the aid of local police departments to canvass every pharmacy and retail establishment known to market poisons for evidence of a sales record in Mrs. Eaton's name or in a name they could link to her.

In 1913, Massachusetts law required any person who sold arsenic, strychnine, and other poisons to anyone without a physician's written prescription to maintain a record of the date of the sale, the name and amount of the poison sold, and the name and residence of the party to whom it was delivered. The law further required every seller to make the record available for inspection by the police. Anyone who purchased arsenic, or any of the other poisons listed under the statute, and who gave a false or fictitious name to the vendor faced a fine of up to fifty dollars. Merchants who sold poisons like Paris green for use as an insecticide were exempt from most of the statute's provisions but were still required to record every sale.

Deputy Sheriff John T. Condon
(*Boston Traveler and Evening Herald*)

When reporters asked DA Barker about the origin of the poison that killed Eaton, he readily admitted, "We don't know. It is known, however, that from the moment Dr. Whitney discovered the traces of arsenic in the body of Admiral Eaton, State Detective Scott and Deputy Sheriff Condon have attempted to locate the place where the poison was procured. They searched all over Plymouth County, among the Boston drugs stores, and also in Medford and Somerville."

Speaking confidentially with a reporter, a source close to the investigation conceded that the search for a sale of poison to Jennie Eaton was like trying to find a needle in a haystack. He said the chances of finding such a record would be enhanced with the help of the press.

"I think that we will have to depend on publicity to discover the place where the arsenic was bought," the source said. "The newspapers have accomplished such things before. We don't know where the poison was bought. Perhaps if the fact is made public, something may be learned."

Newspapers throughout the country had published photographs of Jennie, June, and Dorothy nearly every day since Jennie's arrest. The press had also identified by name every person police had questioned or summoned as a witness in the case. Surely someone would recognize a name or a face and contact authorities with the incriminating evidence necessary to connect Eaton with the crime.

Following up on a tip, reporters identified the mysterious man whose relationship in 1909 with his stepdaughter, June, had angered Admiral Eaton. Even before police had questioned sixty-three-year-old nurseryman James Thom, reporters had been to his modest home next to the Congregational church in Hingham Center to interview him about his association with the Eatons.

Thom was candid with reporters and admitted he had visited the Eaton family frequently. He objected to the treatment the Eatons had received since the admiral's death, and he especially resented the scandalous gossip about an inappropriate relationship between him and June Ainsworth.

Thom attributed the admiral's death to drug addiction and refused to believe anyone in the Eaton family had contributed to his demise. He criticized those who doubted the charges made by Jennie and June about the admiral's attempts to poison them.

One afternoon, Thom related, he called on June and her mother while they were staying in Weymouth after the death of the Eatons' adopted child. The admiral, who occasionally visited his wife and stepdaughter, had just left the house.

Thom found Jennie making a bed that the admiral had been in. When she removed one of the blankets, a "pellet" about the size of a small pea fell from the folds and onto the floor. Jennie picked it up and showed it to Thom, telling him it was "one of the several kinds of poison the admiral carries about on his person and takes." Jennie destroyed the pellet at Thom's suggestion, then emptied the contents of the sugar bowl and salt shakers in the house for fear the admiral had placed poison in them while he was there.

Admiral Eaton bristled when he found out later that Thom had called on June in Weymouth. He suspected a romance between Thom and June and had no intention of allowing it.

Thom told reporters about an episode in September 1909 following Jennie's return to Assinippi and her reconciliation with the admiral. Thom had stopped by the house to collect on a bill for landscaping services. He was in the kitchen speaking with Jennie when the admiral walked in.

Thom claimed that the admiral reproached him for the visit to Weymouth and ordered him to stay away from June. An argument ensued, quickly escalated into violence, and, Thom alleged, the admiral assaulted him. Jennie stepped between them and ordered Thom out of the house. Thom walked out the front door and onto the piazza. June, hearing the commotion from her second-floor bedroom, quickly descended the stairs and followed him outside. She begged him to leave, but he refused, saying he wasn't finished with her stepfather. He waited a half hour, but the admiral never came out.

"If the admiral wants to settle this," he told June before he stepped off the piazza, "tell him I'll be waiting for him at the post office in the village."

The admiral arrived in the village on foot a short time later and found Thom standing outside the post office. The admiral glared in his direction but did not approach him. Instead, he walked over to several men loitering outside Killam's store. After a few moments of conversation, he headed back toward his home. One of the loiterers scurried over to Thom and told him the admiral had threatened to get a gun and shoot him. Thom jumped into his buggy and chased after the admiral. When he caught up to him he said, "Have you got the gun yet, Eaton?"

The admiral ignored him and kept walking. Thom followed Eaton all the way to his house but not another word was spoken between the two. Thom, granted no satisfaction, returned to his home in Hingham.

"If he had continued to quarrel with me, I think I should have struck him," Thom told reporters. "Except as I have told, I have never seen poison in the Eaton house nor in the admiral's possession, but I shall not be surprised if the fact comes out that the admiral was addicted to the use of drugs, very likely to using arsenic. In relation to June, I never say anything that could be honestly construed as detrimental to her character."

~

Reporters posted at the Plymouth County Jail remained alert for new developments. Jennie's first night was uneventful. She rose at 7:00 a.m., donned her prison garb of a dark blue calico wrapper (house dress) with white polka dots, and ate a light breakfast of eggs, toast, and a glass of milk. By noon, she had compiled an inventory of the household furnishings and other property at Assinippi to assist Judge Kelley with the disposition of the admiral's estate and had written several letters, including one to Dorothy, in which she expressed her optimism about an early release and her concern for her mother and the farm.

Attorney Francis Geogan visited his client in the afternoon. Part of their conversation concerned Boston attorney William A. Morse, a former Massachusetts state senator. Geogan had practiced with Morse and considered him an excellent lawyer. He recommended Morse to Jennie as the lead defense counsel in her case.

~

The next day, Saturday, March 22, Dorothy spent a quiet day at the house, taking Jennie's collie, Czar, for a walk in the morning while leaving her mother's other dog, a water spaniel, behind. Her sister, June, left the house a short time later in the company of Norwell constable Frank Hammond who escorted her to Assinippi Village.

Reporters continued to speculate about the police presence at the house. Now that Mrs. Eaton had been arrested, was the rest of the family still under suspicion? Detective Scott later dispelled any theories of additional arrests.

"The members of the Eaton family are not under surveillance," Scott declared. "They are not being guarded except in the sense that the officers have been put there to protect the women who are now there alone."

At the village, June left Hammond, boarded the trolley for Rockland Center and disembarked at the railroad depot in Union Square. Several reporters, who had jumped aboard at Assinippi, followed her into Sullivan's drugstore where she purchased postage stamps. Upon exiting, she returned to Union Street and walked past Maguire's fruit store and up the hill toward Webster Street, stopping occasionally to gaze at clothing shop window displays. She crossed Union Street at the crest of the hill, darted inside the Rice Building at the corner of Pacific Street, and climbed the stairs to Attorney Geogan's office.

June exited the building shortly thereafter and encountered a swarm of reporters. She was reluctant to answer their questions, but in a moment of exasperation she turned to them and said, "It is a shame and an outrage, the way we have been treated. The brain of the admiral should have been examined to show whether he was insane, as much as to find evidence to prosecute his family."

She claimed that an event during his navy career had affected the admiral's mind. "...a big gun – a ten-inch or fourteen-inch – went off close to him one day, and his head has never been right since; he has always been queer."

A reporter asked her if police were wasting their time searching for poison in the house and sales records in drugstores.

"They may search as much as they like," she said, "but they will not find that we bought any, because we didn't."

When asked about the admiral's will and if she would benefit financially, she told reporters the admiral had left her about $5,000, "...but that doesn't mean that I shall get any money. His debts have swallowed up what money he had, long ago."

After reading June's remarks in the newspaper, retired Rear Admiral John M. Hawley immediately came to Eaton's defense. Hawley had graduated from the Naval Academy with Eaton and had served aboard the *Guard* with him during the Darien Expedition in 1870.

"During the four years at the Naval Academy, two years in the

74

tropics, and in all of our forty years' service, Rear Admiral Eaton never mentioned poisons to me nor showed the slightest degree of queerness," Hawley told a *New York Herald* bureau reporter in Washington. "I saw him in Boston just before he retired. He said then he was lucky never to have been injured. I don't believe the report regarding his injury by the firing of big guns."

Boston American reporters spoke with other naval officers in and around Boston who had become well acquainted with the admiral during his career. They all disputed the allegations June and her mother had made about the admiral's interest in poisons. They held the admiral in the highest regard and considered any suggestion that he had conveyed poisons from the South Sea Islands in an old sea chest as preposterous. To a man, they declared "there wasn't a rough or gruff line in him." They described him as "a quiet, refined man, sensitive in a degree, and, under all circumstances, a polished gentleman..." who had "a decidedly artistic temperament," was "intensely patriotic," and "a man of great nerve and quiet bravery."

Inside the county jail, Jennie chatted amiably with *Boston American* reporter Angela Morgan. The two women would develop a lasting friendship over the next seven months. Admitted by Sheriff Porter, Morgan spent an hour with Jennie in her cell on Holy Saturday. On Easter Sunday, March 23, the *American* published Morgan's intimate feature about Jennie's past, "fraught with riddles and weird problems," and the essence of Jennie's struggle as she sat, humiliated but courageous, in her cell.

~

Judge Kelley went with defense attorneys Morse and Geogan to the Eatons' Assinippi home on Easter Sunday and spoke with Jennie's mother and two daughters. After they left, the girls and their grandmother remained quietly inside. Reporters posted outside talked among themselves about the conspicuous absence of June's husband, Ralph Keyes. Keyes had not visited since June's arrival at her mother's home on March 14. Some suspected the couple had been estranged since Keyes's testimony at the inquest.

The suspicions were correct. June's marriage was, for all intents and purposes, dissolved. By April 3, she had moved out of the Summer Street home in Medford where she had lived with her husband for less than two months. With help from Dorothy, June had moved all of her furnishings into storage. Ralph had vacated the house two weeks before. On Saturday, March 29, he and his father had removed several rugs and other personal property.

The press was following June's every move and, aware of her sudden departure and the breakup of her home, dared to ask her what had brought it about.

"Dorothy needs me more than does Ralph Keyes" June replied. "Mr. Keyes and I were never really suited to each other. I would never have married him but for my mother, who insisted that I have a home of my own in case anything happened to her."

Reporters were left to speculate: Was this estrangement due to the accusatory nature of Ralph Keyes's testimony at the inquest? Or was it due to something more sinister? The answers would become evident before long.

~

June had stunned her mother fifteen months before she had married Ralph Keyes when she confessed that she had withdrawn from her studies at the conservatory because she was pregnant. The child was conceived in July 1911, around the time June was completing her second semester. (Ralph Keyes later denied the child was his.)

Jennie was dismayed. The death of her adopted son two years before had been nearly impossible to bear. Now this. She had supported June at every turn, especially when the admiral had thwarted her suitors. The admiral had thought June too young to engage in a serious relationship with any man. Now Jennie was faced with two options: tell the admiral of the girl's transgression and ask for his help, or keep it secret and care for June until the child's birth. She opted for secrecy. Plans were made to send June to Washington, DC, on the pretense of a visit to her family.

When June arrived in Washington, she scanned the classifieds for a place to live and found a vacancy at 425 P Street NW. She went to the address and met the proprietor, Bessie Bursey, who showed her a two-room, second-floor apartment. June agreed to terms and occupied the unit the same day.

Jennie arrived soon afterwards to see to June's needs. June gave birth at Columbian Hospital on April 12, 1912, to a baby girl she named Eleanor. After a two-week stay at the hospital, June returned to P Street with the newborn. They knew they couldn't bring the little girl home to Massachusetts, so they arranged to board the child with a caretaker while they considered their long-term options.

Responding to another newspaper advertisement, they went to the home of Gertie Wallace. After agreeing to pay board of twelve dollars a month, they turned the baby over to Wallace's care. Satisfied that their secret was safe for the time being, Jennie and June returned to Boston.

Sometime in December, Sarah Bucher, an investigator for the District of Columbia's Bureau of Children and Guardians, went to the Wallace place in response to a complaint from a police court clerk. She found little Eleanor living in deplorable conditions. Bucher immediately removed Eleanor from the boarding house and placed her in an orphanage. She then filed a complaint of neglect against June Ainsworth, who by this time had married Ralph Keyes.

Jennie somehow learned of the pending complaint against June – most likely from Gertie Wallace – and of a hearing pursuant to it that was scheduled for December 20. She hurriedly boarded a train for Washington and proceeded to the juvenile court on the morning of the hearing. Jennie confronted Bucher outside the courtroom and pleaded with her to drop the case, requesting that Eleanor be released to her. She advised Bucher that the child's mother had married in November and was now anxious to have her little girl back. Bucher, not quite convinced, went ahead with the hearing. She informed the court of June's marriage and conveyed Jennie's desire to return the child to its parents. The court granted Jennie's request for custody of baby Eleanor. Jennie took her granddaughter back to June in Dorchester, where June and her husband had rented an apartment.

Chapter 13

The special sitting of the Plymouth County grand jury convened, as scheduled, on Monday, March 24. District Attorney Barker opened the session with a summary of the case. He then called his first witness, Annie Rooney, a psychiatric nurse hired by Jennie Eaton in June 1912 to observe the admiral and assess his sanity.

When Rooney exited fifteen minutes later, Barker summoned Effie Cobbett. June Ainsworth Keyes had briefly boarded with Cobbett in her nearby Hanover home following a disagreement with the admiral. On March 19, before she knew she was to be a witness in the Eaton affair, Cobbett had spoken at her home with a *Boston Journal* reporter. Mrs. Cobbett confirmed during the interview that June had boarded at her home in 1910. She likely repeated that information during her testimony before the grand jury.

"Mrs. Keyes first came to my house about two years ago last December," Cobbett stated. "We do not keep lodgers, but she just dropped in one day and said she wished to live with us awhile. She said she was the stepdaughter of Admiral Eaton, and that she had decided to live away from home for fear he would poison her. She repeatedly referred to the subject until it got on my nerves, and I had to stop her."

Cobbett's brief testimony was followed by the examination of twenty-three-year-old Bessie Collamore, another Eaton neighbor. Collamore's appearance surprised reporters, who had never connected her to the case, and left them in a quandary as to what she may have said during the proceeding.

Charles E. Nordstrom, a thirty-one-year-old private detective who Jennie had consulted in 1912 about building a case against the admiral for attempted murder, was Barker's next witness. Nordstrom was assistant manager at the Weyand Secret Service Bureau of Boston. He had granted an exclusive interview to a *Boston American* reporter at his home in Somerville two days earlier and had given a detailed account of his connection to the Eaton case. Nordstrom undoubtedly repeated this account to the grand jury.

Nordstrom told the *American* correspondent that he first spoke with Mrs. Eaton on Wednesday, June 12, 1912, when she telephoned and asked him to investigate Admiral Eaton, alleging that he was trying to poison her and the entire family. He agreed to meet Jennie the next afternoon in the concourse at Boston's South Station.

Mrs. Eaton arrived at the depot with another woman, introducing her as Annie Rooney, a nurse in her employ. They sat on a bench in a secluded part of the station. Nordstrom said Eaton was extremely nervous and exercised the utmost caution as they conversed. She fidgeted on the bench and spoke in low tones, constantly glancing around for anyone who might be watching or listening.

"The admiral is a very well-educated man, but I believe he is a poisoner," Jennie began. "I fear that he is trying to poison me – in fact, the whole family. I shouldn't be surprised to find my daughter Dorothy dead when I get home."

She told him the admiral had become familiar with strange poisons during a cruise to India with his navy squadron and disclosed how he would sprinkle a peculiar yellow poison on his food from a vial at the dinner table. He hid these and other containers of poison in an old sea chest he kept locked in the attic of their home in Assinippi. He kept the keys for the attic and the sea chest with him at all times, she said.

Jennie also told Nordstrom that she had often awoken in the middle of the night to find blood trickling down her arm after the admiral had injected her with a syringe containing poison.

"Why don't you kill me outright?" she claimed she asked the admiral.

Nordstrom said Mrs. Eaton also related a story about the admiral's experiences during the Darien Expedition in Panama. The admiral had told her "men had died like rats about him." She asserted the men did not die of natural causes but at the hands of the admiral who poisoned them all. She further related a conversation with the admiral in which "he boasted of having obtained an extract of snake venom from natives in the South Sea Islands and demonstrated to her how it was possible to secrete a speck of it under a finger nail and then communicate the poison to another person while shaking hands."

The private detective said he had asked Mrs. Eaton for a two-hundred-dollar retainer. She agreed to give him the money when they next met, but he never heard from her again.

At the conclusion of Nordstrom's testimony, the district attorney summoned Hannah Barnes, a housekeeper employed by Mrs. Eaton. Rockland businessman Clarence E. Rice followed Barnes. Later, Dr. Charles Colgate, the Eaton family's first physician, took the stand.

An interview published in the *Boston Evening Transcript* provided a clue to Colgate's testimony. Several days before the grand jury met, a *Transcript* reporter had followed Deputy Sheriff John Condon to Colgate's home in Rockland. When the deputy left, the reporter went to the physician's door. Colgate agreed to an interview and spoke candidly.

"I was the [Eaton] family physician for several years," he said. "During that time, poison was talked [about] continually, mostly by Mrs. Eaton. She constantly asked me to take steps towards the committing of the admiral to an insane asylum." When asked his opinion of the admiral's mental condition and if he knew him to abuse drugs, Colgate answered, "I always regarded Admiral Eaton as a sane, natural, wholesome man. I never saw evidence that he was a user of drugs."

The reporter asked why he no longer attended the Eatons. The doctor replied, "Because of Mrs. Eaton's mental condition and because of her insistence that I use my influence in having the admiral sent to an asylum, I was forced to drop the family from my list of patients."

After Colgate's testimony, Barker called Charles B. Brooks, Admiral Eaton's second cousin, to the stand. Brooks was asked about the admiral's state of mind just prior to his March 8 death because Brooks had received a letter from the admiral on March 7 asking Brooks to consider buying some of his books and valuable papers. Brooks told reporters outside the courthouse that he believed his cousin's letter refuted any theory he had killed himself.

"I believe this letter will disprove any assertion that is made tending to show that the admiral was of unsound mind and committed suicide," Brooks said. "The letter is a splendid example of the work of a well-balanced mind. It proves conclusively, I think, that the admiral not only was sane, but also was of tranquil mind when he wrote it."

Brooks's remarks about the sale of personal effects led reporters to speculate about the admiral's financial condition. They had heard that the admiral was "in a desperate state" and "frequently had to borrow money for carfare and had not been able to meet the expense of Miss June Ainsworth's wedding, which was $300."

Why was a man who was drawing a substantial annual pension so deeply in debt that he considered selling prized possessions? And if he could not meet his expenses, what would motivate his widow to kill him and eliminate the primary source of income with which to pay them?

When Brooks came out, the district attorney called his last witness of the day, Ralph Keyes. The session adjourned at 4:50 p.m. when Keyes finished.

The newsmen had carefully noted the order in which Barker had called his witnesses during the session. They thought it strange he had not called either of Mrs. Eaton's daughters to testify. Both were present in the witness room under court summons. That, coupled with the fact that June Keyes had not been called during the Hingham inquest, prompted some intriguing possibilities.

Newsmen were also anxious to know if the district attorney planned to have Mrs. Eaton examined for mental competence.

Barker addressed that question after leaving the court. He told the waiting reporters that he didn't intend to order a psychiatric examination at the present time, but he reminded them that he "had the power to demand a commission to examine the prisoner at any time." However, he refused to explain why he hadn't called June Keyes to testify, and he sidestepped questions about the possibility of a second arrest.

The prosecutor was more straightforward with reporters about a March 20 *Boston Daily Globe* article that had suggested negligence on the part of Dr. Joseph Frame during his treatment of Admiral Eaton. The *Globe* had quoted an unknown source as saying, "What all the people with whom I have talked cannot understand is why Dr. Frame did not take some action on Friday night and perhaps thus save the admiral's life. He went into action promptly when Admiral Eaton was dead. If he knew of circumstances that were suspicious on Friday night, why didn't he have the patient removed from the danger, or the dangers removed from the patient?"

Barker strenuously objected to the comment and, in Frame's

defense, said, "Any suggestion that Dr. Frame's conduct in the Eaton matter was open to criticism is unwarranted. Quite the contrary, he is entitled to the highest commendation for his course throughout the whole matter. I say this, knowing the circumstances."

~

The next day, Tuesday, March 25, Barker opened the session at 10:30 a.m. and recalled Ralph Keyes. Keyes testified for twenty minutes and returned to the witness room.

Dorothy was the next witness. She testified until the afternoon recess at 12:50 p.m. and continued her testimony when the session resumed at two o'clock. Emerging from the jury room more than two hours later, she wore a "strained and worried look," according to reporters who were in the courthouse corridor.

After a brief examination of Ernest Sparrell, the undertaker, the district attorney summoned June Keyes, his last witness of the day. Barker excused her after a half hour of testimony and adjourned.

~

Defense attorneys Geogan and Morse were waiting for June and Dorothy when the session ended. They walked together to the Plymouth depot and boarded the train for Rockland. Constable Frank Hammond was waiting to escort the women home when they arrived at about 7:00 p.m. Geogan and Morse promised to meet the two sisters in the courthouse the next morning, bid them goodnight, and departed.

As the sisters stood with Hammond on the Rockland depot platform, a number of people recognized them from newspaper photographs and surged toward them. Hammond did his best to disperse the growing throng as he hustled June and Dorothy through the pouring rain to a restaurant near the station.

Inside, Hammond found a table and the three sat down. People gathered outside the establishment and pressed their faces against the windows, straining to get a look at June and Dorothy. Hammond, concerned for their safety, asked the restaurant manager to close the curtains and lock the door. He then called Rockland Police Chief

Michael E. Stewart for help. Several officers responded and tried to disperse the crowd, but they had little success.

When Chief Stewart reached the restaurant, he and Hammond decided it was best for the two sisters to leave the area as soon as possible. Stewart and his officers escorted Hammond and the women through the crowd to the trolley stop where they boarded the 7:30 p.m. car bound for Assinippi. The women were delivered safely at home a short time later.

~

Judge George Kelley appeared at Plymouth County Probate Court on Wednesday, March 26, to file a declaration of trust on behalf of Jennie Eaton. Uncertain of her fate, Jennie feared losing all of her possessions if she did not take legal action to protect them. For one dollar and other considerations paid, she conveyed the Assinippi farm and its accouterments to Kelley to hold in trust. The judge agreed to keep the property in good repair and, if necessary, rent or lease it to pay taxes and two outstanding mortgages held by Rockland Savings Bank.

Attorney Francis Geogan met June and Dorothy at the Rockland depot early the same morning for the trip to Plymouth. When they reached their destination and alighted from the train, newspaper snapshot artists were waiting and photographed them as they made their way up the hill to the courthouse.

Once inside, June resumed her testimony before the grand jury. About an hour later, she was followed by Dr. Joseph Frame. After Frame came Harry S. Cate, a twenty-one-year-old Rockland resident and acquaintance of June Ainsworth; Medical Examiner Dr. Gilman Osgood; and Harvard pathologist Dr. William Whitney. The session adjourned at 4:30 p.m. after the examination of Detective Scott.

~

Attorneys Morse and Geogan again met June and Dorothy in the courthouse corridor at session's end. The two sisters were anxious to visit their mother. They had not seen her since the day of her arrest. Morse engaged a horse-drawn carriage, and all four crowded into it for the two-mile journey to the jail.

Deputy Sheriff Tower met them at the jail and escorted them inside. June and Dorothy waited in a reception area while Morse and Geogan conferred with Jennie in her cell. The two lawyers returned a half hour later. Tower led the sisters to a conference room just outside the female ward and left them. He returned with Jennie a few moments later. The three women looked at each other in silence for a few moments. Suddenly, June rushed forward and embraced her mother. Both began to weep.

"Cheer up, dear. Don't worry," whispered Jennie and, in tears, turned to Dorothy. "My own little Dorothy," she sobbed.

"Mother," cried Dorothy and ran to Jennie who hugged her tightly. Dorothy pressed a bouquet of mayflowers into Jennie's hand.

"Thanks for the flowers," Jennie said tenderly. "They will stay with me in my room, dead, and it will be but a short time now when they and I will be at home again with you."

An hour later, when it was time for June and Dorothy to leave, the three women again embraced sorrowfully.

"Don't worry," Jennie told her daughters. "I have done nothing that I am sorry for and nothing that I should not do. All will come out right.

Dorothy, Attorney Geogan, and June depart Plymouth depot for the courthouse
(*Courtesy of F. Joseph Geogan II, Esq.*)

It is only a matter of time."

~

District Attorney Barker presented two more witnesses to the grand jury on Thursday morning, March 27. After instructing jurors about the law, he dismissed them to begin deliberations. A court officer escorted the jurors to the court's first-floor jury room.

Just before 3:00 p.m., a court officer was sent to Judge Hugo Dubuque's second-floor courtroom where the judge was presiding over a civil trial. The officer got the attention of clerk Edward E. Hobart and informed him that the grand jury had reached a decision in the Eaton matter. When the clerk relayed the information to the judge, he called a recess, cleared the courtroom, and instructed Hobart to bring the jury before him.

At 3:05 p.m., court officers accompanied the jury from the first floor to Judge Dubuque's courtroom and seated them in the jury box. When the jury's written decision was handed to the judge, he scanned it quickly then, glancing up at the jurors, thanked them for their service and dismissed them. The jury filed out of the room.

Judge Dubuque informed District Attorney Barker that the jury had returned a true bill, indicting Jennie Eaton for her husband's murder. Barker told the judge that Mrs. Eaton was in custody at the county jail and that her lawyers were not at the courthouse. Given the late hour, Dubuque postponed the defendant's arraignment until ten thirty the following morning. He instructed a court officer to notify the jail and defendant's counsel about the scheduled proceeding.

Barker left the courtroom. Reporters surrounded him in the corridor. He related the grand jury's findings and provided copies of an abstract of Mrs. Eaton's indictment for murder. The abstract outlined six counts of poisoning in its indictment against the admiral's widow.

Barker told reporters his office would dismiss the murder charge against Mrs. Eaton still pending in Hingham District Court and reported that Judge Dubuque had scheduled her arraignment for the next morning. He also admitted that his investigation into the admiral's death was not complete; that he would continue the inquest in Hingham to develop additional evidence for use at Mrs. Eaton's trial.

Clerk of Court Hobart gave Sheriff Henry Porter a copy of the indictment to serve on Mrs. Eaton at the jail. Porter returned to the jail at 5:30 p.m. He went to Jennie's cell, handed her the document, and announced, "Mrs. Eaton, the grand jury having found a bill against you, it is my duty to serve you with a copy of the indictment by order of the court. Also, you will be obliged to appear at court tomorrow morning."

"Oh, dear! Oh, dear!" Jennie gasped as she held the indictment in her trembling hands. Tears filled her eyes. She was stunned and disheartened. She had never expected the jury to find sufficient evidence to indict her.

However, her sadness quickly turned to anger, and her anger to resolve. The indictment was merely a setback, she thought to herself. She'd prove her innocence and win her freedom at trial.

At about 10:00 a.m. on the morning of Friday, March 28, Sheriff Porter and Deputy Sheriff Joseph Collingwood escorted Jennie from her cell to a prison wagon with curtained windows for the two-mile journey to the courthouse. She was dressed in the same mourning dress and black hat she had worn when police arrested her in Hingham.

Aware that the press and a crowd of onlookers anticipated Mrs. Eaton's arrival at the courthouse entrance on South Russell Street, Porter directed Collingwood to drive to the back of the building. Collingwood pulled up to a door where Deputy Sheriff James Hurley was waiting. Porter and Collingwood hurriedly assisted Jennie from the car and led her into the courthouse and up the stairs to a small anteroom the sheriff had reserved for her detention.

Sheriff's deputies brought Jennie before Judge Dubuque at 10:20 a.m. According to one newspaperman, she "looked very well indeed." Her cheeks were "rosy after her ride in the crisp air and the fresh breeze." He detected a sparkle in her eyes, "and her expression betrayed no trouble within."

The only spectators were women employed in offices within the

Sheriff Henry Porter (*Courtesy of Plymouth County, MA, Sheriff's Office*)

86

courthouse and members of the press. June and Dorothy were absent.

A court officer declared the court in session, and District Attorney Barker stood to address Judge Dubuque. Clerk of Court Hobart also stood, as did Jennie and her counsel, when Hobart read the indictment's seven typewritten pages. When he finished, the clerk asked, "Jennie M. Eaton, to this indictment what say you, are you guilty or not guilty?"

"Not guilty," Jennie murmured from beneath the thin black veil covering her face.

Judge Dubuque turned to Jennie and said, "The plea of not guilty is understood, is entered subject to the right of the defendant to file any objection to the indictment. The motion of the district attorney, that the defendant be remanded to jail without bail, is granted." The judge allowed the defense two weeks to examine the indictment and file exceptions. No trial date was set.

The arraignment was over eleven minutes after it began. Deputies returned Jennie to the anteroom where she conferred with her attorneys for more than three hours as Deputy Collingwood stood guard outside the door. When the conference ended, Collingwood led Jennie to the waiting prison wagon for her return to the county jail.

Concerned about the sizeable crowd outside the courthouse, Sheriff Porter devised a ruse for Jennie's safe and unimpeded conveyance back to the jail. He stepped outside the south entrance and informed newsmen that the prisoner had already left for the jail. A wave of derisive protests rose and echoed off the courthouse façade. Porter's attempts to quell the uproar failed miserably.

District Attorney Barker suddenly appeared at Porter's side and raised his hand. The throng grew silent. "I will make a statement if you will take it exactly as I make it," he said. "The mental condition of Mrs. Eaton will be very carefully examined." Barker and Porter turned and stepped back into the courthouse.

Reporters, hungry to explore this new angle, rushed to the Plymouth depot to intercept attorneys Morse and Geogan before they departed. They found the two men on the station platform and solicited a reaction to the district attorney's comment. Both men seemed surprised. Barker had never discussed his intention to challenge their client's sanity. Morse told reporters that he and Geogan would oppose any attempt by the prosecutor to have Mrs. Eaton examined by an "alienist" and, if necessary, they would demand a public hearing before the court to prevent it.

~

Jennie kept herself busy in the jail while she waited for a trial date. The accommodations were Spartan but reasonably comfortable. Her twelve-by-fourteen-foot cell was actually an enclosed room with a ceiling and walls of white. It was furnished with a bed, dresser, small table, and chair. She was located in the front of the jailhouse, facing east, and she had a view of Massachusetts Bay through her window framed by red iron bars.

Sheriff Porter honored Jennie's request for books but prohibited access to newspapers. She exercised faithfully each morning and labored at her table in the afternoon. She worked on her memoir, and she wrote letters to family and friends proclaiming her innocence, the absurdity of her predicament, and expressing confidence in her exoneration and imminent release.

On March 29, a *Washington Times* reporter reviewed an article in *The New York Times* in which Mrs. Eaton had discussed the circumstances of her marriage to Admiral Eaton. Jennie had told *The New York Times* reporter that the admiral's first wife had died in her arms and, with her last breath, had implored the then Mrs. Ainsworth to watch over her husband after she was gone.

The *Washington Times* reporter contacted Dr. Frank Fremont-Smith to ask about Annie Eaton's death. The physician related that the admiral's wife had died as the result of a stroke that had paralyzed one side of her body. She was unconscious from the day she was stricken until the day she died, a period of about one week. The contradiction must have been obvious to the reporter. How had the unconscious Annie Eaton asked Jennie Ainsworth to "take care of Joe" and "marry him…?"

Fremont-Smith corroborated Jennie May Eaton's version of her assignment to the Eaton household by Mary Struble. He remembered Jennie as "a plain, well-spoken woman…evidently of a respectable family." The doctor believed Mrs. Ainsworth was an "ideal nurse," who was "clean and neat of appearance and very attentive to her patient." Never during their interactions had she said or done anything eccentric or out of the ordinary.

The reporter's next question took the doctor by surprise. "Would there have been any possibility that she (Annie Eaton) died from poison or some other cause, doctor?"

"Not the slightest," the physician replied.

"Did you see her every day during the time she was stricken and her death?"

"Every day and sometimes more than once, if I remember correctly."

The correspondent wanted to know if Fremont-Smith had detected any unusual reaction from Mrs. Ainsworth immediately following Annie Eaton's death.

"If I remember correctly," the physician said, "there was not the slightest action on the part of the woman to lead anyone to believe she did anything but her duty toward the patient."

Fremont-Smith knew little of the circumstances surrounding the admiral's marriage to Mrs. Ainsworth but admitted he had heard that Mrs. Ainsworth and her two daughters had moved in with the admiral shortly after Annie Eaton's death. He thought Mrs. Ainsworth and the admiral had later married in Chicago, but he wasn't sure.

The reporter next asked the doctor if he had ever heard "that Admiral Eaton was an expert on poisons."

"That story is absurd," the physician snapped. "It is true the admiral as a sailorman made numerous trips all over the world, but that he was an expert on poisons – that is a silly fabrication. Admiral Eaton was a fine citizen. He wouldn't have taken an interest – a peculiar interest – in sordid things such as poisons or death-dealing instruments excepting such as concerned the defense of his country in war."

Chapter 14

Jennie's defense team filed pretrial motions at Plymouth Superior Court on Wednesday, April 9. The first motion requested a "bill of particulars" citing the type of poison allegedly used and how it was allegedly administered by the defendant. The second motion sought the names of all witnesses who appeared before the grand jury. A third requested an order from the court allowing the defense to inspect any and all exhibits the district attorney intended to present at trial. The final motion sought a transcript of testimony and a list of evidence presented before the grand jury prior to indictment.

On the same date, Judge Kelley sent his personal secretary to the Plymouth County Registry of Probate to file Rear Admiral Eaton's will. Dated and signed on November 30, 1906, at Brookline, Massachusetts, the admiral appointed his wife, Jeanie [sic] May Eaton, executrix, without bonds. When she declined to serve as executrix, the court appointed Clarence E. Rice of Rockland as the estate's administrator.

The admiral bequeathed all of his estate, save $600 and a naval memento, to his wife, Jennie May. He entrusted the $600 to his nephew, Joseph Parker Varnum of Dracut, directing him to expend $200 of that amount for the "erection of suitable headstones in the Oakland Cemetery, over the graves of his aunt, Annie Varnum Eaton, and myself," and an additional sum of $100 for the perpetual care of the burial plots. The admiral also left his nephew one of the loving cups presented to him by the men under his command.

The admiral had provided for his two stepdaughters in the event that his wife, Jennie May, predeceased him. He set aside $5,000 specifically for June, then gave, devised, and bequeathed "all [his] property left to [his] said wife under this will" to his beloved stepdaughter, Dorothy.

~

Nearly two months after Jennie's arrest on March 20 and her

indictment on March 27, District Attorney Barker reopened his inquest into Admiral Eaton's death. Barker's case was still circumstantial and much was at stake. His term was coming to an end, and he faced a serious challenge for reelection in the coming months. The trial's outcome might very well determine his future.

He considered possible motives. By law, he was not bound to prove motive, but he could not overlook its importance. He started with the admiral's financial affairs and found that his annual pension was a respectable $4,700. The average annual income in 1913 was $800. Yet the admiral was in substantial debt. Eaton had apparently squandered the bulk of his assets, some $30,000, in the stock market, forcing him and his wife to give up the comfortable lifestyle they had enjoyed in Brookline and relocate to the Assinippi farm which they had purchased with a $500 down payment and a mortgage.

Even though the admiral's pension and the farm's income afforded them an adequate subsistence, Barker wondered if Mrs. Eaton had become embittered. She had expected to live lavishly as the wife of a wealthy retired naval officer – a woman of power, privilege, and social stature. Because of her late husband's financial misfortunes, her dream had devolved to the mundane life of a housewife and chicken farmer heavily burdened with bills. Was this dissatisfaction motive enough for her to have engineered the murder of her husband?

Perhaps it was the difference in their ages. The admiral, at sixty-six, was twenty-four years older than his wife. Had this been a contributing factor in Mrs. Eaton's desire to do away with her husband?

Did Mrs. Eaton regret her divorce from her first husband and hope to reunite with him? Barker had received reports about her ex-husband's visits to the Eaton home and the cottage in Scituate. He wondered if this signified a rekindling of their relationship. But why wouldn't Mrs. Eaton just sue the admiral for divorce as she had done with Harry Ainsworth before him?

Did she poison the admiral to protect herself and her children from a perceived threat? From 1909 until the day of his death, Jennie Eaton and her daughter, June, had accused him of dabbling in drugs and poisons and of attempting to poison them. Did she consider his murder a matter of self-defense?

Had all of her complaints about the admiral's drug and alcohol abuse, her allegations of his interest in poison, and her attempts to have him committed to an institution been part of a plan to rid herself of the admiral while retaining his pension benefits? It would make no sense to kill him if she knew her husband's benefits would cease at his death.

Did she continue to blame the admiral for poisoning their adopted child, even though a medical examiner had declared the death due to natural causes? Had she convinced herself that Eaton had killed the child and conspired with the medical examiner to conceal the truth? If so, did she poison the admiral in retaliation? Or was this accusation another part of her scheme to free herself from the admiral by having him imprisoned or institutionalized?

Did June's sudden departure from the Assinippi house factor into the equation? Witnesses had described the contentious relationship between June and the admiral. Whether she had vacated the house on her own or had been forced by the admiral to leave was still a matter of conjecture, but it was clear that June was her mother's favorite and that her absence from the household was a source of bitter resentment between the admiral and his wife.

Was it jealousy? Mrs. Eaton had accused many women – maids, neighbors, store clerks, church members – of flirting with the admiral. She had also accused the admiral of similar transgressions. Were these justifiable accusations or the delusions of an unbalanced mind? Was Mrs. Eaton unable "to distinguish right from wrong to the extent that the law requires in order to constitute capacity to commit crime?" Was she "unable to control her impulses and desires?"

The defense had thus far prevented the district attorney from having Mrs. Eaton examined formally for mental competency, but DA Barker turned to Dr. Gilman Osgood for a psychiatric opinion. The two men discussed at length the testimony and evidence presented during the inquest and the grand jury proceedings. Osgood believed Jennie suffered from a persecutory form of paranoia known as "paranoia sexualis." Her demeanor, her delusions about the admiral's attempts to poison her, and her groundless suspicions about the admiral's flirtations with other women were characteristics of the paranoiac wife.

Barker reserved judgment. So many questions remained unanswered. He needed more evidence to firmly establish which of these motives had compelled Jennie to murder her husband.

As for means and opportunity, Barker had no doubt that Mrs. Eaton had the ability and the capacity to commit the crime. Her own admissions, as well as statements by family members, indicated that she had an exclusive opportunity to poison the admiral. But the prosecution lacked the physical evidence to prove that she possessed the poison. Investigators had failed to find any white arsenic on the Eaton property. Barker considered the idea that Mrs. Eaton had ample time to dispose of any unused poison, or evidence associated with it, before alerting authorities about her husband's death. She had either hidden it so well that police could not find it, or she had destroyed it.

The chances of recovering a sales record for poison grew increasingly remote with each passing day. State and local police had scoured a fifty-mile area around Assinippi and had failed to find evidence of a sale. Searches in Washington, Alexandria, Virginia, and Chicago had also proven fruitless.

Barker had learned during his interviews with Dr. Frame that Mrs. Eaton and the admiral had separate post office boxes. According to Frame, Jennie had insisted he send her medications to her box "because she didn't want anything of hers to come in contact with the admiral." Was it possible that Mrs. Eaton had acquired the poison through the mail? If so, who had sent it to her and how could it be traced?

Extensive publicity about the case in the press had failed to generate any leads. Months of dramatic front-page headlines and photographs of the Eaton family had generated a great deal of interest in the case, yet no witness had stepped forward with information that might link any of them to the purchase of poison.

~

Because the criminal and civil sessions at Hingham were closed, the inquest reopened at the district court in Abington on May 16. The press was in full attendance outside the courthouse as the witnesses, many now familiar to the reporters, entered the building. Among those who provided testimony during the morning session were the Eatons' neighbors and friends as well as *Rockland Standard and Plymouth County Advertiser* newspaper manager M. Warren Wright and Rockland druggist Chester L. Estes. James Thom, the nurseryman whose relationship with June Keyes had caused a rift with Admiral Eaton, also returned.

Wright testified about a transaction between Mrs. Eaton and a clerk at the Estes drugstore on March 1. He had seen Mrs. Eaton accept a small white parcel from the clerk and hurry from the store. Estes was asked to explain the incident. He denied that the parcel given to Mrs. Eaton contained poison and insisted that neither he nor any of his employees had ever sold or given arsenic to her.

Thom also denied that he had ever supplied anyone in the Eaton household with arsenic. Eaton neighbor Helen Jacobs testified about conversations she had had with Mrs. Eaton about the admiral, as did her husband, Andrew Jacobs, after which Barker adjourned the inquest until "…some future date."

~

On July 22, 1913, Chief Justice John A. Aiken, who would preside over the Eaton trial, ruled on the defense's pretrial motions. He denied defense requests for access to the grand jury transcript, government exhibits, and particulars about the specific poison used and when it was allegedly administered. Aiken deferred on the motion for the release of the names of grand jury witnesses because the defense was entitled to the names as a matter of record. At the conclusion of his ruling, Judge Aiken set a trial date of October 13, 1913.

~

With less than three months to prepare a defense for their client, Morse and Geogan began to develop a strategy. After an extensive review of witness statements and physical evidence, the lawyers theorized that Admiral Eaton had died by his own hand. The defense intended to prove that during his wife's absence on the Wednesday before he died, the admiral had self-administered a single, lethal dose of arsenic. Whether he had taken the lethal dose accidentally or as an act of suicide would be left for the jury to consider.

The defense intended to show that Mrs. Eaton was a selfless, devoted woman; a woman who was incapable of committing the heinous crime for which she was charged; a woman of sound mind whose accusations against her husband were wholly justified. They would show that the admiral was not the cultured gentleman and officer depicted by the prosecution, but a charlatan whose veneer belied his true character. They would attack his reputation with testimony and physical evidence that showed him to be a coarse, vile man who was frequently inebriated and under the influence of drugs.

Lastly, the defense intended to dispel any questions in the jurors' minds that Mrs. Eaton had murdered her husband for financial gain. They would establish that the admiral was deeply in debt and show that the defendant was fully aware that her only source of income, the admiral's comfortable pension, would end with his death.

~

District Attorney Barker reconvened the inquest into the admiral's death for a third time on October 2, 1913. Among the new witnesses were Eaton neighbors Mr. and Mrs. Charles Hilt, Mr. and Mrs. William Magoun, and Herbert Simmons; Frank Alger, owner of the *Rockland Standard and Plymouth County Advertiser*; and Annie Rooney, the nurse hired by Mrs. Eaton to assess Admiral Eaton's mental condition. Assinippi grocery clerks Earl Forsman and Adelbert Gooch, both witnesses at the first hearing, were called to testify once more.

With only eleven days before Jennie Eaton's trial, the district attorney was tying up loose ends. He remained silent about the purpose of this latest session, leaving reporters and the general public to speculate. Rumors again began to circulate about a possible second arrest in the poisoning mystery, but they subsided when the trial began without further action by the district attorney.

Barker returned to his Brockton office after the inquest and conferred with his two assistants. For months the three men had familiarized themselves with the evidence, identified strengths and weaknesses of the case, reviewed the law, discussed and prepared for all possible defenses and arguments, and met with potential witnesses to prepare them for their testimonies.

Although he lacked the physical evidence to connect Mrs. Eaton to the arsenic found in the admiral's organs, Barker believed that the testimony of key witnesses would establish a compelling circumstantial case and would show that she had the opportunity and means to commit the crime. The evidence would show that Mrs. Eaton, motivated by jealousy, greed, and rage, had administered more than one dose of arsenic to her husband and, by her overt act, had caused his death. Medical testimony would confirm that the admiral ingested the first dose on Thursday night and the last dose two to six hours before his death on Saturday.

As to criminal responsibility, Barker intended to present to the jury every fact at his disposal. Some of these facts tended to show malice with complete responsibility. Others suggested an overt act by a person of diminished mental capacity. But the district attorney would present them all and let the jury decide whether Mrs. Eaton was guilty of murder or not guilty of murder by reason of insanity.

~

The trial promised to be a sensation. Daily press coverage had generated extraordinary interest in the case. Plymouth town and county officials, expecting large numbers of spectators and a bevy of newsmen, made immediate plans for security and crowd control.

Sheriff Porter devised a detailed plan for Mrs. Eaton's protection and for security within the courthouse. The sheriff would allow access to the courthouse's south entrance to court officials, deputy sheriffs from his office, and all others with a direct role in the case. He designated separate rooms for the district attorney and his associates, the defense attorneys, and the jury. Spectators and newspapermen would utilize the north entrance, and a guard, stationed at the stairway to the second floor, would check credentials.

The small courtroom had limited seating. The sheriff reserved fifteen seats for reporters at a table on one side in a section ordinarily occupied by witnesses. Rather than issue tickets for admission to spectators, Porter provided seats on a first-come, first-served basis. Hopeful spectators would form a line outside the courthouse, and deputies would admit them one by one until all available seats in the gallery were filled. If a spectator vacated a seat, the deputies would admit the next person in line to fill it.

The sheriff arranged for the installation of telephones and telegraph wires for reporters inside the old jail that stood behind the courthouse. He set up a long table in the guardroom for telegraph instruments and authorized three telephone booths in a corridor beyond.

In deference to Mrs. Eaton, Porter removed from the front of the courtroom an iron cage used to confine defendants during criminal trials and restored a mahogany railing that enclosed members of the bar. He placed a leather-cushioned armchair for her in the center of the courtroom just outside the railing, about thirty feet from the witness stand.

The stage set, counsel for the prosecution and defense appeared before Judge Aiken on Monday, October 13, to discuss preliminary matters in anticipation of jury selection the next day. Jennie was not present for these proceedings.

Early the following day, Deputy Sheriff John Geary drove Jennie from the jail to the courthouse where two other deputies met them and escorted her to the second-floor anteroom.

One hundred forty-seven prospective jurors chatted quietly inside the courtroom awaiting the arrival of Judge Aiken. Present at the bar were District Attorney Albert Barker and his assistants, Frederick G. Katzmann and George E. Adams. To their left sat counsel for the defense, attorneys William A. Morse and Francis J. Geogan. Reporters filled the fifteen seats at the table set aside for them by Sheriff Porter. The limited capacity allowed for very few spectators, and many were left standing in the drizzle outside the building, waiting for a chance to fill a vacated seat.

Mrs. Eaton entered the courtroom in the custody of Deputy Sheriff Collingwood a few minutes before ten. A hush descended as every eye turned to gaze at the woman on trial for her life. Jennie looked down at first, startled by the penetrating stares, but quickly regained her composure and strode confidently to the seat she would occupy for the next nineteen days.

All rose upon the entrance of Judge Aiken who immediately began the jury selection process. Aiken excused eighty-two prospective jurors from the panel after his examination determined they were unable to serve. Sixty-four were eliminated for cause when they professed their opposition to capital punishment. The judge excused five for poor hearing, four for illness, one whose wife was ill, and one who was a student. Seven were excused after claiming they had already formed opinions about Mrs. Eaton's guilt or innocence. The prosecution exercised eighteen peremptory challenges and the defense, thirteen.

DA Barker proceeded with utmost discernment as he considered each candidate. His experience led him to believe that jurors always looked for reasons to acquit, especially in a capital case. No juror craved the responsibility for sending a man, let alone a woman, to a life in prison or execution. It was easier for them to acquit and rationalize their decision by blaming the prosecution for failing to prove guilt beyond a reasonable doubt.

By 4:30 p.m., the court, the prosecution, and the defense had agreed on a jury of twelve men. The median age was forty-six years. The oldest among them was seventy-two, the youngest twenty-six. Five were shoemakers, two were farmers, and one was a cranberry grower. A millwright, a streetcar conductor, a wagon driver, and a general laborer made up the rest of the panel.

Aiken dismissed the rest of the jury pool. Then he turned to the newly empanelled jury, administered an oath, and instructed them on their duties and obligations.

He was keenly aware of the widespread publicity the Eaton case had generated. He would not allow newspapers or any other outside source to unduly influence the jurors as they weighed the evidence and decided on a verdict. He informed the jury that he found it prudent to sequester them in the interests of a fair and impartial trial until its conclusion. Many had feared this would happen. Darkness swept over their faces.

The judge told the jurors to notify their families and arrange for clothing, toiletries, and other necessities to be sent to the Samoset House hotel. They would remain there, isolated and under

Chief Justice John A. Aiken
(*Courtesy of the New England Historic Genealogical Society*)

98

guard, for the duration of the trial. Court officers led the panel to the jury room.

An hour later, after all jurors had settled their affairs, they were taken back to the courtroom.

Judge Aiken appointed sixty-four-year-old James A. Thomas, a millwright from Middleboro, as jury foreman and directed the panel to return to the courtroom at 9:00 a.m. the next day. He then released them to the custody of court officers who escorted the twelve men on foot to the Samoset House, three blocks away.

After they had left, Barker asked the court to authorize transporting

Samoset House Hotel *(Furnished by the author)*

the jurors to Assinippi for a view of the Eaton home. Aiken gave attorneys Morse and Geogan an opportunity to respond. After conferring briefly with their client, they offered no objection. With that, Aiken allowed Barker's motion, instructed bailiffs to plan the visit, and adjourned for the day.

Chapter 15

The second-floor courtroom at Plymouth County Superior Court filled up quickly on the morning of Wednesday, October 15. Reporters, spectators, court officers, and attorneys took their places before Judge Aiken entered the room. Bailiffs, dressed in smart, double-breasted frock coats and silk top hats, had marched the jurors from the Samoset House to the courthouse early in the morning. The panel waited anxiously in the jury room.

Plymouth County Courthouse *(Furnished by the author)*

Jennie, dressed in the same black ensemble she had worn the day before, arrived from the jail about a minute before court convened at 9:05 a.m. Spectators had gathered outside for a glimpse of her. As she alighted from the prison wagon, a gust of wind swirled about her and shifted the veil covering her face. Jennie recognized an acquaintance in the crowd and, as she passed by her, said with a confident smile, "Well, I'm one day nearer home."

Jennie showed little emotion as Deputy Sheriff Collingwood led her to her designated seat in the courtroom. She spoke briefly with her attorneys.

Judge Aiken emerged from his chambers and promptly signaled for the jury. The twelve men filed in and assumed their seats inside the jury box located to the judge's right. Satisfied that all jurors were present, the judge directed Clerk of Court Hobart to read the indictment. Hobart stood, faced the defendant, and recited the specifications listed in the document.

Reporters paid close attention to Jennie's reaction as she listened to the charges against her. They noticed that she bit her lips when Hobart said the words "...did feloniously kill and murder Joseph G. Eaton." As Hobart continued, Jennie became more and more uneasy in her seat, shifting from side to side, her eyes darting nervously about the courtroom.

When Hobart finished after fourteen minutes, Judge Aiken nodded to District Attorney Barker who stood and approached the jury. Barker was a tall man who appeared shorter than he was due to his stooped posture. He had thinning gray hair and a bushy, gray mustache, and he wore round, silver-framed glasses. In a voice barely audible to the jurors, he told them that bailiffs would convey them to Admiral Eaton's place of death in Assinippi where he would take them through the interior of the house to facilitate their understanding of testimony the prosecution intended to offer during the trial. When Barker finished, Aiken offered Attorney Morse an opportunity to address the jury, but Morse declined. Asked by Aiken if Mrs. Eaton would accompany the jury to the crime scene, Morse stated that she would not and waived her right to do so.

Aiken summoned four bailiffs to the bench and assigned them to the jury's transport and care. He reminded the jury of the instructions he had given them the day before and admonished them not to speak about the case with anyone while travelling to and from Assinippi.

Before he excused the jury and recessed, Aiken announced it was his intention to avoid a prolonged trial by extending the usual court hours and by trying the case on Saturdays. He also ordered the sequestration of all witnesses for the trial. By sequestering the witnesses, the judge hoped to prevent the occurrence of perjury and, just as importantly, prevent one witness's testimony from being inadvertently molded by the testimony of other witnesses. He would, however, at the request of either the prosecution or the defense, exempt certain witnesses if counsel could show cause. Prosecution and defense witnesses would wait in two separate rooms – one for men and one for women – until called to take the stand.

The prosecution and defense indicating they had no more business before the court, Aiken adjourned. After a few words with her attorneys, Jennie was escorted from the courthouse for the return trip to the jail.

Attorney Morse, District Attorney Barker,
Assistant District Attorneys Katzmann and Adams (seated);
Sheriff Porter and Attorney Geogan (standing)
(*Courtesy of F. Joseph Geogan II, Esq.*)

With court in adjournment, District Attorney Barker, Assistant District Attorneys Katzmann and Adams, Sheriff Porter, and attorneys Morse and Geogan posed inside the courtroom for a Boston newspaper photographer.

Four bailiffs bearing white staffs assembled the jurors in front of the courthouse where they boarded the special trolley that would carry them the twenty miles north to Assinippi Village. They arrived at 12:05 p.m. and boarded a large horse-drawn coach for the quarter-mile ride along Washington Street to the Eaton farm.

Jurors and bailiffs were gathered on the Eatons' front lawn when the district attorney and defense counsel arrived twenty minutes later. Barker asked one of the bailiffs to keep the jurors outside the house until he signaled for them. He wanted to speak first with Jennie's mother, Virginia Harrison, to prepare her for their visit. Barker emerged from the house a few moments later and motioned to the bailiff for the jury.

Inside, the jurors followed Barker, Morse, and Geogan up the front staircase to the second floor. Barker directed the jury's attention to the front bedroom on the north side used by Dorothy Ainsworth and Mrs. Eaton. Barker then led the group across the hall to the south side and identified Mrs. Harrison's bedroom in the front and the admiral's in the rear. He also pointed out a rear stairway leading down to the kitchen on the first floor.

Satisfied that the jury now had an adequate visual reference with which to relate the upcoming testimony and other evidence, Barker asked the bailiffs to escort the group downstairs and back to the courthouse.

~

Assistant District Attorney
Frederick Katzmann
(Courtesy of F. Joseph Geogan II, Esq.)

The next morning, Assistant DA Frederick G. Katzmann presented the prosecution's opening statement to the jury in front of the courtroom packed with reporters and spectators. Katzmann stood directly in front of the jury rail, his hands clasped behind his back. His argument was straightforward.

"The prosecution contends and expects to show," he said as he pointed his finger at Mrs. Eaton, "that Admiral Eaton met his death at the hands of his wife by the administration of poison to him.

This poison was of the variety known as white arsenic. The Commonwealth expects the jury to render a verdict of guilty of murder in the first degree, if the jury believes the prosecution has maintained its contention."

He admitted to the jury that the prosecution could not provide a witness who had actually seen the defendant poison her husband. The prosecution would rely on circumstantial evidence, which, by inference, would prove that no one but the defendant could have committed the crime.

Jennie, sitting in the defendant's chair with her hands in her lap, showed only mild interest in Katzmann's oration. She glanced about the courtroom, seemingly untroubled by the prosecutor's bold, accusatory remarks.

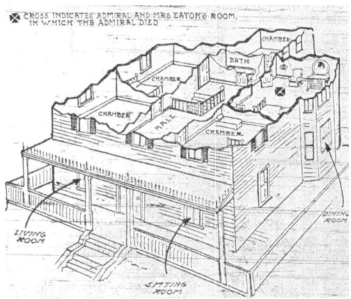

Edward B. Hayward's drawing of Eaton home
(*Boston Traveler and Evening Herald*)

The assistant district attorney provided the jury with a brief account of the Eaton family history – the death of the admiral's first wife; his first meeting with the defendant; the defendant's divorce from her first husband; and her marriage to the widowed naval officer in 1906. He described the admiral's affectionate feelings toward his two stepdaughters and his desire to provide them with the comforts of home and a good education. Katzmann told jurors that June, unlike Dorothy, had disappointed the admiral when she failed to concentrate on her studies and eventually withdrew from the music conservatory.

Katzmann went on to explain how June's romantic affairs had heightened the tension between her and the admiral.

"June began in her early girlhood to have love affairs," Katzmann said, "some of which were not to the liking of the admiral, and so a friction grew between the girl and her stepfather, and this friction further developed and spread between Mrs. Eaton and her husband because June was her firstborn, and the defendant cares more for her than for any other living being. Mrs. Eaton loves her daughter June. She has always been eager to answer to her beck and call. Mrs. Eaton soon began to take the admiral to task."

For the first time, Jennie looked perturbed and moved restlessly in her chair.

"We will show you that she is a woman of irascible temper, and that she was prone to violent outburst," Katzmann declared, "and that the rear admiral bore it all patiently through his short, married life. There was a reason for this. He had had a long training in the navy and knew how to control himself. But there was another reason in addition to this spirit of discipline; that was that he was a man of refinement – a gentleman. The State will show you that the defendant manifested a consistent and extreme jealousy. She was jealous of her housemaids when they lived in Brookline. Maid after maid had to be discharged owing to her outbursts. We will show you by the evidence that these suspicions, that these manifestations of jealousy, were absolutely unfounded in fact."

Jennie leaned forward, her face hard, and placed an arm on the rail in front of her, visibly agitated by Katzmann's allegations.

"We will show that Mrs. Eaton was jealous of neighbors as well as the maids, and it made no difference whether the neighbors or the maids were old or young, or good or bad looking," Katzmann continued. "We will show that she accused the admiral of flirting with women on the street, and that she berated him from time to time, and that he accepted it all patiently. We will show that she upbraided him because, as she claimed, a woman a quarter of a mile down the road waved to him while he was at work in the backyard. We will show that the daughter June became an ardent accuser like her mother, and that she received the aid and support of her mother. We will show that the mother repeated what June told her."

Katzmann delved into the tragic death of the Eatons' adopted son and the unfounded accusations against the admiral by his wife and stepdaughter.

"In the summer of 1909, the whole family engaged a cottage in Scituate," Katzmann continued. "A little boy they had adopted was with them. This little boy became ill and died within a few hours after being taken sick. We will show you that this defendant and her daughter, June, made the accusation that the admiral had brought the little one to his death by poison. An autopsy was held and showed that the death of the boy was due to perfectly natural causes. But from that day this defendant never withdrew her accusation, and from that time she has said that the admiral was trying to poison herself, June, and Dorothy.

"Gentlemen," he asserted, "she went even further than that, and in 1909, she was constantly telling Tom, Dick, and Harry that Admiral Eaton must be committed to an insane asylum, and for years she never ceased trying to have a sane man committed to an insane institution. We will show how she urged certain women to write letters stating that the admiral so annoyed them that something must be done. We will show that she was prompted to do this in order to get the admiral committed to an insane asylum. Even after the little boy died, she told a doctor that she would rely on his finding of poison in the boy's stomach to send the admiral to an insane asylum."

Katzmann next turned to the events leading up to the admiral's death. He described June's marriage to Ralph Keyes and her decision to separate from him. June and her husband, he explained, as well as Admiral and Mrs. Eaton, were to meet at South Station on the Wednesday before the admiral died to find a way to salvage the marriage. The meeting never occurred. That same night, Katzmann told jurors, Ralph Keyes, June, and her mother were at the Keyes' home in Medford. During a conversation there, June described a visit to Assinippi and a talk she had with the admiral.

According to June, the admiral had asked, "June, would you mind if

I put your mother out of the way?" When Mrs. Eaton heard this, said Katzmann, she "became very excited and said, 'I'll have him attended to the very first thing in the morning.' "

Katzmann summarized the last three days of the admiral's life for the jury. He told how the admiral, after eating cold roast pork on Thursday night, became ill and went to his bed where he remained until the discovery of his dead body on Saturday morning. Katzmann related that when doctors appeared at the Eaton household to perform the autopsy on the admiral's body, Mrs. Eaton said to one of the physicians, "I don't know anything about poisons. I never studied them." This, he declared, was said before any of the doctors mentioned poison as a possible cause for the admiral's demise.

Katzmann next told jurors the Commonwealth intended to produce a witness who would testify she overheard Mrs. Eaton say the loss of her husband's income would not cause a problem for her financially because she had "a wealthy lover in the West who wanted her to leave her husband and come to him."

Before he closed, Katzmann stated he was confident that jurors would agree that Mrs. Eaton had murdered her husband. But he also suggested that the prosecution would not be disappointed if they returned a verdict of not guilty by reason of insanity.

"It all depends," he said, "upon whether you judge that her acts, her malice aforethought, her deliberate intentions and plans were those of a sane or insane woman."

Judge Aiken announced a brief recess. When court resumed, the prosecution called Edward B. Hayward, a civil engineer, as its first witness. The district attorney's office had retained Hayward to prepare a floor plan of the Eaton home for court presentation. DA Barker and his assistants had affixed Hayward's oversized drawing to the wall behind the jury box during the recess.

Barker oriented the jury to what they had seen the previous day by having Hayward take them room-by-room through the house. At the district attorney's request, the judge directed the court clerk to mark Hayward's floor plan as Commonwealth Exhibit No. 1 and ordered that it remain on display throughout trial.

When the next witness, undertaker Joseph Wadsworth, took the stand, Barker directed his attention to Hayward's plan and asked him if it was a fair representation of the house's interior. Wadsworth responded that it was. Then, at the DA's prompting, he described the conditions he had found in the admiral's bedroom when he and Ernest Sparrell first arrived at the Eaton home on the morning of Saturday, March 8. He told of Dr. Frame's telephone call and Frame's clear instruction to leave the body undisturbed. He then recollected the postmortem examination performed on the admiral's body later that afternoon.

Medical Examiner Dr. Gilman Osgood of Rockland was next sworn.

Dr. Gilman Osgood
(*Courtesy of the Dyer Memorial Library, Abington, MA*)

Osgood testified about the message he received from Frame on the morning of March 8 and his response to the Eaton house at 10:45 a.m. He spoke of his conversation with Mrs. Eaton and her summary of events leading up to the admiral's death. Osgood described the autopsy he performed on the admiral's corpse, his observations about the stomach, and the inflammation he noted in the brain, stomach, and membranes of the intestines. He told the jury that he had refrained from making a final determination as to the cause of death until Dr. William Whitney of Harvard Medical School had completed a chemical analysis of the organs.

The district attorney questioned Osgood about the conditions he found in the admiral's bedroom when he first arrived. Osgood said he saw the admiral lying on the edge of his bed in his nightclothes, obviously dead. When Barker asked Osgood if the bed in which the admiral was lying was large enough to accommodate two people, as Mrs. Eaton had claimed, Osgood replied it was not; it was designed for the comfort of one person.

Barker asked the medical examiner about his conversation with Mrs. Eaton after the autopsy. Osgood told the court that Mrs. Eaton had drawn him aside at the bottom of the stairs and said, "I don't know anything about poisons." She then asked him what had caused the admiral's death. Osgood said he told her gastroenteritis was suspected, but more testing was required to make a final determination, to which Mrs. Eaton asked, "Didn't you find any indications of homicidal mania?" Osgood informed her it was impossible to determine such evidence through an autopsy. Mrs. Eaton, Osgood testified, went on to repeat her assertions about the admiral's use of poisons, adding that the admiral smoked opium.

A brief recess ensued, after which Osgood resumed his testimony. The district attorney asked the doctor for his impressions of Mrs. Eaton's demeanor during their conversation after the autopsy. Osgood said he thought she was cool, collected, and without emotion.

Barker next tried to draw an opinion from Osgood as to Mrs. Eaton's mental condition. When Osgood began to respond, Morse immediately objected because any questions about the defendant's mental state were deemed not admissible. Judge Aiken sustained the objection, and questioning along that line ceased.

Before he excused Osgood, the district attorney introduced into evidence various articles that Detective Scott had seized from the Eaton home and given to Osgood for analysis. He then turned his witness over to the defense.

"Who first called your attention to the death of Admiral Eaton?" asked Attorney Morse.

"Dr. Frame. He called me up at six a.m. He said he had just received a message saying Eaton was dead. He said he had seen him on the previous day and had not expected him to die," the medical examiner answered.

"Did he ask you to go to the house?"

"No. I assumed he wished me to."

"Did you go?"

"Yes."

Morse stepped to the diagram of the Eaton home and, with a pointer, asked Osgood to explain his movements within the house during his two visits on the day the admiral died.

"You remember Mrs. Eaton's emotions very accurately, don't you?" asked Morse.

"I do," replied Osgood.

"Do you remember whether you told Mrs. Eaton you were going to perform an autopsy?"

"My memory is indistinct," the physician said.

"How long did it take you to perform the autopsy?" Morse asked.

"About three hours."

Morse and Geogan had interviewed Osgood during their preparation for Jennie's defense. Morse tried to pin the doctor down as to when he first suspected poisoning during the autopsy.

"Did you tell Mr. Geogan and me that you took a book on arsenical poisoning to the autopsy?" Morse asked.

"I took a book on autopsies," Osgood replied, "and in that was a section devoted to the symptoms of arsenical poisoning."

"Did you tell us that you opened the book to the symptoms of arsenical poisoning and then and there discovered that the symptoms were found in the admiral's case?"

"No," answered the doctor.

Morse challenged Osgood's recollection of his March 8 conversation with Jennie. He suggested that the doctor may have misheard what Mrs. Eaton said, and when he asked Osgood if he had written down Mrs. Eaton's alleged statements, Osgood admitted he had not.

Morse then asked the medical examiner if it was possible that the admiral had taken poison as a matter of habit. Osgood suggested that arsenic was sometimes used to dispel the aftereffects of alcohol.

Barker, on redirect, asked the doctor to describe the properties of a medicinal dose of arsenic. Osgood said the dose was usually made from Fowler's solution and ran from one-fortieth to one-one hundredth of a grain. Barker then asked Osgood to estimate the number of arsenic eaters in America. Morse immediately objected, and the judge sustained the objection.

During arguments about the objection at sidebar, Aiken stated that the doctor was not competent to provide a number, or even an estimate, of arsenic eaters but was qualified to comment on the prevalence of the practice. He suggested that Barker rephrase his question. "If you will ask, Mr. District Attorney, to what extent there is arsenic eating in this country, I will allow it," said the judge. When Barker inquired as suggested, Osgood replied that arsenic eating was practically non-existent in the United States.

Barker then asked, "What is the result of arsenic eating, as to formation of habit or poisoning?"

Morse again objected before the witness could respond. The judge sustained the objection, turned to Osgood, and posed a theoretical question.

"Can a man in this country contract the habit of arsenic eating?"

"He can, but he doesn't," Osgood answered.

When Morse, on recross, asked the physician why this was so, Osgood said there was no explanation.

"It [is] simply a known fact, just as it is known that the miners of some countries are poisoned by arsenic they mine, while those in Syria and Styria (an Austrian state) eat it without a poison effect," he said.

Satisfied the prosecution and defense had no further questions, Aiken excused Osgood.

The prosecution called Dr. Frank Wheatley, who had assisted Osgood during Eaton's autopsy, and asked him to tell the court about his activities on Saturday, March 8.

"I went to the Eaton house about three p.m.," Wheatley testified. "Dr. Osgood, Dr. Frame, and an undertaker's assistant were there. I met Mrs. Eaton in the front hall, and she asked whether I was professor somebody; I didn't catch the name. I said no, I was Dr. Wheatley, and went upstairs. She seemed somewhat excited."

Wheatley then conveyed the observations he had made during the admiral's autopsy, all of which concurred with Osgood's testimony.

Morse, on cross-examination, asked Wheatley if he or Osgood had said in Mrs. Eaton's presence that they intended to perform an autopsy on the admiral. Wheatley said he couldn't recall. Barker then asked him on redirect if anyone had said anything about poison in Mrs. Eaton's presence.

"Not to my knowledge," replied Wheatley. At this point, Judge Aiken excused Wheatley and ordered a short recess.

Court resumed shortly after 3:00 p.m., but there was a delay while waiting for the next witness. In the interval, Morse re-called Osgood to the witness stand to ask him several questions about the evidence introduced during his direct examination.

"In anything that was given you by the officers, or in anything you saw in your search of the Eaton premises, did you find any white arsenic?" asked Morse.

"I made no analysis of any of the things that were given me," replied Osgood. "Officer Scott gave me some Paris green, but I saw nothing about the premises, or anything that came into my possession, that was arsenic, except that Paris green."

"Mrs. Eaton made no objection to your search?" Morse asked.

"No, she assisted me, at first," Osgood answered.

Barker quickly rose and asked, on redirect, if Paris green contained white arsenic. "I believe it does," Osgood replied. His second examination over, Osgood again stepped down from the stand.

As soon as Osgood left the courtroom, it occurred to the district attorney that the doctor's statement about Paris green containing white arsenic was in error. Dr. Whitney's analysis of the admiral's organs had confirmed the presence of white arsenic. Whitney had also confirmed that Paris green and white arsenic were two common, but distinct arsenicals of diverse chemical properties. Whitney's grand jury testimony had led to the indictment against Mrs. Eaton for poisoning the admiral with white arsenic and no other arsenical compound. Rather than recall Osgood to rectify his testimony, Barker decided he would resolve the issue with Whitney when he took the stand later during the trial.

The prosecution's witness had still not arrived. The district attorney assured the judge that his witness's arrival was imminent. Suddenly, all eyes shifted when the doorway to the judge's left opened and there stood Dorothy Ainsworth, the expected witness. She appeared somewhat tentative as she entered, not sure where she was supposed to go, until a court officer motioned her in his direction. She wore a black gown with white lace at the throat under a black jacket and a black velvet hat with a chinstrap and two quills. A sheer veil covered her face. More than one spectator remarked on how attractive she was.

Dorothy limped noticeably as she walked to the court officer. He directed her to the witness stand. Taking her seat, she gave Judge Aiken a nervous smile. The young woman was about to reveal the innermost secrets of the Eaton household.

Chapter 16

District Attorney Barker questioned Dorothy gently – "as if she was his own daughter," in one reporter's opinion – throughout her testimony. Asked by Barker for her name and age, she identified herself as Dorothy Virginia Eaton and said she was sixteen years old, although she admitted this was a guess because she didn't know her exact birth date. Asked if Eaton was her legal name, she said no; that she had assumed the name.

"Where have you been living for the past year?"

"In Assinippi and West Norwell," she replied.

"And with whom?" the prosecutor asked.

"Father and mother."

"And by 'father' you mean whom?"

"Admiral Eaton."

"And prior to that?" asked Barker.

"In Brookline, one year," the girl answered.

Dorothy spoke so softly that her answers were barely audible, forcing jurors to lean forward in their seats. Judge Aiken, who was also struggling to hear, interrupted Barker's examination and asked Dorothy to speak up.

"How long is it since June has lived at the house?"

"Two years," said Dorothy.

Barker, knowing Dorothy's answer was incorrect, rephrased his question.

"Is there any event," Barker asked, "by which you can fix the time when June went away from the others in the family?"

Dorothy hesitated as if confused, and Barker tried again.

"Do you remember the baby which your mother adopted and its death?"

"Yes," said Dorothy, her memory now refreshed. "June has not lived with us since. She has stayed with us, but has not been a regular member of the family. She has lived mostly in Boston; she was in East Somerville at one time, and at the academy at Fredericktown [sic],

Maryland."

Barker tried to elicit an explanation from Dorothy as to why June left the house.

"Do you know the circumstances of her going?" Barker posed.

"What do you mean by 'circumstances'?" Dorothy asked.

"Why she went – whether she went against her will," the prosecutor answered. When Morse objected to the question, Barker withdrew it and moved on.

Dorothy's apprehension and anguish were palpable. Spectators observed her frequent troubled sighs and fidgeting – obvious indications of the stress put upon her as a witness against her mother. But she proved to be an extremely credible, articulate witness who endeared herself to all present for her courage and candor.

Barker now returned to the adopted baby and questioned Dorothy about statements she had heard her mother make after the baby's death.

"Do you remember when your mother got the boy she adopted?" asked Barker.

"I think it was in March, about three years ago," said Dorothy. "She got it at the Catholic Protectory in Boston, and it lived with the family up to the time we were at the Sand Hills in the summer."

"What happened then?"

"Why, the baby died," said Dorothy.

Barker asked her to recall any statements her mother made following the baby's death. Dorothy said her mother claimed the admiral had poisoned the child and that her mother never wavered from this belief. In fact, Dorothy said, her mother thought the doctor's autopsy report as to the cause of the baby's death was erroneous, telling her, "...One of the doctors who made it had afterward been sent to an insane asylum, and that he was probably insane when the report was made."

"Who made the first complaint that the baby had been poisoned?" Barker asked.

"I think it was made simultaneously by mother and June."

"What did they say?"

When Dorothy answered, "I never heard any actual conversation, but I know they both believed it," Morse raised an objection, and the judge sustained it. He instructed the jury to disregard Dorothy's answer and ordered her statement stricken from the record.

The district attorney asked Dorothy if her mother had accused the admiral of poisoning others in the household besides the adopted baby.

"I heard her say that she didn't believe the baby was the only one who had suffered by the administration of poison. She said she believed he (the admiral) was insane; she said also that she thought he had administered poison to myself and to her."

"What about giving it to June?" Barker asked.

"I don't remember," Dorothy answered. "Mother used to be angry when she said these things."

"What were the occasions?"

"Whenever any of us was sick – when I had a headache, or some perfectly natural ailment."

"And as to herself?" Barker continued.

"It would be when she had little marks on her arm; she believed that he had injected poison into her in her sleep."

"Did she show you these marks?"

"Yes," Dorothy said. "They looked like perfectly natural scratches, or perhaps mosquito bites."

When the prosecutor asked her to recall other incidents, Dorothy said she could not remember. Barker went to the prosecution table and retrieved the transcript of testimony taken during the inquest. He read aloud Dorothy's statement about an incident in which her mother had complained about a tooth. Her memory refreshed, Dorothy told the jury that her mother had insisted that the tooth had loosened after the admiral had injected it with poison.

Barker asked her about another incident that had taken place in the Brookline house. Again, Dorothy claimed she could not remember. Barker read aloud once more from the transcript. Dorothy remembered that the admiral had taken some food to June while she lay sick in her bedroom. Her mother had prevented June from eating any of it, claiming the admiral had laced it with poison.

Barker asked her if she remembered testifying at the inquest about her mother's behavior during meals. Dorothy said her mother wiped the plates with a towel to remove a film of poison before any food was placed on them. When Barker inquired if her mother had ever thrown any food away because it was poisoned, Dorothy said she had not. She also denied ever hearing her mother say that the admiral had poison under his fingernails.

Barker wanted to know how often her mother made allegations about poison. Dorothy said her mother made the claims "whenever anything happened that put her out."

"When she was angry she was more likely to make these claims?" Barker asked.

"Whether she was angry or not," Dorothy replied.

"What would she be angry about?"

"Any illness of myself, or June, or grandmother," said Dorothy. "Sometimes this would happen once a month, sometimes once in two months," she added.

"And with whom would she be angry?"

With an astonished look, Dorothy answered, "I have been speaking of the times she was angry with father."

"Now to the question of any other cause for your mother being angry," Barker resumed.

"Well, it was mostly because she was jealous," said Dorothy slowly. "She was jealous of various women."

"Can you name any of them?"

"Sometimes they were indefinite – people I didn't know at all – people they met in Rockland, in stores, or on the street, or in the cars. Some of them were people I did know; there was Miss Howard (the nurse) and the baker's girls and Mrs. Lewis, principal of the school."

In a moment of retrospect, or perhaps because of a look from Jennie, Dorothy said, "I don't know, mother wasn't necessarily jealous, but she accused them of flirting with father."

Barker asked if she recalled others.

"One was a young girl up the road, named Miss Farrar. There were the servants when we were in Brookline; she was jealous of them on some grounds. She was jealous of Miss Griffith (the Eaton housekeeper in May 1912), too."

"What did your mother say on these occasions?"

"That she didn't think very much of it," Dorothy replied. "That she didn't like it and didn't think he ought to do it (entertain such attention)."

The district attorney asked Dorothy if she had ever seen the admiral flirt with a woman. The judge overruled Morse's objection to the question and allowed Dorothy to answer. She told the court she had never seen him flirt with a woman and knew him to act always as a gentleman.

Barker asked her how the admiral responded to her mother's upbraidings about his dalliances.

"Sometimes he was provoked," Dorothy said. "Sometimes he would deny the charges, sometimes he would make a joke of them."

The district attorney asked Dorothy if there were any other women her mother had accused. Dorothy remembered incidents with neighbors, Mrs. Simmons, Mrs. Collamore, and Mrs. Collamore's daughter, Bessie.

Asked about the number of maids her mother had fired from the Brookline household, Dorothy said she was not positive but estimated that her mother had dismissed more than six during the one year the family lived there.

Barker asked if she could recall the last time her mother had accused the admiral of flirting. Dorothy remembered an incident with one of the Coolidge twins at a Rockland bakery shop on the Monday before the admiral died. Barker was somewhat surprised by her reference to Monday. She had testified during the inquest that the incident had occurred the day before her mother left the house to stay with June for a week to ten days.

"No," Dorothy replied. "I think it was after she came back."

The prosecutor returned to the transcript and refreshed Dorothy's memory. She then changed her testimony and agreed with what Barker had read. Her mother had returned from June's home in Medford on Saturday, March 1. The incident at the bakery shop had occurred on Tuesday, March 4.

In response to Barker's further questions, Dorothy testified about her mother's trip to visit June in Medford the next day, Wednesday, March 5. She said her mother went there to discuss June's intention to separate from her husband, Ralph Keyes. June and her mother were to meet the admiral at South Station the same afternoon to determine how best to proceed.

Dorothy said her mother was not at home when she returned from school at 3:30 p.m. June surprised her at about 4:00 p.m. when she came to the house without her mother. June apparently hadn't realized that her mother had gone to Medford to see her. June departed after a half hour, hoping to connect with Jennie in Medford.

The district attorney turned his attention to the admiral's health during the days leading up to his death. Dorothy said she hadn't noticed anything unusual about the admiral on the day her mother left to visit June in Medford. Dorothy said she and the admiral were having breakfast on Thursday morning when her mother came down from her room at about eight thirty and joined them in the kitchen. Dorothy left for school after breakfast, and when she returned home in the afternoon, she found the admiral in his usual good spirits.

"Do you remember where you had tea that night?" Barker asked.

"In the kitchen," said Dorothy.

"You are sure about that?"

"Yes."

"Was it customary to have it there?"

"No. We did have it there once in a while."

"Who was at tea that night?"

"Mother, father, and myself."

"Where was your grandmother?"

"She was in the dining room."

"Do you recall what you had for tea?"

"I don't remember all we had, but there was some fresh pork, cold."

"And some tea or a substitute for coffee?"

"Yes."

"You drank milk?"

"Yes."

"And the admiral, tea or coffee substitute?"

"Yes."

"Who prepared the supper?"

"Mother."

"Who prepared the tea or coffee?"

"I think father did; I'm not sure."

"Do you recall whether your mother drank any of the tea or coffee?"

"I don't remember whether she drank any."

"How long were you at the table before the admiral got up?"

"About an hour. We sat there and talked and laughed. Father was telling stories."

"Then what happened?" Barker inquired.

"Father excused himself and went out into the back room and was sick," Dorothy replied.

"As he left the room, what did he do with his hand?"

"I don't remember distinctly, but he placed it either on his stomach or over his mouth."

"And after he went out of the room what did you hear?"

"He was sick. He came back into the room, and mother asked him how he felt and what was the matter with him. We all got up from the table. I helped mother clear the table. Then she said she wanted me to go right to bed. I said that I had some lessons to get, and she gave me one hour."

Barker returned to the prosecutor's table and retrieved the inquest transcript. Dorothy was confusing Thursday night's events with Friday's. After Barker read her earlier testimony, Dorothy conceded her error and testified she had gone to bed early Thursday night and had gone to her grandmother's room. The admiral came upstairs about 9:00 p.m. and spoke with her and her grandmother briefly. Mrs. Harrison asked the admiral how he felt. The admiral said he was better. In fact, he told them, he had finished Dorothy's algebra homework for her.

"I was surprised for he had never done it before except when I was there," Dorothy testified. "It was all done when I looked next morning, however." She said she slept in the back bedroom with her mother on Thursday night and neither had heard anything from the admiral's room.

Barker turned to the transcript once more and asked Dorothy if she remembered that she told grand jurors that the admiral had been sick all Thursday night into Friday morning.

Dorothy, her memory refreshed, said the admiral told her the next morning that he had been sick. When she saw him Friday morning he was in bed and looked "weak and pale." When she returned from school in the afternoon, she went to his bedroom and found he had not improved. In fact, he was much worse. She told the court that Dr. Frame had visited him while she was at school and had told the admiral his illness was due to biliousness.

"He asked me about my report card; then he wanted to know if the

119

room was not very cold," Dorothy said. "I told him it was, but that the furnace fire had gone out. He asked me to fill a hot water bottle, and I went downstairs to get some hot water from the kettle. Before I went, he said his head ached and asked for something for that. I gave it to him, but on my way downstairs I heard him throwing it up."

"Where was your mother?" Barker asked.

"Downstairs."

"Did she come in when you gave him the headache medicine?"

"No."

"What was said downstairs?"

"She said she didn't see why I should wait on him, and seemed provoked. She said she had been waiting on him all day and was capable of going on, and grandma said mother had been up and down all day, waiting on him."

Dorothy said that as she walked back to the admiral's room, she met her mother in the hallway. Her mother scolded her for waiting on the admiral.

"Did she talk to the admiral about your waiting on him?" asked Barker.

"Yes. She repeated what she was saying to me in his presence."

"Did you hear her say anything about the medicine she had been giving him?"

"Nothing except that she had been giving him medicine; I think once in three hours."

"What time that night did she say she would give you an hour to get your lessons?"

"About five minutes after seven."

"What time did you go upstairs?"

"Few minutes after eight. She was in our room and in bed. I got ready to go to bed. I think it took me half an hour, as she had given me till half past eight to be in bed."

"Were the doors shut?"

"Yes, both of them, and both locked."

"Did you go to sleep?"

"Yes, we both went to sleep. Mother went to sleep first, lying on her back."

Dorothy said the next thing she heard was her grandmother

knocking on the bedroom door. She said Mrs. Harrison seemed "very agitated."

"She said, as near as I could understand, just waking up that way, that the admiral had fallen on the floor."

"Do you know whether your mother had been up in the meantime?"

"No, but I think we woke up together. We ran into father's room and found him on the floor, sitting against the bed. I should say he was only partly conscious. We got him into bed again, and changed his night robe and his bed linen. After we got him into bed, he murmured, 'doctor.' Mother said that Dr. Frame was coming again in the morning and asked if that would do, and he said, 'Yes.' Then we asked if he was comfortable, and he said he was very cold. We went back then to our bedroom and got into bed. This time the door was closed but not locked.

"We had been in bed only five minutes when I heard him say something about the bedclothes choking him. It was always a fear of his, mother said when I wanted to get up, that the clothes were all right when we left him, that we hadn't been gone five minutes and that the clothes could not be choking him. She told me I'd better not get up, as I had a cold and it was very cold in the house. But I thought that if he believed the bedclothes were choking him, it was as bad as if they really were. So I got up and went in."

When Dorothy checked the admiral, she found no problem with his clothing. She stood quietly watching him. She said he seemed to be mumbling numbers to himself and then asked, "What's the next example, Dorothy?"

"I knew then that he thought he was helping me with my algebra, and finally, thinking it would make him easier, I made up a problem for him. He said, 'I can't solve that, Dorothy.' 'Oh yes, you can,' said I. And then in a moment he came to, as I was stroking his head. He saw me there and said, 'You'll take cold, Dorothy; you'd better go back to bed.'

"Mother said then that if he called again, she would get up and would stay with him the rest of the night. And after a while he did call again. He called my name three times. Mother said, 'I'll get up and go, and I'll stay with him.' She went over and shut the door behind her. I lay awake a long time; it seemed like hours. Finally I fell asleep, and it seemed as if I had been asleep only a few minutes when she woke me up and said, 'Dorothy, I believe your father is dead.'

"I don't know what time it was. The sky was light, but the sun hadn't risen. We dressed. Mother seemed distracted; she didn't seem to know what to do. Finally she suggested that we ought to call the doctor. I didn't know what the doctor could do but said that if she felt that we ought to, I would telephone from Mrs. Simmons's."

Jennie went with Dorothy to the Simmons house where Dr. Frame as well as Ernest Sparrell, the undertaker, were called.

Dorothy had testified for almost two hours, and it was after 5:00 p.m. Judge Aiken suggested that the district attorney continue his direct examination the next morning. Barker agreed, and court adjourned for the day.

Chapter 17

Dorothy returned to the witness stand the next morning, Friday, October 17. Seated behind the defense table inside the bar with permission of the court was Dr. A. Everett Austin, a Back Bay physician and chemist hired by the defense as a rebuttal witness.

District Attorney Barker resumed his direct examination by asking Dorothy to recall her life in Chicago. Dorothy said she had lived there with her biological father, Harry Ainsworth, her mother, and her sister for more than a year. Her sister June had returned to Chicago for extended visits on two other occasions after the family had left. On the second occasion, her mother went with June and stayed for a month and a half.

Judge Aiken, recalling the difficulty he had hearing Dorothy during the previous day, interrupted the district attorney and asked Dorothy to remove her hat and veil. When she struggled to loosen the knot securing the veil, the judge asked Dorothy if someone could help her. Dorothy suggested her mother, and Aiken consented.

Dorothy left the stand, walked to her mother, and sat on her knee. The two women smiled warmly at each other. Jennie untied the veil and, after removing it, tenderly stroked Dorothy's face. Dorothy returned to the witness stand and removed her hat, which she placed in front of her. A black velvet ribbon held her hair tightly in place.

Barker's next line of inquiry concerned the "will" Detective Scott had found in the typewriter at the Assinippi home. Barker was unable to elicit detailed testimony from Dorothy. When Dorothy said she didn't write the will but that her mother may have, Attorney Morse objected and asked the judge for permission to approach the bench. Morse and Barker spoke briefly in hushed tones with the judge at sidebar and then returned to their tables. Barker abandoned his questioning about the will and moved on to statements Dorothy had overheard her mother make about the admiral's sanity.

"I think she did not believe the admiral was always in his right mind," Dorothy said.

"Have you heard her say anything about having him committed?" asked Barker.

"Not that, but I have heard her say he needed an attendant, whenever she got talking about his insanity."

"Did she ever bring anybody there?"

"Yes, Miss Annie Rooney, a year ago last June."

"Where did you first meet Miss Annie Rooney?" Barker asked.

"In Rockland, with mother," Dorothy replied. "Mother had been in Washington a month or six weeks and was bringing Miss Rooney home with her. I was told why she was coming."

Barker then asked Dorothy if the admiral had ever found out the purpose of Miss Rooney's presence in the home. Dorothy said the admiral did find out. She had overheard her mother, Miss Rooney, and the admiral discussing it one afternoon.

The district attorney filled in additional details about the night of Admiral Eaton's death with Dorothy's testimony. He then sought her impressions about his drinking habits. Dorothy admitted the admiral used liquor, sometimes drinking a pint or as much as a quart. She said he was "talkative" and "full of good spirits" when he imbibed.

Barker asked Dorothy if her mother and June had ever searched the Assinippi house for liquor. When Dorothy said she couldn't remember if they had, Barker read her inquest testimony. Her mind refreshed, Dorothy recalled they had searched the attic but did not find any liquor.

The prosecutor returned to his questioning about June's relationship with the admiral.

"Was there any friction between your father and mother on June's account?"

"Yes, there was," Dorothy replied. She related how her mother and the admiral had argued about a Hingham man named Thom who was over seventy years old. (He was actually closer to sixty when the incident occurred). According to Dorothy, the admiral was angry with Thom, who he believed was romancing June.

"When did you hear of this friction?" asked Barker.

"When he (Thom) began paying too much attention to June."

"How long did this continue?"

"Till June got tired of the man herself."

"How long ago was this?"

"Four or five years."

"How long did it last?"

"Little more than a year."

When Barker asked Dorothy when her mother had gone to East Weymouth with June, she said Jennie had left in September and had stayed for five months.

"Did Mr. Thom visit there?" the DA inquired.

"I saw him there once."

"Did the admiral come there?"

"Yes."

"Did he try to get his wife to return to him?"

"I didn't know of it."

"Did your mother later on become better pleased with Mr. Thom?"

"She tolerated him; she never liked him."

"And the admiral?"

"He couldn't bear him."

Aiken suspended the direct examination and called for a short recess. As Dorothy left the courtroom, she tried to approach her mother but was diverted by a court officer.

Dorothy returned to the stand when court resumed, and the district attorney continued his queries about June's relationship with the admiral. Barker wanted to know if June's relationships with any other men or boys had caused hostility between the admiral and his wife. Dorothy said she didn't know of any.

Barker asked her whose money supported June and if any friction existed between the admiral and June about her studies. Dorothy said the admiral provided for June's support. She admitted that June did not like to study and said the admiral was not happy about it, "But I don't know that it caused friction."

"What was your mother's attitude toward June?" the DA asked.

"She was very fond of her," Dorothy answered.

"As to June's influence over your mother?"

Morse objected, but the judge overruled and permitted Dorothy to answer.

"June had a great deal of influence over her," Dorothy said.

When Barker asked, "Would she do almost anything June asked?" Aiken immediately deemed that the question was too speculative and excluded it.

"Did you ever hear your mother regret that June couldn't be with her?" Barker asked next.

"Yes," Dorothy said. "Whenever we were talking of June, she would say what a shame it was June couldn't be at home."

When Barker asked if she had ever heard her mother mention June's absence to the admiral, Dorothy said she had.

Questions about June's illegitimate child followed. Dorothy said her mother was fond of children, but the baby was never brought to the Assinippi home. When Barker asked Dorothy if her mother had ever discussed why the baby had never visited, Dorothy said she had not.

Dorothy told the court her mother had brought the baby from Washington in December 1912 after June had married Ralph Keyes. She recalled that her mother had spent two or three days at June's home after bringing the baby there and had then returned to Assinippi. Jennie revisited June in March for a week or ten days and went back to her home just before the admiral died. When Barker reminded Dorothy that she had previously testified that her mother had spent practically half of her time at June's and half at Assinippi, Dorothy replied: "Well, she went over often, but most of those times were merely calls."

The prosecutor asked about the church social held in the Eaton home on the Tuesday before the admiral died. Dorothy described it as a gathering of the Young People's Christian Union and told the court her parents were present, as were fourteen neighbors. Mrs. Harrison remained in her bedroom upstairs during the entire affair.

"Now, Dorothy, did your mother ever call your father insane or a lunatic?" asked Barker.

Dorothy said she didn't remember her mother using the term "lunatic." But when Barker read Dorothy's inquest testimony from the transcript, she conceded that she had heard her mother call the admiral a lunatic the night after the incident with the baker's daughter at the bakery shop. She also told how the admiral, from that time on, had sent postal cards to her mother on several occasions when she was away, informing her, in French, what was going on at home with the "inmates" in Assinippi and signing the cards "The Lunatic Asylum."

When the prosecutor asked Dorothy if she knew of any plans the admiral had made for the Tuesday after his death, Aiken interrupted, ruling the question immaterial. Barker, along with Morse, again conferred with the judge at sidebar. Barker informed Aiken that his line of questioning would establish before the jury the improbability that the admiral had committed suicide. Satisfied with Barker's explanation, the judge allowed him to proceed.

Barker posed his question to Dorothy once more, and she told the court he had planned to attend a "smoker," an informal social gathering for men only, in Rockland on the Tuesday in question.

The prosecutor revisited the events leading up to the admiral's illness and death. Morse objected, saying the questions had already been asked and answered. Some were allowed while others were not. Nearing the end of his examination, Barker finally asked Dorothy if she remembered the admiral saying he wanted to get out of bed on Friday, the day before his death.

"Yes, he wanted to get up and go to the doctor's but wasn't able," Dorothy answered.

"Did you hear your mother say that he didn't get up at all on Friday?"

"No."

Judge Aiken interrupted at this point, called for a recess, and excused Dorothy from the witness stand. Dorothy lingered momentarily, folded her arms across the witness box rail, and rested her head atop them, obviously exhausted after nearly five hours of testimony. As the jurors filed out, they could not help but notice Dorothy's actions and looked upon her sympathetically.

When the trial resumed, Dorothy identified her mother's handwriting on several letters the prosecutor presented to her. After the letters were admitted into evidence, Barker informed Aiken that he had concluded his direct examination of the witness. The judge then signaled for Morse to begin his cross-examination.

Dorothy sat in the witness box with her head again on her arms. Morse helped Dorothy, through a series of questions, to describe her first meeting with the admiral and her life with him since that time. The attorney intended to show the jury that the admiral was not as healthy or happy as Dorothy had depicted during direct examination.

Dorothy admitted the admiral was frequently intoxicated when they first moved to Hull and had become sick to his stomach whenever he drank to excess. She said her mother was opposed to the consumption of liquor and had tried to keep the admiral from using it, both in Hull and in Brookline where the admiral continued to drink.

"Why did your mother say she moved to Assinippi?" Morse asked.

"Well, we all knew the admiral was not normal," Dorothy said, "and she thought if she could get him away into other conditions, it might be better for him."

"Did she say anything about her inability to pay the bills at Brookline?"

"She said it was too expensive for us to live that way."

"Was the admiral ill at Brookline?"

"He wasn't in bed, but he wasn't strong or vigorous. He had constant trouble with his stomach."

"Was the admiral willing to move to Assinippi?" asked Morse.

"I think not, at first," Dorothy replied.

Dorothy told the court they usually had three servants in the Brookline house and at one time had four. She maintained that her mother had let the servants go because of the cost, not because of jealousy.

"When did your grandmother come to live with you?"

"She came up north just after June and I did, but has made frequent trips back again."

"Who has done the household work at Assinippi?"

"My mother, except when she was away at East Weymouth."

"The admiral didn't do much work about the place?"

"Not indoors."

"Did his health improve there?"

"Yes."

"Did he like the place?"

"Not at first. Later."

"How did your mother treat him?"

"Always kindly and with patience, except when she was provoked."

"Was there any discussion in the family about the adoption of the baby?"

"Not before me."

"He was fond of the baby?"

"Yes."

JOHN F. GALLAGHER

"Did he write to the papers saying a son had been born to him?"
"Yes."
"Did he drink at Assinippi?"
"Yes."
"Did you ever see him when he was greatly under the influence of liquor?"
"Yes."
"Did your mother ever say that the admiral was a habitual user of drugs?"
"Yes."
"And did she say that she feared that he might, under drug influence, poison somebody?"
"Yes."
"She never said she was afraid he would poison somebody when he was in his normal condition?"
"No."
"June never came home to live after the baby's death?"
"No."
"The admiral never said she couldn't come home?"
"No."
"When June was married, he gave her a wedding?"
"Yes."
"Was she always pleasantly received when she came to visit at home?"
"Yes."
"And as far as you know, there was no reason why she couldn't come home?"
"No."

Dorothy repeated her testimony about the visit June and her mother had made to Chicago several years before and their return to Boston. She said that June and her husband lived in Dorchester with the baby after they got married in November 1912. Before that, her mother rarely left Assinippi to visit June, but after the marriage she was frequently at June's house, often for days at a time. Asked about the admiral's relationship with Ralph Keyes, Dorothy said they liked one another.

Morse's next line of questioning led Dorothy to admit the purpose of her mother's recurrent visits to June's home.

"You knew that June and her husband weren't getting along well together?"

"Yes," Dorothy answered.

"And wasn't it to keep June and her husband together that your mother spent so much time with June?"

"Yes."

"And the admiral knew of this purpose?"

"Yes."

"The time came when June and her husband decided to separate?"

"Yes."

"Wasn't it then that your mother sent some trunks to June?"

"I don't know."

Dorothy readily admitted that her mother's complaining about the admiral's use of alcohol and drugs and his flirtations with other women caused friction between her parents. But, she averred, her mother and father were kind and affectionate to each other most of the time. Dorothy suggested the admiral was more apt to drink when her mother was away. He needed her constant vigilance to keep his drinking under control, and whenever Jennie was away he wrote to her, pleading for her to return.

Morse appealed to the jury's sympathies by asking Dorothy a question designed to reveal that she had testified for three and a half hours at both the inquest and grand jury proceedings. Surely, having told the story so many times, it was understandable that she was confused on certain points during her testimony on direct examination.

Morse hoped to rehabilitate Dorothy's statements about the events leading up to the admiral's death, so he brought her back to the Wednesday when her mother had left for June's house in Medford and June had appeared unexpectedly in Assinippi. Dorothy repeated what she had told the district attorney on direct; that June had become upset when she realized that she and her mother had unknowingly passed each other in transit.

At Morse's prompting, Dorothy described the events of Thursday evening, telling the jury that the family had enjoyed supper together and remained at the table for some time afterward, "laughing and joking." She said the admiral and her mother were "pleasant, even jovial and affectionate" throughout the meal. In fact, she said, "they seemed even fonder of each other than usual."

Once again she explained how the admiral had suddenly left the room to vomit. Morse asked how her mother had responded when the admiral returned to the kitchen.

"She seemed very much worried, asked him what was the matter and whether she could do anything for him. He said he didn't know what was the matter, but there was nothing she could do."

Morse led Dorothy through Friday's episode. Her testimony reflected, in every detail, her statements made on direct. Morse next asked her how the admiral's death had affected her mother.

"She cried and cried, and she couldn't stay in one room but was roaming back and forth," Dorothy told the court.

"Now, Dorothy, did your father in all the time you knew him ever show any fear of your mother?" asked Morse.

"No," answered Dorothy. "They ate together. He sat at the table with her and ate the food she prepared, down to the very day of his death."

Morse returned to Thursday's events and asked Dorothy if she could yet recall who had prepared the tea that night. Dorothy remained unsure, just as she had on direct. When the lawyer asked her if she was mistaken about the date of the "smoker" the admiral had hoped to attend, she remained firm and said she was sure it was planned for the Tuesday following the admiral's death.

Morse showed Dorothy several letters. She confirmed which were in the admiral's handwriting and which were in her mother's. Morse then advised the judge he had no further questions and returned to the defense table.

Barker rose for redirect and questioned Dorothy about the medicine her mother had surreptitiously given to the admiral.

"Did your mother show you a prescription for a medicine which she administered to him?"

"Yes – it was a medicine which she put into what he drank. She gave it to him for three months, and he found it out."

"You said something about a pill being found in a cup of tea?"

"I don't remember whether I saw it in the cup or the saucer, in my mother's room or downstairs. It was my mother who spoke to me of it."

"Did you ever see your father take a drug?"

"No."

"Did you ever have any knowledge of his taking drugs, other than what your mother said?"

"No."

At the conclusion of Barker's examination, Judge Aiken excused Dorothy from the witness stand for a short recess. Barker asked her one last question when she returned to the stand.

"In all your acquaintance with the admiral, did you ever see anything that made you think he was not of sound mind?"

Morse objected, but the court overruled and allowed the question.

"No, I never did," said Dorothy.

The judge excused Dorothy after determining the defense had no more questions for her. She rushed from the stand and threw her arms around her mother's neck. The two women wept as Dorothy whispered into her mother's ear and kissed her, telling her, as jurors and spectators in the courtroom looked on, that she believed her mother was innocent. Nearly ten minutes elapsed before Aiken ordered officers to intervene and remove Dorothy from the courtroom.

Chapter 18

The district attorney called Jennie's mother, Virginia Harrison, as the prosecution's next witness. Deputy Sheriff George Hersey assisted her to the stand. She walked past her daughter without acknowledgment.

Barker began by going over her past and explored her relationship with her daughter's family. She related that she had been living at Assinippi with the Eatons for the past sixteen months except for a brief return to Washington for two months. Prior to that, she had lived with her daughter, son-in-law, and granddaughters in Brookline. She had first met the admiral seven years earlier, just before her daughter married him. She expressed her affection for the admiral and said she was greatly saddened by his death.

"Did you ever see anything to indicate that he was not of sound mind?" the prosecutor asked.

Morse objected to the question.

"I will save the defendant's exception to that question and permit it to be asked," Judge Aiken said.

Mrs. Harrison then answered, "No."

The district attorney questioned Mrs. Harrison about the Thursday night preceding the admiral's death. She said she had not eaten at the kitchen table with her daughter, the admiral, and her granddaughter, Dorothy, that evening. She had taken her supper in the dining room, alone.

"What did you observe about the admiral after he had eaten his supper?" Barker asked.

"I don't think I saw him till after he had become sick," she testified. "Then he came in and lay down on the end of the lounge in the library. I stayed in the dining room."

Mrs. Harrison said she had returned to her bedroom upstairs after she'd finished eating. The admiral came up about an hour and a half later and told her he had done Dorothy's algebra for her. He then retired to his own room. She heard him purging that night and early the next morning, she added.

"Did you hear anyone go into his room Thursday night?" Barker inquired.

"No."

"Did you have any talk with your daughter about the admiral's condition?"

"Yes, she came into my room Friday morning about nine o'clock. She said he was very sick and she was going to send for the doctor. She looked out the window and there was Dr. Frame who had come to see me."

Barker did not get the answer he expected from Mrs. Harrison. He consulted the transcript of her testimony at the inquest and read several lines to her. He then asked if that helped her recall what had happened Thursday night. She said it did and then changed her testimony, saying she remembered hearing her daughter in the admiral's room that night.

"What did your daughter say as to giving him medicine on Friday?" Barker continued.

"My daughter said she had tried giving him tea, both hot and cold, but he could not retain it. I said I thought she should keep on giving it."

The prosecutor turned to the transcript once more. He read Mrs. Harrison's testimony about hearing the admiral purging not only on Thursday night and Friday morning but on Thursday morning and all day Friday as well. Her memory refreshed, Mrs. Harrison agreed her previous testimony was correct.

Barker led her to the events of early Saturday morning. She remembered hearing the admiral fall out of his bed, that she had called to her daughter and granddaughter to assist him. After they had tended the admiral, Mrs. Harrison said, she went back to her room and slept. She was awakened about dawn by a noise and overheard Dorothy say, "He's gone."

"I was very much alarmed," Mrs. Harrison said. "I thought the admiral had got up and gone out. And I called out 'Jennie.' She came in, and I said, 'What has happened?' She said, 'I'm afraid the admiral's dead.' "

Mrs. Harrison became visibly emotional at this point. Her head dropped to her chest and she used her handkerchief to dry her eyes. Barker gave her time to recover before resuming. She could not tell the prosecutor if or when her daughter had given any medicine to the admiral on Friday. She didn't know how many times her daughter had tried to feed him but remembered that Jennie had given him milk that he couldn't hold down.

"He was sick at dinnertime on Wednesday?" Barker asked.

"Yes," she replied.

"What did he have for dinner?"

"Roast pork."

Barker tried to establish the exact times at which Mrs. Harrison had seen or heard the admiral purging, but her answers did not coincide with her testimony during the inquest before Judge Pratt at her Assinippi home on March 17. Barker read the transcript to her several times, but it didn't help. She would not change the testimony she was now giving. Barker tried a different approach.

"You were ill on Thursday and did not come down till noon?"

"No, but I knew about his being sick and about his bad stomach."

"Did you take breakfast with the admiral at any time within ten days before his last illness?"

"No."

"Did you breakfast with him prior to that?"

"Regularly," replied the witness.

"Do you remember the incident about two weeks before his death, of the baker's girl in Rockland?"

"I don't know what you mean."

"Don't you recollect what Jennie said about it?"

Morse objected, but the court allowed the question. No matter how many ways Barker posed the question, Mrs. Harrison remained puzzled. Finally, she said the admiral "had bought a pie, or something of that sort, and Jennie thought he remained in the place too long."

Barker was now conducting his entire examination by refreshing Mrs. Harrison's memory with the inquest transcript. Morse protested and asked the court to allow Mrs. Harrison to answer the prosecutor's questions based on what she presently recalled. Judge Aiken overruled Morse's objection and Barker continued.

Barker asked Mrs. Harrison about June's visit to the Eaton home on the Wednesday before the admiral's death. She said June had stayed for about twenty minutes and then left for home. The admiral said good-bye to June before she left, and June said she was sorry she had missed her mother.

"The admiral then said, 'Never mind, June; we all love you and are going to help you.'"

Barker then asked Mrs. Harrison to give the jury a detailed account of what had transpired during June's visit. She said she was lying on the couch in the library when the admiral came in and told her he was not feeling well. He was standing in the doorway, and as he looked out a window he saw June walking toward the house. She heard the admiral say, "Why here's June."

"I said, 'That means that Jennie won't be home tonight,' and he answered back that she had promised to come back. June came in and said, 'Why, grandma's sick.' I said I was better than I had been. Then the admiral said, 'June, you'd better go right home. You can't get there now, before seven o'clock. Your mother has gone to meet you.' She said, 'Yes, I know, I'm going right home.'"

"Was there any conversation after that?" asked the district attorney. Before Mrs. Harrison could answer, Morse raised an objection and requested a conference at the judge's bench. At sidebar with Barker, Morse expressed his concern that Mrs. Harrison was about to offer hearsay statements made by June during their conversation. Barker insisted that it was not his intention to elicit any such statements. Judge Aiken ruled Mrs. Harrison competent to offer testimony about her observations, but any statements made by June were inadmissible under the hearsay rule. Aiken called a recess when the conference ended.

When court reconvened, Barker tried unsuccessfully to get Mrs. Harrison to cite a specific instance when she had observed her daughter criticize her husband for his flirting. He asked her if Mrs. Eaton was jealous of her husband occasionally. The court overruled an objection by the defense, and Mrs. Harrison responded that she thought her daughter was jealous of the admiral but that she couldn't provide any specific examples.

"And you lived with the family how long?" asked the prosecutor.

"About four years," Mrs. Harrison replied.

"And that is all you can remember?"

"Well, there were foolish remarks. She thought he was too polite to people. I didn't."

"Did you ever see him as anything other than a perfect gentleman in

136

his conduct toward women?"

"No. I didn't go out with them much," the witness answered.

Morse continued objecting to Barker's line of questioning, but the court overruled him each time. Barker resumed his examination.

"Can you name any specific instances where Mrs. Eaton accused the admiral of being too familiar with women?"

"No."

When Barker asked if she remembered her daughter castigating her husband for his behavior towards Miss Howard, Mrs. Cobbett, Miss Farrar, or any other women in Rockland, she said she did not.

"You don't recall that she talked to the admiral nearly all evening, the day before she went to June's, about a girl in Rockland?"

"No," Mrs. Harrison said emphatically.

The prosecutor next turned to the defendant's attempts to have the admiral committed to an institution and June's influence over her mother.

"What, if anything, have you heard her say with regard to his being of unsound mind or insane?"

"I have heard her say that," Mrs. Harrison said.

"How frequently have you heard her speak of having him committed to an asylum?"

"I never heard that. I have heard her say she would like to have him examined."

"When did she do anything about it?" asked Barker.

"Never, except that time she brought Miss Rooney, a nurse, to the house."

"When the little boy died, did she not write to you claiming Mr. Eaton was insane, and didn't you in consequence come on here?"

"Yes."

"Have you heard her express or display any affection for June?" Barker inquired.

"All June's life she has expressed the greatest warmth of affection," the witness said.

"Whether June has great influence over her?"

"I think she has."

"How long is it since June has made her home in the house?"

"I think between three and four years."

"Have you heard your daughter express a wish that June could be there and express keen regret to the admiral that June couldn't be there?"

"Yes."

"Did she display a good deal of feeling and become hysterical about it?"

"Yes."

Barker asked Mrs. Harrison how frequently her daughter and the admiral discussed June's situation. The witness said the couple discussed the subject quite often. Then Barker completely altered his course and asked his witness if she knew anything about June's baby.

"I decline to answer any questions on that subject," she said in a firm but irritated tone. "I don't know anything about it."

That answer surprised Barker, and when he repeated his question she gave him the same answer. Convinced he wasn't going to get her to change her testimony, the DA dropped the subject.

"Have you ever heard any talk between June and her mother as to the admiral's mental condition, and his use of poison?"

"Yes, but I can't say how often," Mrs. Harrison replied.

"Have you ever heard your daughter express her fear that the admiral would poison her or other members of the family?"

"I have heard her say she was afraid he would poison June."

"Did you ever hear her attribute illnesses in the family to his using poison?"

"No, I never heard her say that."

Barker was on the verge of declaring Mrs. Harrison a hostile witness. He read to her the statements she had made during the inquest and asked her if she had in fact testified as the transcript reflected. She told the prosecutor she didn't remember making the statements, and in some instances she flatly denied making them at all. Exasperated, but determined to get his witness to testify as she had during the inquest, Barker persisted.

"Who was the first one to talk about poison?" Barker asked.

"June," replied the witness.

"Who was the first one to talk about women?"

"June."

"And what women were they?"

"I don't know."

"Don't you remember saying to me the other night that they were the servants at Brookline?"

"Yes."

"And that June got to believe her own accusations?"

"Yes."

"And that she appeared to believe the stories about poison?"

"Yes, I think she did, too."

"Have you ever known Jennie to search the attic for poisons?" the district attorney posed.

"I don't know that she searched. I know she thought that they were there."

"The admiral was kind to her through all her accusations? He did all that a husband could do? He gave her most of his money? He tried to joke her out of these beliefs?" Barker inquired.

"Yes," replied Mrs. Harrison to each question.

Barker next focused on June's acrimonious relationship with the admiral and the influence she had over her mother, the defendant. He wanted, through Mrs. Harrison's testimony, to establish before the jury how June's separation from her mother may have provoked Mrs. Eaton to murder.

"Along what lines did you notice June's influence over her mother; was it as to believing these things?" asked Barker.

Morse objected, but the court allowed the question.

"I think it was," Mrs. Harrison responded.

"Whether her mother had great confidence in what June said?"

"I think she had."

"And whether June had antipathy toward the admiral?"

"Yes, decidedly."

"To the extent that she said many things against him?" Barker asked. The court sustained Morse's objection before Mrs. Harrison could answer.

"How did June show her antipathy?" Barker continued.

"She spit out at him; she said he had no use for her, and she was afraid of him."

"When did this feeling start?" the prosecutor inquired.

"Directly after he and her mother were married," the witness answered.

"About her studies?"

"Yes. He was anxious that she should have a good education, and June was opposed to studying. Later on she disliked him, exceedingly."

"How was this shown?"

"She wouldn't live at the house. She was afraid of him. She wouldn't eat anything at home, and she had no use for him."

"She was living on his money, however?"

"Yes."

"Do you remember Jennie's saying that she would not force June to come there as long as the admiral was there?" Barker asked.

"Yes, two or three times," replied the witness.

The prosecutor turned to the inquest transcript once more and refreshed Mrs. Harrison's memory. After she had considered this previous testimony, she changed her answer and told the court Jennie made the remark "frequently."

Barker inquired about the admiral's use of alcohol.

"I couldn't say how often [he drank]; I could only see his condition. He'd get pretty full, as the saying is. I should say oftener than once a month; perhaps once a week."

"Was he always kindly when he was [overindulgent]?" asked Barker.

"Always," the witness answered.

"You have said that June was her mother's idol and that she thought the sun rose and set on her?"

"Yes."

"But you don't think so?" Barker suggested.

"What's that?" Morse interrupted.

"I withdraw that," said Barker.

"You should. It's a very improper remark," Morse admonished.

Barker continued.

"Do you remember whether they had tea or coffee substitute on that Thursday night?"

"It was tea," Mrs. Harrison replied.

"You were not in the room where they had tea, or where it was prepared?"

"No."

The district attorney turned from the witness and again walked to the prosecution table where he picked up the inquest transcript. After scanning it briefly and consulting his notes, he again asked Mrs. Harrison when she had heard the admiral last purging on Friday night. She told him it was 10:00 p.m. He eliminated the possibility of some person other than a family member having access to the house on Thursday night by having Mrs. Harrison testify that the only person who had been to the house that day was the grocer's delivery man.

Mrs. Harrison never lost eye contact with the district attorney during her entire examination. It was only when Barker returned to his table for the last time that Mrs. Harrison stole a glance at the jury, as if looking for some recognition or approval of her performance. When Barker approached her for the last time, she again gave him her undivided attention.

"Do you remember the admiral saying, 'Am I not a fascinating man, according to you? Don't you think I must have love on tap?' "

Mrs. Harrison said she didn't remember saying such a thing during the inquest. Barker persisted in his efforts to refresh her memory, but she insisted she had no recollection of it. Barker informed the court he had no further questions for his witness.

Attorney Morse began his cross-examination. After a few preliminary questions about her living arrangements at Assinippi, Brookline, and Hull, the defense attorney repeated the questions he had asked Dorothy. Mrs. Harrison testified that she had seen the admiral frequently intoxicated at all three residences. She admitted that her daughter and the admiral often quarreled about his drinking.

Morse suddenly changed his course and asked Mrs. Harrison if the admiral had ever tried to assault June. When Barker objected to the question, the court sustained it and directed Mrs. Harrison to refrain from answering.

Morse rephrased his question, asking if June had ever told her the admiral had attacked her. Barker objected to the question as hearsay, and Aiken excluded it. Morse persisted – this time asking Mrs. Harrison if she had spoken to June about the subject. But this too failed to elicit an answer after objection.

Morse tried a different approach.

"You say that she (June) had a dread of the admiral?"

"Yes, so she said," the witness answered.

"June's mother said she would not insist on her coming home?"

"Yes."

"Do you know of your own knowledge why?"

Mrs. Harrison began to answer but stopped when the court sustained the district attorney's objection.

"Did you ever hear from the admiral anything about his having made a fool of himself with June?" asked Morse.

"Objection," shouted Barker.

"Sustained," ruled Aiken.

"Do you know, when the mother wished to have June come home, whether the admiral said anything?" Morse inquired.

Mrs. Harrison paused as if anticipating another objection, but none came.

"I have forgotten; June never wanted to come."

Morse revisited the subject of the admiral's health. Mrs. Harrison told the court she had never seen the admiral as sick as she had seen him during the days just before he died. He had always had stomach trouble and nausea, but usually only in the morning after a night of hard drinking. The admiral's deleterious habits had subsided after the family had moved from Brookline to Assinippi, mostly because he had fewer opportunities to imbibe.

"Do you recall an occasion when he was intoxicated, when he had no smell of liquor about him?" asked Morse.

"Yes," said Mrs. Harrison.

She then related how the admiral had come into the Assinippi house one day and complained that he felt dizzy. He stretched out on a couch in the library to recover. When a delivery arrived from the grocer, the admiral got up to help with the packages and, as he did so, he lost his balance and fell against the kitchen oven and onto the floor. Mrs. Harrison and the deliveryman helped the admiral back to the couch. He slept there for hours.

Mrs. Harrison next corroborated Dorothy's testimony about the admiral's predisposition to abuse alcohol when Jennie was away from home. Whenever Jennie was absent, she recalled, the admiral was "crazy to get her back." Mrs. Harrison said she never saw the admiral act any way other than affectionately toward her daughter and that she heard him complain constantly that Jennie worked too hard around the house.

Attorney Morse asked if her daughter was concerned in any other way about the admiral's behavior. Mrs. Harrison said her daughter believed the admiral also abused drugs; that she was in constant fear that the admiral, while under the influence, might poison someone in the house.

Morse brought up an incident that had occurred on the Saturday before Jennie returned home from visiting June in Medford. The lawyer asked Mrs. Harrison if the admiral was intoxicated that day.

"He was beginning to be," she answered.

"She (Jennie) called attention to it?" Morse inquired.

Barker immediately objected to the defense's attempt to lead the witness. "Let Mrs. Harrison tell it," Barker said. But the judge overruled him and allowed Mrs. Harrison to respond.

"Jennie said, 'He fell into my arms, dead drunk,' " Mrs. Harrison recalled, and added that her daughter had "tried everything" to break the admiral of his habits. Her daughter managed the household budget and worked hard with his monthly stipend to pay off $18,000 the admiral owed.

Morse anticipated that Aiken would soon call for an adjournment. He was determined to present the evidence of the admiral's assault against June. He asked to approach the bench and, with Aiken's consent, he and the district attorney conferred with the judge at sidebar. It became apparent with Morse's first question that he had convinced the judge to allow him to proceed.

"Did you have any conversation with the admiral with regard to June's coming home to live?" Morse asked.

"Yes," replied Mrs. Harrison. "He said how deeply it grieved June's mother to have her living away from home, and how expensive the arrangement was, and he said he wished she could come home to live. I said, 'What is the trouble? Why can't she come home?' He said, 'One day I made a damned fool of myself and...' " Her voice trailed off and a hush descended upon the courtroom. The jury waited patiently for her to continue. Jurors expectantly turned their eyes to Morse. But the defense attorney was satisfied he had made his point and did not push his witness to elaborate further. Barker sat motionless in his chair.

Morse had adroitly outmaneuvered him and had delivered a damaging blow to the prosecution's case.

Morse returned to the subject of the admiral's illness. He asked Mrs. Harrison to explain once more her recollection of events leading up to the admiral's death. She now testified that the admiral had first become ill after eating roast pork on Wednesday night. She said he became sick after eating more pork on Thursday afternoon, but she later corrected herself and said he didn't become ill until six or seven o'clock.

"Did you see Dr. Frame the morning after the admiral's death?" asked Morse.

"Yes," replied the witness.

"Did he say, 'There's something behind all this'?"

"He did."

Morse informed the court he had no further questions for Mrs. Harrison. Barker had no questions on redirect. Judge Aiken excused her from the stand and adjourned until the next morning.

Chapter 19

Court reconvened at 9:00 a.m. on Saturday, October 18. Judge Aiken announced the session would adjourn at one o'clock. Jurors took their seats in the jury box after sheriff's deputies had escorted Jennie to her assigned chair.

The prosecution called its first witness, Dr. Joseph Frame. After Frame was sworn in, District Attorney Barker established the doctor's medical qualifications and his professional relationship with the Eaton family.

"Do you remember any conversation with Mrs. Eaton during those first visits?" Barker inquired.

"I remember specifically one," the physician answered. "I had prescribed some medicine for her and had taken or sent it to her. Next day I asked her if she had taken her medication. She said she had not, giving as the reason that it had passed through the admiral's hands, or he had had opportunity to get at it – that it was poison and she would not take it. Later on she said to me that he was not mentally right, and that he ought to be examined by two physicians and committed to an institution."

"Whether she ever came to your office, making no other errand than that?" asked the prosecutor.

"She came to my office about eight thirty one night, and was very emphatic about her idea."

"What was her general tendency as to talking of family affairs?" Barker asked. Attorney Morse objected, but Aiken overruled him and told Frame he could answer.

"She talked about the admiral's mental condition, and talked about poisons. She said she was afraid the admiral would poison her. I cannot remember that anything was said about a fear that he would poison other members of the family."

"Come to the time when you visited the admiral."

"It was in August. I found him sitting on the piazza, and he told me he was suffering from cholera morbus. Mrs. Eaton said in my presence

145

that the admiral was a user of drugs. He looked me in the face and said that he was not and never had been a user of drugs."

"Did you see any indications that he was a drug user?"

"No."

"Did you see anything to indicate that he was not of sound mind?"

"No."

The district attorney next focused on the week before the admiral's death. Frame recalled how the admiral had summoned him on March 1 to attend to Mrs. Harrison. The doctor told the court, through questioning by Barker, that the admiral showed no signs of intoxication when he arrived at the house.

Frame testified that he returned to the Eaton house at about eight thirty the morning of Friday, March 7, to check on Mrs. Harrison's progress. Mrs. Eaton greeted him at the side door and expressed relief that he had come because, she said, the admiral had been sick all night. He proceeded up the stairs to the bedrooms on the second floor.

"The admiral told me that he had been purging all night," the doctor explained. "He mentioned also that he had had excruciating pain; I don't remember whether he said in the abdomen or in the calves of the legs. He may have been a little pale, but his pulse wasn't bad. Mrs. Eaton, I think, was in the room all the time. I asked him what he had been eating to bring on this attack, and he said 'fresh roast pork.' He said he had tasted that roast pork all night and he said, 'No more roast pork for Joseph.' I diagnosed his case as indigestion brought on by overeating roast pork. I prescribed subgalate of bismuth and left the tablets. I also told him when he felt a little better to take lime water, or, in the absence of that, saleratus."

"What was his attitude of mind?" Barker asked.

"I couldn't say he was despondent, but he wasn't over cheerful — one hardly would expect it."

"But he did joke with you?"

"Yes."

"What, if any, conversation did you have with Mrs. Eaton about him?"

"I don't remember any," Frame replied.

"When did you next hear from the Eaton house?"

"Next morning, about ten minutes to six, over the telephone. Mrs.

Eaton, whose voice I recognized, told me the admiral was dead. She wanted me to come right down. I told her I couldn't come right down, and said that if he were dead it couldn't make any difference. Then I asked when he died. She made no definite reply. I asked again and this time she said, 'about five o'clock.' Then she wanted to know whether I wouldn't come down to see Mrs. Harrison, and I said I would be down during the day.

"I determined that this should be reported to the medical examiner. The death came as a surprise to me; I had not expected it the day before. I called Dr. Osgood about six twenty a.m., and told him I thought this was a case for him. And at his request, I went down to the house, reaching it about ten forty-five a.m.," Frame related.

"You saw the admiral's body?" Barker asked.

"Yes, it was in the same place where I had seen him the day before."

"Did you have any talk with Mrs. Eaton?"

"Yes. She told me his stomach had refused all medicine he had taken, and every other thing he had taken. She said she was waked about two thirty in the morning by Mrs. Harrison, who told her she thought the admiral had fallen from bed. She and Dorothy got him back into bed, and she said she got into bed with him and put her arms round him, and they both went to sleep. She said she was waked by the coldness of the admiral's body, and found him dead."

Frame testified he was present at the admiral's autopsy with Drs. Osgood and Wheatley and corroborated their testimony.

"Could you observe anything that showed the cause of death?"

"No."

"Did you have any talk with Mrs. Eaton?"

"Yes. I saw her when I came downstairs. She wanted to know what we had found, and whether the brain was all right. I told her it was pretty hard to tell by an autopsy anything about the brain."

The district attorney then turned the witness over to Morse who approached the stand for cross-examination. Morse asked Frame if he remembered treating the admiral for a scalp wound at some time. The doctor replied he had and said the admiral had sustained a laceration to his scalp on the night of June's wedding in November 1912 and had received sutures to close the wound the same night from a physician in Boston. When Morse asked Frame if he knew how the admiral had sustained his injuries, the doctor said someone had told him the admiral had fallen in the street while intoxicated.

Morse questioned the doctor about the events of March 7. He asked the doctor if he had told the admiral there was no need for a follow-up visit the next day, and if his reasons for saying so were because he didn't consider the admiral to be seriously ill.

"If his appearances remained substantially the same through Friday up to Friday night, there was no reason why the family should not go to bed as usual without taking extra precautions?" Morse inquired.

"Providing my diagnosis of the causation of his trouble was correct, he should improve, and if he didn't, there might be cause for apprehension," Frame explained.

Morse did not elicit the statement he wanted from the physician, so he asked in another way.

"Did you think he was going to be sick after you left him?"

"I thought he was going to improve."

"Then what did you mean by saying somebody ought to attend to his needs?" asked Morse.

"Someone was needed to give him the medicine I had prescribed, and the milk I had ordered, when his stomach quieted down," the doctor replied.

"And there was no other need?"

"Providing the nausea and purging ceased, no."

"And if they didn't cease?"

"I supposed somebody would send for me. I think the promise was made."

"But you concluded that they would stop?"

"I thought so."

"Did you look at his tongue?"

"No."

"Take his temperature?"

"No."

"Just took his pulse?"

"Yes."

Morse continued his attack, suggesting Frame had ignored the symptoms of poisoning when he treated the admiral and had incorrectly diagnosed indigestion.

"You don't remember that he complained of pain?" asked the defense attorney.

"I don't remember it clearly," Dr. Frame submitted.

"Did he complain of a burning thirst?"

"I think he did."

"You didn't mention that before."

"No."

"Did you attribute that thirst to indigestion?"

"I attributed it to the nausea and purging."

"Did you attribute nausea and purging all night to the fact that he had eaten roast pork the night before?"

"I did at that time."

"Didn't he tell you that on Wednesday he ate very heartily of roast pork and that he had failed to retain his dinner?"

Frame was not sure.

"Do you remember refusing to talk with Mr. Geogan and me about two weeks ago, without permission of the district attorney?"

"Yes."

"Do you remember later talking with Mr. Geogan? Do you remember telling him that you had told him of all the symptoms of which the admiral complained?"

"I don't remember that I did."

Morse motioned to Drs. Osgood and Wheatley who were seated within the bar enclosure.

"You have been talking with these medical gentlemen over here on the symptoms of arsenical poisoning?"

"Yes."

"And probably they have mentioned thirst as a symptom?"

"Probably."

"Will you now say to the jury that the admiral complained of thirst?"

"I will not say it."

"Will you now say he complained of pain?"

"Yes – but I will not say whether it was in the legs or the abdomen."

Morse brought up the remark that Mrs. Harrison attributed to Frame as he left her room on the day of Admiral Eaton's death.

"Did you say to Mrs. Harrison, 'there is something behind all this'?"

"Yes – I had forgotten it until you mentioned it yesterday. It was when I went in to see how she was, after I had seen the admiral's body."

"How did you happen to call on Friday?"

"When I called on March 1, I told her and told the admiral I thought she was all right and I would not call again. The admiral, however, said he would feel much better if I would call once more the next week, and it was left that way."

Morse turned to the doctor's treatment of Mrs. Eaton for grippe in February 1911 and her refusal to take the medicine he had prescribed.

"Didn't she say she would have taken the medicine if she could have got it direct from you?"

"Yes."

"Didn't she at one time tell you about finding a pill in a cup of tea?"

"I can't recall that she did."

"Didn't she tell you that the admiral was much under the influence of liquor or drugs?"

"Not on that occasion."

"You didn't go to examine the admiral's mental condition when she wished it, because you thought her belief unfounded?" Morse asked.

"Exactly," Frame answered.

Morse asked Frame if the admiral had nausea, or complained of nausea, when he treated him in 1912 for cholera morbus. Frame said he could not remember.

"Did you ever ask him if he used drugs?"

"No."

"Did she ever say he was not right mentally because he was taking liquor and using drugs?"

"Why, she said that continually."

"And that there was no other cause for his unsound mind?"

"So far as I know, she may have attributed all his mental trouble to those things, but I have no memory of her saying it."

Morse asked the physician if he had considered the admiral's use of alcohol or drugs when he diagnosed him on March 7. Frame said he never asked; that all signs pointed to illness brought on by the admiral's ingestion of pork and nothing else.

Morse inquired about the admiral's position on the bed on the morning of his death. The doctor said the admiral was lying on his back, very near the edge of the bed. He noticed a fresh stain of vomit on the sheet in the bed's center.

Morse announced he had no further questions, and DA Barker stood for redirect. He asked Frame about the medication he had sent to Mrs. Eaton in February 1911, when she was ill with grippe.

"When you sent Mrs. Eaton a prescription, was anything said about a post office box?"

"She said she and the admiral had separate post office boxes, because she didn't want anything of hers to come in contact with the admiral's."

"You don't know that the medicine did pass through the admiral's hand?"

"No."

When Barker indicated he had no further questions for the witness, the judge excused Frame from the stand and called a recess. The trial resumed fifteen minutes later, and twenty-seven-year-old Grace Howard took the stand. A native of Assinippi, she now resided in New Bedford where she was employed as a nurse at St. Luke's Hospital.

Under examination by Assistant District Attorney Katzmann, Howard told the court she had become acquainted with the Eatons at the Assinippi Church where she sang in the choir. One day she had occasion to visit with the defendant and her daughter, June, at the Assinippi house. She recalled a conversation with Mrs. Eaton who had told her the admiral constantly flirted with women and neighbors and was insane. When Katzmann asked her if Mrs. Eaton had named any of these women, Howard said no. She could not recall exactly what Mrs. Eaton had said regarding the admiral's insanity.

Katzmann returned to the prosecution's cluttered table, picked up a document, and showed it to the witness. Howard identified it as a letter she had received from Mrs. Eaton in the summer of 1909, about ten days after the death of the Eatons' adopted child. The court clerk marked the letter as an exhibit and returned it to Katzmann who began reading it aloud.

Sand Hills, August 30, 1909 – Miss Grace Howard, Assinippi, Mass., Personal:

My Dear Miss Grace – I have a very disagreeable task to perform, and as I believe you are a very nice, innocent, good girl, and as you know what a poor little child June is, and what a sweet girl she is, I'm going to beg of you to write me a letter stating that my husband, Admiral Eaton's, conduct was not and far from that of a gentleman.

You may remember that last winter when I introduced you, he winked at you as we went into the car, and two hours later, when we all came back, he did it again, and so pronounced that you laughed outright. Then he has stared and winked at you all last year in church until you were confused and finally stopped singing in the choir, and then that night of the minstrel show he was simply disgraceful. Now the darling boy died so suddenly I had 'an autopsy.' And if poison is found, I believe Admiral Eaton will try to fasten it on my daughter or myself.

Now, of course, you know June is too innocent and sweet a child, of too tender a nature to be wicked, and so I want you to write me these straight-forward, honest truths about my husband's conduct toward us, as Admiral Eaton is not (I fully believe) of his mind, and his conduct to you, and dozens of other young women prove it to me. It would be a most pitiful thing that this young life (June) should have to suffer for the wickedness of an old hypocrite.

If you will not tell the truth, write me a dignified letter. I will be compelled to summon you (in court), as a witness, as I do not intend that this innocent girl shall suffer for his crime, insane or not. As you were very fond of June, and know her well and what a simple, trusting, tender-hearted good girl she is, I know you will not allow his conduct toward yourself to go unnoticed. A few discreet lines stating your belief in June, and that his conduct was very distasteful to you, will prevent me from bringing you into the public eye, and save a lovely poor girl's reputation and have a poor, deluded insane man kept from doing greater harm. And if the poison is found in a baby, who had never been ill or had a doctor since birth, you owe that much to the world at large.

I know your kind heart and quick brain, and believe you will let [sic] *the innocent suffer. With regrets I must write you this sort of letter, hoping you will write me for the child's sake. Your heart anxious friend, Jennie M. Eaton. I shall give you my word of honor that no one shall know of you in any way.*

Katzmann handed the letter to the court clerk and turned to Howard. He asked her if the admiral had ever flirted with her or winked at her. The witness said no. She also told the court she never answered the letter and never spoke with Mrs. Eaton again.

Katzmann then addressed Morse: "Your witness."

Morse opened with a hypothetical question, asking Howard if it was possible the admiral had winked at her and she hadn't seen it. She said yes.

"Did you ever speak to the admiral after receiving this letter?"

"Yes. He asked me, at the post office one day, whether he had ever behaved to me otherwise than as a gentleman. I said, 'No,' and told him of the letter, which I had meant to send him but had forgotten. He said he was very sorry that anything like that had happened."

On redirect by ADA Katzmann, Howard said she had met the admiral by chance about two or three months after she had received the letter and when Mrs. Eaton was away from home.

Miss Bessie Collamore, a twenty-three-year-old North Hanover resident and bookkeeper for Rice and Hutchins Shoe Manufacturers in Rockland, was the prosecution's next witness.

She testified she had once lived in Assinippi, about an eighth of a mile from the Eaton home, and had visited the house only once. She said she had become acquainted with the Eaton family at the Universalist Church in Assinippi.

"Do you recall a conversation with Mrs. Eaton at Sand Hills?" asked Katzmann.

"Yes."

Katzmann abandoned this line of questioning momentarily and inquired about her one visit to the Eatons' Assinippi home.

"Now about your call," Katzmann prompted.

"Mrs. Eaton had called, and I was returning the call. Mrs. Eaton called the admiral before I went," Collamore testified.

"Before he came in, do you remember Mrs. Eaton's subject of conversation?"

"She did not speak of the admiral, nor make any reference to household affairs."

Katzmann returned to the conversation at Sand Hills where the Eatons had summered in 1909. Collamore told Katzmann she had gone to Sand Hills to visit a friend who had rented a cottage next to the Eatons. Before she arrived at the friend's summer home, she passed the Eatons' cottage and saw Dorothy sitting on the front steps. She walked up to her, and while she and Dorothy were conversing, Mrs. Eaton and June came out. Mrs. Eaton asked her to come in, but she declined the invitation.

"Then she said she had something of a private nature to say, and I went in. Then she asked if I would go to court to testify that at the last church social the admiral had so annoyed me with attention that I had to leave early. I was in there nearly an hour, and the whole conversation was repeated urgings over and over for me to go to court."

"The same question, over and over, for an hour?" asked Katzmann.

"Yes," answered Collamore.

Suddenly, all eyes were directed toward Jennie Eaton who had laughed aloud at the young woman's statement. Jennie did her best to stifle her amusement, but she failed and tears streamed down her face.

"Do you remember Mrs. Eaton's saying anything more at Sand Hills?"

"She said the court proceedings wouldn't be around her, and that it would cost a good deal, but she would pay my bills."

"Did she say it would help her if you would go, and put her in a strange position if you didn't?" Katzmann inquired.

"No," said the witness.

Morse then began cross-examining Collamore. He asked her if she had received a letter from his co-counsel, Mr. Geogan, asking her to contact his office. She said she had. Morse asked her why she hadn't called. She said Geogan hadn't said what he wanted to see her about, so she didn't see any reason to contact him.

"You didn't think it was about this case?" Morse asked the witness.

"He should have said so," she replied.

The court excused Collamore, and the prosecution called the admiral's second cousin, Charles B. Brooks of Boston. Katzmann introduced two letters Brooks had received from Admiral Eaton – one in February 1913 and the other on March 7, 1913. Brooks read the letters aloud. In them, the admiral had revealed his dire financial condition and had asked Brooks to assist him with the sale of several rare books he had acquired during his naval career.

Morse waived cross-examination. Judge Aiken, glancing at the wall clock, excused Brooks and adjourned until Monday morning at 9:00 a.m.

Chapter 20

District Attorney Barker summoned Dr. William F. Whitney to the stand when court reconvened on Monday morning, October 20. The sixty-three-year-old pathologist carried a small valise. After he was sworn in, he sat down and placed the valise on the floor beside him. Barker's first question concerned the doctor's involvement in the 1909 autopsy of the Eatons' adopted son, Joseph Eaton Jr.

Dr. William F. Whitney
(*Courtesy of the Harvard Medical Library in the Francis A. Countway Library of Medicine*)

Whitney testified that he had examined the child's organs for evidence of poison, had found none, and had attributed the death to natural causes. He said he had received a letter from Mrs. Eaton about a month after the child died. She had declared her husband insane and accused him of poisoning the child.

Barker retrieved the letter from the prosecution table and presented it to the doctor for identification. The district attorney read the letter aloud after the doctor had attested to its authenticity.

In the letter, written in Assinippi on September 11, 1909, Mrs. Eaton asked the doctor how much longer she would have to wait before he finished his analysis. She expressed her fears about being alone with "a dangerous, insane man." She directed the doctor to search for "foreign poisons," saying her husband talked freely about them. He had "all the cleverness of a maniac and cunning enough to use one that would be hard to detect." She alleged that her husband "has been planning my death all day today. I want the state to take charge of him, for he is mad."

In a postscript, she directed the doctor to examine the child's food and medicine because "if it is a poison, it is a subtle one, as he is familiar with cholera and has spoken about poison used for it; and also the 'back bowels,' and as much as said they could not find it." She asked Whitney to respond by mail to the Rockland post office rather than Assinippi and to write "Hold Until Called For" on the envelope "as I fear the letter would not reach me."

When he finished reading the letter, the district attorney handed it to the clerk who marked it as evidence.

Barker next asked about Whitney's analysis of the admiral's organs. Whitney told the court that Osgood had delivered the organs to him on March 8, the day the admiral died. Examining the stomach microscopically, the doctor detected hemorrhaging. Inside the stomach he found 11.2 grains of undissolved and 1.5 grains of dissolved grayish powder that his assistant, Dr. William Balch, later confirmed to be white arsenic. Whitney also discovered traces of arsenic in the brain, liver, kidneys, and heart. Smaller amounts found in the remaining organs combined for a total of 16.67 grains (1.08 grams).

To demonstrate the relative quantity of the arsenic recovered, Whitney removed a pasteboard box from the valise at his feet. The box contained about one fourth of the quantity of arsenic, now in a dry state, recovered from the admiral's stomach. The item was admitted as evidence, and Judge Aiken allowed the district attorney to pass the box and its contents to the jurors for inspection. Morse did not object.

"What, in your opinion, was the cause of death?" the prosecutor asked.

"Arsenical poisoning," replied Whitney.

"Keeping in mind the evidence you have heard here, and assuming that the organs sent to you were the organs of Joseph G. Eaton, have you formed an opinion as to whether the arsenic in the system was taken at one time?"

Morse objected. Aiken suggested that the district attorney ask the question hypothetically. Barker then summarized the facts previously presented during the testimony of Dorothy Ainsworth Eaton and Mrs. Harrison about the sequence of events leading up to the admiral's death. Morse objected again and said, "The question assumes that the admiral's sickness began after supper on Thursday night." It was his contention that the admiral's illness had actually begun on Wednesday morning, when his client was not present. But Aiken overruled him and permitted Whitney to answer.

Whitney was of the opinion that more than one dose was taken, and he believed the first dose was ingested within two hours, most probably within an hour, of the first seizure reported on Thursday night. He believed the admiral received the last dose between two and six hours before he died. He further contended that the admiral's body had probably eliminated several times the amount of poison it had retained.

Jennie displayed distress during this testimony, dabbing tears from her eyes with a handkerchief.

"On what do you form your opinion as to the time when the last dose was taken?" Barker asked Whitney.

"On the symptoms of nausea, and the fact that the arsenic in the stomach was suspended in the fluid and not adherent to the walls of the stomach," the physician replied.

Arsenical poisoning, he said, is typically accompanied by symptoms of pain in the abdomen, arms, and legs; coldness in the extremities; collapse, delirium, and finally death; although the victim may remain lucid during the entire episode.

In answer to the district attorney's questions about the admiral's alleged overuse of alcohol, Whitney said he had found no evidence of alcoholism in any of the organs he had examined.

Barker asked the physician about the use of arsenic as a medicinal therapy. "What is the regular medicinal dose of arsenic?"

"One-sixtieth to one-twentieth of a grain three times a day to improve the health," Whitney replied.

"What is the form?"

"White powdered arsenic or a combination of mercury. It is usually compounded with something else."

"What is the minimum fatal dose of arsenic?" asked Barker.

"From two to three grains," the witness answered.

"Have you an opinion as to how arsenic might have been received into the system, and be found in the stomach in a powdered form?" the prosecutor asked.

Morse immediately objected but was overruled, and Judge Aiken directed the witness to answer.

"It might be swallowed as a powder, or in suspension in a fluid, or mingled with solid food," the doctor offered.

Whitney testified that he had received from the police various articles taken from the Eaton home, and he removed the items, one by one, from his valise. On March 11, State Detective Scott had submitted for his inspection a cologne bottle, a Bromo-Seltzer bottle, a whiskey bottle, a package of bismuth tablets, a box of saleratus, a box of codol, pepsin tablets, chlorate of potash tablets, a box of headache powders, a pharmacist's prescription, the contents of Admiral Eaton's pipe, and "a paper containing a dry vegetable substance." Scott had submitted additional items on March 18, including "a bottle containing about an ounce of a fluid smelling like whiskey," and some white powder mixed with lint; and on March 25, a bottle with a food preparation label containing a pale yellow powder that smelled of arsenic.

Whitney testified that he later received a box of Paris green and a box of medicine tablets from Scott. The doctor did not analyze the Paris green, a form of arsenic. All of the items were marked as evidence with no objection from the defense.

Barker next moved to amend Osgood's prior erroneous testimony that Paris green contained white arsenic to resolve any doubts in the jurors' minds that Mrs. Eaton had used anything other than pure white arsenic to poison the admiral.

"Whether the arsenic in Admiral Eaton's body could have been administered in the form of Paris green?" Barker inquired.

"It could not," the doctor replied.

Morse took up the cross-examination. Referring to the arsenic shown to the jury, Morse asked Whitney how much it contained. The doctor told him it contained about two and one-half grains.

"What became of the rest of the arsenic?" Morse asked.

"It was used in analysis," replied Whitney.

"Was it necessary to use it?"

"Yes."

"What would you have done if there had been only three grains?"

"I would have used half of it."

"A large quantity of arsenic is easier to detect in a body than a small amount?"

"Yes."

Morse asked his next question to support the defense's theory that the admiral had committed suicide. He had done his homework. Any lawyer worth his salt knew the answer to a question before he asked it.

"When a large quantity of arsenic is found in a body, the presumption of fact by the best authorities is that it has been self-administered?"

"It is."

"And is it true that when you found fifteen grains in the admiral's stomach, you assumed that a much larger quantity had been taken?"

"Yes."

Morse attacked Whitney's assertion that the admiral had ingested his first arsenical dose on Thursday, March 6. It was important for the defense to convince the jury that the admiral had received it much earlier and at a time when the defendant was not present. Whitney conceded the admiral might have consumed the first dose on Wednesday morning but thought it highly unlikely. He suggested the admiral's illness was due to another cause as the symptoms displayed that morning were not consistent with poisoning. The doctor held to his belief that the first dose was administered Thursday night. He refused to answer a question about the use of arsenic as a tonic to curtail the adverse effects of alcohol abuse.

"How long does it take arsenic to go to the brain?" Morse asked.

"Authorities disagree. Some say two or three days, and some a shorter time," Whitney answered. He declined to give his personal estimation.

"You found no traces of alcoholism?"

"No."

"If a man had been drinking hard for four or five days, and had been a heavy drinker for four or five years, you would expect to find symptoms of alcoholism?"

"Yes."

"In many cases it has been testified, has it not, that a large quantity of arsenic found in the stomach, even if there has been remission of nausea, may have been from one initial dose?"

"Yes."

"So that you cannot say it is not possible that the arsenic found in the system after Admiral Eaton's death was what remained after taking an initial dose?"

"That is possible – yes."

"You say that in your opinion the last dose was six or eight hours before death?"

Contradicting his direct testimony that the last dose was taken two to six hours before death, Whitney answered, "That is my opinion."

"You say that the taking of fluid would cause the stomach to rebel?"

"Yes."

"Then how do you reconcile it – if the dose six or eight hours before death was given in liquid, wouldn't it have caused him to throw it off?"

"It would have a tendency to."

"A dose of fifteen grains would be noticeable by its taste?"

"Yes; probably."

"If a man had been suffering from arsenical poisoning all night, wouldn't he have had, on Friday morning, marked symptoms of arsenical poisoning?"

"Yes."

"He would have had a burning thirst, pains in definite parts of his body?"

"Yes."

"Are the conditions which you found in the admiral's stomach inconsistent with the assumption of only one initial dose?" Morse asked.

"No," replied Whitney.

Morse then informed the court he had no further questions for the witness.

On redirect, the district attorney asked the doctor if he had an opinion as to exactly how many doses of arsenic the admiral had received. The doctor said it was impossible for him to give an accurate number.

"What would be the effect, as to the difficulty of detecting the taste of arsenic, if it were taken in saleratus and water?"

"It wouldn't make any difference," Whitney replied.

"Whether, in your opinion, there was time for the arsenic found in the brain to have reached it if the first dose were taken as late as Thursday evening?" asked Barker.

"Yes," the doctor answered.

With that, both Barker and Morse indicated they had no further questions for Whitney, and Judge Aiken excused him.

Barker's next witness, Dr. William Balch, a chemist and associate of

Whitney's, analyzed the residue found in Admiral Eaton's stomach. Balch agreed in general with Whitney's testimony, but when the prosecutor asked him to state hypothetically how many doses of arsenic would have been ingested given the symptoms displayed by Admiral Eaton, he said it was taken in more than one dose. He declined to say if the admiral had consumed two large doses but stated he believed he had ingested the first dose on Thursday night, a half hour before the first sign of symptoms.

This testimony differed somewhat from Whitney's opinion that the first dose was taken within two hours, and probably within one hour, of the first sign of illness. Barker asked Balch if the admiral's illness on Wednesday night and Thursday morning after the pork dinner might change his opinion about when the first dose was administered. Balch remained firm and said his opinion would not differ.

"What gives you your opinion that more than one dose was taken?" asked Barker.

"The fact that there was still free arsenic in the fluid of the stomach, and that there was no adherence to the walls of the stomach," Balch answered. He added that death normally occurs within twenty to thirty hours after poison has been ingested.

"Whether white arsenic is likely to remain in the stomach a considerable time longer than arsenic in the mineral form?" Barker inquired.

"The mineral form is heavier, and would be likely to remain longer."

"Whether white arsenic in the stomach a considerable length of time would be likely to be adherent?"

"Not if there was violent nausea," replied Balch.

Balch declined to offer an opinion as to the length of time it took for arsenic to reach the brain, but he did say that, if Eaton had consumed the arsenic on Thursday night there was ample time for it to reach the admiral's brain by the time of his death early Saturday morning.

Barker asked Balch to comment on whether an unsuspecting person could detect the presence of arsenic if it was mixed with saleratus and water. Balch said detection was impossible if the saleratus was not completely dissolved.

"If a man were sick and suffering great anguish, would he be apt to detect a solution of white arsenic in a solution of saleratus and water?"

"No," said the chemist. He added that the same thing applied to arsenic in tea and milk.

Balch told the court that white arsenic was practically tasteless. He then explained the body's digestive process and how it distributes the poison throughout the circulatory system.

The district attorney produced the pasteboard box introduced by Whitney and asked Balch to comment on the color of the arsenic he recovered. Balch said that even though the powder now in evidence was gray, it was probably white before it was ingested.

Barker asked Balch one last question before he turned the chemist over to the defense for cross-examination. He solicited the chemist's opinion as to when Admiral Eaton had received the last dose of arsenic. Balch suggested it was consumed six to eight hours before death.

Morse immediately addressed that point when he took the floor. "You set the last dose at six or eight hours before death. How do you determine that?"

Balch said he based his opinion on the nausea attacks suffered by the admiral following the arsenic's consumption, but he was not sure how many times those attacks had occurred during that period.

"Looking at these particles," said Morse, showing the witness the recovered arsenic, "and going by their appearance do you say that they were part of the first or last dose?"

"I can't say," the witness replied.

"How do you account for its staying so long, if it was part of the first dose?"

"I can't unless it stuck to the mucous membrane," said Balch.

"You couldn't say whether this contains part of the first dose or not?"

The witness could not say whether this powder came from the stomach or not, nor even with certainty that it was white arsenic. Its appearance, however, was consistent with white arsenic that had been in the stomach for thirty-six to forty-eight hours.

"You gave the district attorney your opinion that the poison was first taken on Thursday night?"

"Yes."

"And the fact that the admiral was sick on Wednesday night and Thursday morning did not change your opinion?"

"No."

"What made him sick Wednesday afternoon?"

"Overeating."

"What made him sick Thursday morning?"

"I don't know."

"You pass over that Thursday morning sickness without an opinion?"

"Yes."

Morse asked Balch if a person could take fifteen or more grains of arsenic mixed in water or tea without noticing its presence. Balch stated that detection would be likely under normal circumstances.

At that point, Judge Aiken announced a recess for lunch.

After the recess, Balch allowed under questioning by defense counsel that he had experience in the treatment of chronic, but not acute, poisoning. The chemist recognized the use of arsenic as a tonic, but he didn't agree with Morse's characterization of it as a "splendid" medication.

"Would an amount of arsenic sufficient to cause symptoms shown by Admiral Eaton make a man exhibit symptoms of arsenical poisoning?" asked Morse.

"Yes," the witness replied.

"Would arsenical poisoning to that degree produce a change in a man's appearance?"

"Yes."

Balch testified that a large amount of poison found in the stomach was an indication that a much larger quantity of the toxin had been ingested by the patient. He based that comment on his review of medical testimony in that area.

"You are not able, are you, to say how many doses were taken?" Morse asked.

"We know, approximately."

"How many?"

"At least two," the chemist said.

Morse then informed the court he had no further questions for the witness.

"You said to Mr. Morse that you thought a man could detect a large dose of poison if it were given him, if the man were in a normal condition. What do you mean by a normal condition?" DA Barker asked on redirect.

"I mean a man having his powers of observation, and with his senses active," Balch replied.

"Do you consider a man who has been sick all night Thursday night, who has been sick all day Friday, and who is found unconscious on the floor Friday night, in a normal condition?"

Morse objected, but the judge allowed the question.

"I do not," said Balch.

To another question, Balch testified it would be difficult to detect arsenic in tea if undissolved sugar was also present or if the amount of arsenic was small.

Morse followed the prosecutor by asking the chemist to clarify his previous testimony during cross-examination.

"When I asked you that question, did you have in your mind the fact that the tea had sugar in it?"

"I merely thought of a cup of tea," Balch responded.

The judge excused Balch, and the district attorney next called Hannah Barnes, a Rockland restaurant owner who had worked as a domestic for the Eatons at their Assinippi home between February and May 1912.

After she was sworn, Barker asked Barnes to explain to the court how her relationship with the Eatons had developed and what had transpired between her and the defendant early in her employment.

"I met her in the post office," said the witness. "She asked me to stay in the house a few weeks while she was in Washington. She said the admiral was a feeble, old man and asked me to keep him from flirting with a woman across the way. She wanted me also to keep him from going to Rockland, where, she said, he would be flirting with the girls. She told me that he was insane and wanted to see what I thought about it."

The former housekeeper also related how Mrs. Eaton had spoken with her a few days before the admiral's death about an incident at a Boston theater. Mrs. Eaton said the admiral had flirted with women there so brazenly that she would never accompany him anywhere outside the home. She claimed the admiral would flirt with any woman of any age. She told Barnes that she feared for June's safety and would

165

not leave June alone with her husband.

"I had a letter from Mrs. Eaton in Washington cautioning me again about the woman across the way," said the witness.

When Mrs. Eaton returned from Washington, she asked Barnes about the flirting and whether she thought the admiral was insane.

"I told her that about the neighbor it was true, but I said I did not think he was insane."

Barnes told the court she could not recall an instance in which Mrs. Eaton had ever mentioned the adopted child's death or accused the admiral of poisoning the little boy.

She also testified that she had attended the admiral's funeral at the Eaton home on Tuesday, March 11, and had remained for four hours. Besides the Eaton family, she recalled, the undertaker and other neighbors were present. When Barker asked if Mrs. Eaton had displayed any signs of grief, Barnes said she could not recall. However, she did hear Mrs. Eaton remark to June, "It will be a nice day, you can come home now."

Questioned about the admiral's sobriety, Barnes attested that she had never seen him under the influence of alcohol or any other substance. She said the admiral typically rose at six thirty in the morning and worked around the house or read all day. At night he helped Dorothy with her school lessons.

"Did you ever have a discussion with the admiral about his relationship with June?" Barker asked.

"He told me that June would never live under the same roof with him again," the witness recalled. "He said June had lied about him; that she had cost him a great deal of money. He had paid her way at the Conservatory of Music and then had found out that June was not attending. He told me at one time that he had not had a new suit of clothes in five years; that he had a large pension, but he didn't know where the money went."

Barnes related one other conversation she had with Mrs. Eaton – this one occurring the week before the admiral died.

"She said she was going to a funeral and seemed quite excited. She said the admiral had gotten on her nerves so that she was going away to stay, and added that something would have to be done about him. She asked me to come and stay at the house, but I told her I couldn't."

166

The district attorney thanked his witness and turned her over to the defense for cross-examination. Morse established through Barnes the apparently affectionate relationship displayed by the defendant and her husband. Barnes told the court she believed the admiral was genuinely fond of his wife to whom he wrote every day when she was away from home.

The next witness, South Weymouth fish merchant Miles M. Shurtleff, told of his first meeting with Mrs. Eaton in 1910 at the Washington Street home in Weymouth where Jennie and June were boarding. He continued to do business with Jennie after she returned to her husband in Assinippi. Jennie had talked at great length about the admiral during Shurtleff's visits.

"She said he was insane, and showed me a lock on the pantry door, put there to prevent him from getting in to poison the food," Shurtleff related. "The day following a visit to the theater with the admiral, I found her suffering from a headache, due, she said, to poison which he had given her, either in food or in some confectionary."

Shurtleff testified that he had always found the admiral to be a rational man. He told the jury that he saw Eaton during a business call at Assinippi the Thursday afternoon before he died. While there, he asked the admiral for advice on behalf of his son who hoped to join the navy.

"He seemed as bright as I ever saw him in my life, in good spirits and perfectly normal," said the witness. "He told me how to get my boy into the navy, and suggested sending the boy to him for a talk."

Aiken excused Shurtleff after Morse indicated he had no questions.

The prosecution then called Harry S. Cate, a twenty-two-year-old Rockland shoemaker who had courted June Ainsworth before her marriage to Ralph Keyes. Barker began his direct examination by asking Cate to describe for the jury some of the conversations he had had with Mrs. Eaton about the admiral.

"I frequently heard Mrs. Eaton say that the admiral wasn't right in the head. She warned me of him and told me not to eat soup when he had had the handling of it, nor to drink anything he gave me. She said he knew a lot about subtle poisons that other people didn't know about."

"Did she ever express any wish or threat about the admiral?"

"No."

"Do you remember testifying to the grand jury that she said she wished he was dead?" Barker inquired.

"Do you consider that a threat?" asked Cate.

Barker retrieved the grand jury transcript from his desk and read back to Cate his prior testimony. He then asked Cate again if Mrs. Eaton had threatened the admiral.

"I heard her say, 'I wish the admiral was dead,' " Cate answered, adding that he had heard her say it more than once.

"What did she say after the death of the child?" Barker continued.

"She said she believed he poisoned the child," said the witness.

"How frequently have you heard June and Mrs. Eaton talking about the admiral?"

"More than once."

"Whether she ever asked you to go to the house?"

"She asked me, after the baby's death, to go to the Eaton house to see if the admiral was all right, and to go prepared to take care of myself."

"And did you go prepared?"

"Yes, with a pistol."

The entire courtroom erupted in laughter at Cate's statement. Even Jennie chuckled.

"When you got there," continued Barker, "did you see the admiral?"

"Yes – we went into the kitchen."

"Did you get hurt?" asked Barker, and the audience roared again. Sheriff Porter called for order. Cate said his visit with the admiral was pleasant, but he kept his hand on his pistol which he carried in his coat pocket.

Barker asked Cate if he recalled his testimony before the grand jury in which he had stated that Mrs. Eaton had directed him to take a weapon with him. Cate said he could not recall making such a statement, but he did remember Mrs. Eaton telling him not to let the admiral get behind him and not to eat anything the admiral offered him.

Attorney Morse's cross-examination was brief and was limited to Cate's impression of the defendant's relationship with her husband. Cate said both the admiral and his wife seemed affectionate toward one another.

The Commonwealth's next witness, Katherine Griffith, was employed by the Eatons as a housekeeper in May 1912. The admiral and his stepdaughter, Dorothy, were the only family members at home. Mrs. Eaton returned to Assinippi the day before Griffith was dismissed in June.

"Who came with Mrs. Eaton?" asked ADA Katzmann, now conducting direct examination for the prosecution.

"Miss Rooney," said the witness. "She and Mrs. Eaton went right out in the barn – it was early in the morning – and I was getting breakfast. The admiral was upstairs."

Mrs. Eaton dismissed her that very day, she said, accusing her of making the admiral ill and stealing his money "because he was a crazy, old man." Mrs. Eaton demanded she open her valise for inspection before she left the house.

"She had a bad temper and I was afraid of her," said Griffith.

"Did you see any signs of liquor or drugs on the admiral while you were there?"

"No."

"What was the state of his health?" Katzmann asked.

"He was strong and well," Griffith replied.

Morse then asked the witness how she had gotten the job. Griffith told the court the admiral had hired her through a Boston employment agency.

"Wasn't the reason that Mrs. Eaton let you go that she wasn't satisfied with the way you had done the work?" Morse suggested.

"She didn't say so," Griffith replied simply.

The prosecution called Charles Hilt, an Eaton neighbor, to the stand. Hilt told the court that he saw Admiral Eaton almost every day and that Mrs. Eaton had visited his home on two or three occasions. Hilt claimed he had never seen the admiral appear to be intoxicated by liquor or drugs and believed him to be a sound, reasonable man.

"Did you ever hear Mrs. Eaton speak of the admiral?" Katzmann asked.

"She was over to the house one day and said she had seen a doctor relative to getting attendance for the admiral. She said the doctor had told her if anybody was unsound, she was."

Hilt was confined to his home because of illness on the Thursday before the admiral died. He told the court the admiral had dropped by with some reading material and had offered to help Hilt with his chores.

On cross-examination, Hilt, too, confirmed that the admiral and his wife had always been kindly and affectionate toward one another. He said he often saw them walking arm-in-arm on the grounds of their home.

The day's session concluded with Katzmann presenting the court with the marriage certificate of Joseph G. Eaton and Jennie May Ainsworth, the death certificate of the admiral's first wife, Annie Varnum Eaton, the marriage certificate of Daniel H. Ainsworth and Jennie May Harrison, and the divorce decree granted to Jennie May Ainsworth in Chicago. Finally, he produced the admiral's official retirement papers. Defense counsel made no objections, and the court marked each certified copy as evidence.

Judge Aiken adjourned at 4:30 p.m.

Chapter 21

Local police officers and deputy sheriffs struggled to keep order outside the courthouse when the trial resumed on Tuesday, October 21. Spectators, predominantly women, contended for limited seats in the courtroom. The number of women seeking admission had increased noticeably with each passing day.

A sheriff's deputy arrived with Jennie at the prescribed time and escorted her to her seat behind the defense table. She seemed cheerful, smiling at everyone in the courtroom.

The proceedings began with ADA Frederick Katzmann calling Charlotte Hilt, wife of the prosecution's last witness the previous day. Mrs. Hilt, a stout, middle-aged woman, corroborated her husband's testimony about the admiral's visit to their home on Thursday, March 6, and his apparent good health. She testified about statements that Mrs. Eaton had made to her about the admiral's use of drugs and alcohol and about her fear of being poisoned. She also related how Mrs. Eaton had told her she had searched the house for drugs but admitted she had never found them.

Mrs. Eaton repeatedly told her that the admiral had poisoned the adopted child and expressed fears that the admiral would poison her mother, Mrs. Hilt said. In light of these accusations, Mrs. Hilt asked Mrs. Eaton why she had left her mother alone with the admiral. Mrs. Eaton didn't answer.

"Did you have any conversation with Mrs. Eaton the morning of the admiral's death?" Katzmann asked.

"Yes. She came over to my house about seven o'clock and asked me to come over to her house, as she thought the admiral was dead," Mrs. Hilt explained. "I went over at eight. She said the admiral had been sick all day Friday, and had said all day that he was cold. She said she had to keep him supplied with hot-water bags all day."

Morse's only question for the witness concerned her impressions of the relationship between the admiral and his wife. As had all of the witnesses before her, Mrs. Hilt stated the couple appeared to be on the

171

most affectionate of terms.

Catherine Magoun, a thirty-eight-year-old housewife who lived across the street from the Eatons, was the next witness. She related a conversation in her backyard with Mrs. Eaton.

Jennie had asked her to take June as a boarder in her home. When Magoun asked why, the defendant told her "June was ill and the admiral had mixed up a mess for her." When Magoun inquired what kind of mess, the defendant said "soap, vinegar, and pepper or salt."

"I said I didn't believe it, and she made no reply, but I didn't take June to board," Magoun said.

"Did Mrs. Eaton ever say anything about Mrs. Collamore?" asked Katzmann.

"She said Mrs. Collamore winked at her husband. He was in the backyard, and Mrs. Collamore was in the second-story window of her house," Magoun answered.

"Did you see much of the admiral?"

"I saw him about every day."

"Did you ever see anything to indicate that he was of unsound mind?"

"No," she replied.

On cross-examination, Morse asked Magoun if she had ever visited the Eaton house. Magoun said she had not. Morse then told the court he had no other questions, and the witness stepped down.

Barker examined the next witness, Rockland businessman Clarence E. Rice. Rice told the court he had first met the Eatons at their home in Assinippi just after they had moved there in 1907. He went to their house frequently, helping them select carpeting and wallpaper for their new home.

"What has Mrs. Eaton told you about the admiral?" Barker inquired.

"In March of 1908 she told me, explaining why there wasn't ready money to settle their bill, that the admiral gambled and drank in Boston, and they were in debt. She said he was not right mentally," Rice responded.

Rice told the court how he had invited the admiral, in the presence of Mrs. Eaton, to speak at the Rockland Men's Club. Before the admiral could respond, Mrs. Eaton had said she didn't allow her husband to go out at night alone. She consented only when Rice promised to pick him up and bring him home.

As he had with every other witness personally associated with the Eatons, Morse asked about the Eatons' spousal relationship and found Rice's response consistent with the testimony of others.

Abbie Cornelia Cottrell, a seventy-five-year-old Hingham resident and widow, told the court she had been the admiral's housekeeper for three months during the winter of 1909-10 while Mrs. Eaton and June had lived in East Weymouth. She said Mrs. Eaton stopped by the house once a week during her employment.

Barker asked the witness if Mrs. Eaton had ever spoken about the admiral during any of the visits.

"On one occasion that I remember, I think both the admiral and Dorothy were away. She began criticizing the admiral, and I told her I didn't care to listen to any talk of that kind."

As to Barker's questions about the admiral's use of alcohol and drugs and his rationality, the witness replied, "I never saw any evidence of the undue use of liquor by the admiral. Nor was he of unsound mind."

Judge Aiken excused Cottrell when Morse indicated he had no questions. Mrs. Eaton smiled at Cottrell and bowed her head and shoulders as the witness passed her while leaving the courtroom.

Forty-one-year-old optometrist and jeweler Samuel W. Baker was the next witness. Baker owned and operated Baker Brothers, a retail establishment on Union Street in Rockland. He testified that he knew both the admiral and the defendant and had frequently seen the admiral on Union Street.

Baker told the court that Mrs. Eaton had visited his shop one day looking for a pair of glasses and, once inside his examination room, had asked him if he thought the admiral was insane. The district attorney asked the witness if he could recall exactly what Mrs. Eaton had said to him.

"She asked me if I wouldn't help her to have him examined. She said that whenever anybody was sick in the house, the admiral insisted on waiting on them and wouldn't let anybody else do so. She said that he had, she believed, foreign drugs, that these were kept under lock and key."

Baker said he last saw the admiral on February 17, 1913, when he and Mrs. Eaton came into Baker's shop together.

"The admiral told me that they were going to Panama; that acting under commission from President Grant, I think in 1871, he had made a survey for a canal route across the isthmus, and that he looked forward with pleasure to the trip that he and Mrs. Eaton were to take to see the completed cut. He had an invitation from the government to go on a naval vessel."

Morse took his turn and asked Baker if Mrs. Eaton had ever told him the admiral had studied poisons in the Far East. Baker said she had not. To Morse's standard question, Baker said he thought the admiral and his wife always seemed happy together.

Grocery clerk Frank L. Booth was sworn and, under questioning by Katzmann, said he did business with the Eatons and stopped by their house every week for grocery orders and deliveries. Booth said he seldom engaged Mrs. Eaton in conversation at the house, but he had once driven her in his wagon from Mann's Corner to her home at Assinippi.

"Did she ever talk with you about the admiral?" the prosecutor asked.

"Yes, most any time when he wasn't present," Booth recalled. "She said he was taking some kind of poison, and that he was trying to poison her. She told me she thought he kept it hidden in the attic, but she could not find it. She had put talcum powder on the stairs, hoping to trace his footprints to where it was hidden, but failed. One day it was cold, and the admiral asked me if I didn't want a cup of coffee. I declined. Later, Mrs. Eaton told me it was well I didn't drink it, because it was poisoned."

"Another time she wanted to know if I didn't think it advisable to have a detective come to watch the admiral and find out about the poisons. She said she didn't care to sleep with him at night for fear he would do away with her before morning, and she said that Dorothy, who was sick at the time, was being given something by the admiral to keep her from getting well. The admiral never talked about these things. One day, I was talking with the admiral when he had a 'spell,' fell backward and struck the stove. Mrs. Harrison came from the other room, and between us we carried him in and laid him on the couch. After a bit he came to and thanked me for getting him in there."

The witness said he had never seen the admiral do or say anything to suggest he was unsound.

Under questioning by Morse, Booth estimated he had been doing business with the Eatons for about a year and a half. Contrary to his previous statement that conversations with Mrs. Eaton were infrequent, Booth now said she talked about poison every time he stopped by.

Morse pursued Booth's account of the admiral's fall, suggesting the admiral had collapsed because he was intoxicated or drugged.

"Did you say that he reeled and staggered like a drunken man?" asked Morse.

"He naturally staggered," Booth answered. He refused to say that the admiral smelled of liquor and insisted Eaton did not seem under the influence of any substance. Mrs. Harrison asked Booth not to tell her daughter about the admiral's mishap, and Booth never discussed it with the admiral.

The district attorney called another witness to verify the admiral's soundness of mind. Elizabeth Lambert had worked at the Eaton house for one day during Mrs. Eaton's absence in 1909. She and the admiral had lunch and conversed in the kitchen. She noticed nothing irrational about the admiral's speech or behavior. To Morse, she declared the admiral had been exceedingly polite to her that day.

Twenty-eight-year-old Grace Coolidge Booth, wife of previous witness Frank Booth, took the stand as the Commonwealth's next witness. She and her twin sister worked in their father's bakery on Union Street in Rockland Center, and the Eatons were occasional customers. She testified that the admiral always acted like a gentleman when he stopped in the shop and had never flirted with her.

Morse had no questions.

Grace's twin sister, Maud Coolidge Powers, followed her on the stand. She recalled a visit that Mrs. Eaton made to the shop about a week before the admiral died.

"She said she was going to June's house for six or seven weeks and wanted to know if I could get a girl to stay with the admiral while she was gone. I said I didn't know of any, but asked why she didn't get Mrs. Barnes. But she said she wanted a young woman.

"She said the admiral was getting childish and was always thinking about girls. She said he had been to the theater the week before and had acted disgracefully."

"Was the admiral ever unduly familiar with you?" Barker asked.

"No," she replied.

"Ever try to flirt with you?"

"No."

Morse, on cross-examination, asked Powers if it was the admiral who had asked for the young girl and not Mrs. Eaton. She said no; that it was Mrs. Eaton's idea. Powers said the admiral and his wife always seemed on good terms whenever they visited the store.

Following a brief recess, Frank S. Alger, owner and editor of the *Rockland Standard and Plymouth County Advertiser*, took the stand. Alger testified he had visited the Eaton home on at least six occasions. In 1909, he brought the admiral and his wife the results of Dr. Whitney's postmortem analysis of their adopted son.

"They came out on the piazza and I told them the news. Mrs. Eaton said there must be some mistake and that the child couldn't have died unless something had been given to it. The admiral was present."

"Did you ever talk with the admiral about the reason June didn't live there?" Barker asked.

"In August 1909, he said she couldn't live there – he would not have it because she told stories about him," Alger answered.

"Has the defendant ever said that the admiral wouldn't have June there?"

"She did once, and may have at other times, I'm not sure."

"On an occasion shortly after you went to Assinippi you met Mrs. Eaton in a train, and she spoke of the admiral?" asked Barker.

"Yes. She spoke of his not being well, childish in his actions – that she had great care with him. On other occasions she spoke of his liking to study poisons, play with them, and dabble in them. I asked where he got them, and she said she didn't know. She said she didn't dare to eat food nor drink anything without first examining the plates and saucers to see that they were all right."

"How many times did she speak of her fear of being poisoned?"

"If she ever did," Morse interjected.

"Several times – I can't say how many," Alger said.

"Whether you ever saw anything about the admiral to indicate that he was of unsound mind?"

"I thought he was peculiar in his manner of expressing himself. I don't know that I can describe it – I thought that perhaps it resulted from his being a naval man."

Morse asked Alger about the notice of the adopted baby's birth that was published in his newspaper. Alger confirmed that the admiral had sent him a letter about the birth and that Alger had printed it soon afterwards. He said he did not mention how he had received the birth notice because he didn't consider it "a matter of news."

Alger corroborated the testimony of previous witnesses when he stated a cordial relationship existed between the admiral and his wife. He also told the court he had never seen the admiral under the influence of alcohol.

John H. Prouty of West Norwell, nephew of Eaton neighbor James L. Prouty, testified next. Prouty was a real estate agent for Chapin's Farm Agency and had brokered the sale of the Dunham property in Assinippi to the Eatons in 1907.

Prouty told the court he had visited the Eaton home several times after the sale. Mrs. Eaton had stopped at his own home twice, the first time about two weeks before she went to Weymouth to live with June. Mrs. Eaton asked Prouty to find her and June a cottage to rent for the summer. She said she didn't dare to live with the admiral who she described as an insane man who dabbled in poisons.

"I asked her if she thought it was prudent to leave Dorothy with an insane man, and she said the admiral was very fond of Dorothy and wouldn't hurt her. I told her I had no place I could rent her, and advised her to go home. She promised to do so. About the time the child died at Sand Hills, Mrs. Eaton came to my house at eleven at night. She talked to me about an hour, and was very positive that Admiral Eaton had poisoned the child. She considered him an insane man."

"Did she say anything about him poisoning other members of the family?" Katzmann asked.

"No," Prouty replied.

"Did she show any fear herself of being poisoned?"

"No."

On cross-examination, Prouty said he had first met the Eatons when they came to him and inquired about purchasing the Assinippi farm.

"With whom did you talk?" Morse inquired.

"With both of them," Prouty answered.

"Did the admiral talk about his financial circumstances?"

"He told me he could pay only five hundred dollars down."

"What was the house sold for?" asked Morse.

"Fifty-five hundred dollars. They paid five hundred dollars to the owner and a mortgage was taken," the witness said.

"Did Mrs. Eaton say to you subsequently that the reason she came to Assinippi was because the admiral was in poor health and she wanted to get a home?"

"She said she wanted to get away from the city, where expenses would be less. She never mentioned to me that the admiral was addicted to drugs," Prouty insisted.

Morse, not satisfied with Prouty's answer, questioned him repeatedly about whether Mrs. Eaton had mentioned the admiral's drug and alcohol problem as a reason for moving to the country. But Prouty held his ground and refused to acknowledge that the defendant had said anything of the kind.

On redirect, Katzmann asked Prouty if he had ever seen the admiral under the influence of liquor or drugs. Prouty said he had either seen or conversed with the admiral fifteen or twenty times, and the admiral had never shown any signs of intoxication or addiction.

On recross-examination, Morse sought to establish exactly when and where Prouty had spoken to Mrs. Eaton about renting a cottage. Prouty said he had visited the Eaton home just after Mrs. Eaton had returned from her extended stay in Weymouth following the death of the adopted child. Morse asked Prouty if he had detected any animosity between the couple on this occasion. The witness said the admiral and his wife had appeared to be on friendly terms.

Charles E. Nordstrom, the private detective Mrs. Eaton had planned to engage in 1912 to investigate the admiral, recalled the circumstances of his first meeting with the defendant at South Station in Boston, an appointment she had made with his office by telephone.

"I met her between eight and nine in the morning (on June 13, 1912). She had a woman with her who was introduced by the name of Rooney. Mrs. Eaton said Miss Rooney was going out to take care of her husband. She asked me if I would take her case, to get evidence against her husband as a poisoner. She said I should have to be very careful; that he had a chest of poisons in the attic and she wanted me to find the chest, to get complete evidence and to have him arrested," the detective testified.

"She said her husband was a retired naval officer of great influence, that he had studied poisons in the Orient. She also said that he had been in Panama, and that he had gloated over the way people were dying there.

"I told her I should have to have an operative in the house, and that if she had hired Miss Rooney, she would have to discharge her in favor of my operative. I made an appointment for the following Tuesday, which was not kept. I asked her for two hundred dollars for a retainer; she said she hadn't any money, but owned the house, and offered me a mortgage on it. This not being feasible, she said she thought she could raise fifty dollars.

"She told me she often woke in the night and found blood streaming down her arm, and when she found this she said she used to say, 'Why don't you kill me outright?' "

The witness said he understood Mrs. Eaton to mean this was her husband's way of poisoning her.

Morse tried to discredit Nordstrom when he asked the detective if a Boston newspaper had paid him for an interview it published about the Eaton case. Nordstrom admitted he had received twenty-five dollars. Further questioning by defense counsel was aimed at portraying Nordstrom as a publicity seeker intent on promoting his investigative proficiency and his fledgling detective business.

After a recess for lunch, Katzmann assumed the prosecution's direct examination. His first witness, Bessie Bursey of Washington, DC, managed the lodging house at 425 P Street NW where June and Mrs. Eaton had occupied two rooms in April 1912. Katzmann asked Bursey to tell the jury the circumstances of her meeting with the defendant and her daughter.

"I was keeping a rooming house and June came there, after seeing my advertisement in the paper," the witness said. "Mrs. Eaton came later. They stayed there altogether till July, and went away together. They had two rooms on the second floor of the house and did light housekeeping there. In April, June went to the Columbian Hospital, where she gave birth to a girl. I saw her while she was a patient there."

"Did you see much of Mrs. Eaton?" asked Katzmann.

"Yes. She and I had many talks, some of them lasting an hour or two."

"Anything that concerned her husband?"

"Yes, a right smart," replied the witness.

"What?" Katzmann asked.

"A right smart," interrupted Morse, "is Southern for 'a good deal.' "

"I am aware of it," an annoyed Katzmann retorted.

"What name did the mother give you?" Katzmann continued.

"Mrs. Eaton."

"Where did Mrs. Eaton tell you her home was?"

"When she first came, she said it was in Chicago."

"Did she ever tell you of any other home?"

"No."

"What did she say about her husband?"

"She said that she was afraid of him and that he used poisons," Bursey replied. "She said she wouldn't go to sleep in the same room with him. She told me that once she waked in the night and found the blood running down her arm. She asked him what had happened, and he told her that he had injected some medicine into her arm. She said that when she had business letters come, her husband opened them. Then later, when her correspondents wrote asking why she had not answered the earlier letters, she would ask her husband if he knew anything about it. He would reply that perhaps if she looked under the carpet she might find the letters.

"She said that she had a man friend in Chicago who was all the time writing her letters, asking her to leave her husband and come to him," Bursey continued. "She said that when the Chicago man died she was to inherit all his money. He had a beautiful home in Chicago, Mrs. Eaton said, and was a rich businessman. He owned many houses. I don't think she spoke of this Chicago man so often as she did of her husband, but she told me a great many times that she thought the world of the Chicago man."

"Did you ever see any of her postal matter?" Katzmann asked.

"Yes, she had letters from Chicago, New York, and Boston."

"Where did Mrs. Eaton spend her time?"

"In and out of the house, in the afternoon. She was almost always in the house by six or seven o'clock, and then she and June would go out in the evening. I was always in bed and asleep when they returned. I go to bed at ten or eleven."

"Have you any knowledge of where they went when they went out in the evening?"

"No."

"Anything else Mrs. Eaton told you about her husband?"

"She said that at one time he pulled down a pair of portieres (curtains hung over a door or doorway) in the house, and painted them in stripes, asking whether they didn't look prettier that way. On another occasion, he tore up some of June's music and when asked where it was, he told Mrs. Eaton to look behind the piano and she would find it."

"Did Mrs. Eaton say anything about her plans?"

"She said she was going to take a detective back from Washington with her – that if her husband was insane, they would find it out within two weeks, and have him put away," the witness answered.

"After the baby was born, where was it kept?" Katzmann inquired.

"At my house."

"Where was it left when June and her mother went out?"

"Upstairs in their rooms, without any attendant."

"How long was June in the hospital?"

"For two weeks after her baby was born."

"What did you say to Mrs. Eaton about the baby?"

"She had been to the hospital one day, and I asked her how June was. She said she was all right and that she had a big girl baby. I asked whether she had notified the father, and she said she had. I said, 'Well, I guess he'll be glad,' and she agreed with me."

"Did you know that Mrs. Eaton lived near Boston?"

"Not until after she left. She had said her home was in Chicago, and described it as a beautiful home with a beautiful lawn, close to some driveway."

"Just prior to their leaving, what happened with respect to the baby?" Katzmann asked.

"Mrs. Eaton asked me on the Friday before – they left on Sunday – to wash some dresses for the baby, saying she was going to take it to a friend's house. That evening she took the baby away, and I never saw it again. After their departure I went through their rooms to clean them up and found a letter from Mr. Eaton. I tore it up. It was addressed to Mrs. Jennie Eaton and signed, 'Your husband.' "

On cross-examination by Morse, Bursey related how June had arrived alone and had told her she lived in Chicago. She gave her name and said an aunt would join her later. June was obviously pregnant and had explained to Bursey that she was on a business trip with her husband, a traveling salesman. June told her that when they reached Washington she had consulted a physician who advised her not to travel any farther in her condition.

"Did Mrs. Eaton ever tell you the name of the Chicago man who loved her so much?"

"Yes, but I have forgotten it."

"What name did Mrs. Eaton give?"

"She said she was June's mother-in-law," said the witness, apparently to Morse's discomfort.

"You said that she and Mrs. Eaton stayed out late in the evenings. Did June do this within a month of the birth of the baby?"

"Yes."

"You weren't curious about who they really were?"

"It was none of my business."

"Did you ever see Mrs. Eaton write a letter to Chicago?"

"No."

"Did any man ever call on these two women?"

"No."

Bursey told the court that letters postmarked "Assinippi" arrived for Mrs. Eaton at the lodging house every day. She admitted she had never seen Mrs. Eaton address a letter to Assinippi, nor had Mrs. Eaton ever asked her to mail one for her.

"Did she pay you when she left?" asked Morse.

"Yes."

"How much has been paid you to come here?"

"Nothing. My way was paid here, and I was promised that my expenses should be paid," Bursey answered.

"Did Mrs. Eaton say that her husband and the man in Chicago both loved her?"

"Yes."

"Did she say she loved her husband?"

"I don't think she ever told me that," said Bursey.

"Now, as a woman, didn't you find at once that Mrs. Eaton was simply trying to conceal facts because of her daughter's condition, and the circumstances under which her baby was born?"

"Well, I knew as soon as she came that she was the girl's mother," said Bursey. "The resemblance alone would have told me, and their manner was alike, too."

"You saw that the whole plan was to mislead you because of the circumstances?"

"Yes."

"I have no further questions," Morse told the court.

Katzmann, on redirect, asked Bursey if Mrs. Eaton had told her she had a husband and a man in Chicago other than her husband who she was fond of. The witness replied in the affirmative.

Morse momentarily consulted with his client and then approached the witness for recross. He asked if Bursey had written a letter to Mrs. Eaton after Admiral Eaton had died. She admitted she had.

"You knew then that Mrs. Eaton was his wife?"

"Yes."

"And you wrote to her in Plymouth Jail?"

"Yes."

When Morse asked Bursey what she had written, she said she could not recall. Morse turned to Mrs. Eaton and quietly conferred with her once more. He turned again to the witness.

"Did you write that you knew she could not be guilty of the offense because she told you in Washington of her love of her husband?" asked Morse. The witness shook her head.

"When did you discover that she was Admiral Eaton's wife?"

"When I saw the story in the newspapers with her picture. I recognized her," Bursey replied.

"Hadn't she told you that her husband loved her, and she loved him, and he wanted her to come home?"

"Yes."

"But," said ADA Katzmann, rising from his seat at the prosecution table, "she didn't say the letters from Assinippi were from her husband?"

"No."

When the prosecution and defense acknowledged they had no more questions for the witness, Judge Aiken dismissed Bursey and called a brief recess.

When court reconvened, Sarah Bucher, a thirty-five-year-old investigator with the District of Columbia Bureau of Children and Guardians, took the stand.

Bucher testified that she had received a complaint from the clerk of the Washington Police Court about the improper care of a child being boarded at 1377 L Street SW. Bucher went to the address and spoke with Gertrude Wallace, caretaker for the five-month-old girl. As a result of her investigation, Bucher immediately took custody of the child and placed it in a state ward pending action for child neglect against the child's mother, June Keyes, in Washington Juvenile Court scheduled for December 20, 1912.

At the hearing, Bucher related, she was approached by the defendant, Mrs. Eaton, who identified herself as the child's grandmother. Mrs. Eaton asked to see the investigative records and then asked Bucher to destroy them and dismiss the case.

"The defendant said there was no need to bring a case," Bucher recalled. "She said she was the child's grandmother, and that she wanted to take the baby away with her. She first told me she was Mrs. Owens of Chicago. I asked her if Ainsworth wasn't her name; after that she gave me the name of Eaton and then denied it. I asked her again if her name wasn't Keyes, for I had got three names when I investigated the case. She then said that Ralph Keyes was the father of the child, and that her daughter was eighteen years old. She said her daughter and Keyes had been married one month before and that they intended to take the child into their home. She wanted to take the baby then and there, but I told her I couldn't do that. She was exceedingly angry at that and said that if I proceeded I could go to – I guess I needn't say the rest."

"I think you may as well tell us," said Katzmann.

"Well, she said that I could go to hell," Bucher continued. "I asked her whether she had been to see the baby since she had placed it in the home, and she said 'no.' And then I asked her how she heard of the court proceedings, and she said she had had a bad dream in regard to the baby's being mistreated."

"Please go on," prompted Katzmann.

"Later in the afternoon, she spoke to me again, and told me of her affection for the baby, and the love its mother bore it. She said the young people were thinking of adopting it. She said she would not board it out again; she would not trust it for one night out of her house, after what had happened."

"Did she tell you who she really was?"

"No more than when she said she was Mrs. Eaton, the wife of a navy man. She told me about coming to Washington the previous spring – not, however, in detail."

"Did you discuss the condition of the child?"

"Yes. She was very much distressed when she found what had happened, and said that she had not known what Gertie Wallace was like. She had gone in answer to an advertisement, had found a very nice, clean place, and had thought that it would be all right. She said that she didn't think the child looked so very bad, on the whole."

"How long did she remain in Washington?" Katzmann asked.

"Overnight. She took the child away with her next day, going to Boston," the witness replied.

"Did she say where she lived?"

"She mentioned the Franklin Square House as a place where she and her daughter had both stayed, and said that her daughter's address was Dorchester."

"Your witness," Katzmann said to Morse.

"When you called at the home where the baby was, did you ascertain that Mrs. Eaton had sent money for its keeping?" Morse inquired.

"Gertie Wallace told me that it was the child of a niece of hers," said Bucher.

"You didn't know, and couldn't find out, that Mrs. Eaton had sent twelve dollars a month to pay its board?"

"Found that out later."

"She told you that in some way the child was connected with a naval man of some distinction?"

"Yes."

"And that she was very anxious to prevent a scandal, for the sake of the officer, and to prevent reflections on the department?" Morse asked.

185

"Yes," said the witness.

"You felt it was all right to let her have the child, and you did allow her to take it?"

"The court did," corrected Bucher.

"You knew that she was the wife of Rear Admiral Eaton when she took the child, and that she was doing what she could to avoid publicity?"

"No, not that," said the investigator.

At the conclusion of Bucher's testimony, Judge Aiken adjourned for the day. The jury filed out and a sheriff's deputy escorted Mrs. Eaton to the prison wagon for her trip back to the jail.

Reporters rushed to the temporary communications center set up for them behind the courthouse and filed their stories to meet deadlines. The prosecution and defense teams huddled for a short time in their courthouse offices to discuss the day's events and prepare for the next. Court would reconvene on Wednesday with the prosecution's final witnesses and possibly the defense's opening statement. The trial was moving quickly, primarily because of Morse's very brief cross-examinations of witnesses during the past few days and Judge Aiken's shortened recesses and extended sessions.

Chapter 22

In an interview outside the courthouse before the trial resumed on Wednesday, October 22, defense attorney William A. Morse surprised reporters by confirming a rumor that Mrs. Eaton would take the stand near the end of the trial. He could not say if the defense would call June Keyes. "That will depend upon developments," he said. "If we feel that the occasion demands it, we will summon her."

Judge Aiken called the court to order, and the Commonwealth called State Detective John H. Scott. The veteran policeman told the court that he and his partner, Deputy Sheriff John Condon, had first visited the Eaton house at about 8:30 p.m. on March 10, two days after the admiral's death. Scott said Mrs. Eaton had expressed surprise at their appearance, stating it was her understanding that the medical examiner had already ruled the admiral had died a natural death. When Scott explained that police were required to investigate every unexplained death as a matter of routine, Mrs. Eaton agreed to answer their questions.

Scott testified about Mrs. Eaton's account of the events leading up to the admiral's illness and death in the early morning hours of Saturday, March 8. Jurors noted that her version concurred with the accounts given by her daughter, Dorothy, and her mother, Mrs. Harrison, during the early days of the trial.

Scott testified that the defendant had accompanied him and Condon as they inspected the house and searched for evidence. He recalled that she was extremely "excited" and nearly knocked over the stretcher bearing the admiral's body. She told Scott she had searched the admiral's bed but had found no poison. Scott remembered her saying at the same time that she wanted to hire "some Sherlock Holmes or a noted detective" to solve the mystery of her husband's death.

Scott related that Mrs. Eaton had talked so incessantly during the search that her mother had admonished her to be quiet. She had dismissed her mother's reprimand and explained to Scott and Condon, "She thinks if I talk too much they will put me in Taunton (insane asylum). I hope they won't. I'd rather go to jail than to an asylum with the monkeys hopping round the bars."

The prosecution strengthened its contention that Mrs. Eaton was the only person with the exclusive opportunity to administer poison to the admiral when Detective Scott testified that Mrs. Eaton had acknowledged that she alone had cared for the admiral on the night before his death.

"Nobody gave him anything but myself," Mrs. Eaton had told him. "Dorothy did not give him anything, nor did my mother. I gave him the first dose of medicine left by the doctor in hot water. He threw it up. I gave him another dose later in water not quite so hot. He threw that up. Then I took some milk. He could not stand that. The next dose with water I mixed with a small pinch of soda. He did not leave his bed from Thursday; he was too weak."

Scott asked Mrs. Eaton where she had gotten the soda, and she pointed to a box in the pantry. She showed Scott and Condon how much soda she had given the admiral by removing a small amount from the box with a table knife. Scott asked her if she was sure it was the same box from which she had taken the soda. She said she was positive and added that the admiral had thrown up the soda as soon as she had given it to him.

"The doctor gave him a dose of soda about noon, and I gave him one about three o'clock," Mrs. Eaton had told the two investigators. Scott testified he took the box of soda and later gave it to Dr. Osgood for analysis. Osgood forwarded it to Dr. Whitney, who found no arsenic mixed into the soda.

Scott said that he and Condon had visited the Eaton home on four other occasions between March 10 and March 20. Scott testified about his discovery on March 11 of a purported "will" in a typewriter in one of the bedrooms. He had not seen the document since then. It was the same "will" DA Barker had failed to have admitted as evidence during Dorothy Ainsworth's testimony on October 17.

When Scott suggested that the document was Mrs. Eaton's unfinished will, bequeathing all her real and personal property to her daughter, June, Morse objected. The judge instructed the jury to disregard Scott's statement and ordered it stricken from the record.

Barker asked Scott if Mrs. Eaton had ever shown any signs of grief during his interactions with her. Scott said Mrs. Eaton was crying when he stopped by the house after she and Dorothy had returned from the admiral's burial, but he believed it reflected neither sorrow nor sadness but anger at the aggressive press people who had followed her to Dracut. She said to him, "I wish you had gone with me yesterday from the funeral to protect me from the newspaper photographers and reporters. It was horrible."

On cross-examination, Scott told Morse that he and Condon had searched the Eaton home and grounds three times for a total of eleven hours. They searched the entire house, the attic, the cellar, the sheds, and the barn, but found no white arsenic. He said they visited drugstores in Malden, Medford, Boston, Brockton, Rockland, and Hanover. They went to Alexandria, Virginia, and the Georgetown section of Washington, DC, but found no record to confirm a sale of arsenic to any person under the name of Ainsworth, Keyes, or Eaton.

Morse wanted the jury to hear just how cooperative Mrs. Eaton was whenever the two investigators visited the house.

"She talked fully and unreservedly, didn't she?" Morse asked Scott.

"Yes," he replied.

"There was no disposition on her part to conceal anything?"

"No."

Morse sought to clarify Scott's interpretation of Mrs. Eaton's emotions following the admiral's burial in Dracut.

"There was sorrow and grief on her part after she returned from the burial?" Morse inquired.

"There were tears," said the detective.

"Didn't she say that she thought it was a shame that so distinguished a man as the admiral should be humiliated by the presence of the newspaper reporters and cameramen at the burial?"

"She did."

Deputy Sheriff John Condon was the next witness, and his testimony corroborated Scott's almost verbatim. Under cross-examination by Morse, Condon also acknowledged that their search had failed to produce evidence of arsenic on the Eaton property or any record of a sale of arsenic to the defendant.

Condon was excused, and Barker called one-time Eaton family physician Dr. Charles Colgate to the stand. Colgate testified that he had first met Mrs. Eaton when she came to his office on Webster Street in September 1908. She asked for medicine to put into her husband's tea without his knowledge. She said the medicine was needed for his stomach ailments. Colgate said he prescribed a small dose. Mrs. Eaton had returned sometime later, and he wrote another prescription.

The doctor further testified that Mrs. Eaton came to his office in February 1909 and asked him to have the admiral committed.

"Mrs. Eaton told me the admiral was insane and was trying to poison her and that she had to put a lock on her daughter June's door. She brought some preserves for me to analyze, saying the admiral had placed poison in it [sic]. She also brought a bottle of antiseptic wash to my office to be analyzed, saying it was not clear, and she thought the admiral had placed poison in it."

The witness said he later told Mrs. Eaton that he had found no evidence of poison in the stuff she had brought him.

Colgate said he visited the Assinippi home about six weeks later to observe the admiral's behavior.

"On April 17, 1909, at her request, I called on the admiral. The admiral said, 'My wife has the idea that poison has crept into our little household, but it is all a mistake.' I felt convinced his mind was all right."

Mrs. Eaton had written three letters to the doctor, all of which were marked as exhibits. In one, she castigated the doctor for his failure to recognize the admiral's obvious insanity. In the second, she declared the admiral had poisoned the child and blamed the physician for not preventing it by not having the admiral put away.

> *I hold you morally responsible for the death of my boy. Had you examined the admiral for his sanity, it would have saved the life of my dear little boy.*

In the third letter, she repeated her complaints about the admiral's insanity and the need for committal. She implored the doctor to take his wife to an upcoming lecture the admiral would give on the Spanish-American War. "Ask your wife to speak with the admiral," she wrote, and he would quickly see how the admiral behaved toward women.

When Morse got his turn, he strode determinedly to the witness stand and went on the attack. He laid into the doctor with a ferocity that astonished the jury.

"You were willing to give Mrs. Eaton medicine to be given to her husband without his knowledge?" Morse bristled.

"Yes, sir," Colgate calmly responded.

"Is it your custom to treat women's husbands upon their statements, without the husbands' knowledge?"

"I can't remember any other such case," the doctor said with an air of indifference.

"Did you tell Admiral Eaton, when you saw him professionally, that his wife had been to you and received medicine to be given to him without his knowledge?" asked Morse.

"No," replied Colgate.

"Did you ask Admiral Eaton whether he took drugs or whiskey?"

"No, because we can usually find out in some indirect way," said the doctor.

"Did you ask him directly or indirectly whether he used drugs or whiskey?"

"No."

"Did you take into consideration Mrs. Eaton's statements that he was a drug eater, a poison taker, a hard drinker?"

"She never said any of those things," DA Barker interjected.

"Perhaps you would better take the witness stand, Brother Barker," Morse retorted.

Barker repeatedly objected to Morse's line of questioning, but the court overruled him every time. Colgate finally admitted he had never tried to find out if the admiral used either substance. When Morse asked him why not, the physician calmly stated he could not give any particular reason.

Morse delved into the admiral's physical shortcomings. Colgate initially claimed he was unaware that the admiral had procured a truss as a remedy for a hernia, but, under redirect by Barker, said he had recommended one after the admiral complained of pain in the groin during an examination. The motive for this questioning was unclear and caused Judge Aiken some consternation. He interrupted both attorneys and directed them to move on. Both sides conceded further questioning, so Aiken excused Colgate.

Unexpectedly, Barker recalled Dr. Gilman Osgood. Osgood produced two bottles containing white arsenic, one with two grains and the other fifteen, and both were submitted as exhibits for comparison. Osgood testified dramatically that he had obtained the arsenic an hour before at a store in Plymouth and affirmed that the sales clerk had not required a signature for receipt of the drug.

That testimony surely had an impact on jurors. Osgood's easy procurement of the arsenic without a signature helped to explain the investigation's failure to produce a record of purchase by the defendant.

Morse had no questions for Osgood, so the judge recessed for lunch.

The spectators present during the morning session remained inside the courthouse, anxious to retain their seats. Outside, the crowd had swelled considerably. When a sheriff's deputy announced that no seats were available for the afternoon session, the crowd became belligerent. The deputy ordered the people to disperse, but they ignored him. When he stepped back inside and closed the door, the throng surged forward and knocked the door off its hinges. Officers stationed inside and outside the courthouse rushed to the deputy's assistance and scattered the belligerents, forcing them into the street and beyond.

When court resumed, Barker called June's husband, Ralph Keyes. Keyes testified about his marriage to June and their separation six days after the admiral's death. When the district attorney asked him if he had any children, the witness answered "No."

Aiken immediately ordered the question and answer excluded from the trial record.

"I am not going to allow the paternity of the child born in Washington to be made the subject of inquiry," the judge told Barker. "If you wish to inquire whether there was a child in the household you may do so."

"You knew a child was born in Washington?" Barker continued.

"Yes, on April 20, 1912," Keyes replied.

"When did you first learn of such a child?" Barker asked, but Morse raised an objection, and the judge sustained it.

"When did the child come to your house?" the district attorney asked.

"Mrs. Eaton brought it a few days before Christmas. It lived with me and my wife until the separation. Mrs. Eaton visited us from time to time up to the admiral's death," Keyes answered.

He related how Mrs. Eaton had two trunks and a bed and bedstead delivered to his house in Medford on February 20, 1913, and had arrived there herself later that day. She stayed with them until March 1.

Keyes said he next saw his mother-in-law on Wednesday, March 5, when he returned home from work at about 5:45 p.m. and found her sitting in his kitchen. He said June came home about eight thirty the same evening. He related that his wife had gone to Assinippi thinking she was to meet her mother there and had returned to Medford when she realized her error.

"What conversation did you hear between Mrs. Eaton and June?" Barker asked.

"June said the admiral was planning to go to Europe and that she thought he was planning to put somebody out of the way before he went," Keyes recalled. "June said he had asked her whether she would care very much if her mother were put out of the way, or if I were put out of the way. Mrs. Eaton was very much excited. She said she would have to go and look after him, and she went away about five o'clock the next morning."

The significance of this testimony was not lost on jurors. The prosecution, through previous witnesses, had shown that the admiral had received the first dose of poison on Thursday, March 6. Keyes corroborated Dorothy Ainsworth's testimony about Mrs. Eaton's presence at Assinippi on Thursday morning. Through Keyes, Barker believed he had also established deliberate intent based on Mrs. Eaton's statement that "she would have to go and look after him."

Keyes testified that he, his wife, and Mrs. Eaton talked until 10:30 p.m. when they all went to bed. Mother and daughter spoke mostly about their fear of being poisoned by the admiral. He overheard Mrs. Eaton say the admiral had caused the deaths of more than one hundred men on a ship he had commanded during his service with the navy. He said she told him the admiral had pricked her arm with a hypodermic needle while she slept, and she thought he had injected her jaw with something that loosened one of her teeth. She also said the admiral had put tablets in her tea and poisoned the food he had given to June while she was ill.

Barker asked Keyes if, during the conversation, anyone had

mentioned the admiral's sanity. Keyes said he could not recall, though he remembered Mrs. Eaton saying she had planned to hire a detective to watch the admiral but had not followed through because of the expense.

Morse began his cross-examination by asking Keyes if he knew what Mrs. Eaton had inside the trunks she brought to Medford. Keyes said he had seen linen, pillows, and silverware. He also admitted that Mrs. Eaton had exhorted him and June to keep their marriage intact. She was well aware of the strife the couple had been going through and knew the baby's unexpected arrival was the primary cause of dissension between them.

Morse asked Keyes to recall his first meeting with the Eaton family. Keyes said he had first met Mrs. Eaton and June at Nantasket about three years before and had met the admiral a short time afterward.

"How long was it after you met Mrs. Eaton that you heard her say that the admiral was a user of drugs or whiskey?" asked Morse.

"I can't remember," the witness said.

"What I want to get at, Mr. Keyes, is whether you had heard this talk of poisoning before, a great many times."

"Yes," Keyes admitted, and, upon further questioning, agreed that Mrs. Eaton and her husband had always shown affection for one another whenever he was in their company.

Keyes testified that he had visited the Assinippi home on two occasions and had been welcomed by the admiral. Keyes admitted that the admiral had given him seventy or seventy-five dollars to assist him with his financial obligations.

Morse asked Keyes if he knew the admiral had hoped to visit Medford with his wife to discuss a separation between Keyes and June. Keyes said he was aware of that and realized after Mrs. Eaton had arrived that the admiral was not going to come. He acknowledged that Mrs. Eaton had received letters from the admiral during her ten-day stay in Medford. Apparently, Mrs. Eaton had shared the contents of those letters with him, because he characterized them as affectionate in tone.

After Keyes was excused from the stand, Barker approached the bench with Admiral Eaton's probated will, offering it as evidence. Judge Aiken ordered it marked as a government exhibit. ADA

Katzmann submitted the property records for the Assinippi home. Two mortgages were outstanding on the property; the last one dated November 1912. Barker also offered copies of the federal statutes under which Admiral Eaton had retired. Aiken admitted all of those documents, and they were also marked as exhibits for the Commonwealth. Barker then announced that the government was resting its case. The judge called attorneys for both sides to his bench and, after a brief conference, adjourned for the day.

~

Jennie Eaton's ex-husband, Daniel Henry Ainsworth, had been noticeably absent from the courthouse since the start of the trial. Newspapermen could not confirm that Ainsworth was on a witness list for either side. Both Barker and Morse were reticent when asked about the possibility of Ainsworth's appearance.

A reporter asked June Keyes if her father was expected to testify at the trial. "My father has promised to come from Arizona (where he was living)," June said. "He will do everything in his power for Mamma [sic]. I know he will, because he loves her as much today as he ever did, and it just about broke his heart when mother was divorced from him. My sister, Dorothy, and I will be happy to see our father, and I feel that Mamma will, too, because he can help her a whole lot.

"Just think," June added, "what a terrible ordeal it has been for poor mother – to be held up as a murderer of her husband, to be torn away from those she loves, and to be kept all these months in jail. But we shall stand by her, and so will father, and in the end it will all come out fine, and the people will see what a mistake has been made and how mother has suffered."

Asked about her marital troubles and the paternity of her child, June said, "Talk about my baby is neighborhood gossip, and I want to say right now that my husband knows all about the baby and everything. Just as soon as mother's trial is finished, I shall enter suit for divorce. Any statement that the baby is not the daughter of Mr. Keyes is false."

In a new development, newspapers reported that Mrs. Eaton's defense was being funded in part by a $6,000 death benefit awarded by the Army and Navy Club, of which the admiral was a member. A

$3,000 life insurance benefit that would be paid at the end of the trial was also expected to defray additional defense costs.

Chapter 23

Court opened at just after 9:00 a.m. on Thursday, October 23. Judge Aiken entered the courtroom and, after the jury was polled, nodded in the direction of defense attorneys William Morse and Francis Geogan. Geogan rose from his seat and approached the jury box. He was about to deliver the most important opening statement of his career.

He began his remarks by reminding the panel of the solemn duty placed upon them as jurors in a capital case. They had the power to take a human life, he declared, "and life is sacred, the life of the defendant, no less than the life of the deceased. You cannot take her life unless you can come to no other reasonable, logical conclusion than that she is guilty of murder."

Mrs. Eaton gazed at him, expressionless and immobile, as the twenty-eight-year-old lawyer paused momentarily for effect, then resumed.

"Let me at this point suggest to you what I apprehend that the court will later instruct you as to insanity. Unless you find that Jennie May Eaton committed the overt act of which she stands accused, and by that overt act killed her husband, you cannot consider insanity. She does not raise the plea of insanity; she is here on the charge of murder, and she has denied that charge and has gone to trial."

Geogan described for jurors the events surrounding the defendant's early life, from her birth in Alexandria, Virginia; the move to Michigan; the drowning deaths of her father and sister; her family's return to Washington, DC; her early education and employment; and her marriage, at age seventeen, to Daniel Ainsworth.

Soon after she married, Geogan recounted, the defendant learned that her husband was an alcoholic whose intemperate ways cost him position after position. The defendant was forced to seek employment to support her family and sold books and engravings door to door throughout the Midwest. Eventually, she left her husband, returned to Washington, and placed her two daughters in a convent school.

"Through Miss Struble, head of the George Washington Hospital and Nurse's Home," Geogan said, "she found employment at nursing, and she was sent to the home of Admiral Eaton to nurse his wife, who died the following February. This was the beginning of her acquaintance with Admiral Eaton. She remained in his home as housekeeper after the death of the first Mrs. Eaton, and her mother came to live with them.

"The body of the first Mrs. Eaton was not buried immediately. In May, Admiral Eaton brought it to Massachusetts, and it was buried in Dracut. He remained here, and in June sent for the defendant to come on, as his housekeeper. She came, and later the children were also brought here in the care of a woman. The admiral took a cottage at Hull for the summer. In July the defendant's divorce was granted in Chicago; on July 25th she was married to Admiral Eaton by Dr. A. Z. Conrad of the Park Street Church."

Geogan advanced to 1909 and called the jury's attention to the subject of the adopted child, explaining why the defendant and her husband had kept the adoption secret.

"Admiral and Mrs. Eaton thought that it would be to the advantage of the boy in the future if it could be given out that he was their own and not adopted," Geogan said. "Admiral Eaton sent out the announcement to a Rockland newspaper and to a naval officer's magazine in his own handwriting."

Turning to the days and weeks preceding the admiral's death in March 1913, Geogan assailed the prosecution's contention that Mrs. Eaton had deserted the admiral when she left Assinippi for Medford on February 20. He insisted that a harmonious relationship existed between the pair at her departure and continued when she returned home on March 1.

"We will show you," Geogan continued, "that Mrs. Eaton's purpose was not to leave the admiral, but to help June arrange things in her new home. When she got back to Assinippi on the afternoon of Saturday, March 1, the admiral, badly intoxicated, met her and fell into her arms. She got him to bed, and next morning made him get up and go to church. Monday and Tuesday she spent cleaning up her house, which had been left while she was away with June. Wednesday morning she went to Boston. It had been arranged that the admiral was to accompany her, that they were to meet June, and that these three were then to make arrangements with Mr. Keyes, looking to a separation between June and her husband. The admiral was not feeling very strong, and did not go. A man named Russell Henry of Hanover came to buy a load of hay, and the admiral was in the barn with him, loading hay, when Mrs. Eaton came out to start away. She bade her husband an affectionate farewell, and went. And after she had gone he turned to Henry and said: 'There's a fine woman.' "

Geogan next attacked the prosecution's interpretation of a statement attributed to Mrs. Eaton by Ralph Keyes. He decried the implication that the phrase – "she would have to go and look after him" – was a veiled threat. The defense would show she intended to do just that – look after him – in the same way she had cared for the admiral since their first meeting.

"Mrs. Eaton and June minded one another at their agreed place of meeting," continued Geogan, "and Mrs. Eaton stayed at June's home in Medford that night because when June got back from Assinippi, it was too late to start home again. Then came that conversation you heard reported yesterday. We shall show you that the expression, 'I'll go home and attend to him,' had no sinister meaning, but meant just what Mrs. Eaton had been doing for years – taking care of her husband. When she reached home the next morning, there was absolutely no antagonism nor misunderstanding between the admiral and his wife. She had not had breakfast and set about getting some. She asked the admiral if he would have some, and he replied, 'No, I've lost one breakfast this morning. I don't want another.' He suffered from nausea after breakfast, again at eleven o'clock, and during the whole afternoon – and you have heard the description of his condition for the rest of the time he was alive."

Geogan summarized the details leading up to the admiral's death as told under oath by the defendant's daughter and mother, by Drs. Frame, Osgood, and Wheatley, and by Detective Scott.

"After the funeral at Dracut, Mrs. Eaton came back to her home to take up the course of her life again, but on Saturday the inquest was begun at Hingham. The members of her family were summoned to testify against her, and on Thursday, March 20th, she was arrested and held for a hearing in the lower court on March 28th. Before that date came, the grand jury indicted her, and on March 28th she was brought into court here, the indictment was read to her; she pleaded not guilty, and was placed in jail to await this trial."

Geogan next explained how the defense intended to prove Jennie's innocence. The entire courtroom sat in stunned silence as they heard the lawyer paint a picture in sharp contrast to the prosecution's portrayal of the admiral as a refined man and reputable naval officer.

"We shall show that many of the statements which Mrs. Eaton made against her husband had a foundation in fact – that they were not malicious, nor mistaken, but founded on fact. We shall be obliged to violate the adage which says that nothing but good should be spoken of the dead. This is our duty to do. For this man had a dual nature; he was a veritable Jekyll and Hyde. We shall show you that when his first wife lay dying, he was in the house, drunk night and morning, and morning and night. He did not attend her funeral, because he was in no condition to do so.

"At Hull he was drinking constantly, steadily, heavily. At Brookline he spent most of his time in his club, and drank constantly. At Assinippi he was somewhat better, but even there he had occasional drinking sprees. We shall prove that he had a more insidious habit, the drug habit. We shall put on officers of the battleship *Massachusetts*, at the time he commanded her, to show his habits. We shall show that he came, captain as he was, on deck in his pajamas, his voice thick, and that he gave orders so dangerous, so contradictory, that the officer of the deck had to change them in transmission.

"Again at Bar Harbor, he gave orders so contradictory and illogical that they were disobeyed and disregarded. Once, coming into New York Harbor, he gave orders that if obeyed would have wrecked his ship. Again they were disregarded. His officers couldn't detect a smell of liquor about him, and the common talk of the wardroom mess was that Captain Eaton was using drugs of some kind. At one time an officer of the ship saw a lot of black bottles dumped overboard out of the captain's cabin window. And a witness will tell you of an admission by the admiral himself that he was a drug user; that when he was thought to be under the influence of liquor, it was really a drug which bound him.

"We shall show that Mrs. Eaton did at times think the admiral deranged and dangerous. On one occasion he brought up a cup of tea when she was sick in bed. By some miracle the tea was spilled, and in the bottom of it was found a white tablet. We shall show you that under the influence of drugs, he was the vilest, coarsest of men. We shall show letters from him, so coarse that anybody would have thought him a degenerate; and we will show you that, as a matter of fact, he was unduly attracted by women."

Murmurs rippled through the courtroom when Geogan told jurors about the admiral's dependence on arsenic to ease the pain associated with alcohol abuse.

"We shall show you that in 1910 he consulted a physician and said that his stomach was in bad condition and that he drank heavily. The doctor gave him a prescription, and the admiral came back and said it was too strong, that he wanted something weaker. He was given a prescription which contained one-hundredth of a grain of bromide of gold, one-hundredth of a grain of bromide of arsenic, and two grains of pepsin. He went a number of times to this physician, who delivered to him in all four thousand, six hundred of these tablets, containing in the aggregate forty-six grains of arsenic. Admiral Eaton knew arsenic and its use. He was directed to take these tablets four times a day, and the physician warned him of the danger of cumulative poisoning."

Geogan challenged the testimony of prosecution witnesses who suggested that the defendant had no intention of returning to the admiral when she left Assinippi for Weymouth in September 1910.

"We shall show that there never was any permanent break between Mrs. Eaton and her husband. When she was in Weymouth, he visited her; when she was in Washington, there were daily letters. We shall show you these letters from him, alternately loving and then coarse beyond belief. We shall offer her letters to him, advising him to live quietly and not to drink, asking him to quit his pipe, advising him as to the payment of a note which was soon due. And we shall show you his reply by saying that he would wait before making any new arrangements until she got home again. She was his guide, counselor, and stay.

"We are prepared to show you a book in which Mrs. Eaton kept the details of her plan for paying off the admiral's debts. Finally, Mrs. Eaton will take the stand herself and will deny that she committed this murder. We shall show you that the admiral left no estate and no heritage save debt. We shall show you that Mrs. Eaton had no motive for killing her husband, that she would lose her own support by doing it. We shall show that she was jealous, but jealous of the admiral's position, which she didn't want him to jeopardize by his attentions to other women.

"We are to put on the stand a man eminent in his profession of medicine, who has listened to the testimony presented by the State, and he will say that the condition of the organs and the symptoms which have been described by the State's witnesses were entirely consistent with the assumption that a dose of arsenic was taken on Wednesday and that dose was the only one."

"I think that I have now stated to you the essential features on which we shall rely," said Geogan in conclusion. "But there is one thing more. You were asked in the prosecution's opening to be fearless and to make your verdict regardless of the sex of the defendant. Let me, too, urge you to do that very thing. This defendant does not try to raise the insanity plea. She asks no special privilege on account of her sex. She realizes that the sympathy of all men must be hers in her situation, but she does not ask for it in their verdict. We ask no favors, no mercy, except that of honest, earnest, painstaking consideration of our case and a fair, honest verdict."

The courtroom was silent. Geogan's powerful presentation had left an indelible impression on the audience. His delivery was articulate and even. He never referred to notes, nor did he resort to theatrics. Veteran trial lawyers who were present in the courtroom later commented on the young attorney's exceptional performance and the force and logic of his address.

After Geogan took his seat, Morse called the first witness for the defense. Dr. Frank Fremont-Smith, the Eaton family's physician in Washington who had attended the admiral's first wife before her death, stood to be sworn and then settled into the witness chair.

Fremont-Smith told the court he had first met Admiral Eaton around January 1906 at the home of the distinguished inventor, Alexander Graham Bell. Bell invited guests on Wednesday evenings to discuss scientific advancements. The physician said he was struck by the admiral's "peculiar, prolonged, and irrepressible laughter over small things, and his incapacity to control himself."

Fremont-Smith recalled a telephone call that he had received from the admiral about his first wife who had taken ill. The physician went to the admiral's home and found that Annie Eaton had suffered a stroke and was paralyzed. He informed the admiral that his wife's severe condition would require the constant attention of a nurse.

The physician said he called Miss Struble, director of nurses at George Washington Hospital, who sent Jennie May Ainsworth.

"What do you say as to the qualities of the nurse you obtained?" Morse asked.

"She was faithful and true to her charge by day and by night," answered the physician. "She attended to her as carefully as any trained nurse could do, though she was not and did not claim to be a trained nurse. I saw Admiral Eaton frequently; for the first week, four or five times a day, because his wife was desperately ill. The second week, I saw him about as often, on account of his own condition. The third week I saw him at least once a day."

Morse asked Fremont-Smith to describe the admiral's condition to the jury. The doctor said the admiral was constantly under the influence of liquor. He was incapacitated for the first two weeks following his wife's stroke, sober by the third week, and by the fourth he had become well enough to leave his home and walk to Fremont-Smith's office with the help of Mrs. Ainsworth.

"To what extent was he under the influence of liquor at those times?" asked Morse.

"To complete stupefaction at night; to incoherence of speech and incapacity of memory at other times," the witness replied.

"Was your attention called to the quantity of liquor he took?" Morse inquired.

"Yes. Mrs. Ainsworth and a colored cook both mentioned it, and the cook showed me a great many whiskey bottles, empty," the doctor answered.

"Whether you and Mrs. Ainsworth made any effort to get the admiral sober?"

"We tried to reduce the amount of alcohol he took every day and to get him to a realizing sense of his condition," Fremont-Smith explained. "We succeeded so far that he was able to come to my office for further treatment. We talked over his condition freely. Mrs.

Ainsworth said in his presence that she was trying, with my assistance, to sober him up."

"Do you know whether he attended his first wife's funeral?"

"I don't know personally."

"Then please don't tell us," DA Barker interjected. Courtroom spectators snickered.

"Is arsenic sometimes given as a tonic for the stomach?" Morse asked as he glared in Barker's direction.

"Not necessarily for the stomach; it is given as a general tonic."

"Would a man be likely to be affected mentally by the amount of liquor Admiral Eaton was taking?"

"Yes," the doctor asserted.

"If such a man had had syphilis, would he be likely to be more affected mentally by the amount of liquor that Admiral Eaton was taking?" Morse asked hypothetically.

Barker rose to his feet and objected strenuously. Judge Aiken overruled his objection and instructed the witness to answer.

"The liquor would affect his mind more seriously and more promptly," the physician said. "It is well known that a man who has had this disease cannot, and should not, be allowed to drink alcohol."

"Is arsenic sometimes given for this disease?"

"Yes, in all its stages."

"If the system becomes accustomed to the use of arsenic, can a person take larger and larger doses with safety?"

"Yes. In large quantities it is an irritant to the stomach; in smaller doses, a general tonic."

Morse returned to the defense table and picked up a document containing an excerpt from the navy surgeon general's report about Admiral Eaton's physical condition. The report revealed that naval medical staff members had treated Eaton in 1869, and again in 1880, for syphilis and had prescribed opium pills as treatment. Morse submitted the report as a defense exhibit, and the judge ordered it so marked.

Morse next asked Fremont-Smith to describe the symptoms of syphilis in an effort to point out that Dr. Colgate had misdiagnosed the admiral's condition as a hernia. The physician testified that certain symptoms of syphilis might be mistaken for a rupture.

Morse finished with the witness. The district attorney approached for cross-examination and asked the doctor to explain the cause of Annie Eaton's death. The doctor testified that the primary cause of death was cerebral apoplexy and that the admiral's syphilis may or may not have indirectly contributed to the stroke. A gasp came from the courtroom audience. Barker, displeased with Fremont-Smith's inference, asked the court to strike the doctor's comment. He was overruled.

"You still called at the house after her death?" asked Barker.

"Yes, on account of the admiral's condition."

"At whose request?" Barker inquired.

"There was no need of any request; the man was too low. And there was nobody to make a request. The man was drunk, and I stayed with him until I got him partly straightened out. He never did get wholly straightened out," said the doctor. His choice of words was not lost on spectators who laughed until Sheriff Porter restored order.

"When did you last see Admiral Eaton?" Barker continued.

"About March 1 of that year," replied Fremont-Smith.

"Was he in grief over his wife's death?"

"I think he was hardly conscious of his wife's death. He probably knew she was dead, but he was not keenly conscious of it."

"How often did you see Mrs. Ainsworth?"

"She was always in the house when I called there."

"When did you last see Mrs. Eaton?"

"You mean the first Mrs. Eaton?"

"No, the present Mrs. Eaton."

"Just this second," said Fremont-Smith, leaning over the rail of the witness stand to glance at the defendant.

"You know what I mean," said the district attorney, displeased with the doctor's sarcasm. "When before this?"

"When she came to my office with the admiral leaning on her arm."

"Were they married then?"

"I know nothing about their marriage. He needed her support on that day."

"I didn't ask you that question," Barker said brusquely.

"Well, I answered it," said the witness indignantly.

The prosecutor and witness continued to spar.

"A great many men drink to excess who are not insane afterward?" Barker inquired.

Fremont-Smith hesitated. Judge Aiken turned to him and said, "That is a question."

"Oh, I beg pardon, Mr. Justice," said the witness and bowed toward the bench.

"Please read the question," Fremont-Smith asked the stenographer. "I thought it was a statement."

Barker interceded, putting the question to the doctor once more.

"I can't follow you, sir," said the witness.

When Barker asked a third time, Fremont-Smith said, "They are sometimes not all insane."

"You think some do go insane?"

"It depends very largely on what disease they may have had."

"How many cases have you had brought to your attention in which the disease ascribed to Mr. Eaton, forty years ago, with some drinking later on, has caused insanity?"

"Since 1883, being constantly in hospitals, I have seen a good many go insane from alcohol – probably thousands."

"How many thousands should you think?"

"I will not answer that question unless you require me to do so," the witness said to Judge Aiken.

"This court will not require you to make any particular answer," the judge replied. "You may answer as well as you can."

No matter how the district attorney phrased the question, he could not elicit the answer he wanted. Barker finally gave up, and Aiken excused the physician.

Morse next called retired Rear Admiral Charles E. Clark, USN. Clark had served with then Commander Eaton during the Spanish-American War. Clark was the captain of the battleship *Oregon* during the Battle of Santiago. Eaton commanded the transport *Resolute*.

The defense attorney began his direct examination by asking about Eaton's request for an appointment to the navy's Examining Board in 1905, after Eaton had been promoted to captain.

"Did you talk with Admiral Eaton with reference to his becoming a member of this board?" asked Morse.

"Yes," said the admiral. "He asked me to approve his application, or to help him to get appointed to the board, but I told him I could not do this. I don't recall all our talk, but the substance was that I couldn't apply for him, and that if he applied I should oppose his appointment because he had become addicted to habits of intemperance and that he had even been intoxicated on shipboard. He said that it was rather rough on him, because that really was not liquor, but something he had to take, which made it seem he was under the influence of liquor. He told me that he knew where the report of his being intoxicated came from."

Morse indicated to the district attorney that he was through with the witness, and Barker began his cross-examination.

"Admiral, whether this something he had to take was taken by orders of a physician?"

"I inferred that."

"How long had you had the information on the strength of which you refused to approve his application?"

"A year."

On redirect, the admiral told Morse he had come to the trial voluntarily at Morse's urgent request.

Aiken excused Clark from the stand, and Morse called navy Lieutenant Holden C. Richardson.

"Were you at one time on the battleship *Massachusetts* with Joseph G. Eaton?" asked the defense counsel.

"Yes," the officer replied. "I think it was May 11, 1903, when he took command at the Boston Navy Yard. He was then Captain Eaton, of course. I was on the ship until July 20, 1904. I was the junior watch officer. I noticed his peculiar condition shortly after we left Boston. He would go about with a stare, his eyes were fixed and his voice thick. He didn't stagger, but he had the appearance of a man under the influence of liquor or of some drug."

"At one time," Richardson continued, "I think on a cruise to the Azores, I was officer of the deck one night in the mid-watch. I had control of the ship and was on the bridge. Shortly after I went on watch the captain came on the bridge in his pajamas. There were four vessels, steaming in column – the *Alabama*, *Kearsarge*, *Indiana*, and *Massachusetts*. We had to keep position four hundred yards off the ship ahead, I think, the *Alabama*. I shortly noticed that the captain was not himself. He attempted to give orders to keep the ship in her proper position. He took up his own position at the starboard, aft end of the bridge, and looked off toward the starboard quarter – not toward the ship ahead.

"Presently he asked for the position with reference to the ship ahead, and I told him. He ordered the number of revolutions changed. Presently he ordered another change, and this occurred time after time. I found that if I carried out his orders, we should be out of position and might put the ship in danger of collision from the other ships. When I found that this was the state of affairs, I went to the captain's speaking tube on the mast, as if I were talking to the engine room, giving his orders. Really, however, I spoke only to the mast, as I had closed the tube. By giving the proper orders at the proper time I kept the ship in her position. The captain remained on deck half an hour and then left."

"Do you recall any other instance of peculiar actions?" Morse asked.

"I recall one time when the captain was so much under the influence of something that he staggered. I noticed it more because he proceeded to 'hold mast,' which consists of bringing men who are accused of offenses against the rules to the 'mast,' which is really a place on the quarterdeck. Here a court is held in a small way, and the captain gives the sentences. On this afternoon, two men were brought before Captain Eaton, who were accused of being under the influence of liquor aboard ship. The circumstances of his sitting in judgment, in the condition in which he was in, on men accused of the same thing attracted my attention."

DA Barker rose to cross-examine the naval officer.

"You and Captain Eaton didn't get along very well?" Barker asked.

"On the contrary. We got along very nicely," Richardson answered firmly.

"You considered these things which you noticed constituted a danger to the ship?"

"Yes."

"To whom did you report them?"

"I spoke to the ship's surgeon, Dr. Leach, and I talked with the navigator, Lieutenant Commander C. H. Hughes. We talked the matter over generally in the wardroom."

"So far as you know, no official action was taken, however?"

"No."

"And did you think you had done your duty to the United States when your ship was in danger and the lives of all those men were in danger?"

Richardson hesitated and looked to Judge Aiken for guidance.

"You may answer that or not as you see fit," Aiken advised in a serious tone.

"I decline to answer because I'm not on trial here," the lieutenant answered promptly. "I disregarded his orders. I think I did my whole duty."

The prosecutor asked the witness why other officers who had been assigned to the *Massachusetts* had not come forward to testify about the admiral's conduct and if he knew their present whereabouts. Richardson could not answer either question. Barker asked his questions in other ways, but he did not get satisfactory responses. Finally, Barker abandoned his line of questioning and declared he was finished with the witness.

Morse recalled Charles Clark to the stand. He asked if the retired rear admiral knew Lieutenant Commander Hughes's present assignment. Clark informed the court that Hughes was currently assigned as chief of staff for the Atlantic Squadron. When Morse asked if Clark knew whether the squadron was preparing to sail on a Mediterranean cruise, the district attorney objected.

"If you are intending to make any adverse comment on the absence of Commander Hughes from this case, I will permit the inquiry," the judge told Barker, who replied that was not his intention. When Morse heard Barker's response, he stopped questioning Clark.

A spectator in the courtroom suddenly jumped from his seat and hurried to the reporters' table. In a hushed tone, he asked a reporter to tell Morse about a rule in the navy forbidding a subordinate officer from reporting a superior for an infraction. The district attorney overheard this comment and turned to Clark. He was about to break a lawyer's cardinal rule: Never ask a question to which you do not know the answer.

"Is it a rule in the navy for minor officers to report a superior officer for intoxication?" Barker asked.

"No," said Admiral Clark with a smile on his face. "It is never done, except as a witness in a court of inquiry. It is a rule in the navy for officers not to comment on the acts of superiors, but to let any comment be known to their own seniors." Barker immediately realized his mistake and quickly concluded his examination.

Morse seized the opportunity and asked Clark to give his perspective on Lieutenant Richardson's actions during the episode in question.

"I think that the lieutenant might have reported the matter to the executive officer rather than to the navigator; but he was a very young officer and did what he thought was right," Clark said.

When both defense and prosecution indicated they had no further questions, Aiken dismissed Clark and adjourned for the day. The defense attorneys looked forward to the next day's session. They would present additional witnesses to undo the government's glowing characterization of the admiral as a man of civility and temperance.

Chapter 24

The courtroom, as usual, was filled to capacity when court opened at its usual time on Friday, October 24. Jennie took her assigned place just outside the defense bar, dressed in the black ensemble that had become her habit.

Defense attorney William Morse wasted no time calling his first witness, forty-eight-year-old Peter S. McNally, a newspaperman who had worked as a Boston Navy Yard correspondent for *The Boston Daily Globe*.

Attorney William A. Morse
(Courtesy of F. Joseph Geogan II, Esq.)

McNally told the court that he had become acquainted with then Commander Eaton in 1897 and 1898 at the Boston yard when Eaton was commander of the training ship *Enterprise* and later served as the yard's ordnance officer.

"Did you see anything peculiar about him?" asked Morse.

"He was intoxicated," McNally replied.

"How many times?"

"Three or four times at the yard, more times at Boston hotels."

"To what extent?"

"He would be befuddled. He would laugh immoderately at things that seemed not worth it, and his talk was on subjects that one would not expect from a man like him. I have seen him moody, despondent, talking to himself, pulling at his beard, smiling. And ten minutes later he would be bright, quite himself. Sometimes he would not see me at all, though he knew me very well. And within a few minutes he would know me perfectly well."

"Did he ever entertain you with stories?" Morse inquired.

"Many times," said McNally.

"Has he indulged in obscene stories?"

"He frequently indulged in ribald stories. Nearly every time he told a story it bordered on the obscene."

"Did he tell you of his experiences with women of immoral character in foreign ports?"

"Yes," McNally replied, but he did not elaborate.

"What have you noticed about his conduct toward women?"

"I've seen him indulging in flirtations – rolling his eyes at women. He invariably brightened up when women approached."

"How did he act when they came near him?" asked Morse.

"He would dust himself, throw out his chest, and, in general, spruce up."

District Attorney Barker approached for cross-examination. He asked McNally if he had told the court everything he knew about Admiral Eaton. When McNally said he knew much more, Barker backed off, fearful that McNally's unknown testimony might hinder his case.

Judge Aiken excused McNally, and the defense next called Judge George Kelley, the Eaton family's counsel. Kelley told the court he had known the Eatons since 1907.

"What was their manner toward each other?" Morse asked.

"In my office they were always holding hands. Their affection was a little out of the ordinary. It was more pronounced than is usual with married couples," Kelley responded.

Morse asked the witness for his impression of the admiral during their first meeting.

"He was depressed and in a very serious spell of blues. I was alone in my office and never saw him before. I think about the first remark he made was, 'Does the good judge think the voyage is worthwhile?' I argued with him that it was. I quoted some poetry to him."

"What did he say regarding his wife?"

"He said, 'I have a remarkable wife. She has been a great help to me, but she has one obsession, and that is her daughter, June.' "

"Did you ever hear Mrs. Eaton speak of her husband?" Morse inquired.

"A great many times. She told me innumerable times that she loved him. On one particular occasion she very emphatically stated that she would not allow me or anyone else to harm a hair of his head."

Morse next turned to financial affairs and asked Kelley if he was the administrator of the late admiral's estate. Kelley acknowledged that he was and estimated the current value of the estate at less than $1,200, although the final property appraisal had not been completed. He said he had received bills in excess of $1,700.

When Kelley tried to present the declaration of trust assigned to him as trustee by Mrs. Eaton, the district attorney raised an objection. Judge Aiken sustained it. Morse tried to introduce the document in another way and, again, Barker objected. After a brief sidebar, Aiken ruled that Kelley could only testify to that section of the trust that set aside Navy Mutual Aid Association insurance benefits for Mrs. Eaton's daughters in the event of her death. Kelley, again questioned by Morse, read the section into the record, and it was admitted as evidence.

Judge George W. Kelley (*Courtesy of the Dyer Memorial Library, Abington, MA*)

The defense turned to the admiral's excessive habits. Morse asked Kelley if Mrs. Eaton had spoken to him about the admiral's use of drugs and whiskey.

"I don't remember any mention of whiskey. She did say that he used drugs, and that the effect of these was to make him insane – that when he was in this condition she feared poison. I should say that I talked with her perhaps twenty-five times, but after a certain time – I should say within six months prior to April 1st, 1912 – she ceased to mention it."

Morse returned to Kelley's testimony about his conversation with Mrs. Eaton and her comment that "she would not allow me or anyone else" to harm the admiral. Morse asked Kelley if the subject of poison had also come up during this conversation.

"Yes. She began the old story and I cut her short by saying, 'I have decided on one of two things – I will have the admiral arrested or committed to an asylum.' She became very excited and said, 'You will do no such thing. I won't allow you, or anybody else to harm a hair of his head. He is a good, kind man, except when under the influence of drugs and except for those times there is no danger of poison.' "

Morse turned to Barker, indicating he had completed his direct examination. Barker approached the witness and asked him if he was counsel for Mrs. Eaton.

"Not in this case."

"Didn't you say you had done more work in this case than I had?"

"Not as counsel. I did say that I had done more work investigating this case than the district attorney and his officers."

"In what capacity?" asked Barker.

"As a friend," Kelley replied.

Kelley denied that Mrs. Eaton had asked him to get Admiral Eaton committed. He admitted, however, that he had asked Dr. Osgood to assess Mrs. Eaton's mental state about two and a half years ago, but the examination had never occurred.

"She pestered you with her talk about the admiral?"

"I shouldn't say she pestered me. She took a great deal of my time, but I always felt kindly toward her and wanted to be helpful to her."

"Did she always lay his condition to drugs?"

"I think so. She never mentioned liquor, that I remember, nor women."

Barker turned to the declaration of trust and asked Kelley if he had advised Mrs. Eaton to draw it up. Kelley explained that Mrs. Eaton had asked him to take the money from the Navy Mutual Aid Association insurance policy to provide financial support for herself, her mother, and her two daughters. He said he declined to take any money unless a declaration of trust was drawn up.

Kelley said he had received $3,653.84 in total and had already expended much of it on the financial needs of the defendant's family. He stated he had heard that other insurance policies on the admiral's life existed but knew nothing more about them.

Barker dug out more details regarding the admiral's assets. Kelley told of the admiral's interest from estates owned by two uncles but said the admiral had borrowed against his interest, leaving no equity.

"Do you know of any other property?"

"I have heard that the admiral had once a lot of land in Lowell. I was also told that it was long ago sold for taxes."

"Did he own property in California?"

"The admiral himself told me that he long ago disposed of it."

Morse asked Kelley on redirect about the other insurance policies brought up by the prosecution. Kelley said he had confirmed during conversations with insurance company executives that the admiral had borrowed money on the other policies.

"Did Admiral Eaton ever say anything about your acting for his wife as counsel?"

"Yes, he asked me, if anything happened to him, to take care of her, and I promised that I would."

Asked about Mrs. Eaton's present financial condition, Kelley told the court that she had no money at all. In fact, she had to borrow ten dollars from him the Monday after the admiral's burial. When Morse asked about his personal observations regarding the admiral's intemperance, Kelley said he had never seen the admiral intoxicated or under the influence of drugs.

Barker had no questions, so Kelley was excused.

The court was now about to hear the most astonishing testimony of the trial.

Morse called Dr. Jacob Wales Brown. From the rear of the courtroom, the frail, eighty-four-year-old physician slowly shuffled to the stand with the assistance of Attorney Geogan and a deputy sheriff. He wore a shabby suit and an old gray-blue shirt with a makeshift necktie. His face was pale and wrinkled with age, his hair silver-white and sparse. Once he was seated, a bailiff brought him a glass of water that he clutched with uncontrollably trembling hands.

Brown had arrived at the courthouse in the custody of guards from the Bridgewater State Farm. On March 22, 1912, Suffolk Superior Court Judge Henry Sheldon had sentenced the disgraced physician to serve five to seven years in Charlestown State Prison. He was convicted of performing an illegal abortion that had resulted in the death of Mrs. Margaret LeFevre. Prison authorities had transferred the physician to Bridgewater because of his poor health. Brown had served time in 1884 at Concord Reformatory and again in 1895 at Charlestown for similar offenses. He had also served time for forgery.

Morse established Brown's medical credentials. The doctor told the court he had set up his first practice in Meriden, Connecticut, in 1860 but had moved to New York soon afterwards. He had enlisted in the Union army at the outbreak of the Civil War and was assigned to a surgeon's staff. The army had transferred him to a hospital in Philadelphia after the December 1862 Battle of Fredericksburg. He had moved to Boston at war's end and had practiced there ever since. Brown was confident and unabashed in his testimony.

"I knew Joseph G. Eaton. He came to my office in February 1910, on Berkeley Street in Boston. He had the circular of a dyspepsia cure I had written. He told me his stomach was bad, that he couldn't keep his food down, and that the cause was his overdrinking. I gave him a box of dyspepsia tablets, and he paid half a dollar.

"About a week later he came back and said they had helped him," Brown continued. "He then told me his real trouble; he was worrying himself to death. He told me he was suffering from an organic weakness. I advised him to cut down his whiskey and gave him one hundred tablets, made purposely for that trouble. They contained one-hundredth grain of bromide of gold, a like amount of arsenic, sugar of milk [sic] and a chocolate coating. He paid a dollar for them; a week or ten days later he came back. On this next visit he told me his name and his naval experiences. The next time, I sold him five hundred of the tablets at a rate of seven dollars and fifty cents a thousand. He said he had taken everything and done everything he ever heard of for his trouble."

Brown was reluctant to define the admiral's "organic weakness," but, by then, the jury had likely inferred that the admiral was afflicted with syphilis. Bromide of gold mixed with arsenic was a common treatment for various forms of syphilis at the time.

"On his next visit," Brown continued, "he bought one thousand tablets. He said he had taken other remedies, including phosphorous pills. He said he thought these last were dangerous to take. He said one of them was swallowed by a young child, which took sick and died. He said his adopted baby had eaten one of these tablets and died, and he was afraid there had been poison in the tablet. He said he had, therefore, destroyed the remainder. He feared the pill might have had something to do with it and destroyed the rest of the pills.

"I saw him many times, the last about March 18, 1912. In this time I sold him four thousand six hundred tablets. He always scraped off the labels, before doing them up. He said he didn't want the neighbors to know his condition, and for that reason he would not put himself under the care of his family physician. I said, 'You should tell somebody. If you should die suddenly and your body were [sic] examined, arsenic would be found in it. If it isn't known that you are taking it, somebody will be accused of giving it to you.' He said, 'You know it, and that's enough.' He told me that unless he got back to his normal condition, he didn't care how soon he died. He told me he had drunk whiskey and champagne enough to float a battleship."

"Did he come to you with some arsenic tablets?" asked Morse.

"In June 1911, he brought me a package containing about sixty gelatin capsules, each containing, he said, about a grain of arsenic. I asked him what he was doing with arsenic at that rate, and he said that it was handy for destroying cats or dogs about the place. He left them with me. He wanted me to keep them for him. I kept them two weeks."

Morse asked Brown to tell the jury how he had become a witness for the defense. Brown said he had read about the Eaton case in the papers and had mentioned to a fellow inmate at Bridgewater, Cardenio F. King, that he had treated Admiral Eaton at one time. King, a well-known financier and newspaper publisher, was serving time for fraud and larceny. He, too, had been incarcerated at Charlestown State Prison and was transferred to Bridgewater due to illness.

After hearing Brown's story, King sent word to Morse who immediately visited Brown at Bridgewater to obtain a statement and enlist him as a defense witness. King died at Bridgewater in July 1913, shortly after contacting Morse.

Morse said he had no more questions.

DA Barker approached the witness with fire in his eyes. Desirous of impeaching Brown's testimony, he asked the physician to reiterate his previous convictions.

"I don't see what it has to do with this case," the aged doctor replied, his hands trembling. "If you want my whole history, you can have it."

"To what other persons were you giving these tablets containing arsenic?" the district attorney asked.

"You must excuse me from giving away the secrets of my patients," Brown replied.

Barker turned to Judge Aiken to compel Brown to answer, but Aiken ruled against him on the basis of doctor-patient privilege. Barker, however, was not about to give up. He asked Brown if all of his patients were local. Brown said he had patients all over the country.

"Where were some?" Barker asked.

"Well, San Jose, California. I should say probably I had two or three patients there, and sent these tablets to them by mail."

"How many did you send to the first?"

"I don't remember."

"How many to the second?"

"I don't remember."

"How many did you have in Boston?"

"I had patients all over Boston."

"Pick out any one patient. How long did you treat him?"

"I can pick out one whom I treated a year."

"How many tablets did you sell this patient?"

"I don't remember."

"Can you say how many tablets you sold to any one patient whom you treated for any length of time?"

"One hundred to a thousand."

"That is as near as you can tell as to the amount you sold to anybody except Admiral Eaton?"

"I could tell by my records, but they are not now in my hands."

"Did you keep a record of the number of tablets you sold?" asked the prosecutor.

"No," replied Brown.

"Then you have no record of the number of tablets you sold Admiral Eaton?"

"I haven't now – I had, however."

"In what form was the record?"

"A memorandum of money taken and what for."

"You are testifying now, however, wholly from memory?"

"Yes."

"When was it he brought the gelatin tablets there?" Barker asked.

"I think it was in June 1911. He left them with me six weeks or two months, and then took them away again," said Brown.

"What were the capsules in?"

"A glass bottle; it was about half full."

"When did you first see counsel for the defense?"

The witness didn't remember.

"Did you tell them about the arsenic capsules then?" Barker pressed.

"No."

"Did you tell them at the next interview?"

"No."

"When did you tell them?"

"At a recent interview, two or three weeks ago."

"Why didn't you tell them before?"

"It wasn't necessary."

Barker glowered at Brown. He strode to within a foot of the witness stand, shook his finger at the old man, and raised his voice.

"It isn't necessary to speak so loud," Brown said calmly.

"I want you to hear," said Barker. "Of how many other crimes have you been convicted, beside those you have told?"

"None."

"You can't give a single word of conversation with any other patient?"

"I refuse to," Brown said. "Other patients are alive."

"But you are willing to damn a dead man?" Barker asked reproachfully. Morse jumped to his feet and objected. Aiken found the question argumentative and instructed the jury to disregard it.

Barker was furious. This convict, this charlatan, this man who flaunted the law for personal gain was taking the moral high ground with no qualms about publicly revealing the most intimate medical details of a man who could not defend himself. Barker was powerless to continue. The rules of evidence permitted Brown to invoke doctor-patient privilege to protect the privacy of patients still living.

The district attorney changed course and turned to Brown's previous testimony about an alleged conversation he had with Eaton, in which the admiral had allegedly told him that his adopted child had swallowed one of his pills and died.

"When was it that Mr. Eaton had the conversation about the baby

219

and the tablets?"

"I think it was in 1911. I don't remember what season of the year. He didn't say the baby was in the family, and I never thought of it again until this matter of the adopted baby came up."

Barker asked Brown to recall once more the substance of that conversation. Brown repeated his prior testimony word for word.

The prosecutor then asked the witness about phosphorous and if it was a "rank poison." (Phosphorous was used at the time for a variety of diseases but was considered extremely dangerous.)

"I shouldn't want to take much of it," Brown said.

"You have sold phosphorous pills?" Barker inquired.

"Yes," said the doctor.

"What is the dose?"

"It varies. I have given one-tenth of a grain."

Barker tried to find out where the witness's records were kept, but Brown was not helpful. He told the prosecutor he didn't know where they were.

"How much money did you take from any other patient in a year?"

"My business ran to four thousand dollars a year."

Barker considered Brown's answer evasive and asked him again. Brown told him he wouldn't tell him.

"You can't, can you?" Barker demanded.

"I could if I saw fit to," the witness replied smugly.

"Well, sir, you see fit to, please," said Barker sarcastically.

Morse objected, and Judge Aiken, agreeing, refused to compel the answer.

"And that's your only reason, to protect patients that you don't tell us?" Barker continued.

"It has nothing to do with this case," Brown replied.

"How much of your income was from the sale of tablets?"

"About two-thirds."

"And your tablets brought in about a cent apiece?"

"From half a cent to a cent."

"How many at half a cent and how many at a cent?"

"I don't propose to tell you. Wouldn't do you any good, nor anybody else."

Barker reminded Brown that he had taken an oath to tell the whole truth. Brown said that he took the oath to tell what he knew about the case. The district attorney was determined to convince the jury that Brown's testimony was unreliable by suggesting that Brown's "selective memory" allowed him to recall details of his interactions with Admiral Eaton yet not a single fact related to other patients or to his records. What the felonious physician hoped to gain by lying about his association with the admiral was a mystery to all but Barker.

The district attorney next moved to the doctor's last meeting with Eaton. Brown said he saw the admiral about a year before his death but couldn't remember the exact date. Barker, shaking his head in disgust, turned to the judge and said he had no further questions.

On redirect, Morse asked the doctor if Admiral Eaton had ever shown up at his office while intoxicated. Brown said he had on two occasions. Morse then informed Aiken he was finished with his witness. Aiken excused Brown and recessed for lunch.

When court resumed in the afternoon, the defense called fifty-year-old Mary McSkimmon, principal of Brookline's Pierce School, to the stand.

"Did you ever meet Admiral Eaton?" asked Morse.

"Yes," she said. "He came to the school in September 1906, and brought June and Dorothy with him. He spoke of them as his 'motherless children,' and called attention to the mourning band he wore on his arm. He spoke of his wife's death, as if it had been recent, and said, 'I am bringing these children to put them in your charge, and I hope you will find them as good places in the school as possible.' "

"What was his condition at that time?"

"He was intoxicated. His breath was heavy with the fumes of liquor and his speech was confused. He showed a desire to talk at great length about personal matters and to make personal speeches to me. He explained that his wife had been a Massachusetts woman and had wished to have the children brought up in a Massachusetts school."

"What was his manner?"

"He was very effusive. He held my hand a long time when he was going away, bowing very low over it. He held my hand at his coming, and again when he was going, much longer than was necessary."

Barker's cross-examination was brief. He asked whether the principal had seen the admiral again, and she said two times.

"You are sure he was intoxicated on this occasion?"

"Yes."

Aiken excused the witness, and Morse called navy Lieutenant Commander Raymond S. Keyes, who was not related to Ralph Keyes, June's husband. Keyes had served under Eaton on the battleship *Massachusetts*.

"Did you notice anything peculiar about Captain Eaton's condition on the ship?" asked Morse.

"On a few occasions he seemed to me to be under the influence of some intoxicant," replied the officer. "His speech was more or less thick and his walk more or less unsteady. On the night when we left the Azores, returning to the United States, Captain Eaton came on to the bridge and remained during my entire watch. His voice was thick, his gait unsteady, and he kept his hands on the bridge rail during the entire watch."

When Barker indicated he had no questions for the witness, the defense called Patrick J. Ford of Rockland.

Ford, a bookkeeper and musician, testified that he had visited the Eaton home at Assinippi to give Dorothy violin lessons. One of the lessons took place about the time of the adopted baby's arrival.

Ford said the admiral greeted him when he arrived and expressed regret that he had not notified him not to come. He explained that Mrs. Eaton was confined to her room and that he wanted the house quiet for the next several weeks. He asked Ford to return for Dorothy's lessons as soon as Mrs. Eaton was up and about.

"Whether anything was said about the baby?" Morse prompted.

"Not at that time. I went down again later and Admiral Eaton came into the room with Mrs. Eaton, carrying the baby in his arms. He asked me if I wanted to see it and I went over and looked at the youngster. He said, 'This is little Josephus,' and seemed very much pleased with the baby. I went to the house once a week for seven months."

"What was the behavior of the admiral and Mrs. Eaton toward each other?"

"It was always strictly business between them and me until I finished giving the lessons, then they would come into the room and spend ten or fifteen minutes chatting with me. As far as I could see it was a happy home."

The defense recalled Lieutenant Commander Keyes and asked him if he had detected the odor of liquor about Captain Eaton on the *Massachusetts*.

"On several occasions I did detect it, but on the specific occasion of which I have spoken, when we were leaving the Azores, I could not," the officer replied.

On recross, Barker asked the witness where he was on the ship when it left the Azores.

"On the bridge, in charge of the ship," Keyes explained.

"And where was he?"

"On the bridge, also."

"How big is the bridge?"

"On the *Massachusetts* it is very small, hardly more than a narrow passage round the mast. I was very close to him, and I remember thinking it remarkable that he didn't smell of liquor."

The defense next called Dr. Benjamin S. Blanchard of Brookline. The doctor testified that he first met Admiral Eaton at his Brookline office on October 5, 1906. The doctor visited Eaton at his home in Brookline that November to treat him for nausea that Blanchard recalled was caused by the admiral's excessive use of alcohol.

"Was this cause apparent from his appearance?" asked Morse.

"Perfectly," replied the physician.

"Did you visit the family in a professional way after it had gone to Assinippi?"

"In April 1909, Mrs. Eaton wrote asking me to come out there," Blanchard replied. "She had written me before that she and her husband wanted to adopt a baby. She said they wanted a boy, who might grow up, get into the navy, and follow in the admiral's footsteps, and she said she wanted the adoption kept secret in order that the boy might have the fullest advantages that his parentage could give him. I told her I did not know where to find a baby that fulfilled her requirements, and I added that she would better go to one of the Boston institutions, which she afterward did. In April, upon receiving Mrs. Eaton's letter, I went to Assinippi. I saw the admiral at that time and he had undoubtedly been drinking."

"Were you paid for the services you rendered in Brookline?" Morse asked.

"Yes."

"How?"

"Mrs. Eaton sent me fresh eggs once a week, and very often sent vegetables. She continued to do this until the bill was paid."

On cross-examination, Barker asked the doctor if Mrs. Eaton had come to see him in Brookline for medicine. Blanchard said that Mrs. Eaton had written to him in 1911, and he had sent her a prescription for the admiral.

"To be administered without his knowledge?" Barker inquired.

The doctor said he didn't think so. He remembered Mrs. Eaton's reasons for wanting the prescription, but he was sure she hadn't mentioned giving the medicine to the admiral without him knowing it.

"Did she tell you the admiral was crazy?"

"She didn't use that word. She said that he had a subtle knowledge of poisons and that she was afraid he might use them. She talked in this fashion three times, once when she asked me if I could get her a nurse or an attendant for him."

"Did she apply to you personally, or by letter, to help her get him committed?" Barker asked.

"No, but I suggested that if he were insane I would be willing, perhaps, to be one of two doctors to examine him."

Judge Aiken excused the witness when Barker concluded his examination. After consulting with the prosecution and defense, the judge adjourned until nine o'clock the following morning. Acknowledging that it was a Saturday, he assured the jury that he would recess at 1:00 p.m.

A deputy sheriff led Jennie to the anteroom where she met with Morse and Geogan. The two lawyers remained for the entire afternoon to prepare Jennie for her testimony the next day. When the courthouse closed, Deputy Sheriff John Geary returned Jennie to the jail. The lawyers went with her and stayed until late into the evening. When they left, the two men were confident Jennie would be a credible, compelling witness.

Chapter 25

Word that Jennie Eaton would testify in her own defense drew an immense crowd to the courthouse on Saturday, October 25. Sheriff Porter deployed additional security inside and outside the building to prevent a repeat of the disorder that had taken place the previous Wednesday.

Jennie arrived from the jail at 8:50 a.m. She had a broad smile on her face as Deputy Sheriff Joseph Collingwood assisted her from the prison wagon and led her inside and up to the courtroom.

"I shall establish my innocence beyond a doubt when all the facts are heard by the jury," she told a reporter. "I have long waited for such an opportunity."

Attorneys Morse and Geogan conversed quietly at the defense table.

When the judge had taken his place on the bench and the jury was seated, Geogan called the first witness. William Gammons of the Massachusetts Mutual Life Insurance Company had in his possession two original insurance policies. Admiral Eaton had taken out both policies, which were valued at $3,000 each, in 1870. He had designated his mother, Sarah Eaton, as the original beneficiary. By 1879 the admiral had paid the premiums in full.

In 1907, the admiral borrowed against the first policy in a series of small loans totaling $1,385. He borrowed an additional sum against the second policy.

District Attorney Barker, on cross-examination, asked Gammons how much the policies were worth on the day the admiral died. Gammons told the court the first policy was valued at $1,700 and the second at $2,000. The admiral had named the defendant, Mrs. Eaton, as the sole beneficiary.

Judge Aiken excused Gammons.

Morse called Jennie to the stand at 9:20 a.m. All eyes were on her as she left her seat behind the bar and walked to the witness stand. With her left hand on her hip and a faint smile on her lips, she raised her right hand and listened as the court clerk asked, "Do you swear to tell the truth, the whole truth, and nothing but the truth, so help you God?" Jennie replied with perfect composure, "I do," and took her seat. Morse poured a glass of water from a pitcher at the defense table and placed it on the stand in front of her. A persistent cough had nagged her all week.

Seated within the bar enclosure was Dr. Gilman Osgood. At the district attorney's request, he watched Mrs. Eaton closely, jotting notes from time to time on a notepad he had in his lap. Seated behind the defense table was a noted Boston physician, Dr. A. Everett Austin, who had attended the trial from the outset and was expected to testify on Jennie's behalf before the defense team rested its case.

Jennie calmly identified herself, gave her age as thirty-nine years, and said she was born in Alexandria, Virginia. She recounted her formative years, the drowning deaths of her father and sister when she was seven, and her return to Washington, DC, with her widowed mother and siblings. She said that during her teens, she acquired a stenographer's position in the federal Land Office, earned sixty dollars a month, and gave half of her earnings to her mother.

She told of her marriage in 1891 to Daniel H. Ainsworth, a clerk at the Interstate Commerce Commission, and of June's birth the following year. She testified that Ainsworth was an alcoholic who was unable to hold steady employment. Her husband left Washington in 1897 to work as a clerk in a land office in Guthrie, Oklahoma. She joined him there three weeks later.

"When I got to Guthrie, he was already twelve hundred dollars in debt from gambling and drinking," Jennie testified. "Mr. Ainsworth's father sent me some money, and I bought a little cottage house. I had to sacrifice it when I went away."

"Where did you go?" asked Morse.

"I went to St. Louis to see if we could get anything done at the McLean Hospital for Dorothy's lameness. For three years I took Dorothy to the hospital from eight thirty to one thirty every day. All that we could do for Dorothy failed to help her. I remained there fully three years."

Jennie described how her husband made his living in St. Louis as a salesman selling books door to door. When he was fired because of his drinking, she replaced him at the same company and "made considerable money selling fine editions of rare books. I think I stuck to the bookselling about a year."

"Where did you go from St. Louis?" Morse asked.

"Mr. Ainsworth persuaded me to make a tour of the Midwestern states with him, selling books. Then I drifted back, finally, to Washington (with her husband). I had quite a little money – fifteen hundred or seventeen hundred dollars. I got my brother-in-law, a real estate man (John Edwards, husband of her sister, Gertrude), to help me find a home. And I bought a pretty ladylike little place for four thousand seven hundred dollars, paying twelve hundred or fourteen hundred dollars down."

Jennie said that Ainsworth eventually moved into the house in Washington with her.

"Was Ainsworth drinking?" Morse asked.

"Yes, almost hopelessly," Jennie replied

"Did you go to work again yourself?"

"Yes, but on the outskirts of Washington, and in Baltimore and Norfolk. My people were so well connected in Washington that I didn't like to do work in the city itself.

"Ainsworth continued to drink so that I lost hope. I sold my house, stored my furniture, and put my children in the Convent of the Visitation (in Frederick, Maryland). I made up my mind to train myself to be a nurse and went to Miss Struble, head of the George Washington Hospital. I told her what experience I had had nursing my children and husband. She called me on the telephone a few days later and got me a position to nurse Mrs. Siegel, which lasted a month. Mr. Ainsworth kept coming to the house and wanting money, and it mortified me so that I left before the case was really finished."

"Miss Struble next gave me a telephone order to go to Admiral Eaton's house. I got there about six p.m. and found in the house, beside the admiral and his wife, a maid-servant and a colored cook. I stayed there until Mrs. Eaton died – about three weeks. The shock to which Dr. Smith testified was six or seven days before the death."

DA Barker made note of that comment. It contradicted Dr. Fremont-Smith's testimony that he had secured the services of the then Mrs. Ainsworth immediately after Mrs. Eaton had suffered her stroke, which was six days before she died.

"What was the admiral's condition as to intoxication?" Morse inquired.

"Worse than I ever saw Mr. Ainsworth."

"Did he go to his first wife's funeral?"

"No."

"Why not?"

"He couldn't."

"After Admiral Eaton went north with the body of his wife, did you get another position?"

"Yes, I was up on Columbia Heights and had been there three weeks. Admiral Eaton's card was brought to me, and when I went down he was so intoxicated that the butler and I had to hold him up. I told him I would see him in an hour, and the butler helped him into his carriage. But when I got to the house, he was still so befuddled that I couldn't do anything."

Jennie told the court the admiral asked her to "help straighten him out, to take care of him." He agreed to pay her twenty dollars a week. He took her to Boston, but "he was in such a pitiable condition" she suggested he take a trip to improve his health and outlook. She accompanied him with her two daughters to Niagara Falls, Montreal, and Chicago, "where I stopped to get my divorce papers." She stated she had instituted divorce proceedings eighteen months before.

After the trip to Chicago, she returned with the admiral and her children to Massachusetts where the admiral had rented a cottage in Hull for the summer. Jennie's mother joined them, as did two servants.

"Had the admiral spoken to you of marriage?" Morse asked.

"Yes," Jennie replied. "He said that he thought it would be the best thing I could do for myself and for him. He said this before he left Washington, but I did not consider myself engaged to be married when I came to Boston."

Jennie said she married the admiral in July and summered in Hull. At summer's end, the newlyweds left Hull with Jennie's two daughters, her mother, and two servants, and moved into a rented house, for seventy-two dollars a month, at 56 Harvard Avenue in Brookline.

"How long were you in Brookline?" asked Morse.

"Eleven months."

"Why did you leave?"

"Well, when the children had gone to school, there was nothing for him (the admiral) to do, and he began to live mostly at the clubs – the Somerset, Algonquin, and the Army and Navy – and was drinking too much. The bills had begun to pour in, tradesmen's bills and bills of all sorts; bills from Washington, lawyer's letters. When we first went (to Brookline), I did not know the admiral's financial condition."

Jennie testified that some of the bills were seven or eight years old and that the admiral had never concerned himself with them. She decided that the only way to repay the debts was to find a less expensive place to live, somewhere in the country, a farm perhaps, where the admiral could keep himself occupied and away from the clubs and the temptations of alcohol.

Morse asked Jennie about the servants she had hired to work in the Brookline household. She stated she had replaced at least three servants. Morse then asked her if she remembered a conversation she had with the admiral, in June's presence, about the servants. Ignoring Morse's question, Jennie described an incident in which the admiral had made improper advances toward June.

"I had a seamstress who was fitting a dress on June. She left June standing only partially dressed while she went upstairs for material. The admiral came in and seized June. I came in from the library where I was sitting, took him into the library, and talked to him."

"Was he under the influence of liquor?" Morse asked.

"I don't think so," was the reply.

"Was there another occasion?"

"Yes. He and June had been to walk, and she came back crying. She said, 'Oh mother, this horrible man!' and she told me he had hugged her. I said, 'Joe, you ought to be ashamed of yourself.' He didn't seem to know what he was doing – and I don't think he did."

"Did you discharge a servant because of improper conduct with the admiral?"

"Yes."

"Did you discharge any other?"

"No."

Morse next focused on family life at the Assinippi farm and Jennie's efforts to reduce the admiral's debts. Jennie stated she and the admiral moved into the house with June, Dorothy, and Mrs. Harrison on the last day of August 1907. She stocked the place with hens, a cow, and a pig, and bought some books for the admiral. She estimated her annual household budget at $1,200.

"The admiral drew one hundred eighty-seven dollars on the first of every month and one hundred eighty-seven dollars on the fifteenth," Jennie explained.

"Was the rest of the forty-seven hundred dollars a year, over expenses, used to pay debts?" her counsel asked.

"Many months I had four hundred to five hundred dollars to meet, and only three hundred seventy-five dollars to pay it with."

"How much of his debts did you pay off?"

"If the admiral had lived another year, we would have been out of debt."

"Then thirty-three hundred or thirty-five hundred dollars a year went for debts?" inquired Morse.

"Yes, fully that," Jennie responded.

Morse asked his client about the admiral's health and habits at Assinippi. She testified that the admiral was in poor health when they first moved there. She forced him to curtail his drinking and within a year had limited him to two drinks a day. She recalled one period of about twenty-two months in which he was nearly sober, but it didn't last, and he began drinking again.

Morse retrieved a ledger from the defense table and showed it to Jennie. She confirmed that the entries in the book were in her own handwriting. Morse asked her the meaning of an entry on May 18 marked "birthday gift, paid mortgage on home - $100."

"The admiral always meant on my birthday to give me a hundred dollars," Jennie said. "I put the money, in 1912, on my mortgage. This year on my birthday I was in Plymouth Jail."

Morse offered the ledger as evidence over the objection of the district attorney. Judge Aiken overruled Barker and ordered the ledger admitted and marked as an exhibit.

Morse shifted to the story of the adopted baby. Jennie testified it was her idea to adopt a child. She thought that having a child in the home would change the admiral's disposition.

Morse stepped to the defense table and picked up a copy of the probate court adoption order, which he read aloud.

"Did you conceal the fact that your child was adopted?"

"I didn't say much about it. I didn't want to gratify the curiosity of the country people. And I thought that the admiral would take more interest in it, that way. And I didn't want the boy later on to be taunted," Jennie explained.

Morse asked Jennie to comment once again on the admiral's behavior up to the time of the baby's adoption. Jennie related how one day, while she was in bed after a long day of work about the farm, the admiral brought her a cup of tea. A necklace she was wearing around her neck caught in the teacup's handle and overturned it. When she picked up the cup, she noticed a pill in the bottom that looked like a chlorate of potash tablet but which she believed to be poison. She showed it to June and confronted the admiral about it.*

Morse returned to the adopted child. He asked Jennie to relate the circumstances of the child's sudden illness and death at Sand Hills in the summer of 1909. Jennie testified that the baby was three weeks old when he arrived and that by August he had become "a fine, big, healthy, strong, rosy baby."

"When was your attention called to the baby's illness?" Morse asked.

"The day he died," Jennie answered. "I had bathed the baby in salt water, and he laughed and crowed. I then gave him his bottle and put him to sleep. I then went in bathing, about as the admiral, the children, and some friends were coming out. I stayed in about twenty minutes, and when I came out, Joe was buttoning his collar as I came to the house. I said, 'Wasn't the water fine?' but he made no reply."

Jennie then testified that the admiral's face appeared to be greenish-gray, an indication that he was under the influence of drugs. Fear gripped her. Had the admiral harmed the baby?

"When I got back [to the crib], the baby had a bottle, and the baby looked sick," Jennie continued. "I said, 'Joe, you've got to come with

---

*Admiral Eaton, in 1909, had related the story of Jennie's allegation to a reporter and was quoted as saying he had given the tablet, which was in fact chlorate of potash, to his wife because she had complained of a sore throat. Chlorate of potash tablets were commonly used to alleviate or prevent sore throats. If taken in large doses, the tablets could act as a poison. But the typical dose of one tablet was not considered dangerous.

me to the doctor's with the baby.' He came along as soon as I had dressed, and I pushed the baby in its carriage to Dr. Cleverly's office. I said, 'Doctor, I think Joe has done something to this baby. I'll give you one thousand dollars if you'll save the baby's life.' He gave me some medicine for the baby. Joe went over to the drugstore, and when he came back he did smell of liquor. It seemed to have straightened him out, for he helped me to push the baby carriage back home. But he seemed determined to have the medicine the doctor had given me. I, on the other hand, demanded the brandy and the 'drops' that he had."

"When did the baby die?"

"That night. It didn't vomit anymore, but had quivering fits from time to time."

Morse led his witness to the baby's burial. Jennie recalled how she and the admiral had taken the child's remains in a casket to Assinippi where it was temporarily placed in a vault. When asked why the child wasn't buried at once, she said she couldn't recall the reason. She said she returned to Sand Hills and the admiral remained at Assinippi. She thought the admiral was going to notify her when the baby was to be buried, but he never did.

She eventually returned to Assinippi with Dorothy but not with June. June refused to go back to the farm and went instead to Weymouth where Jennie later joined her.

"June was too nerved up over the affair," Jennie said. "I wanted June to have a three-month rest, to be ready for her examinations at the conservatory."

Morse prompted Jennie to tell how the admiral had visited her at Weymouth every Tuesday from 10:00 a.m. until 6:00 p.m. He wrote her a letter every other day. Morse went to the defense table and picked up several papers. He asked Jennie to identify them. She acknowledged they were some of the letters she had received from her husband during her stay in Weymouth.

Morse began to recite the contents of the letters, all of which carried mundane messages about life at the Assinippi farm. They also revealed how desperately the admiral missed his wife and how much he loved her. He gave several to Jennie to read aloud when he had trouble deciphering the handwriting.

In one, the admiral wrote:

> *Dearest Jane* [sic],
>
> *Just a hasty line to say I love you and am still true. I miss you always. I miss the touch of your tender hand. I am utterly disconsolate. Everything is all right, but a house without a mistress is a poor place to be in. Be careful of yourself, dearest, and don't get cold. I think of you all the time.*
>
>

With a warm kiss,
Your Joe
>

Jennie said she remained in Weymouth for three months before returning to Assinippi. She had lived at Assinippi since then other than, of course, during her incarceration and two trips she had taken. Jennie elaborated on the trip to Washington in April 1912 and the birth of June's baby. She said she received two or three letters a day from the admiral during her stay with June at Mrs. Bursey's house.

Morse hesitated momentarily and then asked Judge Aiken for a sidebar. The defense attorney intended to introduce as evidence the letters that Admiral Eaton had sent to Jennie in Washington. But Morse was concerned about some indecent content. The letters, apparently, were the ones that Geogan had referred to during his opening statement as "so coarse that one would think they were written by a degenerate."

Morse asked the court to excuse the defendant and to permit him to read the letters within the hearing range of only the judge, the jury, and counsel. Aiken called a brief recess and continued to confer with the two lawyers as jurors filed out and Deputy Collingwood assisted Jennie from the stand to the anteroom.

Chapter 26

Jennie did not return to the witness stand but resumed her seat behind the bar enclosure when court reconvened. During the recess, counsel for the prosecution and defense agreed on how the admiral's obscene letters would be presented to the jury.

Morse approached the jury box and began to read aloud from one of the letters the admiral had sent to his wife in Washington. He came to a sentence – "I am all love for you." – and then moved closer to the jurors and continued in a hushed tone, well outside the earshot of the spectators, the press, and the defendant. He read several more letters in the same manner. When he finished, Jennie returned to the stand.

"Upon receipt of these letters did you come home and engage a nurse?" asked Morse.

"Yes," Jennie replied.

"And it was in consequence of them (the letters) that you believed, as you did before, that he was under the influence of a drug?"

"Yes. I first thought I would take a nurse from Washington. I found that would be rather expensive, so I came to Boston, looked up a nurses' directory, and found Miss Annie Rooney. She said she had been caring for insanity cases. I did not tell her the admiral was insane, but that I needed some skilled help in taking care of him, and I wanted her to see what was the matter with him. She stayed just six days. She was tired and ill, I think, from trouble for which she later had an operation."

Morse returned to the subject of June's pregnancy and had Jennie explain the reason for her return to Washington.

"How long were you in Washington?"

"From April 4th to June 13th."

"And did you go back?"

"Yes, about a week before Christmas, after June was married."

"Why?"

"June was wild to have her baby."

"Did you know the baby was ill-treated?"

"No – and I don't know that it was."

Morse knew his next line of questioning was an important juncture in Jennie's testimony. He needed to show that Bessie Bursey, the Washington lodging house proprietor, had misunderstood Jennie during their conversations about the mysterious Chicago lover.

"Did you tell Mrs. Bursey you had a rich lover in Chicago?"

"I did not. I hadn't a man friend in Chicago."

"Had you been in Chicago?"

"Yes, with June. She had gone to Chicago with her own father, but found him impossible. She only stayed a few days, for he was worse than ever."

"What was your purpose, when you went with June?"

"June had met a young man there, and they had become sweethearts. I went on to become acquainted with this man, and see whether I approved of him."

Satisfied that he had made his point, Morse turned to Jennie's relationship with her ex-husband to dispel any notion that Jennie had any residual feelings for him or had used the admiral's money to support him.

"Did Ainsworth come to see you?" Morse asked.

"Yes, he came to Assinippi when the baby was about three months old," Jennie replied. "Ainsworth was intoxicated. The admiral was there, and I said that I would not stay. I went to my room and locked myself in; the admiral got a carriage and drove Ainsworth to the train in Rockland. Ainsworth came to Scituate when the baby died. He was intoxicated. Again the admiral took him away. A few days later Ainsworth came again and was intoxicated. The admiral was away, having taken the baby's body to Assinippi. I think I gave Ainsworth fifty cents and told the chauffeur to drive him to Cohasset. And I told Ainsworth that if he came around again I would have him arrested."

Having explained Ainsworth's visits, Jennie next told the story of an injury the admiral had sustained on the night of June's wedding in 1912. She confirmed that the wedding had taken place at the Hotel Vendome in Boston and the reception had followed at the Algonquin Club on Commonwealth Avenue. She testified that she had seen the admiral at the end of the reception apparently licking what she believed to be drugs from the palm of his hand. The admiral walked Jennie and Mrs. Harrison the short distance back to their rooms at the hotel. The admiral bade them goodnight and returned to a room at the club where he spent the night.

The next morning, Jennie said, the admiral appeared at the hotel with his head bandaged. He told her that a horse-drawn carriage had knocked him down in the street, but Jennie thought it more likely he had fallen because of his drug-induced state.

While Jennie spoke, Judge Aiken checked the clock to his left. He had announced he would end that day's session by 1:00 p.m. and was concerned that Morse still had much to ask his client. Aiken called the lawyer to his bench for a brief conference. Morse stepped away and continued his examination.

Jennie's stay in Medford in February 1913 was his next line of questioning. He hoped to remove any belief in the minds of jurors that Jennie had gone to Medford with the intention of leaving her husband permanently. Ralph Keyes had suggested that Jennie intended to stay when she arrived at his Medford home on February 20 with two trunks and a bed.

"Did June and her husband visit Assinippi?" Morse began.

"Yes."

"How did the admiral treat them?"

"He was always very fond of June; he didn't care so much for Keyes," was Jennie's reply.

"What was the occasion of your nine-day visit to June?"

"I had found the house in Medford for them, paid the rent, and went to help them get settled in their housekeeping."

"Did the admiral know you were there and why you went?" asked Morse.

"Yes," Jennie asserted.

"Was this the time you took two trunks?"

"Yes. One trunk was filled entirely with bedding, blankets, and quilts. The other had some fancy pillows, a bathrobe, and a black skirt of mine. That was all the clothing I took, as I expected to stay only a few days – all I had except my little handbag with my dressing things."

Despite his promise, at one o'clock Judge Aiken called for a recess until 2:15 p.m. Jennie returned to the stand when court resumed. Morse and Geogan spent the entire recess reviewing Jennie's testimony and realized that Morse had failed to ask her about two other occasions when she had dealings with her ex-husband.

"Since the noon recess, have you recalled another time when you saw Ainsworth?" Morse asked Jennie.

"Yes, when June and I were at Weymouth he called twice. I saw him once. He was intoxicated. I requested him emphatically to keep away, and I saw him one other time in Chicago."

Jennie related how she had set Ainsworth up in a cigar business there. She signed off on the purchase of a cigar stand with a seventy-five dollar deposit and assumed responsibility for a $325 balance. She said she only agreed to help Ainsworth if he promised to stay sober. But Ainsworth didn't keep his part of the bargain, and the business failed. Jennie said she settled the debt by selling some of her clothing and a ring the admiral had given her. She sold another ring, this one given to her years ago by Ainsworth, and she bought Ainsworth a railroad ticket with part of the proceeds and sent him to his father in Arizona. She was practically penniless after this unfortunate episode.

"The first two years at Assinippi I literally went without a coat," she told the jury.

Satisfied he had left the jury with an impression that his client was a devoted, unselfish, and caring woman, Morse moved to her dealings with Dr. Charles Colgate, the family's first physician at Assinippi.

"Now, Mrs. Eaton, you called on Dr. Colgate?"

"Yes, the first time I think was about four years ago. I took the little baby to consult him about the wax in his ear. The doctor said it was all right."

Morse referred to the letter she had sent to Colgate and which the prosecution had introduced during Colgate's direct examination. When Morse asked if Jennie had written the doctor for advice on how to deal with the admiral's drug and alcohol use, she said she had.

"Did you make efforts after you went to Assinippi to have the admiral work about the place and keep his brain occupied?" Morse asked.

"Yes, incessantly. He really didn't have brain enough to keep himself occupied," said Jennie.

Morse returned to the Colgate letter and asked the defendant what she had meant when she wrote: "I proved to myself that the trouble was deeper than whiskey."

"Why, for twenty-two months he had had practically no whiskey," Jennie asserted. "He had seen no women; he had eaten mush and milk for supper and gone to bed. And if he still had the trouble, it proved conclusively that it was caused by something else than whiskey."

"You complain in this letter that Dr. Colgate did not treat you courteously. What did you mean?"

"Why, I went there to get advice about a sick man. I wanted doctors, nurses, attendants, and he told me I wanted a lawyer. He treated me as if I were a young woman, tired of an old man, and anxious to get rid of him."

Morse momentarily diverted from his line of questioning, establishing through his witness that she and the admiral could not have marital relations at that time because of his bad health. Moving on, he asked if Jennie had ever requested any physician to have her husband committed to an asylum. She emphatically denied she had done so.

Morse returned to the defense table and picked up several more letters. He showed them to Jennie, and she identified the handwriting as Admiral Eaton's. DA Barker objected and asked that he be allowed to see the letters before they were introduced. He and ADA Katzmann reviewed the documents and consented to their admission as evidence.

The letters were consistent with previous correspondence introduced by the defense that demonstrated the admiral's extraordinary fondness for his wife. One letter, written by the admiral on February 11, 1913, to Mrs. Montgomery Sears, was offered by Morse to show the admiral's state of mind and financial condition. Jennie explained that the admiral had borrowed $300 from Mrs. Sears's father, Charles F. Choate, a wealthy New England attorney and businessman, many years before.

My Dear Mrs. Sears – I wrote to you in 1911 asking that you give me time to pay a note to which you are heir. As you did not do this, your brother threatened me with imprisonment, using the influence of his law firm. The note has now been paid in full and he can no longer bully me under cover of the law. Owing to my financial inability I was put to an expense of $176 above the amount due on the note to protect my liberty. Part of this accrued to him. Part of my distress is that this has made me discontinue violin lessons of my lame daughter, who must some time earn her own living, as I am now nearing the portals which

> *should open into loving kindness. Thus do the innocent suffer. I cannot believe that the daughter of so Christian a mother as yours was, would have the feeling of charity to none, malice toward all. I write this to say that the pound of flesh is now exacted.*

Judge Aiken had all of the letters marked as defense exhibits at Morse's request. He then nodded at Morse to continue. Morse took Jennie through the testimony given by Miss Howard and Miss Magoun about her husband's flirtatious behavior. She explained that she had written the letter, introduced by the prosecution, to Miss Howard because at the time she was awaiting the results of her son's autopsy, believing he had been poisoned. She needed Miss Howard's support to prevent the admiral from blaming her or June for the death.

Jurors at this point appeared disinterested and listless. Many yawned and a few drowsed occasionally. Their languor quickly dissipated, however, when Morse finally arrived at the events leading to the admiral's death.

Morse began his questioning at the point of Jennie's return to Assinippi on March 1, after her visit to June's house in Medford.

"What was his condition when you got home on Saturday, March 1st?"

"He fell into my arms, intoxicated; I got him to bed, gave him sandwiches and coffee," Jennie testified. "Next morning I gave him a Turkish bath, got him up, and made him go to church. Monday morning he had an engagement to go to town meeting. But on Monday morning he vomited after breakfast and was too sick to go. My impression is that he vomited every day that week. Tuesday we spent at home. Dorothy was to have a party Tuesday night. I thought it would brighten him up to go to Rockland and to get the supplies for the party. During Tuesday evening he vomited once or twice."

"Were you and the admiral in the party?" Morse continued.

"Yes – and there were, I should think, eighteen people there," Jennie said.

"Had you any arrangement with the admiral on Wednesday?"

"Yes, we were going to talk with Ralph Keyes, to talk over his and June's affairs. I got up early and straightened out the house after the party. About eleven, I had a postal from June reminding me to come.

And I started about noon."

"Why didn't the admiral go?" inquired Morse.

"Because he had extreme nausea, and also because he was very busy helping a man load hay. I went on the eleven-fifteen car from Assinippi to Rockland, and by train to Boston, arriving at one twenty. In the station I had a club sandwich and a cup of coffee. I then went on to June's house in Medford. She wasn't there, and the colored woman (housekeeper) said she had gone to my house. I sat down and hemmed six little curtains till Ralph Keyes came home. Then we had supper.

"June came in about seven thirty," Jennie went on. "I asked how her father was, and she said, 'If I hadn't known he was an insane man I should have fallen in love with him. He was fascinating.' June said he had said something about going to Europe. And she quoted him as saying, 'June, what do you want me to do about Ralph? Do you want to get rid of him?' June said he had asked her if she would like to go with him to Europe. She said, 'With mother?' and he replied, 'No, not with mother.' June said, 'Mother, I guess he wants to get rid of you, too.' And I said, 'That's the drug. I'll have to get home and take care of him.' "

"Had you any sinister meaning when you said that?" Morse asked.

DA Barker objected strenuously but was overruled.

"No," said Jennie, contradicting the testimony of Ralph Keyes. "I merely meant that I recognized the effect of the drug."

Jennie related how she had left June's house at 5:00 a.m. to return to Assinippi. She said that when she arrived home she found Dorothy at the breakfast table. She repacked a lunch the admiral had prepared for her daughter and sent her off to school. She then sat down to have her own breakfast.

Morse asked Jennie if the admiral had mentioned his illness and nausea on that Thursday morning and on the day before. But before she could respond, Judge Aiken sustained an objection by Barker who argued that any answer given by the witness would be self-serving and unreliable without corroboration. Morse tried to rephrase his question several times, but Barker objected every time, and the judge upheld every objection.

Morse finally asked if Jennie had seen the admiral vomit on Thursday morning. She said she had. She did not see but heard him retching again later in the afternoon.

Barker was satisfied with this curtailed response. If the court had allowed Jennie to testify that the admiral had complained of being sick on Wednesday, the day before she returned home, it would have undermined his theory by suggesting that admiral became ill while she was away.

Morse next asked Jennie to describe the supper she and the admiral ate on Thursday night.

"We had a light soup – I think a chicken soup – and a pitcher of milk," Jennie related. "We had neither tea, nor coffee substitute. We had finished and were sitting talking, when he clapped his hand over his mouth and ran into the woodshed, where he was nauseated. I worked at cleaning the kitchen."

"What happened next?" Morse asked.

"About eight thirty I went to bed. I think the admiral and Dorothy did a little mathematics. I was in bed when they came up together. And I think I got up and made the admiral comfortable. I had seen the admiral vomit before in terrible paroxysms. I talked with him about five minutes, and he said he would call me if he needed anything. I then went to bed and slept until the sun was shining. I suppose it was about six. I dressed and went into the admiral's room. I saw that he was a little feverish and that he had vomited. I straightened out the bed clothing and got hot-water bottles and some six whiskey bottles, putting them at his feet and at his sides. He said he was cold."

"Please continue," Morse encouraged her.

"I went downstairs, got an egg and beat it up in a cup of tea with some toast. I took it up to him. But he said he didn't care for it."

Barker jumped to his feet and objected to Mrs. Eaton's hearsay statements. He pleaded with the judge to advise Mrs. Eaton to refrain from repeating conversations when no third party was present to corroborate her testimony. Aiken agreed and warned Jennie that the rules of evidence prohibited her from sharing a statement made outside of court by a person who is not available to testify.

Jennie carried on. Just as she was about to telephone a doctor for the admiral that Friday morning, Dr. Frame pulled up to the house in his carriage to see her mother. When he came in, Jennie asked him to assess her husband.

"Did you tell Dr. Frame what you had done for the admiral?" Morse asked.

"Yes, but we didn't have very much talk."

"Did [Frame] order lime water?"

"Yes, and I told him there was none in the house."

"What was your husband's appearance?"

"He looked perfectly natural, though weak from vomiting. I gave him the medicine Dr. Frame left, at noon and at two o'clock, at four and at six. But Admiral Eaton never got any of the medicine Dr. Frame left, at all. He would take a swallow, and back it would come, pill and all."

"What were you doing that afternoon?"

"Everything I could think of. I was up and down, every twenty minutes. About four thirty, Dorothy came home. I sent her out of the room. The water bottles were very hot, and I was afraid she would scald herself. I preferred her to be out in the air."

"Were you provoked with the admiral?"

"No."

"Did you have any talk with reference to his having sold a pipe or cigar holder?"

"I don't remember that I did."

Morse led Jennie to Friday night.

"What was the admiral's condition when you went to bed?"

"About the same. Dorothy and I went in, and I asked him if there was anything I could do, and if he wanted me to sleep with him. He said, 'No.' I went to my room across the hall. I went to sleep almost in no time."

"What aroused you?"

Jennie said she heard her mother or the admiral or both calling for her and Dorothy.

"I rushed out and heard Mama say something about the admiral," Jennie elaborated. "So I ran in there with Dorothy and found him on the floor. I said, 'Dorothy, for goodness' sake, take your father's feet and let's get him into bed.' And we lifted him into bed by main strength. I had come out in my night gown and I got thoroughly chilled. I asked the admiral if he wanted anything, refilled the water bottles with hotter water, and put a light blanket over them. We went back to bed, Dorothy and I, and got into bed. We hadn't been there more than ten minutes when he called again. Dorothy jumped right over me and went into the admiral's room. When she came back she was like an icicle. I said, 'Don't you get up again – you'll catch your death of pneumonia.' "

Jennie testified that the admiral called again about ten minutes later. She told Dorothy to stay put and went to the admiral's room with a blanket, which she put around him. She got into bed with him and they both fell asleep quickly.

"I was awakened by the feeling of cold," Jennie continued. "I shook Joe, but I found that he was dead. Then I jumped up, went first to the bay window. Then I ran across to Dorothy's room, and said, 'Dorothy, I think your father is dead.' Then we told my mother."

Jennie explained that she and Dorothy went to the Simmons house to telephone Dr. Frame and the undertaker. The undertaker informed her that an autopsy would be performed on the admiral's body.

"After the autopsy I asked Dr. Osgood, 'Would you mind telling me what was the matter with the admiral?' " Jennie said. "I'm not sure what he answered. I asked him if he had examined the brain, and he said, 'No.' I think he also said that hallucination or delusions wouldn't show."

"Did you fear that the admiral might have died from other than natural causes?" Morse asked.

"I think I did," Jennie answered.

"Mrs. Eaton, did you ever buy any poisons?"

"I never saw any in my life," the witness answered emphatically.

"Did you ever have any white arsenic?"

"Never in my life."

"Did you ever administer arsenic to your husband?"

"It is the most absurd thing I ever heard. Never, never in my life!" she declared.

"Did you love your husband?"

"I was very fond of Admiral Eaton."

Morse indicated he had completed his direct examination. Judge Aiken, aware that he had broken his promise to end the Saturday session at 1:00 p.m., immediately adjourned. Jennie stepped confidently from the witness stand and smiled broadly at her two lawyers. It was an expression of both relief and self-satisfaction. She had testified for more than five hours. She believed she had acquitted herself well, but she knew the real test would come on Monday when the prosecution would begin its cross-examination. She spoke briefly with Morse and Geogan, then she left the courtroom in the custody of Deputy Sheriff John Geary who drove her back to the jail.

Reporters at the jail spoke briefly with her before Geary led her inside.

"How do you feel after the ordeal?" one newsman asked.

"Fine," she replied, "except that my head is tired, because I had to think quickly and keep my mind constantly alert while on the stand. I am thankful that I have at last had an opportunity to tell just what I had waited so long to say. I have felt no ill-effects from the trial at any time, on the whole. I feel tonight that before another Saturday night I shall be at home."

Morse and Geogan lingered in the courtroom. They were pleased with how they were managing the case. They had completed direct examination during the day's abbreviated session and had left the prosecutor no time for questions. Sunday's respite would allow their client ample time to recuperate. It would also provide them an opportunity to review her direct testimony and prepare her for questions the district attorney would likely ask on Monday.

~

At the jail on Sunday, Jennie busied herself reading and writing notes to friends, family members, and other supporters, telling all that she expected vindication before the week was out. Her defense team spent several hours with her during the afternoon. When the two lawyers exited the building, waiting reporters asked Morse if his client was anxious about her appearance on the witness stand the next morning.

"She regrets of course that she must undergo the cross-examination," Morse said, "but she knows it is a necessary part of this experience and she says that she is ready for it and not afraid of it."

Chapter 27

Bright sunshine filled the courtroom on the morning of Monday, October 27. Judge Aiken briskly emerged from his chambers, took the bench, and signaled for the jury. As soon as the jurors were seated, Morse re-called Jennie to the stand. Spectators in the packed gallery watched in eager anticipation as the defendant, a smile on her face, strode purposefully to the front of the courtroom.

Exempted from sequestration by Judge Aiken at the request of the district attorney, Drs. Osgood, Wheatley, Carroll, Whitney, Balch, and Frame sat together on a bench inside the bar. Barker intended, if necessary, to use each of the doctors as rebuttal witnesses.

Once sworn, Jennie took her seat and nodded in greeting to the jurors. Morse approached and asked one final question before turning Jennie over to the district attorney.

"Did you know that your husband's income stopped at his death?" Morse asked.

"Yes," said Jennie.

District Attorney Barker rose and, with a transcript of Jennie's testimony in his hand, ambled over to the sheriff's desk where he paused momentarily, gazing out the window for effect. At last, he put his right hand on his hip and gently turned to pose his first question.

"Did I understand you to say you were born in 1874?"

"Yes," Jennie replied.

"What was your father's business?"

"He was in the wholesale fish industry."

Barker asked her to talk about her parents and siblings. When he asked her to give more specific details, Morse interrupted him, objecting that the prosecutor's questions were immaterial. Aiken, however, overruled him, observing that Mrs. Eaton's answers might reveal the influence of her upbringing.

Barker resumed.

"How many children did your mother have?"

"Twelve," answered Jennie.

"How old is Dorothy?"

"Sixteen last September."

"Where is her birth record?"

"In Washington, I presume."

"Do you not know that there is a question as to her age?"

"No, I do not. There is no question in my mind. I never heard of it being raised."

After her marriage to Ainsworth, she recalled, they boarded at the Franklin House on I Street NW in Washington, and after June's birth they rented a flat on I Street SW. They moved to another flat six weeks later and then rented a house on D Street SE.

"After Mr. Ainsworth lost his position, I talked to his father and he got him a position in Guthrie, Oklahoma," Jennie offered. "He had lost four or five positions from drink. He was a chief clerk."

"The chief clerk?" Barker asked.

"No, I guess he was a head clerk – there was a chief clerk over him. He received one hundred twenty-five dollars a month," Jennie added.

"Did you know he drank before you married him?"

"I heard so, but I did not understand then what drinking meant. I was a very young girl."

"When did you go west with Mr. Ainsworth?" Barker continued.

"I followed him to Guthrie in three weeks, after I broke up housekeeping. He drank badly in the three years we were there. He lost a year's pay playing faro with the cowboys. The boss there, a Mr. McKinley, wanted to get him out of his job. But a congressman whom he had helped kept it for him. We had bought a little house there. After a time, they pressed heavily on him and I advised him to get out."

"Where did you go then?"

"To St. Louis. I wanted to see about Dorothy's lameness. Her foot would double under her when she tried to walk. I found an institute and took her to it every day. I devoted my time to her. Later I took up canvassing and made some money."

"What was Mr. Ainsworth doing?" Barker inquired.

"Selling books two days a week and being intoxicated the other five days. Then, in three or four years, we drifted back to Washington. The treatment did not do Dorothy any good. I had bought seven pairs of braces for her at thirty-five dollars a pair."

Barker asked her to recall what transpired upon her return to Washington.

"At first I lived with my mother, and then got my own little house. Ainsworth was drinking heavily; he had to have half a pint before breakfast, and five times a week he would get dead drunk. Then it got too bad, and I left him. He would break up the furniture, and he acted disgracefully. He got to look like a tramp. I would buy him a complete outfit, and next morning the clothes would be gone, and he would be shabby again, but would have a five-dollar bill."

"You found it was a pretty serious thing, living with a drunkard?"

"Yes."

"You didn't think your children should be brought up in such an environment?"

"I thought it was horrible for little children to grow up seeing such things."

Jennie said she left Ainsworth and began selling books in the Washington metropolitan area. She earned forty or fifty dollars a week. She put June and Dorothy in the Visitation School while she worked. But she was not happy with what she called a "wandering life." She wanted a home. It was then that she decided to take up nursing and went to Miss Struble at the Washington Hospital and Nurse's Home.

"Who sent you to the Eatons?" asked Barker.

"Dr. Fremont-Smith telephoned me," she replied.

"Did you go before or after the shocks she had?"

"Before, I am sure, because I used to read Shakespeare and Browning to her. Dr. Smith was mistaken, I think, on the stand when he said she had had the shock before he sent for me. Why, her friends used to run in and out to see her. I was very fond of the first Mrs. Eaton. She was attached to me. She wouldn't allow me to leave the room."

A subtle smile crossed Barker's face. It was quite obvious that Mrs. Eaton was more than willing to offer more information than she was asked for, and he wasn't about to stop her. He'd give her all the rope she wanted. His primary goal was to evoke her mental state for the jury rather than discredit her direct testimony for the defense.

Some who attended the trial must have considered the idea that Barker's focus on proving that Jennie was insane might come at the expense of proving her guilty. Barker seemed confident that he had already convinced the jurors, albeit circumstantially, that Jennie was the only person who had opportunity to administer the deadly poison to her husband. He still had to prove motive, and there his case, based on a premise of jealousy, was weak. He had a stronger case for securing a verdict of not guilty by reason of insanity. Still, to reach such a verdict, jurors would first have to find that the defendant had, in fact, administered poison to her husband.

"The admiral was drunk during this time?"

"Yes. In a way he needed more attention than [his wife] did," Jennie said. "I used to run his bath, and Mrs. Eaton asked me to attend to him. He couldn't give any orders to the servants even. I used to try to open his mind by reading little humorous stories to him. It was six weeks before he came to himself. I gave him a course of treatment."

Dr. Osgood shook his head and scribbled furiously on his notepad. Barker asked Jennie to describe her "treatment."

"Well, I made him go to bed at eight o'clock, for one thing."

"Oh, I see," said Barker sarcastically. "But he was dead drunk all this time?"

"He wasn't staying in bed."

"I see. What else?"

"Well, I wouldn't let him sit with the decanter by him. I took it away from him."

"I see. Why did you do this?"

"Well, I thought he ought to go to his wife's funeral."

"You laid the law right down to him, didn't you? What did you do next?"

"Well, I tried to cut down his supply of liquor."

"Oh, yes."

"I got him so he could walk to the doctor's by leaning on my arm."

"I see."

"He was so weak."

"Oh, yes," Barker said mockingly.

Morse resented the district attorney's sarcasm. He asked Judge Aiken to instruct the district attorney to refrain from commenting whenever Jennie answered. Aiken agreed with Morse and instructed Barker to keep his remarks to himself.

"Was he very ill?" Barker continued.

"Yes, he vomited terribly," Jennie answered. "I never saw such spells of vomiting in a human being. He would fall over. I would get him to bed at eight and up at ten in the morning. I would telephone for a barber to shave him. I had him looking like a gentleman by luncheon time. Then I would take him driving and drop him at his club."

"You controlled him entirely?"

"Yes, like a child. He was like a child until the day he died. He was never serious. I never had a serious talk with him in my life. He couldn't eat an egg or anything in all this time."

"How did he keep alive?"

"By stimulants, I suppose. I had let him have a little or he would have died. Gradually I weaned him away from drink."

"So you kept after him until you got him thoroughly weaned? How long was that?"

"Well, I never thoroughly got him weaned," Jennie said with a smile.

"Then you did not get him weaned?" the district attorney asked with a slight rise in his voice.

"I don't know as I did." Jennie replied.

"Did you attribute the admiral's drinking to his sorrow over his wife's illness?"

"Yes, at first."

"Wasn't he drunk when you went there?"

"Yes, Mrs. Eaton had no control over him whatsoever."

"And you thought he needed a wife to look after him?"

"I thought he needed Mrs. Eaton's care, and I was sorry she was too ill to give it to him."

"You said Saturday he did not attend his wife's funeral. Are you quite sure of that?"

"He did not," Jennie insisted. "I am quite sure he didn't. I remember a Mrs. Tuckerman of New York, a very warm friend of Mrs. Eaton, came on from New York and was very highly incensed because he didn't go to the funeral."

"Where was he during the funeral?"

"Upstairs in his house."

"You are positive he didn't go?"

"I am."

"Why didn't he go?"

"He was too much under the influence of liquor to do so."

She recalled how it was necessary for her to stay at the top of the stairway just outside his room to prevent him from coming out in his nightgown and toppling down the stairs. She said she was in a position to watch the funeral services from above. Barker walked back to his table, picked up a piece of paper, and returned to the witness.

"It wouldn't make any difference to your statement, would it, if I held in my hand a telegram from the minister who conducted that funeral, saying Admiral Eaton was there?" Barker inquired.

"I know he didn't attend that funeral. I, from the head of the stairs, saw the services and I know he wasn't there," she said defiantly.

Barker dropped the matter. He never offered the paper in his hand as evidence.

"Did your mother come there to the admiral's house in Washington?"

"Yes, she came there to live either the day after, or before Mrs. Eaton's death."

"How long did she live there?"

"She lived there until the house was closed."

'Did you run the house in the admiral's absence?"

"Yes, I had an old colored servant to help me."

"Did Admiral Eaton leave Washington soon after his wife's burial?"

"He went on a trip to Boston. I think he stopped at the Algonquin Club, and then went up to Dracut, outside Lowell, to visit some relatives."

"Did he ask you to take charge of his Washington home in his absence?"

"He did."

"When he came back to Washington, did he behave any better than before his wife's death?"

"No. He got very badly intoxicated soon after he returned from the trip."

"Did you stay in his house all the time he was away?"

"No. I locked it up shortly afterwards and secured another position as a nurse."

"Did you see the admiral soon after his return?"

"Yes. He drove up in a carriage to the house where I worked, rang the bell, and was admitted."

"Did you have quite a talk with him?"

"Yes. He said he wanted me to take care of him."

"Did you go back to live at his house?"

"Yes, I did."

"How did he behave after that?"

"He behaved well at times, but I had to keep my eye on him. He wouldn't drink when I was with him."

"Did he drink any?"

"Oh, yes. He was taking a pint of whiskey before breakfast."

"How did you manage to cut down his drinking?"

"I had great influence over Admiral Eaton, so I cut down his supply. I hid the whiskey. In spite of that he used to get hold of it sometimes. If I hadn't limited him, he would have taken fifteen at each meal."

"That would be forty-five during the day," Barker smirked.

"Did he often express affection for you?" he then asked.

"Yes. He said he couldn't live without me. He said I wasn't fitted to be a nurse and his trip away from Washington proved to him how much he wanted me. He asked me to marry him."

"Did you then promise to marry him?"

"I don't think I ever promised to marry him. But I saw that he needed somebody to take care of him. I saw that he would die or kill himself unless somebody took hold of him, and of course there would be a great deal of gossip if I went with him and didn't marry him," Jennie declared.

"You really married him to save his life, then?" Barker asked disingenuously.

"I really married him to save his life," Jennie said softly.

"What was the exact date you made up your mind to marry him?"

"I can't exactly remember."

"Was he paying you wages all the time you were taking care of him?"

"Yes, he was paying me twenty dollars a week."

"How long after his wife's death before you left Washington?"

"About three months or so. I was going out to Chicago to get my divorce. The admiral suggested that he go along and that we take in Montreal, Toronto, and other cities, so we went together."

"Of course you had made up your mind to marry the admiral by that time, hadn't you?"

"Yes, I had."

"And though you had had such an experience with drinking once, you could take a chance again?"

"I thought," said Jennie, "that the admiral had brain enough to realize that he couldn't drink as he did, at his age, and that he really wanted to stop."

"You felt that though you had failed with the first husband, you could reform the second?" asked Barker.

"I believed that he would realize his situation," she replied.

"Who got your divorce?"

"Marshall B. Gallion, a lawyer in Chicago."

"You had previously lived in Chicago, hadn't you?"

"Yes, I spent three or four months of one winter."

"What year?"

"A couple of years before I went to Washington."

"How long were you on that trip with the admiral?"

"About sixteen days."

"How much of that time were you in Chicago?"

"Only about three days."

"And you were married shortly after to the admiral?"

Barker intended to show with his next line of questioning that the defendant had married the admiral for his money and not "to save his life." He also intended to refute Jennie's claim that she was forced to deny herself while paying off her husband's alleged indebtedness and making payments on the Assinippi home which was purchased in her name.

He began by asking her if the admiral's first wife had left him any property. Jennie disavowed any knowledge of it. Barker then inquired if Annie Eaton had left the admiral a large sum of money that he had lost while speculating in stocks.

"I don't know where he got the money with which he speculated; I know he did speculate and that he lost money," said Jennie.

"Wasn't it because he had lost money speculating in stocks, and was unable to bear the expense of the Brookline house, that you moved to Assinippi?"

"No, we went into the country to help build up his health. We could have lived in Brookline longer if we had wanted to."

"How was it if you had such influence over the admiral you didn't know the amount of money he was losing in stocks?"

"I had too much pride to ask about his money matters."

"Did you ever ask him to stop playing the stock market?"

"I did. He said he guessed he would."

Judge Aiken interrupted at this point. Mrs. Eaton had, on several occasions during her testimony, adroitly offered into evidence statements made to her by her husband. Aiken cautioned her that any statements uttered by her husband were protected under the rules of evidence and were not admissible at trial.

"Your place in Assinippi was mortgaged back to the seller?" Barker continued.

"Yes," the witness replied.

"Was the house in your name all the time you lived there?"

"Yes."

"Did you try to pay off the mortgage?"

"Yes. Every month one hundred dollars was paid."

"Did that come out of the admiral's pension?"

"Yes."

"How near did you come to paying off the mortgage?"

"If the admiral had lived another year or two it would have been all paid off. As it was, we brought it down to eighteen hundred dollars."

"Did you make a great many improvements in the house after you moved in?"

"No, not a great many. We only made necessary improvements."

"Did he help fix up the house?"

"Yes."

"You had it fixed up so that you considered it a beautiful country home, didn't you?"

"Yes, I am very fond of it."

"Do you remember telling Mr. Scott that while you were living in Brookline the admiral gave you thirty thousand dollars, and you gave him back twenty thousand dollars, which he lost?

"I think he did give me thirty thousand dollars."

"And that thirty thousand came from his first wife's estate?"

"I don't know that it did."

"You later learned that that thirty thousand dollars was lost?"

"Yes."

"How long did you have that thirty thousand dollars in cash in your possession?"

"About three weeks."

"You knew when you married him that he had forty thousand dollars in cash, didn't you?" Barker asked sharply.

"I didn't know he had forty cents," Jennie said with reproach.

"Didn't you tell Mr. Scott you gave him back twenty thousand of the thirty thousand dollars?"

"I did not."

"How much did you give him back?"

"I gave him all of the thirty thousand dollars back."

"Then you did not spend for your own uses ten thousand dollars?"

"I did not."

"Where did you keep that thirty thousand dollars?"

"I locked it up in my jewel box. I didn't know where the money came from, or how he got possession of it."

"How did you happen to give him back all of the thirty thousand?"

"By reason of talks I had with him. He begged it back from me."

"You told the jury you had so much influence over him that he was like a child," Barker reminded Jennie. "How is it you didn't know where he got that thirty thousand dollars?"

"He never volunteered to tell me and I didn't ask."

"Whom did he do his stock trading with?"

"I don't know."

"During the time you lived in Brookline, did he give you any other large sums of money besides the thirty thousand dollars?"

"No, he didn't."

Cutting off Barker's cross-examination, Judge Aiken called for a brief recess.

Chapter 28

District Attorney Barker continued his examination when the session resumed. Jennie retained her cool, pleasant demeanor, sipping occasionally from a glass of water on the stand.

"Did you ever milk the cow you had in Assinippi?"

"Yes, sir, I did. I had to."

"Didn't the admiral milk the cow?"

"He made attempts to. He never could learn to do it properly."

"Did you want a boy to raise up in the navy?"

"I did want one."

"You wanted him to become a naval man because of your husband's naval associations?"

"Yes."

"And as a result you adopted a boy as your son?"

"Yes."

"Did you go to see Dr. Colgate about having the admiral committed?"

"I told him the admiral acted queer and was not himself. I wanted him to form his opinion as to what was the matter."

"Did he go down to your house?"

"He did. Dr. Colgate stayed about fifteen minutes."

"What did you think was the matter with the admiral about that time?"

"I thought the admiral was under the influence of drugs when he acted so peculiarly."

Jennie offered that Colgate never made a serious effort to determine what was wrong with the admiral. When Colgate learned that her child was adopted, she stated, he became indignant and refused to continue as the Eaton family's physician.

"He seemed to think that the trouble was chiefly in the fact that I was a young woman and the admiral was an old man," Jennie declared.

"How often did you go to see Dr. Colgate in all?"

"Three or four times."

"And you quit going to him because you thought he was rude, didn't you?"

"He did act rudely."

Barker asked the court clerk for the letters that were marked as government exhibits during Colgate's direct examination. Scanning the letter she had written to Colgate in February 1909, he called Jennie's attention to her phrase, "his poor, diseased brain."

"Did you think the admiral had a diseased brain?" Barker asked.

"Yes, I did," she responded.

"What did you think made his brain diseased?" Barker asked.

"Why, the drugs he used."

"Did you think he was deluded?"

"I thought at times he had delusions."

"Do you think he took the drugs because his mind was diseased, or did you think that the drugs he took made his mind diseased?"

"I think it was both."

"Did you believe that you were being poisoned?"

"Well, that's a strong way to put it. I think I was being given a medicine, though I don't believe he would have done anything wrong when he was in his right mind."

"Did you believe he would burn the house?"

"Yes, sir, I did. I thought that in a careless, semi-dreamy state, he would do so. He was dropping ashes all over the place when he wasn't himself."

"Did you ever speak to any member of your family of the fact that your husband sent away one thousand dollars' worth of silver?"

"I never mentioned my troubles to anyone else in the family. My mother was an old lady and Dorothy was a cripple, so I thought it best to bear all my troubles myself."

"And yet you consoled the admiral like a child and didn't make an effort to find where this silver went?"

"I spoke to the admiral about it."

"You never really found where he sent it?" Barker asked.

Jennie made a number of attempts to explain where the silver had gone, finally admitting that the silver had been returned.

"Ah, then you do remember it. When did you think of it?"

"Since we have been talking about it," replied Jennie.

"Mrs. Eaton, in the letter you wrote to Dr. Colgate you state: 'I am a woman now at the best time of my life.' Were you at the best time of your life?"

"Yes, I was."

"And you believed that you were being poisoned?"

"Yes."

"Had this affected you very much?"

"Yes, it affected my ankle."

"Have you been entertained by aristocratic people, as you said in your letter to Dr. Colgate?"

Osgood watched Jennie's reaction closely and waited expectantly for her answer.

"Yes, I have been entertained by aristocratic people in Washington."

"And did you entertain aristocratic people?"

"Yes, I did in Brookline, after my marriage to the admiral."

Barker did not pursue the identities of these "aristocratic people." Instead, he quickly shifted to Jennie's assertion that the admiral had injected her with poison while she slept.

"Did the admiral give you a hypodermic injection of some drug?" Barker inquired.

"I do not know that he did. I know I found some blood on my arm one morning and I couldn't account for the blood in any other way," Jennie replied.

"You told Dr. Colgate that he had injected something, didn't you?"

"I told him I thought it was possible."

"Did you hunt much for those drugs?"

"I hunted everywhere."

"Did you scatter white stuff on the stairway in an effort to trace him to the place where he had his drugs?"

"No sir, I didn't," Jennie replied, directly contradicting government witness Frank Booth.

"Didn't you tell somebody you did?"

"No, I never did," she said crossly.

"Were there other places on your body where you thought the admiral had injected something?"

"Yes, I thought he had injected it in several places on my arms, my ankles, my back, my ears, and other places."

"Where else?"

"One morning when I woke up one of the gums in my mouth was all swollen. My mouth was all right when I went to sleep."

"And you thought he had tried to inject something there?"

"Yes, I did think so. What else was responsible?"

Jennie added that she had also seen punctures on Dorothy's legs but that she'd never said anything to her daughter lest she frighten her.

Jennie told Barker she had always prided herself on the condition of her teeth and was especially upset because the injection had affected one tooth in particular. Barker asked if he could inspect the tooth and, with Jennie's consent, he approached the stand. The courtroom audience laughed when she lifted her upper lip with the fingers of both hands and submitted her teeth and gums for the prosecutor's inspection. Barker peered briefly at her mouth, thanked her, and stepped away.

"Tell us about the time you thought he harmed June in Brookline," Barker prompted.

"June was a strong, beautiful girl at the time. She weighed one hundred forty, had a fine shape. All of a sudden she went down in health. Her weight dropped until she weighed only one hundred ten. She lost seven inches from her waist. I know that the admiral insisted on treating her all the time, and I allowed him to."

"Did he insult her?"

"Yes. I saw it. I remember taking hold of his arm and drawing him into the library so he wouldn't keep it up. I knew he didn't know what he was doing."

The district attorney asked Jennie if she recalled any other instances of subterfuge by the admiral. She told of how she had often detected white powder on her dishes and never sat down to eat without dusting them off. Barker asked her about a comment attributed to her about the admiral having poison under his fingernails. She flatly denied she had ever said anything of the sort.

Barker questioned her again about her allegations of her husband's drug abuse. Jennie testified about an incident that occurred in Chicago as she was dining in a restaurant. On the sidewalk outside, she had seen white smoke emanating from a pipe in the hands of a Chinese man. She stepped outside and asked the man what he was smoking. When he told her it was opium, she concluded that because the smoke was the same color emitted from the admiral's pipe, he too, was an opium user.

Judge Aiken called a recess at twelve thirty. As self-confident as ever, Jennie stepped down from the stand as the jury left for lunch. She and her lawyers retreated to the anteroom and sent out for sandwiches. They reviewed her testimony and discussed what she might expect during the afternoon. Morse gently told her not to offer any information beyond the questions asked by the district attorney. Her tendency to elaborate on her answers only helped the prosecution, he cautioned.

When the trial resumed, Barker questioned Jennie about the death of her adopted child. She reiterated, in practically every detail, the testimony she had given to Morse during his direct examination.

Barker asked her to explain remarks attributed to her in newspapers after the baby's death.

"I went to Boston to get some advice from people whose opinion I valued and saw there in the newspapers a headline which said, 'Admiral Eaton's wife says he poisoned baby,' " Jennie said. "Now, I would like to clear myself of the charge that I gave out this story. When I got back to Sand Hills I found that the reporters had been there all day. They were still there and in my excitement I probably said more than I might have done at another time, but I did not start that story, and would not have brought notoriety on the admiral."

Barker asked the court clerk for the letter that Mrs. Eaton wrote to Dr. Whitney in September 1909. This was the same letter the government had offered as evidence during Whitney's direct testimony. Seeing it, Jennie admitted she had written it. Barker read pertinent excerpts aloud.

"What did you mean when you wrote that your husband was a 'dangerous, insane man?' " Barker asked.

"Wouldn't you think a boy being poisoned showed him insane?" the witness responded.

"You wrote that 'he can fool others, but not me?' "

"After two and a half years with him, yes."

"You wrote, 'He has been planning my death all day.' What did that mean?"

"He handed me a glass of water. He had his gray-greenish look upon him, and I said, 'Why don't you drink it yourself, Joe?' He purposely dropped it on the floor and said, 'Oh, how careless of me. I'll get you another.' But I told him not to bother. I don't think he wanted to kill me, you know, he just couldn't help it. He might next day bring me flowers, jewels, and pretty dresses."

Osgood shook his head again and made another notation on his notepad. He observed nothing in her manner but composure. Regardless of what Barker asked, she never hesitated to answer.

"Shortly after this did you go away from Assinippi?" the DA asked.

"Yes, I did. I was searching for a place for June. Her mind was all wrought up, and she had to prepare herself for the examination at the conservatory. She was afraid of the admiral in two or three different ways, and I thought then it would be a good thing for me."

"Did you visit the admiral while you were at Weymouth?"

"Yes, every two weeks."

"Yes, you went over to see him every pay day?" Barker asked derisively.

"No, not especially for that," Jennie responded with a hint of anger. "I went over every other Sunday, and he came to visit us every Tuesday."

The defendant explained for the court how she always threw out leftover food after the admiral had eaten there. She also admitted that she emptied the salt and pepper shakers, although she kept the sugar, which was in cubes.

Barker went back to the pill she had found in the glass of water given her by the admiral.

"Did you ever have that pill analyzed?"

"No, I was so indignant I didn't have it done. It was such a cold-blooded thing, so horrible, that I didn't keep it."

Barker read from another letter the defendant had written to Colgate in which she had complained of the admiral's flirtatious ways. She had asked the doctor to bring his wife to a lecture the admiral was to give on the Spanish-American War. If Colgate's wife engaged the admiral in conversation, she wrote, he would witness an example of just how obsessively the admiral acted toward women.

Jennie related how the admiral had embarrassed her in public places with women. He would stare at them, nudge them, and be so obnoxious at theaters that women next to him would leave their seats.

In this same letter Mrs. Eaton had expressed her concerns to Colgate about her daughter Dorothy, who remained at Assinippi with the admiral and Mrs. Harrison. Barker read the excerpt aloud: "He will abuse her and then kill her."

"Did you think, when you wrote this that Dorothy was in danger of being killed?" the prosecutor inquired.

"She seemed safe when I saw her. I did think he was liable to kill anything that came along. His brain didn't work properly at all," the defendant replied.

"You say, 'He should be put in the place where he should be put.' What place did you have in mind?"

Jennie picked her words carefully. She was answering questions more reflectively during the afternoon session. She told the court she had not meant that an asylum was the only option available to address the admiral's behavior. She believed an operation could have had the same effect.

As to her reference that she should have "a wife's share," she only meant that she was entitled to some support.

"I cannot live on the trees out there at Assinippi, and they won't let me live in the hospital," she declared.

"You speak of him again as a monster," Barker said. "You lived with him most of the time, did you not?"

"I was very fond of the admiral. I might have called him that for his thoughts," Jennie replied.

Barker asked what she had meant when she referred to the effect of designing women on the admiral.

"His brain was filled with drugs, and I knew there were designing women in the world who would be attracted by a man of his high place. I could see he was easily influenced, and I didn't want to see him subjected to any other influence."

"Did you ever see the admiral take a drug?" asked Barker.

"Yes, dozens of times. I saw him eat from his palm, chew something up and swallow it," was the reply.

Jennie said the admiral was ashamed of his drug habit but not of whiskey. He'd sprinkle whiskey on his mustache to make others believe that his unusual behavior was due to the effects of alcohol, not drugs, she explained.

"Pretty cute, wasn't he?" said Barker. When Morse objected

strenuously to Barker's remark, the judge reprimanded the prosecutor and instructed the jury to disregard it.

Barker next produced the letter Jennie had written to Grace Howard in August 1909. Jennie had asked the young churchgoer to write a letter that confirmed the admiral had misbehaved in her presence and in the presence of other women. Howard, the jury knew, had identified Mrs. Eaton's letter during direct examination and had testified she refused to write any such thing about the admiral because he had always acted as a gentleman in her presence.

Jennie admitted authorship when the DA showed her the letter and stood by every word she had written.

If the allegations she had made about the admiral in the letter were true, Barker asked her, why did Howard deny them?

"I was surprised to hear her testimony. I think she's a nice girl and that she didn't want to get mixed up in this case. That's why, I think, she testified as she did," Jennie theorized.

Barker brought up the conversation she had with Bessie Collamore at Sand Hills that same summer. Collamore had testified that Jennie took her inside the Sand Hills cottage and privately asked her to testify in court that the admiral had flirted with her on numerous occasions. Listening to Collamore tell the story on the stand, Mrs. Eaton reflected, was thoroughly amusing.

The district attorney asked Jennie if she believed Collamore had misled the jury with her testimony. The defendant said she believed Collamore had and guessed she had done so because she was just as frightened as Howard.

Barker probed more deeply into the admiral's physical condition. He asked about the medicine prescribed by Colgate that she had administered secretly to the admiral.

"You considered that never since you married him could he have been a father?" the prosecutor asked.

"Yes. I think that was the secret of his actions."

"Did you at one time obtain some medicine from Dr. Colgate for the purpose of secretly treating him for his desires?"

"I got some medicine from him, but it was not for the purpose. It was to build him up," Jennie admitted.

Barker asked if the medicine she had obtained from Dr. Blanchard in Brookline was also for "treating him for his desires." Again the defendant denied it and said the medicine was "to keep [the admiral] from his mania and make him physically better."

The district attorney retrieved another letter from the prosecution table and presented it to Mrs. Eaton. She identified it as a letter she had typed on July 28, 1912, and sent to a neighbor, Mrs. Farrar. Barker showed it to defense counsel who, by their reaction, had obviously never seen it.

Nonetheless, Morse indicated that he had no objection to the letter, so Barker offered it as evidence and Judge Aiken had it so marked. Barker then spent five minutes reading the letter aloud. In it, Jennie had criticized Mrs. Farrar, her daughter, Mrs. Simmons, and other neighbors in Assinippi Village for their lack of kindness and understanding.

When he came to the end of the letter, which Jennie had neglected to sign, Barker asked her about the meaning of certain phrases she had used within its contents. One in particular referred to her belief that the admiral had a tumor in his head.

"You thought the admiral had one?" the district attorney asked her.

"Yes. I did," replied the defendant. But when she added, "The admiral told me so," Judge Aiken reminded her once again about hearsay statements and ordered her last comment stricken from the record.

At five o'clock, Aiken excused Jennie from the stand and adjourned. Barker was expected to finish his cross-examination in the morning, followed by rebuttal witnesses for the defense.

The prevailing sentiment among courtroom spectators was that Jennie Eaton had handled her cross-examination in a dignified, self-assured manner and that her unsolicited responses had not harmed her in any way. To that point, few among them believed jurors would convict her.

Newspapers quoted one veteran lawyer who, as a spectator, had listened to Jennie's testimony and who declared her an exceptional witness.

"She is the most wonderful witness I ever heard," the lawyer said. "I think Mrs. Eaton showed herself the intellectual equal of the district attorney at all times. She baffled him at every critical point. Voluble as she was, she rarely spoke to her own hurt, and she was so adroit that even in apparent innocence and ignorance she managed to get before the jury several times conversation between husband and wife with none other present – which is, of course, against the rules of law."

Chapter 29

Nearly everyone expected DA Barker to abandon the mild, considerate approach he had taken with Mrs. Eaton the previous day. He seemed baffled at times by the defendant's guileless responses to his direct questions. Much to the surprise of everyone in the overcrowded courtroom, however, he was as indulgent as he had been the day before.

Barker opened day fourteen of the trial by exploring the admiral's relationship with his stepdaughter, June. He asked Jennie if she had ever told anyone that the admiral didn't want June living in the Assinippi farmhouse. Jennie denied saying anything of the sort.

"I think he would have paid a large sum to have her live there," said Jennie. "He was very fond of her. He was always sorry June could not live at home."

"One of the great sorrows of his life, wasn't it?" asked Barker in another instance of sarcasm.

"I wouldn't use that expression to describe his feeling, but he was very sorry," said Jennie without a hint of protest at Barker's derision.

Barker turned to the testimony of real estate agent John Prouty, who had told the court that Mrs. Eaton had visited his home late one night, just after the adopted child had died, to agitate over the admiral's "insanity" and her belief that he had poisoned the baby.

Jennie disputed Prouty's testimony. She said she had arrived at his house at 10:30 p.m., not eleven o'clock as he had testified. She had just returned by train from Boston after visiting June and had stopped at Prouty's home, near Queen Anne's Corner, to ask him for a ride because she feared walking the darkened streets alone. As to Prouty's estimation of an hour-long conversation, Jennie said Prouty was mistaken. She also said she could not recall Prouty's advice to leave Weymouth and return to her home with the admiral.

Barker continued down the list of previous witnesses, asking about Charles Nordstrom, the private investigator. Jennie acknowledged meeting with Nordstrom and admitted that the only reason she had not hired him was because his fee was too high.

As for Annie Rooney, Jennie denied she had ever told the nurse that she wanted the admiral committed to an institution; that she had merely asked Rooney to observe the admiral's behavior. Jennie told the court Rooney's presence in the house was a waste of time because she never got out of bed until ten o'clock in the morning and she was a sick woman. Besides, Jennie said, the admiral made it a point to avoid the nurse.

"Did Miss Rooney tell you the admiral was all right when she left your home?" asked Barker.

"No, sir; she did not," replied the defendant. "She was only a companion to my mother and Dorothy. She hadn't observed the admiral talk and act to any great extent."

"How much did you pay Miss Rooney?"

"Twenty-five dollars a week."

"Do you make a distinction between a hospital and an insane asylum?" Barker inquired.

"Oh, yes," Jennie said. "I never wanted Admiral Eaton taken to an insane asylum. I think an asylum would be horrible."

The defendant next refuted the testimony of Harry Cate who had testified that Mrs. Eaton told him she wanted the admiral dead. Jennie said that Cate later divulged to her daughter Dorothy that he was intoxicated when he made the comment before the grand jury and was sorry he had said it. Cate couldn't very well go back on his testimony as a government witness at the trial, she said, when the prosecutor had his sworn grand jury statement in hand.

Barker introduced another letter and asked Jennie to identify it. She admitted she was the author and said she had written it on April 14, 1912, while she was with June in Washington. Addressed to Hannah Barnes, the Eaton housekeeper, the letter depicted Jennie as a loving, sympathetic mother.

...By the way, there is a very nice young boy who goes to school with [Dorothy], and as they are very fond of each other, I will ask you to let him stay Saturday nights till ten thirty and go to church with her Sunday. This may seem silly, as she is too young to have boy or men friends. But in a couple of years Dorothy's eyes will be opened, and she will find that few men will care to call on her or go with her, because

266

she is lame. You can understand how I am anxious for her to have one little romance to carry with her through life. Because of her affliction no one will want her. Of course, this may not be so; she is an attractive child. But I do want to make sure that she has this innocent, short-lived pleasure, so even if the admiral objects, tell him I wish it. Be good to her. I know you will. You know few men marry lame women nowadays, and it is her right to have this while it lasts.

Jennie also thanked Barnes for her help around the house and with Dorothy, asked for news of the admiral, and informed Barnes she was not certain when she would return to Assinippi. Barker sensed a well-disposed reaction to the letter from jurors and spectators. When Jennie revealed that Dorothy was still involved with her suitor, Barker moved on.

Barker turned to the testimony of Frank Booth, the deliveryman who had been present when the admiral stumbled in the Assinippi kitchen. When asked if she had ever told Booth that he had been fortunate when he had refused the admiral's offer of coffee, Jennie admitted she might have made the statement and added, "I still think he was lucky."

"What about that story that the admiral fell up against the stove in the kitchen?" Barker asked.

"Why, he was apparently in a semi-stupor that day. He fell up against the range and knocked the front of it off. I know he spoiled the nickel plating on the front by breaking it."

"Did you know the admiral had received an invitation to attend the opening of the Panama Canal and had planned to go?"

"I didn't know he had received an invitation," Jennie replied.

"You heard him say he was going, didn't you?"

"Yes, he said he was going to take me and we would both have a delightful trip."

Dr. Frame had testified about Mrs. Eaton's insistence that he mail medicines and prescriptions to her separate post office box rather than to the one she shared with the admiral. According to Frame, Mrs. Eaton had said she preferred this arrangement because she didn't want her medications coming into contact with the admiral.

When Barker asked her about the box, however, Jennie had an entirely different explanation. She told the court she got the box only because the admiral continually lost her mail and neighbors would find it along the road and bring it to her home.

Barker turned to the incident at the Rockland bakery where the admiral had allegedly flirted with one of the Coolidge twins. He asked Jennie for her version of the incident.

"The admiral went inside, and I stayed on the sidewalk. I saw him talk and smile. I don't know which young lady it was in back of the counter. Then I beckoned to him, and we just caught a car."

"Did you speak to him about the girl when you got on the car?" the prosecutor asked.

"I said he shouldn't start anything like that so near home," Jennie said.

"You didn't continue to talk about it at home or after you went to bed that night?"

"No, I did not."

"You went to see the bake shop girl later?"

"No. I went in to buy an angel cake, and I asked her if she knew of some nice, pretty, young girl to come and be a companion to Dorothy."

"You didn't say anything about a middle-aged lady and the admiral, as she (Maud Coolidge Powers) testified?" asked Barker.

"I did not," Jennie retorted.

"You are sure?"

"You heard what I told you just now," said the defendant, now defiant.

"Did you tell her he got on your nerves?"

"I may have said that," Jennie admitted.

"And that there ought to be something done?"

"I said something should be done for him; yes, sir. He always needed somebody with him."

Barker moved on to the week before the admiral died. He began with the day Jennie left for June's house in Medford.

"You started on Wednesday and went to the barn to say good-bye to the admiral?"

"Yes. I told him I would be back by six o'clock. I got to June's at twenty minutes of three. Ralph came in at half past six and June about seven thirty. We talked till ten and went to bed."

"The baby was there?"

"Yes."

"You had some talk about the admiral that night?"

"Not very much."

"You did talk about his peculiarities?" Barker pressed.

"I don't know as we did. June said if she hadn't known him so well she would have fallen in love with him," Jennie answered.

"And later you got to talking generally about poisons?"

"No, I don't think we did particularly. We talked about clothing and the house and things I wanted June to do."

"Did you mention the dying off of men on the ship?"

"No, sir," Jennie said emphatically and in direct contradiction of Ralph Keyes's testimony.

"Did you talk about the admiral's having asked her to go abroad?"

"Yes," replied the defendant, and she repeated the conversation June said she had with the admiral. Jennie added that June had told her she had seen tears running down the admiral's face as he asked her to accompany him on the trip.

"That was when I said, 'I guess I had better go home and take care of him.' "

"Was the admiral ill when you reached home?"

"Yes, he vomited. My mother said he had an awful attack while I was at June's."

"What was the rest of the conversation you had at June's?" Barker asked. Morse immediately objected, stating the witness had already answered the question. The judge overruled the objection, and Barker continued.

"Didn't June say, 'The admiral wanted to know if I wanted my mother put out of the way,' and didn't that idea excite you?"

"No," Jennie replied. "I knew it was idle talk of a brain under the influence of a drug."

Morse objected when Barker began another question. Barker's temper flared. "I don't know why you should interrupt me at such a crucial point," he snapped at Morse.

"I am here to protect the interests of my client, and I ask the court to rule on that," Morse replied. Again, Aiken overruled defense counsel, and Barker resumed.

He turned to Jennie's direct testimony about having had "chicken

269

soup" for dinner on the Thursday evening before the admiral's death.

"Do you remember having cold roast pork for supper that night?"

"No, I do not."

"Do you remember having tea or cereal or coffee?" Barker asked.

"No, I do not," the defendant replied again. Suddenly, her tendency to elaborate whenever she answered a question had vanished.

"Your mother testified that you did," Barker stated rather than asked.

"She did not testify anything of the sort," Morse quickly interjected.

(Mrs. Harrison testified that she noticed the admiral had first become ill after eating pork on Wednesday night and became ill again at about six or seven o'clock on Thursday evening after eating more pork that afternoon.)

Barker ignored the defense attorney, and Jennie responded, "My mother could not have known because she was in the library."

Barker left it for jurors to decide whether Jennie was telling the truth. He had already established through several witnesses that the admiral had, in fact, consumed pork on Thursday night.

Barker asked if the admiral customarily drank three or four cups of tea every night. Jennie denied it and said he would have needed a nurse in the morning if he drank that much tea.

The prosecutor came to the events of Thursday night, March 6, and asked the defendant if she had taken care of the admiral that evening. She vehemently denied she had done so. She said she had gotten up early on Friday morning and had tended to the admiral all day.

"I kept six bottles of hot water on him all day. I got fresh eggs from the nest and cream and made some toast. I took it up to him."

"Did he swallow it?" Barker inquired.

"He couldn't take a thing," came the reply.

"Did you give him whiskey?"

"No, I didn't have any. What was the use anyway? He couldn't take a thing. I just kept him warm and let in the fresh air."

"And Dr. Frame came?"

"Yes."

"He left some tablets?"

"Yes."

"Did he keep them down?"

270

"No, they never got down. He threw them up before they were completely swallowed. He couldn't even keep down water. It distressed him to sit up in bed."

Jennie admitted she had tried to give the admiral two pills, but she denied giving him a cup of tea. When asked if she had given the admiral saleratus, Jennie said she put a pinch of soda in water and tried to give it to him, but he couldn't ingest it.

"How often did he vomit?" asked the prosecutor.

"About every hour," Jennie responded.

"You told Scott he did not get up?"

"As I go over it in my own mind, I think perhaps he got up on Friday afternoon – perhaps to go to the bathroom."

"You and Dorothy talked to the admiral Friday night?"

"Yes, I fixed him all up and told Dorothy to go to bed."

"Weren't you in bed when she came up?"

"I was not. I sent her to bed."

"You are sure?"

"I am positive."

"Do you remember telling her to get upstairs, you would give her fifteen minutes to get her lessons?"

"I don't recall that."

"She came up at five minutes past eight?"

"I don't recall the time."

"You both went to bed?"

"Yes, and went to sleep."

"And the next thing you recall was when he called at ten minutes after two?"

"Yes. I went in and he was semiconscious on the floor, leaning against the bed."

"When the admiral was dying, didn't he say, 'Get the doctor, get the doctor,' and you said, 'The doctor is coming in the morning'?"

"No, he didn't say that. He said, 'Doctor, doctor.'"

"When did all that happen?" Barker asked.

"Friday night when he fell out of bed," the defendant replied.

"Who else was there in the room?"

"Dorothy."

"Didn't you tell the admiral that you would get the doctor in the morning?"

"I don't recall saying that."

"How long was Dorothy in there?"

"Just a little while."

"And did she go back to bed?"

"Yes."

"After you put him back into bed, didn't he call for you shortly after?"

"Yes. I went in. I told Dorothy I would stay in there the rest of the night. I told Dorothy to stay in her bed."

"What did you do when you went into his room?"

"I got into bed with him. He was feeling very cold. I soon went to sleep."

"And you woke up about daylight and found him all cold?"

"Yes, it was about four o'clock."

"What woke you up?"

"I was cold. The coldness of his body aroused me."

"What did you do?"

"I couldn't realize the admiral was dead. I shook him. I tried to arouse him. I jumped out of bed and told Dorothy I feared he was dead."

"Getting back to the Thursday night before the admiral died, didn't you tell Dorothy to go to bed early as the admiral wasn't able to help her on her algebra?"

"I don't remember saying that. I know the admiral wasn't able to help on her algebra, but I don't recall sending Dorothy to bed."

"Are you sure you didn't send Dorothy to bed?"

"I don't admit it."

The district attorney persisted with great effort to pry details from Jennie about her actions at the death scene. He did his utmost to ensnare her in a contradiction, but he could not.

Barker wrapped up his cross-examination with questions about the unfinished, typewritten will found by Detective Scott, which Jennie denied as her work; with a review of her visit to Chicago in 1911 to visit June; with an explanation of the admiral's debts before they left Brookline; and with a question about her statement to Dr. Osgood about not knowing anything about poisons.

At 12:08 p.m., after Morse asked her a few clarifying questions, Jennie stepped down from the witness stand.

The defense called Dr. A. Everett Austin immediately after Jennie took her seat. After establishing the physician's credentials, Morse asked him if he had formed an opinion as to when the admiral had received the first dose of poison. In direct contradiction to the Commonwealth's medical experts, Austin stated that the first dose was taken immediately after the midday meal on the Wednesday preceding the admiral's death. The physician was also of the opinion that the admiral had taken the poison in one large dose as opposed to the smaller doses suggested by Drs. Whitney and Balch. He added that an ingestion of fifteen grains of arsenic would, as a rule, bring about death within twenty-four to thirty hours.

When Morse indicated he had no further questions for Austin, Judge Aiken recessed for lunch. Austin returned to the witness stand when court resumed, and DA Barker began his cross-examination.

The prosecutor compelled Austin to agree that the testimony of government experts was consistent with the possibility that a small, initial dose of poison was taken Thursday during dinner and that several other small doses were ingested between then and the time of the admiral's death. Barker did not remind jurors that both Dr. Whitney and Dr. Balch had conceded during their testimonies that it was possible the admiral had ingested one large dose as opposed to smaller doses over a period of time. Austin also concurred that bromide of arsenic, as sold to Admiral Eaton by Dr. Brown, would not appear as white arsenic in the stomach.

Conflicting testimony from medical experts left jurors in a quandary. What bearing this conflict would have on the outcome of the trial was a matter of conjecture for both the prosecution and the defense.

Barker quickly concluded his examination of Austin. Morse asked Barker if he intended to present Whitney and Balch as rebuttal witnesses. When Barker replied in the negative, Morse thanked Austin for his testimony and released him. Morse then declared that the defense rested its case.

The district attorney called his first rebuttal witness, Dr. Thomas F. Carroll of Norwood. Carroll was one of the physicians who scrutinized

Mrs. Eaton's words and actions while she testified. Carroll was a practicing physician at the Boston Medical Dispensary and a graduate of the College of the Holy Cross and Harvard Medical School.

Barker intended to raise questions about Admiral Eaton's syphilis. He believed Carroll would refute Dr. Fremont-Smith's testimony by testifying about overt symptoms displayed by the typical syphilitic person, about underlying symptoms, and the condition of the brain, which Osgood had found to be slightly swollen during the autopsy. Barker further wanted to demonstrate that if he was, indeed, insane, Admiral Eaton would have begun to show symptoms a short time after his second bout with syphilis in 1880.

Carroll testified that he had seen as many as thirty thousand cases of syphilis during the previous four years. He stated that insanity, usually in the form of dementia and paralysis, would develop in a syphilitic patient in the third phase of the disease. He described the physical and mental symptoms of the disease and added that these symptoms were "usually obvious to the ordinary observer."

"What is the longest period in which insanity has been known to develop?" Barker asked.

"Eighteen years," Carroll answered.

"In an autopsy, does the brain of such a patient who has developed insanity usually show any side effects?"

"Yes, lesions – a thickening of connecting tissue, or a softening and breaking down of the tissue."

Morse asked Carroll on cross-examination if a person could contract an infection more than once. Carroll said a second infection was not possible and, if symptoms reappeared, they were a result of the first infection.

"Have you observed that people who have suffered from this disease, and have a recurrence of symptoms, are more easily affected by alcohol?" Morse inquired.

"Yes. Alcohol has a very strong effect upon them. The use of alcohol steadily in such persons would bring on insanity in four or five years," the physician acknowledged.

The district attorney next called Dr. Harry Cleverly of Scituate to the stand. Cleverly was the attending physician for the Eatons' adopted child in August 1909. His testimony contrasted sharply with several points made by Mrs. Eaton during direct examination.

Cleverly related how the admiral and Mrs. Eaton had come to his office with the infant in the afternoon. Mrs. Eaton had testified that she and the admiral left for Cleverly's office almost immediately after the child took sick.

Barker asked the physician to tell the jury what happened when they arrived. Cleverly related that Mrs. Eaton said to him, "Doctor, I'd like to have you see the baby." It didn't take him long to realize how seriously ill the infant was. He told the couple the child had cholera infantum and would not survive another two hours. He wrote a prescription to ease the symptoms and advised them to take the child directly home.

In an effort to controvert Mrs. Eaton's assertion that she had rushed to the doctor's office as soon as she had found the baby sick, Barker asked Cleverly about the visits June had made to his office before Admiral and Mrs. Eaton arrived.

"Had you talked with her daughter June prior to her coming to your office with the baby?" Barker asked.

"Yes, about an hour and a half before," the doctor replied.

"Was this conversation connected with the child?"

"Yes."

"You saw June again before you saw Mrs. Eaton?"

"Yes, about fifteen minutes before."

"What was the purpose of the first visit?"

"She told me of the illness of the child and I gave her some medicine. On her second visit, she said she had broken the bottle and wanted more."

"Was Mrs. Eaton wearing a bathing suit when she came to your office?"

"No, she had on a dress and a hat."

"Did she appear as if she had ran all the way from her home to your office?"

"No."

Jennie had testified that the admiral had taken the prescription given them by Cleverly to the drugstore and that he had smelled of liquor when he returned. She had also stated that she offered the doctor $1,000 to save the baby's life. Cleverly contended that the admiral never left his office during the visit and never appeared to be under the influence of liquor or a drug. He refuted Mrs. Eaton's assertion that she had offered him $1,000 to cure the baby.

Morse had no questions for Cleverly.

Barker called Charles R. Henry, a Hanover blacksmith, to bolster the prosecution's assertion that the admiral first became sick on Thursday night, not Wednesday, as argued by the defense.

Henry was sworn and testified he had first met the Eaton family six years before. He said he had gone to the Eaton farm around 9:00 a.m. on the Wednesday before the admiral died to unload some hay from the barn and had left about 11:45 a.m.

"Was the admiral present?" Barker inquired.

"Yes, but he didn't do much work," said Henry. "He sat on a box and smoked his pipe most of the time. He appeared to be in the best of spirits and was all right as far as I could see."

"Did you see him vomit while you were there?"

"No."

On cross-examination, Morse asked Henry if he had seen Mrs. Eaton on the day he visited. Henry confirmed that he had and said Mrs. Eaton came out of the house and told her husband she was leaving for Boston. When asked by Morse if he remembered any other particulars about that day, Henry said a comment the admiral had made stood out in his mind. "What a lovely woman she is," said the admiral as Jennie walked away from the house.

ADA Katzmann questioned the prosecution's last two witnesses. Minnie Smith and Luella Fairbanks, Eaton neighbors, testified that they had attended the church social at the Eaton home on the Tuesday night before the admiral's death. Both contended that the admiral never left the room where the party was held. Mrs. Eaton had earlier testified that the admiral had vomited once or twice during the party.

Morse, on cross-examination, succeeded in getting both women to admit that the admiral had left the room for a few minutes on one occasion. They conceded they did not know what he was doing when he was absent.

At 3:40 p.m., his evidence all in, District Attorney Barker rested his case. Judge Aiken instructed the prosecution and defense to be ready to deliver closing arguments the following day and quickly adjourned.

Chapter 30

Deputy Sheriff Collingwood escorted Jennie to her seat behind defense counsel just before nine o'clock on Wednesday, October 29. She had a placid expression as she strode, head held high, across the courtroom. Her attorneys briefly engaged her in conversation as the court waited for Judge Aiken's arrival.

Sheriff Porter and his deputies were busy with spectators and newsmen trying to gain access to the courtroom. Much to the dismay of the press, photographers were still excluded from the courtroom because of an order Aiken had issued when the trial started.

The courtroom audience was overwhelmingly women, many of whom had attended the trial every day. The women's suffrage movement was in full swing. A protest held in Washington, DC, the day before Woodrow Wilson was inaugurated as president in 1913 had drawn a crowd of eight thousand women. As a sign of solidarity and support, a loyal group of women had rallied around Mrs. Eaton since the day of her arrest.

Today's group included a celebrity. Lotta Crabtree, a sixty-five-year-old retired entertainer and one of the country's highest paid actresses in the 1880s, arrived by train from Boston's Brewster Hotel at 8:00 a.m. She remained for the entire day, listening attentively and occasionally using opera glasses to scan the courtroom.

Thanks to the efforts of several major newspapers, including *The Boston Daily Globe*, the *Boston Traveler and Evening Herald*, the *Boston Evening Transcript*, the *Boston American*, the *Boston Journal*, and the *Boston Post*, readers enjoyed descriptive accounts of the proceedings in next-day editions. The *Globe*'s Frank Sibley, an astute, veteran reporter, and Charles Parker, a cub reporter from the *Post*, were especially deliberate as they recorded, verbatim, the closing arguments of Attorney William Morse and District Attorney Albert Barker as well as Judge Aiken's charge to the jury.

The *Traveler*'s Solita Solano, a fearless, outspoken woman, who on occasion marshaled suffragist parades in Boston, provided a feminist's perspective on the trial as did the *American*'s Angela Morgan, who was later celebrated for her prolific writing and poetry. Both shared the intimate details of their exclusive interviews with Mrs. Eaton.

The judge and jury entered the courtroom at nine o'clock. Judge Aiken asked Morse if he was prepared to present his closing argument.

"I am, your honor," Morse said in a serious tone as he rose from his chair. He walked to the end of the clerk's desk and leaned against it with his hands in his pockets. Everyone in the packed courtroom focused on him with rapt attention.

Facing the jury, Morse removed his hands from his pockets and began speaking in a quiet, dignified manner.

"Mr. Foreman and gentlemen of the jury, I feel it is an imposition after the strain you have undergone to weary you with any arguments. Since we have met, weeks have gone. I believe that after you have heard all this case, this brave, patient woman, who for several long months has awaited this hour, is going home with us.

"This has been a most remarkable trial, and I cannot with any language portray the awful situation in which this woman has been placed. She is taken from her home, from the midst of her loved ones, and put on trial for her life.

"Was there ever anything like it in human annals? She came here and said, 'I am not guilty. You charge me with an atrocious crime.' And day after day she has had to sit here and listen to accusations.

"She has sat here calmly awaiting her fate. When my colleague, who will render service to this county in years to come because of his ability, arose and said, 'Her life is in your hands,' he made no light statement. It is a fact. Never before have you had such an awful responsibility as is now on your shoulders. You must decide this woman's fate."

Morse diverted briefly to thank Sheriff Porter and his staff for their treatment of Mrs. Eaton while she was in their custody. He then returned to his summation.

"She stands before you charged with an awful crime. The law presumes she is innocent. I want you to look on her and take this case as the law lays it down. She is innocent until the government proves her guilty.

"In great cases like this one, which has attained great notoriety throughout the country, we are sometimes influenced by opinions and sympathies, but the law is not. The law is stern and unyielding, but it is just, and she has the protection of the law.

"The rights of an innocent person are very sacred. This woman is charged with murder in the first degree. It is the most horrible crime. It means willful, deliberate, malicious murder. The government says you must establish beyond a reasonable doubt that she committed the crime before you can convict her. Reasonable doubt means beyond a moral certainty. I hope to establish to you there isn't a fact to prove it.

"She repudiates herself the contention of the government that she isn't mentally responsible. I submit, gentleman, she is a wonderful woman. She wasn't obliged to testify. She had the right to remain silent and make the government prove its case. But this woman, confident of her innocence, said, 'I'll meet my accusers. I will go on the witness stand. Let the jury judge by my words whether I am crazy or not; whether I killed my husband or not.'

"I know you respect her courage. It was the most extraordinary scene that ever happened in a courtroom. I hope there will come a time when the words that pass between husband and wife may become known.

"The story of her life has been that of self-sacrifice. She has fought on in the face of reverses until she could do no more. If you have ever seen an unselfish life, a life like that of a martyred saint, you have seen it in this woman. She is a wonderful woman, a woman of generosity, a woman who has no mean and small traits.

"This woman's life since the day she was born has been searched. They have searched her record, looked into everything she said, and yet she stands before you a woman of a spotless character. Picture her at seventeen, this young girl, happy in helping her mother. Then she married young Ainsworth, and thereafter followed her the curse of drink – alcohol, the curse of the world.

"Mr. Foreman, I want you to appreciate this, that Mrs. Eaton has always given herself and her best efforts to the child who needed her most. She carried little, lame Dorothy day after day to the hospital in St. Louis. She earned money for her and cared for her tenderly. Not June, but Dorothy, had her loving care."

Morse now abandoned the even, reserved tone he had thus far

employed. His voice rose as he spoke of the defendant's troubled first marriage and her attempts to separate herself from the drunken Ainsworth and pursue a nursing career. Then he proceeded with his renunciation of Admiral Eaton's character.

"She wanted to enter a hospital and devote her life to nursing the sick. But she was a victim of circumstances. She, through this decision, met that man who is responsible for her being where she is today. He was vile, corrupt, impure, rotten."

Morse paused for effect, his words hanging in the air. Aiken called for a brief recess. Morse resumed his summation ten minutes later.

"Now you have heard her story of struggle before she met Rear Admiral Eaton. She had made good in her new profession. And she was sent to the home of the admiral. You heard Dr. Fremont-Smith tell you how his attention was first attracted by the admiral's behavior in a company of distinguished scientists and that he inquired who the admiral was. Without cause Admiral Eaton continually laughed long and immoderately that evening. Later, Dr. Fremont-Smith went to the Eaton home to attend the sick wife there. You have heard him tell you of the admiral's condition. He did not accompany his wife's body to its burial place. He lay in an upper chamber in a drunken stupor.

"He was a sensualist, a drug eater. If he had let her alone, she would have gone through life without this awful trial.

"Whenever you see a woman who wants her mother with her, who finds her comfort and happiness with her mother, there you will find a virtuous and upright woman. When Mrs. Eaton went to another nursing place after the admiral's first wife had died, this man, the great admiral, followed her there and would not let her alone. He made her leave and talked marriage to her. She talked it over with her mother.

"I am not going to say, gentlemen, that she fell dead in love with the admiral. But she liked and admired him for the interesting man he could be when he was sober. You know after hearing those parts of his letters that had to be read in a hushed voice to you that only on the exterior was he a polished gentleman. Underneath, his mind was vile and sensual.

"He borrowed money on his life insurance. He didn't pay his personal debts. He gambled and lost in stocks the money he received from the estate of his first wife."

Morse pointed out to the jurors that all of the time testimony was being presented about the loss of this money, Admiral Eaton's stockbroker was present in the courtroom, but the government never called him as a witness, leading one to wonder if his testimony would be damaging to the government.

"Mr. Foreman and gentlemen, Admiral Eaton was up to his eyes in debt. This woman did everything honorable to help him out, to put him on his feet financially, and to build up his physical health. The evidence shows no sane woman could have murdered Admiral Eaton, and you couldn't convict a sane woman on the evidence given here.

"This woman has been examined, re-examined here. Before this she has been through enough tortures, trials, and hardships to wreck an ordinary mortal.

"I don't care what they say about June Keyes. Thank God there was that in her which wouldn't let her submit to the foul embraces of her mother's husband. Look at little Dorothy. Hour after hour she was questioned before the grand jury and in this court to help send her mother to an awful doom. The poor, little girl didn't know what she was falling into.

"A man who could write such letters to his wife as Admiral Eaton did is capable of an infamy that fits this case. He is capable of any act.

"Mrs. Eaton mistrusted him while he was drunk. She knew he would be capable of anything. Isn't he to be condemned for the unhappy agitation of this woman's brain? He spoke to her frequently of subtle drugs, of intoxication, of oriental customs and of his adventures in foreign ports.

"This woman will live in my memory as one of the most unselfish women I have ever known… What is her reward? She even went so far as to adopt a baby to help brace him up.

"She was willing to bring a nameless babe out of a foundling hospital to bear her husband's name and share her husband's fate. Could anything more sacrificing be done? This woman loved this baby boy. She loves children.

"What is the character of the poisoner throughout the world? It's the person who is dark, sly, secret, the person who never allows the word 'poison' to cross his lips. The way of the poisoner is secretive.

"We have had a lot of letters. She often speaks of poison in them. In seven long years in Assinippi, this woman has written only five letters. Three of them were written to one man. What was there so terrible in them?

"All this correspondence, every bit of it circles around the death of her baby. She never wrote a letter accusing her husband until her baby died under circumstances that aroused her suspicions. Is it remarkable that in seven long years' association with one man she should write five letters about him? Three of them went to her physician.

"There isn't any doubt but that Mrs. Eaton wanted a home for her mother and children. And so she married him. The admiral, too, wanted the home he knew they could make for him. He had no one, no relative of his has come forward."

Morse donned his glasses and went to the evidence table where he picked up the letter the admiral had written to Mrs. Montgomery Sears. This was the same letter he had introduced and read aloud during Mrs. Eaton's direct examination. He recited it as an example of the admiral's ingratitude and sense of entitlement.

"I'm very glad that Mrs. Eaton didn't write a letter like that," he said, tossing the document on the table.

"The day the admiral brought in thirty thousand dollars in Brookline and put it in his wife's lap, she was troubled. She did not know where he had got it. He had no money when they went to Brookline. In all the sixty years of his life, he never had more than five hundred dollars at one time.

"You couldn't help believing until this defense opened that she was uttering vile and incoherent statements. You thought it absurd that Admiral Eaton was anything other than the perfect, cultured, polished gentleman. But you later heard his brother naval officers, headed by Admiral Clark, tell stories that corroborated her stories about his drinking and his other habits. They had seen him with their own eyes."

District Attorney Barker and his assistants listened intently as Morse addressed the jury. From time to time they jotted notes on their pads.

Morse returned to the evidence table and picked up several letters. Among them were those the admiral had written to his wife while she was living with June in Weymouth after Joseph Jr.'s death. He read aloud from two, both of which he had introduced during Mrs. Eaton's previous testimony.

He rejected the testimonies of several women who alleged that Mrs. Eaton had expressed fear that the admiral would poison her.

"As I listened to their testimony, it almost seemed to me as if we were back in the days of Salem witchcraft. They drew on their imaginations. They came to conclusions from expressions on her face."

Morse touched on the testimony of Bessie Bursey, the woman who had lodged June and her mother in Washington during June's pregnancy. He denounced the government for making a case based on allegations, rather than facts, to establish the defendant's motive.

"It is a wicked accusation, founded without a fact," Morse said, "that this woman had a rich lover in Chicago who owned blocks and blocks of houses that she sometime hoped to own. They obtained that story from one woman who, before she had been seen by anybody relative to this case, wrote to Mrs. Eaton, 'The whole world may not believe in you, but I do. You always spoke so loving about your husband.' "

Jennie dabbed her cheeks with a handkerchief as tears welled up in her eyes and coursed down her cheeks. She struggled to maintain her composure as she removed her glasses and dried the moistened lenses.

"The prosecution has offered you no definite motive. It has tried to offer several and let you take your choice. This woman has never accused Admiral Eaton of anything more serious in his relations to people outside their household than flirting. And on that alone the government asks you to believe she was jealous.

"Is there a word of impropriety, is there a word of suspicion offered by the government about Mrs. Eaton's conduct while she was in Chicago? Mrs. Eaton went there because she wanted to see the man June was going to marry. The government, with plenty of money and detectives, aided by the Chicago police, traced her movements all over Chicago, yet nothing was found against her. That's the answer to the lover in Chicago."

Morse praised Jennie's actions for sending her unmarried, pregnant daughter to Washington in 1912. It was out of a growing concern for June, her baby, and the Eaton family name that she had made every effort to prevent what was sure to become a scandal in Assinippi, the attorney contended.

"Is there anything in this Washington thing, Mr. Foreman, that you think you can use in convicting this woman of murder in the first degree?" Morse asked.

"This woman in all her life," he continued, "has never spoken a single, unkind word to Admiral Eaton, and furthermore, Admiral Eaton never spoke a harsh word to her. The last word anybody heard him say about her was, 'There goes a lovely woman.' That was spoken on the Wednesday before his death, as she was leaving home to visit June.

"What was Admiral Eaton's record before he married this woman? Admiral Clark refused to endorse him for a position he sought. Admiral Clark went further and threatened he would expose Admiral Eaton's drinking habits if he tried further to get the position. And he had been taking drugs – he took drugs down to the last days of his life."

Judge Aiken once more called for a brief recess before Morse continued his summation.

"I said when I first opened the argument that it was a shame to weary you with all this when you have been shut up for so long. I come now to the final chapter in this case.

"You have heard me say that this woman's heart is as unselfish as a woman's heart can be. I ask you to take it from other lips. You have heard witnesses say that the admiral's mind was sound and he was always a perfect gentleman," Morse said as he moved again toward the evidence table and picked up yet another letter.

"Assuming that, here is his tribute in this letter he wrote when the government said she left him in anger. 'I was so glad to get your loving letter. I wince sometimes under the thought others may think you are of no account because you administer to my wants. I want my queenly wife to come into her own someday.'

"He had lived then with her for seven years. He knew her life and her struggles. Sorrow may have made her unduly suspicious. She may have exaggerated things sometimes. But she never forgot her duty to the admiral.

"I am not obliged to give you any theory of this case," Morse declared. "It is up to the government to prove it – and they can't prove it. Every drugstore in the land has been searched, under different names, and nothing found, because there was never a drop of poison in this woman's hands. I can't give you a theory; I wish I could.

"I have sometimes thought there was a touch of despondency in him. You can almost see it in his letters to Mr. Brooks and Mrs. Sears. I don't argue that he committed suicide. It would be only a guess, and you can't guess or speculate with this woman's life! The motives! Murder has a motive, and it is a strong motive."

Morse turned to the events of Wednesday, March 5, and Jennie's statement to Ralph and June Keyes about her plans to go home the next morning and "look after" the admiral. Keyes had misinterpreted the true meaning of Mrs. Eaton's intentions, Morse declared. Mrs. Eaton's only purpose was to return home and do what she had so devotedly done during all the years she had been married to the admiral – attend to his needs.

He summarized Jennie's testimony about the events leading up to the admiral's death.

"The strongest proof of this woman's innocence," maintained Morse, "is that in all her story there are no inconsistencies."

He recalled the statements of witnesses who testified that Mrs. Eaton had shown no signs of grief at the loss of her husband. He spoke of her strength and composure on the witness stand. He challenged anyone to brand her demeanor as anything less than genuine.

"If she had wept copiously, then they would have called it acting," Morse said. "But you and I saw last Saturday that she can't act."

Pausing one last time before the jury, Morse slowly turned and took his place at the defense table beside Geogan, who whispered his congratulations. When he turned to Jennie, she smiled and nodded appreciatively.

Morse concluded his summation at one o'clock. Except for two brief recesses, he had spoken for four hours. Morse's performance met with immediate approval from spectators.

Frank Sibley of *The Boston Daily Globe* later described it as "constructed with the art which conceals art. Its very quietness marked its power." Morse had "managed to leave with the jurors little maxims which they must have carried vivid in their memories into the jury room…"

Judge Aiken called for a lunch recess, and the jurors filed out. Several women wept quietly in the gallery, moved by the eloquence of Morse's presentation.

District Attorney Barker and his assistants, Katzmann and Adams, retreated to Barker's office on the second floor where they discussed the defense summation, identified several conflicts and discrepancies, and prepared an appropriate rebuttal.

The three government lawyers had methodically constructed a closing argument as the trial progressed. After a final review, they were satisfied it captured the key testimonies, crucial evidence, and all of the points made by ADA Katzmann during his opening statement. They were confident that its logic and reasoning would persuade jurors to return a verdict in the government's favor.

Chapter 31

DA Barker remained standing when the court was called to order, picked up his notes, and walked to the front of the jury box. He greeted the jurors and thanked them for their attentiveness during the trial.

"Mr. Morse appealed to your sympathy, but it is my duty to deal with the cold facts," he began. "It has been my sworn duty to ferret out these facts, and to present them to you. Your duty will be performed when you bring in your verdict in accordance with the facts."

The district attorney first moved to assuage any real or perceived antipathy jurors held against the government for placing Mrs. Eaton's youngest daughter, Dorothy, on the stand as a witness against her own mother. That was an issue that he, Katzmann, and Adams had discussed at length before and after Dorothy had taken the stand. They realized it was risky to make her a government witness, but her testimony was vital to establish both motive and opportunity.

"I have never been as torn as I had been by being compelled to set mother and daughter against each other," Barker told the jury, his voice trembling. "I hope that I shall never be compelled to do such a thing again, but if I am, I will do so, as I consider it my sworn duty."

He made no mention of his failure to place the defendant's other daughter on the stand. As he and his assistants had prepared for trial, they had discussed June Keyes's potential as a witness. After long and careful consideration, they had decided not to call her. Since the first day of investigation, it had become increasingly apparent to Barker that June was the root of the tensions between the admiral and his wife. June detested the admiral and adored her mother. Any testimony she had to offer could be prejudicial and have an adverse influence on the government's case.

Before he continued with his main points, Barker commended Assistant District Attorney Katzmann for the expertise with which he had delivered the government's opening statement.

Barker next drew attention to Morse's assertion that the Commonwealth was asking the jury to consider an option: guilty or not guilty by reason of insanity.

"If we fail to convince you that she committed the act, acquit her; don't stop half way," Barker charged. "The Commonwealth isn't looking for glory in convictions. All it wants is the facts.

"The first question," he next said, "is whether she did the act; but entering into that is her state of mind toward her husband and whether she entertained delusions concerning him. For if you can find the state of mind of a person, his innermost thoughts, we have the clue to his actions.

"I am going to give you six propositions. The first is: Did Admiral Eaton die a natural death? And remember that all the physicians said that every organ was normal, and that Dr. Whitney found in his stomach eleven and one-half grains of undissolved white arsenic. There is only one conclusion possible – that he did not die a natural death, but from arsenical poisoning."

He next questioned Morse's attempt to confuse the matter of how, when, and where the poison was ingested. "It is the very heart of the government's case, and he did not dare to mention the testimony of his own expert," Barker pronounced in support of his second proposition.

He addressed the element of opportunity. There were only four people in the Assinippi house when the admiral fell ill – Mrs. Harrison, Dorothy Ainsworth, the defendant, and the admiral himself.

"Did Dorothy do it?" he asked. "We come next to the mother. You saw her on the stand. I had to draw from her and from Dorothy what I could of the facts. And when you are questioning those nearest in blood, you get only a small part of the facts."

He asked jurors to recall Mrs. Harrison's affection for the admiral when she stated, "He was as good as gold."

"Did she kill him?" he asked. "No. I throw this in the face of the accusation that he was everything damnable. This is when she knew her own daughter had charged him with insanity, with indecency. No, she didn't do it. That leaves us two."

In his fifth proposition, Barker attacked the defense's insinuation that Admiral Eaton had committed suicide. "Admiral Eaton loved his wife," he said. "He knew many of her failings. He knew she thought he wasn't right; he knew she fed him medicine. He was sixty-six years old, in a pleasant home, with a future provided for."

He reviewed testimony showing that the admiral, on the Tuesday night before he died, had offered to buy ice cream for the party the following week. "Was he intending to die? Did he think he'd die?" demanded the prosecutor.

He asked the jurors to recall how witnesses had testified that the admiral was cheerful and healthy on Wednesday morning – not miserable and nauseous as the defense had alleged. On Thursday, the admiral wrote a letter to his nephew asking him to sell some books. On the same day he offered to help a neighbor with his chores. On Thursday night, Barker continued, the admiral was at the dinner table, laughing and telling stories.

"Was he figuring to die? Was he knowingly taking, chewing arsenic as he sat there? Did this man excruciate himself with arsenic if he knew of the existence and use of a poison so subtle that the expert of Harvard couldn't find it?" Barker paused, his hands clasped behind his back, looking at each and every juror.

"You remember when Dorothy went in on Friday night, and he inquired into her school marks, and he asked also, 'How did you feel when you had a bilious turn?' That tells the story. He was suffering in a different way from what he ever suffered before, and he wanted to know what it was.

"We now have excluded every proposition but one, and we hate to approach that one. But it is a thing that has gone on from the beginning of the world. Poison has always been a woman's weapon. And so we come to the sixth proposition – did the defendant administer the arsenic to him?"

The district attorney discussed Mrs. Eaton's first meeting with the admiral and the events surrounding his first wife's death. He vilified Dr. Fremont-Smith and scoffed at his testimony, suggesting the physician had ulterior motives when he appeared on behalf of the defense.

"If you could go underneath the surface, you'd find there was some reason why Dr. Smith came here," the prosecutor said without offering one.

Barker assailed the defendant's testimony about her care for the admiral and their subsequent marriage.

"Could she learn to love a man in that condition in a few weeks? If she couldn't, there was just one explanation. She thought he had money. Could there be any other reason?" he demanded.

A touch of sarcasm in his voice, the district attorney mocked the actions of Mrs. Eaton who "divorced one sot in May in order to marry another worse sot in July." He brought up the summer rental in Hull and the Brookline residence and asked how the admiral could have afforded the expense of both if, as Mrs. Eaton had testified, he was deeply in debt.

"Did he have money or didn't he have money?" Barker posed. "We have her own story that he brought thirty thousand dollars in cash and threw it into her lap. She says he was a child in her hands, but she never knew where he got that thirty thousand dollars. Why didn't she pay some of that mountain of debt that was worrying her so? Ah, gentlemen, there's the trick, there's the turn. They went to Assinippi because the family was losing its money."

The prosecutor addressed Morse's allegation that the government had never called a Boston stockbroker who was present at trial to explain the circumstances surrounding the admiral's investments and losses. Barker countered that if there was a stockbroker in court, he was not aware of it. If there was a stockbroker at all, he added, the defense would likely have summoned him.

Barker defended the admiral's reputation and character. Each and every prosecution witness, when asked for his or her impression of the admiral, had depicted him as a gentleman. Not one testified that the admiral had shown, at any time, signs of inebriation or drug impairment.

"And I stand here to resent the defaming of a dead man," he added. "Nobody, except the defendant, furthermore, has ever put a drug into the admiral's mouth."

The prosecutor admonished the defense for purposely neglecting to ask Judge Kelley's opinion of the admiral's stability.

"They didn't dare to ask the man who's really defending the defendant the thing they most wanted to prove – that the admiral was of unsound mind," said Barker. "He (Judge Kelley) tried to get her (Mrs. Eaton) into the hands of experts long ago in order that they might take care of her. My heart goes out to the woman in pity."

Turning to Dr. Cleverly's testimony and the story of the adopted baby's death, the district attorney asked jurors how they could possibly consider Mrs. Eaton's version of events which he termed "a deliberate lie" or "the manifestation of an unbalanced mind."

"Is it a hallucination, or is it malicious? You alone are to be the judges," said Barker. "The baby didn't start the insanity cry by any means. You remember Dr. Colgate? Nothing was said to him about drugs. She went to him and said the admiral should be committed, and she said just what the Commonwealth has claimed, sane or insane, but she got the impression that Dr. Colgate thought that she was a young wife who wanted to get rid of an old husband."

Mrs. Eaton's accusations against the admiral for poisoning the baby were either "unspeakably malicious" or "hallucination." It made no sense to him, he told the jury, that she would accuse the man she loved of killing the baby both of them adored. "Was it venom, or was it here?" he asked as he touched his forehead at the last word. "My God, what a picture," he cried. "The greatest wonder to me is that Admiral Eaton ever lived four years after the baby's death!"

Reporters and spectators kept an eye on Mrs. Eaton for a reaction. She maintained the composure she had shown throughout the trial. As she listened to Barker's remarks, she slipped lozenges from a bag in her lap into her mouth.

Barker brought up the letters that Mrs. Eaton had sent to Howard and Collamore asking them to support her accusations that the admiral was flirting. He spoke of her letter to Dr. Whitney and her plea for help with the admiral who she claimed was "mad" and "planning her death all day." She had asked Whitney in her missive to examine her husband and, if the doctor should find evidence of poison in the child's organs, to commit the admiral to an institution. Why, Barker wondered, would a woman make such accusations and demands and then, as if in defense of her actions, declare that she "didn't want the admiral's money."

Barker refuted Jennie's claim that the admiral had injected her with a hypodermic syringe while she slept.

"You know and I know that Admiral Eaton never gave Jennie hypodermics in her sleep," he said, "for there is a pain which goes with the insertion of a needle which would wake up any man unless he were [sic] drugged."

The district attorney went over the events at June's house in

Medford and Ralph Keyes's testimony. Barker had no qualms about expressing his interpretation of what Mrs. Eaton meant when she said, "I'll have to get home and take care of him."

"She got up at half past four in the morning. What was her hurry? Did she ever leave June's at half past five in the morning before? Dorothy was eating breakfast when Mrs. Eaton reached home. The admiral had had his, and the evidence of it must have been still upon the table. Yet she tried to get him to sit down and have a second breakfast, for what purpose? Was the idea in her half-crazy mind then? Was it because the conditions were not favorable at noon that the admiral's symptoms did not begin then?" Barker demanded to know.

He asked the jury to consider Bessie Bursey's testimony about the Chicago lover and decide for themselves whether her testimony carried any weight. He also mentioned the separate mailbox Mrs. Eaton had obtained and asked if her explanation – that she needed her own box because the admiral habitually lost the mail that arrived in the box they shared – was credible. Was the box used to correspond secretly with her paramour? Or was there a more evil purpose for the box – perhaps for the clandestine delivery of the arsenic she administered to the admiral?

Barker methodically recalled the events immediately preceding the admiral's death and compared the facts with Mrs. Eaton's version of events.

"Now, gentlemen, Jennie Eaton was never in bed with Admiral Eaton that night. I say to you that her story of what transpired that night is not true. Didn't she show the guilty mind from the time she came home until long after the admiral's death?

"Mrs. Eaton did attend this man every twenty minutes while Mrs. Harrison was in sight, but she went to bed at eight thirty, locking two doors between herself and a dying man, and left him. I say, to die alone. God forgive her. When she was called at two o'clock in the morning, I say God forgive her again – for she had a lie on her lips when he mumbled, 'Doctor, doctor.' She told him the doctor was coming in the morning, when she knew he was not coming.

"She did the deed at night. She got Dorothy to bed early on the first night believing results would come sooner. She was feeding him arsenic all day Friday, possibly after he was unconscious. How are you going to account for the free arsenic in his stomach that the doctors say was taken shortly before he died? Who did it? Nobody else in that house could have done it.

"This woman," Barker charged, his voice rising, "fed her husband arsenic all day Friday with his medicine, and she fed him the poison after he fell out of bed and she kept feeding it to him up to within two to eight hours of the time he died."

The district attorney criticized the defense for putting Dr. J. Wales Brown on the stand.

"You have heard the testimony of the Back Bay physician, a man whom you found had been sentenced to a total of twenty-eight years in prison for his acts. That testimony is some of the dust that the defense has tried to cloud your eyes with.

"It is a disgrace to the Commonwealth to introduce the testimony of a convict doctor, J. W. Brown, that he prescribed arsenic tablets for Admiral Eaton. I brand it a lie. And the same lies have permeated the whole of the defense."

Barker turned his fury on defense witness Dr. A. Everett Austin. Austin's ambivalent testimony left the prosecutor with one conclusion: He "forgot the honor of his profession and came to the stand to say anything that was required of him."

Barker demanded that the jury find Mrs. Eaton "not guilty by reason of insanity" if they found that she had poisoned her husband during a hallucination.

"She is more dangerous than a rattlesnake, and there is no telling whom she may hit next if she is allowed her freedom," Barker charged. "Mrs. Eaton divorced her husband and married Admiral Eaton for his money, and when that money was lost playing the stock market, she reached a turning point which led the admiral to a grave in Dracut."

The district attorney retrieved from the evidence table the two samples of white arsenic marked as Commonwealth exhibits. These two samples, one containing two grains and the other fifteen, had been introduced as evidence during the redirect examination of Dr. Osgood one week before. Osgood had testified that a Plymouth drugstore owner had sold the arsenic to him and had required neither identification nor a signature.

Barker showed the jurors the fifteen grains – less than a quarter of a teaspoon of powder.

"Look at that fifteen grains," he said. "Think it would be difficult to give Admiral Eaton that amount undetected? Why, if I couldn't give any one of you that amount, I'd go out of the poison business."

He stepped away and shook his head as he returned the samples to the table. When he resumed his place in front of the jury box, he wearily uttered these final words:

"May God help you to come to a right conclusion. Be men and do your duty. This thing has bowed me down like a millstone about my neck for six months. God help you, and God help any district attorney that ever in the future has to handle a case like this."

Barker returned to his seat at 5:30 p.m. He had spoken for three hours. Judge Aiken called for a brief recess, informing the court that he would deliver his charge to the jury when court resumed.

Globe reporter Frank Sibley, who was in the courtroom during Barker's argument, later described how the district attorney had "shouted and gestured wildly" and "leaned over the rail of the jury box and thrust his head almost among the jurors." Sibley regarded the prosecutor's delivery as "emotional in the extreme." Still, he wrote, it was "the most merciless, the most logical, the bitterest construction of a theory that has been heard for a long time in this state," and one that "will take its place among the greatest arguments at the Massachusetts bar."

The following day, *Boston Post* reporter Charles Parker offered his impression of Barker's summation. "With fire flashing from his white-browed eyes, his rounded shoulders straightening, his voice thrilling with indignation or growing gentle with praise for the unhonored naval officer, he presented to the twelve good men an argument that long will live in the memory of his hearers – the most masterful piece of summing up of evidence in a capital case in the history of Massachusetts jurisprudence."

Judge Aiken returned to the bench after the recess, moved his chair to the side nearest the jury box, and in a clear, even tone began his charge. The judge had carefully prepared his remarks, and he consulted his notes from time to time as he led jurors through the process of deliberation.

It was impossible, he told the jurors, that all of them would be affected alike by the evidence. He stressed the importance of respecting each other's opinions as they deliberated. After all, Aiken said, they shared a common goal – to reach a fair and just verdict.

"It has been said," remarked the chief justice, "that a jury room is no place for private opinions, and that any man who cannot be reached by the ideas of others is not fit for a juror. Nevertheless, if any of you men find yourselves unable to agree with the others upon mature deliberation, you are not required to surrender your well-formed opinions. On the other hand, you should not be obstinate and hold out for your own opinion until you have first convinced yourself that that opinion is well considered."

He moved on to the defendant's presumption of innocence and the meaning of the "proof beyond a reasonable doubt" standard.

"She is not required to prove herself innocent, nor to offer any evidence," he said. "Nothing is to be taken for granted, neither that she is on trial, nor the fact that she is here under indictment.

"You are not to convict on suspicion, probability, nor preponderance of evidence. If the facts proved can be reconciled with any reasonable theory of the defendant's innocence, she must be acquitted. The defendant must be found guilty to a degree of certainty upon which reasonable men are accustomed to act in important affairs in their own lives. Guilt is not required to be proven beyond any possible doubt, but beyond a reasonable doubt."

The judge directed the jurors to follow a proper order of inquiry, first establishing whether the defendant did or did not administer poison to Admiral Eaton as alleged.

"The Commonwealth charges that this defendant killed Admiral Eaton by giving him, or causing him to take, arsenic. To justify a verdict of guilty, it must be proved that the arsenic found in Admiral Eaton's body got there by the defendant's procurement, with intent to cause his death. Your first inquiry is whether the defendant caused arsenic to be given to Admiral Eaton. It is the underlying inquiry in the case and is of vital importance. You have the opposite views of the prosecution and the defense – that it was so administered and that it was taken by accident or intentionally by the admiral himself. You will take into consideration the declarations of the defendant, her letters and her words, her conduct, beliefs, rational or otherwise."

Judge Aiken delved into the legal principles regarding motive and intent.

"There may be conviction though the motive is inadequate, or even if there is not motive whatever. Where there is question whether the death was caused by the defendant or by the deceased's own act, the question of motive may be of highest importance, and although the government is not bound to prove motive, you may take into consideration whether any profit or advantage would come to the defendant if she killed her husband.

"You may consider whether their relations were affectionate, and in considering this the language she used should not be judged with literal exactness. So far as it is used in letters, of course, there are no doubts. But in the use of the spoken word there may be taken into account, as modifying it, the tone of voice, the expression of countenance, the stress of the occasion.

"In the effort to trace to the defendant the poison that was used, search was made of drugstores, and it is proper for the jury to know that in this state the law requires that a record of all sales of arsenic be kept, and that this record be open to the inspection of the police."

Reading slowly and deliberately from his notes, Judge Aiken continued.

"If the Commonwealth has failed to prove that the defendant caused arsenic to be given to the admiral, the verdict is not guilty, and there is no occasion for you to consider any other aspect of the case." Here he paused, looked at the jury, and repeated his words exactly.

"If it is your decision that the defendant caused arsenic to be given to Admiral Eaton," Aiken continued, "your next inquiry is, what her state of mind was in so doing."

He defined murder as "the malicious killing of a human being." By malicious, the law means "with any unlawful or unjustifiable motive," Aiken added.

"If arsenic was caused to be given," he went on, "there was malice aforethought if the defendant was of mental capacity to come within the rules. If a person has so little intelligence as to be incapable of appreciating the difference between right and wrong, he is excusable. In this case, there was no claim that the defendant was incapable of discriminating between right and wrong. But the law recognizes another limitation."

Here Aiken went into the legal principles pertaining to mental responsibility.

"If a person's mind is in such a disordered state that an uncontrollable impulse takes control of it, this may be regarded as an outbreak, so that he has for the time lost control of his will. Such a person is not held to be a responsible agent, though he may have had an appreciation of right and wrong.

"If the defendant's mind was so far disordered that the impulse was one she could not control, she is not criminally responsible," he continued. "The claim of insanity or uncontrollable impulse is generally raised by the defense. In this case, the district attorney does it, and I say that it is proper for him to do so. It is his duty to present to you any consideration which arises upon the evidence. There is testimony of Mrs. Eaton's statements that her husband was paying attentions to other women, that he was insane, that he took drugs, that he poisoned the adopted child, that he was trying to poison her, and it is urged that these statements indicated a disordered mind or delusions.

"Your inquiry will be whether she was laboring under delusions as to his disease, condition, endeavors or intentions, and if so, whether these delusions had so far affected her mind that in doing the act which is charged – if she did do it – she was acting under an uncontrollable impulse of a disordered kind."

The judge stated that in most cases in which the defendant's mental responsibility is an issue, expert "alienist" or psychological testimony is offered by either the prosecution or defense or by both. No such testimony was offered in this particular case, but Aiken showed little concern.

"There is no reason why, exercising your common sense, you may not pass on the defendant's insanity."

He next turned to the testimony and evidence.

"There is no question in this case as to the arsenic, nor [sic] as to the amount. As to the length of time it was taken before death, there is controversy. It is for you to consider the different opinions of the physicians, and to give them the weight that is their due."

The judge offered jurors several criteria to assist them in determining the veracity of a witness. He cited the witness's appearance, his or her conduct on the stand, and his or her fairness or unfairness. He warned jurors not to disregard any circumstance, no matter how trivial, they perceived as having a bearing on a witness's knowledge and credibility.

Judge Aiken next discussed four possible verdict outcomes. The jurors must decide, he instructed, which of these verdicts best expresses their conclusions.

"The first is not guilty. The second is not guilty by reason of insanity. The third is guilty of murder in the second degree. The fourth is guilty of murder in the first degree."

He stressed once more that the jury must first agree that the defendant did administer poison to the admiral and cause his death before they consider the second verdict – not guilty by reason of insanity.

"The law provides," he explained, "that in such a case the court shall order the defendant to be committed to the state hospital during her life, from which she may be discharged by the governor and council after an examination which may show her to be cured.

"If, however, you find that she was responsible for her acts, then the question of degree arises. Murder in the second degree is 'killing with malice aforethought.' Murder in the first degree is 'killing with deliberately premeditated malice aforethought.' To justify a conviction of murder in the first degree in this case, you must be satisfied that her mind was in such condition that she was capable of deliberate premeditation and that she deliberately decided to give the arsenic.

"If the defendant's mind was somewhat impaired, but not so much as to render her wholly irresponsible, though to such an extent that she was incapable of deliberate premeditation, the verdict should be murder in the second degree. Murder which does not appear to be murder in the first degree is murder in the second degree. The penalty for murder in the second degree is imprisonment for life. The penalty for murder in the first degree is death. There is no discretion allowed on the part of the court."

In closing, Judge Aiken said, "Use the knowledge, intelligence, and discretion that you use in your daily life, and the conclusion which you reach satisfactory to yourselves, must be satisfactory to others."

It was 6:14 p.m. Court recessed for an hour, and when jurors returned, Aiken gave them final instructions before he dismissed them to begin deliberations.

Deputy Sheriff George Wheeler delivered fifty-three trial exhibits to the jury room – letters, photographs, samples of poison, and items found about the Eaton home – and placed them in the custody of jury foreman James Thomas. When Wheeler emerged from the room, he closed and locked the door and stationed himself outside.

Chapter 32

By all accounts, Jennie May Eaton showed no distress as she waited in the anteroom for the verdict. Deputy Sheriff Collingwood brought her dinner that she ate while talking with her attorneys.

About fifty of Jennie's most ardent supporters remained inside the courtroom. Outside, other devotees took up posts on a small rise adjacent to the jury room, peering into the tall, arched windows, trying to get a glimpse of the jurors as they deliberated.

In the old jail, the furious clatter of typewriters and telegraph machines resonated throughout the evening and into the early morning hours as newspapermen wrote and filed their stories about how the case had gone to the jury.

When Morse and Geogan departed for their hotel, Jennie curled up on a sofa and quickly fell asleep. By 2:00 a.m. on Thursday, October 30, many in the courtroom had dozed off and the crowd outside the building had dwindled to about a dozen hangers-on.

At 4:20 a.m., a buzzer in the court officer's room sounded sharply, signaling a summons from the jury. Word was sent to Deputy Sheriff Wheeler, who was still posted outside the jury room. Jury foreman James Thomas answered Wheeler's knock at the door and informed him the jury had reached a verdict. Wheeler immediately alerted Sheriff Porter who telephoned Judge Aiken, District Attorney Barker, Assistant District Attorney Katzmann, and defense counsel. Deputy Collingwood, still on duty outside the anteroom, roused Jennie from her slumber.

His deep sleep interrupted at the Samoset House by Porter's call, Barker threw on a robe, left his room, walked down the corridor, and spoke briefly with Katzmann and ADA George Adams who were sharing a room on the same floor. Pleading fatigue, he instructed them to return to the courthouse without him and returned to bed. A few minutes after Barker's assistants had departed, a reporter knocked on Barker's door and asked him if he was aware that the jury was about to announce its verdict. Barker said he was and, when asked for a comment, admitted he was surprised the jury had reached a verdict so soon. He told the reporter he would make a formal statement later.

At 5:05 a.m., as spectators and newsmen noisily assembled inside the courtroom, Deputy Sheriffs Wheeler, Hersey, Spring, and Condon took their places. Within the bar enclosure, Morse and Geogan, who had arrived ten minutes earlier, conferred quietly with Katzmann and Adams.

Aiken took his seat on the bench minutes later. Before he brought the court to order, he informed the gallery he would tolerate no outbursts at the reading of the verdict and instructed Sheriff Porter to remove anyone who did not comply with his directive. He then gestured for the defendant.

Deputy Collingwood ushered Jennie into the courtroom and to her seat behind defense counsel. Her clothes disheveled and her hair in disarray, she smiled confidently as she sat down. She leaned forward and placed her hands on the rail in front of her. Her attorneys placed their hands over hers.

A hush descended over the room as the jurors filed in, and after Clerk of Court Edward Hobart had ensured that all were present, he addressed them.

"Gentlemen of the jury, have you agreed upon a verdict?"

Jury Foreman James A. Thomas (*Courtesy of Dawn Richards*)

"We have," James Thomas said, rising from his seat.

"Gentlemen, look upon the prisoner," said Hobart. "Prisoner, look upon the jury.

"What is your verdict?" asked Hobart.

"Not guilty," said Thomas in a loud, confident tone.

Everyone in the courtroom remained motionless for several seconds. Jennie gasped sharply, sank back into her chair, then she beamed and squeezed the hands of her two lawyers. Spontaneously, spectators in the back rows erupted with cheers and applause. Sheriff Porter quickly restored order.

"I told you so," said Jennie as she pointed at Morse.

Katzmann and Adams sat stone-faced at the prosecution table.

Judge Aiken turned to the exhausted jurors and thanked each of them for their service. He cautioned them that the press would likely try to interview them when they left the room and advised them to keep the nature of their deliberations confidential. He then excused the twelve men.

Turning his attention to Jennie and attorneys Morse and Geogan, the judge said, "The prisoner is discharged." Then to Jennie directly, Aiken said, "The court orders your discharge from the indictment to go without delay."

"You did it, you did it, you did it," Jennie exclaimed with tears of joy as she turned to her attorneys. Spectators leapt to their feet and rushed toward Jennie to grasp her hand and offer congratulations, but a line of court officers surrounded her and held them at bay. Deputy Collingwood guided Jennie and her lawyers into the anteroom, and he remained outside to prevent intrusion.

As soon as his deputies had cleared the courtroom, Porter walked back to the anteroom and tapped lightly on the door. Opening it, he poked his head in and lightheartedly said to Jennie, "Well, are you coming home with me?"

Jennie laughed and said, "Now you know, I hate to leave you, Sheriff, but I really must decline your kind invitation."

She thanked Porter for the many kindnesses he had extended to her during her confinement. Porter smiled, stepped back, and gently closed the door.

Moments after Porter withdrew, jury foreman Thomas knocked at the door and asked Morse if he could speak to Mrs. Eaton. When she emerged, Thomas and the entire jury, standing in a semicircle in the corridor, greeted her with congratulations. Jennie shook each of their hands and sobbed her gratitude.

She left the building at about 6:00 a.m. after bidding good-byes to other people. Accompanied by her two attorneys and surrounded by a crowd of supporters and newsmen, she walked down the hill to the Plymouth Rock House where her defense team was staying.

When they arrived, the hotel's manager ushered Jennie, her counsel, Judge Kelley, and several newsmen into his private office. While

Geogan arranged for a room and Morse spoke quietly with the manager, Jennie stepped through the French doors leading from the manager's office onto the hotel's piazza and gazed across Plymouth Bay.

"Isn't the sun just lovely," she said to no one in particular as she inhaled the ocean air. "It's the dawn of a beautiful morning, especially for me, for it is a new era in my life, one I know that will never have the sorrows of the one now gone."

Boston American photographer Richard Sears got Jennie to pose for several pictures with her defense counsel. At Jennie's urging, Judge Kelley agreed to have his picture taken as he congratulated her. Sears also photographed Jennie with *Boston American* correspondent Angela Morgan, who had covered the Eaton trial from day one and had become Jennie's staunchest supporter.

Judge Kelley congratulates Mrs. Eaton on her acquittal
(*Courtesy of F. Joseph Geogan II, Esq.*)

Thoroughly exhausted, Jennie left the office and spoke briefly with well-wishers and other reporters in the hotel lobby, then she retired to the hotel room reserved by Geogan. She rejoined Morse, Geogan, and Judge Kelley an hour later in the hotel dining room where they enjoyed a light breakfast.

Jennie and her attorneys held a brief press conference in the hotel lobby after breakfast.

"An acquittal was what we confidently expected," said Morse. "I have felt from the first that Mrs. Eaton was absolutely innocent, and I am as happy as she is that justice has been done this woman who has suffered so much. She is a wonderful woman and has shown marvelous self-control all through her trying experience.

"It was Mrs. Eaton's appearance on the stand, an unusual event in any capital case, and a remarkable one where a woman was on trial for her life, which decided the defendant's innocence in the minds of the jurors," Morse added. "The verdict was what we expected. It frees an innocent woman but leaves as a mystery the end of the admiral, her husband. For six months I have tried to find out what was behind the poison which caused his death, but my investigations have developed no satisfactory explanation. It must probably remain a mystery."

Geogan echoed Morse's sentiments and said, "We never gave up hope for a minute during the trial. We are very grateful to the judge for his fair charge to the jury and for their decision."

Judge Kelley added that he, too, had always expected Mrs. Eaton's acquittal.

"It gives me much satisfaction that this verdict of not guilty has been returned," said Kelley. "I was satisfied that this woman was innocent."

Kelley also expressed his delight in having kept two promises. The first was to Mrs. Eaton – to stand by her until the end. The second was his promise to the admiral before he died – to "look out for and care for Jennie."

As the press conference progressed, *Boston Traveler* columnist Solita Solano placed her arm through Jennie's and asked to speak with her privately. They strolled out of the hotel and stood on the crest of the hill overlooking Plymouth Rock. Solano described Jennie as "radiant" as she spoke softly about her plans for the future.

"I am going back to Assinippi and fight it out," Jennie declared. "I am so happy in my heart that I cannot express it, in words. I feel that I owe everything to Mr. Morse. He seemed inspired as he pleaded for me. And now, I am going home to my little family.

"How glad my girls will be. I am going to keep chickens and bees and sell eggs and honey. I want to make a good income from my labors in the country. And I am hoping to have June and the baby with me.

"I shall buy a pony for Dorothy and little Eleanor to play with. And in the summer, I am going to have two or three children come down on the farm and try to make a small part of their lives bright. My experience in prison has taught me so much; I want to make everybody happy now.

"I have had a dreadful life, you know. No woman has suffered more than I have. Both my marriages were unhappy, but I tried to do the best I could always, and enjoy what little happiness I could find.

"Since I have been in Plymouth Jail, I have written a story of my life. It is stranger than any novel of fiction. They say that truth is stranger than fiction, and I can vouch for that. I am going to have my book published soon.

"They say that June has always been the apple of my eye," Jennie went on. "This is not true. I love my little girl Dorothy just as I do June. But it is as I said in court. I went to the aid of the child who needed me most.

"I shall begin life anew, and live for my mother, June, Dorothy, and the baby. I know we shall be very happy at Assinippi. I love the quiet of the country, and I can be contented to work there and live for those I love and who love me."

A *Boston Traveler* reporter went to June Keyes's home in Quincy Point for a comment on the verdict. The reporter was the first to tell June the news of her mother's acquittal. She reacted with relief and joy.

"Thank God, my prayers are answered," June said. "I am so grateful that my mother has been acquitted that I can hardly find words to express my feelings. I thank God for it. He has answered my prayers. I did not sleep all last night. I was so anxious to hear the outcome.

"My mother is the best mother that ever lived, and I knew all along the result could not be otherwise. I was overjoyed in reading the plea of Mr. Morse in my mother's behalf. I think it was magnificent. As for Mr. Barker, I have nothing to say against him. I am so grateful that I don't know as I can add any more."

Reporters caught up with Barker and Katzmann at Barker's office in Brockton that afternoon and asked for their reaction to the verdict.

Katzmann had nothing to say other than he was surprised at the outcome.

Barker refused to offer an opinion on the jury's verdict, but the terseness of the district attorney's remarks reflected his disappointment.

"My responsibility ceased when I placed this case before the jury," Barker said. "The responsibility is upon them. Whether the verdict is right or wrong is not for me to say. That is all."

~

When the press conference at the Plymouth Rock House concluded, Jennie and her two lawyers climbed into Morse's car and set out for Assinippi. Jennie was anxious to see her family. About a mile from the hotel, a car sped past them, going in the opposite direction. Jennie recognized Dorothy in the car and alerted Morse who abruptly stopped and turned around. Morse pulled up behind the car as it stopped in front of the Plymouth Rock House. Jennie jumped out and rushed to her younger daughter. The two women embraced and cried with tears of joy, oblivious to the onlookers who surrounded them.

Moments later, mother, daughter, and the lawyers returned to Morse's car. With Dorothy at her side, Jennie asked Morse to drive her to the Plymouth Jail so she could retrieve her personal effects and bid good-bye to Laura Porter and other employees who had treated her kindly.

At the jail, they were told that Judge Kelley had arranged for them to join him for lunch back at the Plymouth Rock House. When they arrived, they were greeted at the main entrance by Special Deputy Sheriff and Mrs. Howland Hart of Weymouth. Mrs. Howland presented Jennie with a bouquet of carnations and hosted an impromptu reception in the hotel's lobby where many more supporters had assembled to offer Jennie their congratulations.

~

Jurors left the courthouse and ate breakfast in the Samoset House before retiring to their rooms for some much needed sleep. James Thomas, the foreman, was interviewed by a *Boston Traveler* reporter in the hotel lobby before he went to his room.

"We're about all in," Thomas said. "Every man who sat on the jury is completely fagged out. All we want now is sleep. And we want to forget this case entirely."

When asked to elaborate on how the jury reached its verdict, Thomas declined to answer, citing Judge Aiken's admonition.

A *Boston American* reporter, however, found another juror who was willing to speak with him on condition of anonymity. According to that juror, an informal ballot was taken before deliberations commenced. Five of the twelve jurors voted to convict. On a second ballot, taken three hours later, one of the five had changed his opinion.

A spirited debate continued through the wee hours of the morning. The jurors reached a unanimous decision to acquit at 4:20 a.m. The juror indicated that a crucial element in the decision was the failure of the government to prove that Mrs. Eaton had purchased the poison that killed the admiral.

"How did Admiral Eaton get the poison into his stomach?" a *Boston Post* reporter asked another juror who also asked to remain anonymous.

"We don't know and we don't care, and it's not of vital import in our view of the case, because Mrs. Eaton didn't give it to him, and whether she did or not is what we were here to determine," the juror said.

Jurors drew their own conclusions on whether Admiral Eaton had ingested the arsenic accidentally or intentionally, but none were willing to comment further on the issue.

Having exonerated Mrs. Eaton of murder, the jurors proceeded, as instructed by Judge Aiken, to the consideration of Mrs. Eaton's sanity. To a man, they agreed that the government had presented no evidence to convince them that Mrs. Eaton was insane, citing her rational behavior on the witness stand as a factor in reaching their decision.

Another juror, Daniel P. Murphy of Brockton, found a *Brockton Times* reporter waiting on his doorstep when he returned home at 11:30 a.m. Murphy agreed to an interview and spoke of the long, complicated ordeal he had undergone, saying he hoped he would never have to experience anything like it again.

As for the verdict, Murphy said, "From the time when the arguments were closed, I made up my mind that the evidence put forth by the government was entirely insufficient to create even the slightest possibility of Mrs. Eaton's guilt. Although the government searched thoroughly for evidence to connect the widow with the poison, they were unable to find any trace that she made such a purchase. This point alone was a strong one. The fact that the admiral was a user of the drug stands out in his widow's favor."

The day after the trial, the *Boston Post* reported, based on a "reliable source," that jurors in the Eaton case had deliberately ignored Judge Aiken's instructions for reaching a verdict, having first decided on the question of Mrs. Eaton's sanity before considering her guilt or innocence of the murder charge.

James Thomas was incensed about the *Post* article and contacted *The Brockton Times*. The jury foreman declared the allegations were totally false. He and the other jury members, Thomas insisted, had "followed to the letter the instructions they received from the judge."

~

Morse arrived in Assinippi with Jennie, Dorothy, and Geogan at about 2:00 p.m. He stopped momentarily at the post office so Dorothy could get the mail. Many of Assinippi's residents, aware of Jennie's acquittal, had gathered in the village center anxiously awaiting her arrival. Seeing her in Morse's car, they rushed to greet her and offered congratulations.

"This is a very happy homecoming for me," Jennie said with tears in her eyes after stepping out of the car. "I am glad to get back again. It has been a long, hard trial and I am very tired." She had been away from her home for 224 days; for more than seven months.

Thanking her well-wishers again, she got back into Morse's car, and the little party made its way up Washington Street to the Eaton house. Neighbors stood in their doorways, waving and shouting congratulations as the car passed.

June Keyes had arrived at the Eaton home prior to the homecoming and spoke with one of the many reporters who had gathered outside. She was scarcely able to restrain her excitement over her mother's vindication and her return home.

"O[h], isn't it grand; isn't it fine to have mother home again? She surely is innocent," June said. "Didn't Mr. Morse make a grand fight for her? I couldn't sleep all night. I heard the clock strike every hour. I was so happy when I heard the news and I am glad it's all over."

Boston Globe reporter Frank Sibley described the emotional scene when Jennie arrived at her home.

"Pacing restlessly about the front of the house, as if sensing their mistress's approach, her two dogs watched furtively up and down the street. When the automobile drew up to the entrance of the Eaton homestead, the joy of the faithful dogs knew no bounds. They could scarcely contain themselves as Mrs. Eaton stepped from the auto, and Czar, her handsome collie, leaped upon her, yelping, barking and threatened to throw her down. He licked her hand and would not be restrained. Mrs. Eaton stopped and patted him affectionately and then started for the house.

"As the front door opened, June was the first to greet her mother. The two women fell into a long embrace – one uttering the single word 'June' and the other speaking only once – 'Mother.'

"Standing just inside the door was Mrs. Eaton's mother, Mrs. Harrison, and when Mrs. Eaton could release herself from her daughter's arms, she passed into those of her mother. Tears rolled down their cheeks as they greeted each other. Then, turning to Mr. Morse, who with Mr. Geogan had followed her into the house, the aged Mrs. Harrison grasped the senior counsel's hand and exclaimed, 'Thank God!' Then the four women, mother, daughters, and grandmother, stood looking at each other, each too much overcome to give further expression of their feelings, and the door closed on the reunited family. And so, the few strangers who had followed turned silently away and left them in their happiness."

Epilogue

Jennie May Eaton set about the business of restoring her financial affairs. On November 13, the declaration of trust that Judge Kelley had filed on her behalf was revoked and terminated, conveying the Assinippi property back to her.

Nearly all of the proceeds she had received from her settlement of Admiral Eaton's life insurance policies and benefits had gone to offset a portion of her legal fees which were estimated at between $15,000 and $20,000. This included a $10,000 fee for the services of attorney William Morse and additional fees for attorney Francis Geogan and experts who had testified at the trial.

Unable to meet her obligations, Jennie appealed to Massachusetts Governor Eugene Foss for assistance in paying the balance of her defense costs. She claimed that the Commonwealth had submitted insufficient evidence before the grand jury for an indictment against her and had burdened her with "a great and needless expense."

The governor responded that the state could not reimburse her directly. He suggested that Jennie file for compensation through the courts and informed her of two options available to her under Massachusetts law.

"An Act to Authorize Compensation in Certain Cases to Persons Confined While Awaiting Trial," enacted in 1911, provided that any person confined for more than six months after indictment who is finally acquitted or discharged without a trial is entitled to compensation for any period that exceeds the six months of confinement.

The judge who presided over the claimant's trial would conduct a hearing to decide whether the claimant's petition has merit. If the judge ruled in the claimant's favor, a second hearing would be held to determine an appropriate compensatory award.

Should the judge deny the claimant's request, he or she could file under another previously enacted statute. But compensatory awards under this law were generally limited to $500.

~

Until her appeal under the new statute was resolved, Jennie looked for new sources of income beyond her modest farm earnings. Her book deal with the New York publisher never materialized. She did, however, find an outlet for her literary pursuits and a supplemental source of income by writing for the *Boston Post*. The *Post* published her tales of love and romance in the feature section of its Sunday edition. Among those stories were "The Vampire of the City," "Clothes or the Girl, Which?" "The Boy and the Woman," and "The Love of a Maid and the Love of a Man."

The Post also assigned Jennie as a feature writer for several high profile murder cases. Two cases occurring in 1915 involved socialites. Florence Carman, the wife of a Newport, Rhode Island, doctor, was charged with the murder of Louise Bailey on Long Island in New York. Another socialite, Elizabeth Mohr, was indicted in Providence, Rhode Island, for the murder of a woman she suspected of having an affair with her husband.

In the Carman case, Jennie seized the opportunity to publicly lay bare, for the first time, the fury seething within her regarding her own ordeal. By this time, the Massachusetts courts had denied her request for reimbursement of her defense costs.

In the article, she excoriated the government and the courts for the way they handled murder cases, particularly those in which women were the defendants.

"Few can appreciate the terrible situation in the Carman murder case as can I, who but recently was acquitted from a charge as grave as that lodged against Mrs. Carman. The nameless terror that takes possession of a sensitive woman, the weary months of suspense, the consciousness of overwhelming injustice, the public scorn and the separation from one's friends and family – have I not endured them all? And for what? That a cruel and heartless state, grown callous in the exercise of the barbarous spirit of revenge, shall take toll from someone, no matter whom, for the death of one of its members. It is little short of crime itself for the so-called beneficent state to place one of its members in prison without absolute proof of his guilt."

She expressed bitterness over the harsh treatment she continued to suffer at the hands of her critics despite having been acquitted.

"After one has been acquitted of such a charge, people whom they have never seen in their lives shrink from them and point them out as the person who killed so-and-so. Everywhere one must go there is the gaping, curious throng ready to hold her up to nameless insult and ridicule. And all this even after a woman has been declared innocent. To be a leper is not nearly so bad as to live under such a stigma.

"I earnestly entreat the people of these broad United States to rise to their fine sense of honor and principle, and, as a nation, pass a law so that no official can deprive a person of his liberty until he is proven guilty.

"As things are now, the courts and district attorneys are carried away in their lust to win either by hook or crook so that they entirely forget the sensitive soul of the perhaps innocent prisoner whom they are pillorying in the dock."

Alluding to this unfair treatment and the denial of her claim for reimbursement, Jennie wrote, "If a person must undergo the stigma and injustice of incarceration only to be proven innocent, then I think the state should pay such victims of judicious malpractice the sum of five dollars a day for each and every day they are held in jail, besides defraying all the expense of defending the prosecution by the state.

"I can but add that jails are kindergartens to the madhouse. For a high-strung innocent woman they are doubly so. Yet, after all, life can never be quite the same for Mrs. Carman even if she is cleared of guilt in the eyes of the law. Her misfortune will follow her wherever she goes. When will the Unites States become civilized enough to rise above this relic of barbarism?"

~

Harry Ainsworth, who had remained conspicuously absent during his ex-wife's trial, became a frequent visitor to the Assinippi farm after Jennie's acquittal. His presence soon became the subject of persistent gossip among village residents.

In December 1913, Virginia Harrison left Assinippi and returned to Washington, DC, where she lived with her youngest daughter,

Gertrude. She died at Gertrude's home on December 20, 1918, and was buried three days later at Ivy Hill Cemetery in Alexandria, Virginia.

In March 1914, Jennie, Dorothy, June, and Eleanor boarded a steamship in Boston and sailed to Norfolk, Virginia, where Harry met them. The family remained in the Norfolk area, visiting friends and occasionally visiting relatives there and in Washington.

On June 3, 1914, Harry went to the municipal offices in Washington and applied for a license to remarry Jennie. License in hand, he and Jennie went to the home of the Rev. L. Morgan Chambers, pastor of the McKendree M. E. Church, who performed a brief marriage ceremony.

Newspaper reporters and photographers, who had received an anonymous tip, confronted them as they emerged from the clergyman's house, shouting questions and snapping pictures.

"Won't you tell us where you intend to spend your honeymoon?" a reporter asked Harry point-blank.

Harry began to reply, but Jennie poked him. "Hush," she said as she took him by the arm, elbowed her way past the newsmen, and hastened to a trolley headed for the steamboat pier. The couple boarded a freight steamer bound for Colonial Beach, a summer resort at the mouth of the Potomac River, where Dorothy, June, and Eleanor were waiting for them at a rented cottage. The newly reunited family stayed for a month and then returned to Assinippi.

In late October 1914, the *Boston Sunday Herald* drew attention to the family with the headline "Eatons Worried by June Keyes's Strange Actions." The article reported that June and Dorothy had taken a train from Hingham two weeks before to shop in Boston. When they arrived at South Station, Dorothy stepped inside a telephone booth and called her mother to tell her they had arrived safely. She emerged from the booth and found that June had vanished. In a panic, she sought the assistance of terminal employees and notified police. After a daylong search, they found June at a station platform on board an unoccupied Cape Cod-bound train. Confused and frightened, June stepped from the car with Dorothy and the train's conductor. Asked why she had not waited for Dorothy, June said she had seen the ghost of Admiral Eaton and had fled to elude him.

The *Herald* also reported that June had disappeared from the Eatons' home in Assinippi several days after the South Station incident.

When Jennie realized she was gone, she and Dorothy mobilized a search with neighbors and friends. They found June later that evening almost four miles from home, sitting on the steps of an abandoned grocery store on Webster Street in Rockland.

On March 31, 1916, Ralph Keyes filed for divorce from June at Middlesex County Superior Court in East Cambridge. Keyes alleged that June had "utterly deserted [him], and has continued such desertion for over three consecutive years…"

~

It wasn't long after Jennie had reunited with Harry Ainsworth that she realized he was still drinking. He never recovered from his alcoholism. Boston police arrested Ainsworth six times in one year for public intoxication. He served a short jail term or paid a fine each time.

On November 7, 1916, Ainsworth returned home from Boston. In a drunken rage, he expelled Jennie and Eleanor from the house and locked them out. Jennie ran with Eleanor to a neighbor's house and called police. When Deputy Sheriff John Condon arrived, Ainsworth refused to let him inside. Condon later testified during a court hearing before Judge George Kelley that he had to help Jennie through a window so she could unlock a door from the inside. He found Ainsworth, inebriated and half-dressed, lying on a bed in an upstairs bedroom, and arrested him.

Judge Kelley sentenced Ainsworth to four months in the Plymouth House of Correction. While incarcerated, Ainsworth appealed the judge's ruling and he appeared at Plymouth Superior Court before Judge Philip J. O'Connell on February 21, 1917. O'Connell agreed to suspend Harry's sentence if he promised to leave the state and never return.

Outside the courtroom, a *Boston Herald* reporter overheard Ainsworth say, "I suppose I made a great big mistake in marrying Mrs. Ainsworth the second time." He then had a few choice words for Judge Kelley, whom he described as a "too close" friend of his wife's. Five months later, Jennie filed for divorce from her husband for the second time.

Ainsworth returned to Washington, DC, and boarded with his

brother, Judah. He went to work in Washington as a sales representative for his father who was president and general manager of the Orion Gold and Copper Company in Arizona.

A year after his court appearance in Plymouth, after Ainsworth had stayed clear of the law and kept his promise to stay out of Massachusetts, Judge O'Connell dismissed his case.

~

On successive, frigid evenings in February 1917, June left the Assinippi house, barefoot and scantily clad, and wandered neighborhood streets, through snow and slush, pleading for someone to free her from the specter of the admiral's face.

She told Jennie that a "secret son" of the dead admiral – "a real, young gentleman of flesh and blood" – had climbed a ladder placed against her bedroom window and glared at her through the glass. June was so adamant about the prowler that Jennie employed detectives to watch the house. After several all-night vigils, they recorded nothing suspicious.

Jennie, concerned about June's safety and mental well-being, filed a petition with the Second District Court in Abington to have her daughter hospitalized for psychiatric care. Judge Kelley committed June to the Taunton State Hospital.

In April, the *Herald* reported that Jennie had taken June from the state hospital and brought her home to Assinippi. Jennie explained that June's physical condition had deteriorated to such an extent during her ten-week confinement that she feared her daughter would not survive. What she failed to say was that June's delicate condition was not because of illness. She was five months pregnant.

On June 16, 1917, Jennie sold the Assinippi farm and took June, Dorothy, and Eleanor to Madison, Connecticut. Anxious to keep her identity and past a secret, Jennie purchased a home in Madison's East River section under her maiden name, Harrison.

Dorothy married twenty-nine-year-old William B. McMahon, a Maine native and 1913 Bowdoin College graduate, two weeks after moving to Madison. After the ceremony in New York City, the couple spent time in Washington, then they moved to Boston where they rented an apartment in the Dorchester neighborhood.

June's baby, a boy, was born in poor health with an unspecified deformity on August 5. The paternity of the child and the circumstances of his conception were never publicly revealed. Jennie named him Woodrow Wilson Keyes.

Knowing that June was incapable of caring for the infant, Jennie took him to Dorothy's home in Boston. The following night, Jennie and Dorothy, who was four months pregnant with her first child, took the infant to Brookline, Massachusetts, where they left him, swaddled in a blanket, on the doorstep of Dr. Harold Bowditch. Inside the blanket they had placed a jar of baby food, a can of condensed milk, Vaseline, a piece of white castile soap, some corn starch in a paper, and a white rubber nipple.

Bowditch discovered the child together with a note that was typewritten and signed cryptically.

This little baby is born of American educated parents. Mother dead and young father not situated so he can care properly for child. If a good Christian woman should raise this boy she will be repaid by having a son that will be a credit to her, as well as an affectionate, lovable child, with a bright, quick mind that will excel in all studies. A lawyer would be a fine profession for this child to be trained for. It is a most highly-connected child, but reasons that are most pathetic make this step enevetable [sic].

Trusting it to your Mercy and Care,
I am with regretts [sic] that come from my heart,
O. O. M. N.

Bowditch called the police. A matron took custody of the baby and brought him to her home. She turned the child over to the State Board of Charity's Department of Minor Wards the next morning. The child was placed with a family in Stoughton but died in October of complications unrelated to his abandonment.

Frederick Katzmann, who had succeeded Albert Barker as district attorney in the Southeastern District, convened a secret grand jury in Dedham in December 1917. After a single day of testimony, the jury returned an indictment against Jennie and Dorothy, charging them with child abandonment. Boston police arrested Dorothy on January 12, and she was released on $500 bail. Guilford, Connecticut, police arrested Jennie two days later in Madison.

A reporter from *The Hartford Courant* interviewed Jennie several days after her arrest. Jennie related that the infant was deformed and, according to the doctor who had attended the birth, would not survive. She said that she and Dorothy had done all they could for the child. She insisted that she had tried to place him in several institutions, but none would accept him. She felt her only other alternative was to leave the infant in Dr. Bowditch's care.

Taking advantage of the opportunity, the reporter abruptly changed the subject and off-handedly asked Jennie why she had remarried her first husband. To his surprise, Jennie answered him. She said that Ainsworth had followed her and her children to the resort in Virginia where they were staying. He had threatened to shoot her and kill himself if she did not remarry him. She knew he was a drunkard, she said, but she would "have married a Chinaman than face another scandal."

~

No jail existed in Guilford or Madison, so Jennie remained under house arrest until Massachusetts authorities took her into custody on January 17 and returned her to Dedham for trial. During her confinement, she had confessed to Madison police that she had abandoned the baby.

"Yes, I am guilty as charged, but when the world hears why I did it, it will forgive me," she later told a reporter who had learned of her admission. "Mother love alone prompted me. If the situation were to confront me tomorrow, I would do the same thing again."

Attorney William Morse met Jennie in Dedham and posted $1,000 bail. On her release, Jennie visited Dorothy at her Dorchester apartment and returned to Madison the next morning.

The Hartford Courant published a story the following day about the birth and disappearance of June's baby. Beneath the banner, "Child Gave Clue That Led to Arrest of Mrs. Ainsworth," the article revealed that five-year-old Eleanor, in a burst of excitement, had announced the baby's birth to a neighbor. A month later, Eleanor naively told the neighbor that the infant had disappeared during the night. The neighbor contacted Madison police. Under questioning by two officers at her home, Jennie admitted she had taken the infant to Brookline and had left him on Dr. Bowditch's doorstep.

On April 17, 1918, Jennie appeared with Dorothy, whose own daughter had been born in February, at the Norfolk County Court House in Dedham before Judge Philip J. O'Connell, the same judge who had banished Harry Ainsworth from Massachusetts. Both women, represented by Morse, entered guilty pleas. Morse requested a delay in sentencing so that Jennie could return home to take care of June who was reportedly dying. O'Connell agreed to a stay of sentence and continued the case until September. The case was ultimately dropped.

~

Jennie sold the Madison property in August 1919 and returned to Washington with June and Eleanor. They reunited with Harry Ainsworth who was living at 40 C Street NW. (Jennie had apparently dropped her divorce suit against Harry.) They later moved into a larger apartment on New Jersey Avenue.

By 1925, the couple had purchased a three-story, multi-unit dwelling at 65 K Street NE which they operated as a boardinghouse. June lived with them briefly but was later admitted to St. Elizabeth's Hospital, a Washington psychiatric facility.

Back in Boston, Dorothy's husband, William McMahon, found work as a machinist at the Fore River Shipyard. The couple welcomed their second child, a daughter, in 1921.

The U. S. Customs Service appointed William as an immigration officer three years later and assigned him to the Canadian border at Rouses Point, New York, and later, Cornwall, Ontario. They rented a home in Cornwall and remained there until 1936 when William was reassigned to Chateaugay, New York.

In the early morning hours of June 14, 1957, Dorothy, driving alone from St. Albans, Vermont, to her home in Chateaugay, lost control of her vehicle and struck a utility pole on darkened Route 11 at Ellenburg Depot. She died instantly. She was fifty-nine.

After a funeral in the Chateaugay Presbyterian Church, Dorothy's remains were sent to Norwell where she was buried beside the grave of her adopted brother, Joseph Eaton Jr., at the Washington Street Cemetery plot purchased by Admiral Eaton in 1909. A simple granite stone, inscribed "Dorothy E. McMahon," marks her grave.

Dorothy's husband died in an Ormstown, Quebec, hospital the following year. His remains were returned to his birthplace in Brunswick, Maine, where he was buried in a family plot.

~

By 1937, Harry and Jennie had sold the building at 65 K Street and had moved into an apartment at 900 11th Street NW. Harry died of pneumonia on October 28, 1937. A funeral was held in Washington where his body was cremated.

Jennie found herself destitute and barely surviving on her meager savings and Social Security benefits of twenty-three dollars a month following the death of her husband. She asked U.S. Senator David I. Walsh of Massachusetts for assistance in obtaining a pension as the remarried widow of Rear Admiral Joseph Eaton. Walsh, chairman of the Committee on Naval Affairs, referred Jennie to the Navy Department where she received assistance with her application. The Veterans Administration notified her four months later that the remarried widow of a Spanish-American War veteran was entitled to a thirty-dollar monthly allowance.

Jennie was not satisfied with that amount and appealed to President Franklin D. Roosevelt's secretary, Marvin H. McIntyre, to intercede on her behalf.

My dear Mr. McIntyre:

I am writing you to beg of you to assist me in some way to get an increase in a pension of $30.00 allowed to me a month ago as the former widow of Admiral Joseph Giles Eaton of the United States Navy. My husband give [sic] 44 years of his life to the Navy and his country, and this pension is not enough to support me, and I am now 66 years of age and have no one to give me a home or in any way help me.

The Admiral was an Annapolis graduate and commanded 7

battleships. His family are [sic] *a great family up in Massachusetts — all Harvard and Yale men, judges, etc., etc. It does not seem possible that I, his widow, should have this very small pension, about what his cabin boy would receive, for his valuable services, his social standing and wonderful record (Naval record). I do wish you would appeal to President Roosevelt and suggest some way where I may be given an increase so that I can live.*

I wrote you some months ago in reference to a daughter of mine who is over in St. Elizabeth's hospital (June), who is very frail and ill, and whom I want to devote the rest of my life to trying to cure her or at least leave her a happy person. Your letter over there helped her a great deal. She gets better care, but in her condition, she needs a mother's care and <u>normal surroundings</u>. With this pitifully small pension I can do nothing for this gentle, sweet, refined young woman, and she can only stay there and await death if I cannot feed and house her properly. If this pension could be raised to $70.00 per month, I could support myself and this dear girl (who has not lived at all) and you would have saved her life and <u>mine</u>, for I worry so over what other patients may do to this sensitive, gentle, timid girl, I am afraid I will lose my senses. They frighten me and her to death. They curse, scream, and she sees such suffering it tears her to pieces. She begs me each time I see her to "Take me away, Mamma, from all this disease and misery. I can't stand it, Mamma!" So please, in Mercy's name, see if you cannot help us two helpless ladies.

The pension is through the Veteran's Bureau. Please write me after you talk to the President, and don't delay if you please as my daughter cannot stand it over there <u>much longer and live</u>.

I thank you for the good your writing them did. They now at least see that she has water regularly and are kinder in many ways, but they have not time enough to give individual care to her, and she can't live without it. The Admiral loved this beautiful girl greatly and in memory of his truly great record, I hope you will do this kindness to her for his sake.

Thanking you again for your past kindness, I am,
Cordially yours,
Jennie Eaton Ainsworth
900 11th Street Northwest

P. S. I wrote the President a few weeks ago asking for a five minute interview, as I wished to talk this matter over with him so I may save my daughter's life. But you were (according to papers) very busy at that particular time, and I presume the President did not see my letter. I hope I did not offend any Secretary who may have read my letter to him. I asked him not to take the time and red tape by having his Secretary answer me, as I had visited my daughter and found her so frightened and ill I was afraid she would pass away before I would hear from him. Please remember I meant not to offend you or anyone, only was wild about my daughter's situation and my seeming helplessness to save her. Hope you will understand, pardon and help me.

Jennie Eaton Ainsworth

P. S. Please talk this over earnestly with the President, for he is a man full of mercy and Christian Charity and believes in his God, for I read what he had written in the Great Clock in his Hyde Park home about serving God and each hour of our lives as the moments ticked our lives away to help each other and be kind and good. These are not the exact words but their meaning, and President Roosevelt I know will help me. Tell him I have a daughter by the Admiral, a wonderful girl who is paralyzed from infantile paralysis, and I need his help. She has two lovely girls but is partially paralyzed in one limb, and he is a sufferer and can understand and will help me save my daughter, June Keyes, at St. Elizabeth's, I believe. I am relying on you both to help.

J.

McIntyre contacted the Veterans Administration for a review of Jennie's case. In May, McIntyre sent Jennie his regrets and informed her that the Veterans Administration had determined that because she was not married to Admiral Eaton during the period of his Spanish-American War service, and because his death was not related to his naval service, she was entitled to only a thirty-dollar monthly allowance, the maximum rate permitted by law.

Undeterred by McIntyre's response, Jennie wrote directly to President Roosevelt, First Lady Eleanor Roosevelt, and Secretary of the Navy Frank Knox, seeking relief. Those letters were referred to the Veterans Administration's director who promptly denied her requests.

Jennie petitioned Presidents Truman and Eisenhower and other government officials for increases in her benefits during the next twenty years.

On March 1, 1944, Congress enacted Public Law 242. Under its authority, the Veterans Administration increased Jennie's monthly pension from thirty to forty dollars. Legislation passed in January 1949 authorized an additional monthly stipend of eight dollars. That increase and the welfare assistance she was receiving from the District of Columbia provided her with a total monthly income of $121.

Jennie fell while walking in a local park and fractured both legs in May 1949. After several weeks of confinement in Washington's Gallinger Hospital, she convalesced at her granddaughter Eleanor's home in Suitland, Maryland, until she was well enough to return to her own apartment.

On January 27, 1959, impoverished and alone in her apartment at 229 Pennsylvania Avenue SE, Jennie suffered a heart attack. She later died at the District of Columbia General Hospital. She was eighty-six. An autopsy attributed her death to acute congestive heart failure, heart disease, general debility, and emaciation.

Following a funeral at St. Peter's Catholic Church in Washington, Jennie's granddaughter, Eleanor, sent the body to Norwell where it was laid to rest with Jennie's daughter Dorothy and adopted son Joseph Jr. at the Washington Street Cemetery. Jennie's grave is not marked.

It is believed that June Keyes, who was mentioned as a surviving daughter in Jennie's 1959 *Washington Post* obituary, remained hospitalized at St. Elizabeth's until her death. There is no record of her death between 1959 and 1963. The District of Columbia prohibits releasing the records of residents who have died within fifty years, so the details of June's passing remain a mystery.

~

Dr. Gilman Osgood shared his opinion about Mrs. Eaton's mental condition with no one except the district attorney until 1934 when he addressed a group of colleagues at the Massachusetts Medico-Legal Society. Osgood firmly believed that the jurors in the Eaton case had rendered a mistaken verdict – not because they were imprudent but because no expert psychiatric testimony had been offered during the trial to assist them in evaluating the defendant's sanity.

After careful analysis of Jennie's demeanor before, during, and after the trial, Osgood concluded that she was paranoiac; that her accusations against the admiral represented a persecutory form of the illness characterized by delusions of jealousy. It was known in psychiatric circles as "paranoia sexualis."

The doctor described as symptomatic Jennie's "calm, undisturbed, unemotional" demeanor as she testified in her defense and her delight at being the center of attention. He cited examples of Jennie's delusions; specifically, her allegations of inappropriate behavior by the admiral toward women in general and toward her daughter, June, in particular. He expounded on instances in which Jennie had accused the admiral of poisoning their adopted child and attempting, on many occasions, to poison her and June.

"When these attempts on one's life are thought to have been made; when it is believed that the husband brings into the house dissolute women, and here orgies are held, while the wife is lulled into unconsciousness by hypodermics of drugs, then the paranoiac wife may become furious and not infrequently murders her husband," Osgood declared.

In Osgood's view, both the community and Mrs. Eaton suffered an injustice. As laymen, he expounded, jurors were ill prepared to make an informed decision about Mrs. Eaton's sanity. They did not possess the knowledge or sophistication to see through her charade. They did not realize that Mrs. Eaton was outwitting them with her composure and acuity as she told the story of her life and jousted with the district attorney during cross-examination.

In 1921, Massachusetts enacted an insanity reform bill known as the "Briggs Law." Proposed by noted psychiatrist L. Vernon Briggs – a Hanover resident, coincidentally – the law required Massachusetts courts to appoint an impartial psychiatrist or psychiatrists from the state's Department of Mental Diseases to examine every person indicted for a capital crime or for repeated felonies.

The psychiatric report was to be made available to the court, the prosecutor, and the defense attorney, but it was not admissible at trial. A defendant found to be insane was committed to a state mental hospital until he or she was determined to be fit to stand trial. A defendant found guilty by reason of insanity was sentenced to a state hospital for life.

In his 2008 book, *Murder and the Death Penalty in Massachusetts,* Boston College Professor Alan Rogers states that Briggs "believed this procedure would spare the mentally ill defendant the bewildering experience of a trial, or, if a trial occurred, the neutral psychiatric report would eliminate the confusing courtroom spectacle of dueling psychiatrists. The reform, he boasted, 'practically does away with the necessity of expert testimony or the trial of mentally ill persons in criminal cases.' "

Osgood praised the Briggs Law in his presentation and expressed his regret that the state legislature had not enacted it before Jennie May Eaton stood trial. Had the law existed at that time, Osgood reasoned, she would have avoided the incredible pressure of having to fight for her life. It might also have spared her friends and family "the ignominy that comes from the logical acts of a mentally ill person."

Notes

CHAPTER 1

1   His thick wool clothing: U.S. Dept. of Agriculture, Weather Bureau, *Surface Weather Observations*, (Boston: Boston Signal Service, U. S. Army, Division of Telegrams and Reports for the Benefit of Commerce, 1913). (Weather Bureau reported sunrise as 6:07 a.m.; temperature between 5 and 6 a.m. was 10 degrees).

2   Osgood agreed to meet: Frank P. Sibley, "Asked Aid of Girls; Wanted Eaton Confined; Wife's Letter of 1909 Before Jury; She Called the Admiral 'An Old Hypocrite;' Dr. Frame Testifies to Death Incidents." *The Boston Daily Globe*, October 19, 1913, 1.

2   Frame instructed Sparrell: Frank P. Sibley, "Traced Anew to Dr. Frame; His Order to Undertaker Starts Eaton Inquiry; This Given before Physician Had Seen the Body; Widow to Be a Witness at the Hingham Inquest Today." *The Boston Daily Globe*, March 17, 1913, 1.

2   It acquired its name: Jedediah Dwelley and John F. Simmons, *A History of the Town of Hanover, Massachusetts with Family Genealogies*, (Hanover, MA: Town of Hanover, 1910), 219.

3   Delivery men rolled along: Hanover Historical Society, under the direction of Fanny Hitchcock Phillips, *History of the Town of Hanover, Massachusetts, 1910-1977*, (Hanover, MA: Hanover Historical Society, 1977), 39, 40.

3   A popular summer resort in Hull: Barbara U. Barker and Leslie J. Molyneaux, *Images of America: Hanover*, (Charleston, SC: Arcadia Publishing, 2004), 119.

3   The Eatons' yellow: Angela Morgan, "Eaton Denounced as Maniac by Elder Stepdaughter; Younger One Sounds Admiral's Praise as the 'Best of Daddies.'" *Boston American*, March 16, 1913, 1.

3   The admiral and his wife purchased: Plymouth County Registry of Deeds, Plymouth, MA. Land Records, book 968, page 400. The admiral and his wife purchased the home for $5500 on July 16, 1907, from Mrs. Ella Bristol Dunham, widow of Henry Dunham, a wealthy Abington shoe manufacturer and inventor. The couple put $500 down and secured a mortgage for the balance.

3   Built in a Folk Victorian style: Robert Cowherd, PhD., "Architectural Style Question." Message to John F. Gallagher, December 18, 2012. Email. Note: Franklin Jacobs inherited the property, which was without buildings, on November 29, 1860 (Plymouth County Registry of Deeds, Land Records, book 303, page 258). By 1870, Jacobs and his family were living on the property. *1870 United States Federal Census*: Census Place: *South Scituate, Plymouth, Massachusetts*; roll: *M593_639*; page: *762A*; image: *692*; Family History Library Film: 552138.

3   Off the dining room: Arnold (Sewell), Lois (former owner/resident of Eaton

place), interview by John F. Gallagher, Norwell, MA, "Description of home's interior and exterior." October 11, 2012.

3   Stairways front and back: "Eaton Murder Jury Visits Home of the Dead Admiral; Accused Widow Hears Reading of the Indictment and Barker's Opening Statement; Judge Orders Recess Till Tomorrow Morning." *Boston Traveler and Evening Herald*, October 15, 1913, 1.

3   The rooms were well-appointed: Angela Morgan, "Arrival of June's Baby Completes Mrs. Eaton's Joy at Home Coming; Widow to Devote All Her Time Now to Literary Work, She Tells Angela Morgan." *Boston American*, November 2, 1913, 3B.

3   Behind it were the outbuildings: "Real Estate – Well Known Poultry Farm Sold." *Boston Evening Transcript*, July 29, 1907, 5.

4   When he spoke to her: Sibley, "Asked Aid of Girls."

5   Frame reiterated his belief: Ibid.

6   "No more roast pork…": Ibid.

7   "There's something behind…": Frank P. Sibley, "Eaton Defense Scores upon the State's Case; In Hard Battle, It Opens before Jury Story of the Reason for June Keyes' Feeling toward Admiral; Once Baffled, Morse Renews Attack Successfully; Defendant's Mother, Aged and Infirm, an Alert Witness; In Dramatic Contrast with the Youthful Dorothy." *The Boston Daily Globe*, October 18, 1913, 1.

CHAPTER 2

8   A portable "cooling board": Kate Sweeney, *American Afterlife: Encounters in the Customs of Mourning* (Athens, GA, University of Georgia Press, 2014), 4.

10   He gathered the admiral's: Jack Eckert, Public Services Librarian, Center for the History of Medicine, Francis A. Countway Library of Medicine, Boston, MA. "William F. Whitney and Joseph Eaton." Message to John F. Gallagher, June 28, 2012. Email. Note: Whitney article at MA Medico-Legal Society on autopsy procedures, "Suggestions in Making Autopsies in Cases of Suspected Poisoning," volume 4, pages 49-54 (1913).

10   The three doctors were taken aback: "Rear Admiral Eaton Poisoned; Slayer Escapes; Jennie May, His Wife, Wins Quick Acquittal On Charge She Fed Old Sea Dog Arsenic; Testifying, Spouse of Officer Claims That Navy Officer Intended to Kill Her and Got Doped Solution Himself; Justice Conducts Long Fight; Search Ends in Complete Defeat; War Hero Found Dead in Bed but All Members of Strange Family Deny Guilt; Still Mystery" *The Syracuse Herald*, March 22, 1925, section 3, 3.

10   When Jennie asked: Frank P. Sibley, "Chided by Mother for Going to Father's Aid; Dorothy Ainsworth Eaton Testifies to This; Daughter Recites Dramatic Story of Night of Death; Frequent Outbreaks of Jealousy and Family Quarrels; Talk of Poison Constant With Woman Accused of Murder." *The Boston Daily Globe*, October 17, 1913, 1.

10   She asked if they had found: Ibid.

10   ...to determine through autopsy: Sibley, "Asked Aid of Girls."

10   Osgood, who had served: Albert Nelson Marquis, *Who's Who in New England - A Biographical Dictionary of Leading Living Men and Women of the States of Maine, New Hampshire, Vermont, Massachusetts, Rhode Island and Connecticut. 2nd Edition,* (Chicago: A. N. Marquis & Co., 1916).

11   The article disclosed that police: "Secret Inquiry on Eaton Death; Dist. Atty. Barker of Brockton among Those Active in It; Cause of Rear Admiral's Sudden End at Norwell Not Determined." *The Boston Daily Globe,* March 12, 1913, 1.

11   "That's all I care to say...": "Mystery Increases as Eaton is Buried; 'I Feared They Would Blame Me, and They Probably Will,' Says Admiral's Widow; Chemist's Report Awaited; State Police Investigating Retired Officer's Death; Absence of Naval Honors Marks His Funeral." *The New York Times,* March 13, 1913, 11.

11   "As to anything else...": "Expect Inquiry as to Widow's Sanity; Member of Eaton Household Lets Fall Only Clew [*sic*] of Day to Death Investigation; Fear of Blame Admitted. Mouths Sealed by Officials; Chemical Analysis Is Under Way; Conference at Brockton at End of the Day; Rear Admiral Is Buried at Dracut." *The Boston Daily Globe,* March 13, 1913, 1.

11   It was the era: Herbert A. Kenny, *Newspaper Row: Journalism in the Pre-Television Era,* (Chester, CT: The Globe Pequot Press, 1987), 71.

CHAPTER 3

13   He practiced law: *Record of the Class of 1837 in Yale University,* 7th edition, (Privately printed – not published, 1887), 56-57.

13   Joseph's mother, Sarah: Samuel Abbott Green, *Groton Historical Series: A Collection of Papers Relating to the History of the Town of Groton, Massachusetts,* Vol. IV, (Groton, MA: University Press, 1899), 167.

13   James Brazer, in 1793: Samuel Abbott Green, *Groton Historical Series: A Collection of Papers Relating To the History of the Town of Groton, Massachusetts,* Vol. I, No. VII, (Groton, MA: University Press, 1885), 4.

13   The couple met: Eaton, William P., *Correspondence of William P. Eaton,* 1836-1864 (bulk 1841-1856). Huntington Library, San Marino, CA. Letter dated February 13, 1845, Lowndesboro, Alabama, from William P. Eaton to his stepmother, Pamela Eaton.

13   Shortly after their marriage: Thomas McAdory Owen, L.L.D., *History of Alabama and Dictionary of Alabama Biography*: Volume III, (Chicago: S. J. Clarke Publishing Co., 1921), 527.

13   In the fall of 1849: *Catalogue of the Officers and Students of the Cahaba Male and Female Academy, 1848-1849, Cahaba, Alabama.* Printed at the "*Gazette*" office, 1849. New York Historical Society Museum and Library, December 28, 2011.

13   William and Sarah resigned: Eaton, William P., *Correspondence of William P. Eaton*, 1836-1864 (bulk 1841-1856). Huntington Library, San Marino, CA. Letter dated December 16, 1850, Cross Keys, Macon County, Alabama, from William P. Eaton to his brother, Giles Eaton.

14   Once settled: Ibid.

14   In December 1850: Ibid.

14   In October, the Board installed: *100 Years of Education, 1847 – 1947*, (Lockport, New York: Board of Education, 1947), 33.

14   That contentment: *Record of the Class of 1837 in Yale University*, 57.

14   Friends and relatives: "Funeral Obsequies of Prof. Eaton; The Union School – Sorrow among the Scholars." *The Lockport Journal*, March 19, 1857 (copy of article in Eaton file at Dracut Historical Society, Dracut, MA).

14   The academy instructed: *Places of the Past, Highland Military Academy*, Worcester, MA.

15   He placed first: Robyn Christensen, Librarian, Worcester Public Library, "Rear Admiral Joseph Eaton." Message to John F. Gallagher, September 21, 2011. Email. Attached document, *Catalogue of the Officers and Cadets of the Highland Military Academy from 1856-1870*.

15   The Naval Academy returned: Benjamin Park, *The United States Naval Academy: Being the Yarn of the American Midshipman (Naval Cadet)*, (New York: G. P. Putnam's Sons, 1900) 234-235, 262.

15   Joseph G. Eaton reported: Department of Veteran Affairs, Regional Office, Federal Building, Baltimore, MD 20201. VA File #XC-02-726-440. Veteran Records of Rear Admiral (Retired) Joseph Giles Eaton.

16   …Atlantic and Pacific Oceans: David G. McCullough, *The Path Between the Seas – The Creation of the Panama Canal 1870-1914*, (New York: Simon & Schuster, 1977) 20, 26.

16   He received promotions to ensign: Department of Veteran Affairs, Regional Office, Federal Building, Baltimore, MD 20201. VA File #XC-02-726-440. Veteran Records of Rear Admiral (Retired) Joseph Giles Eaton.

16   He married Mary Anne: Massachusetts Registry of Vital Records and Statistics, Boston, MA. Marriages, 1871, Dracut, volume 236, page 176, record 4.

16   The couple managed: Massachusetts Registry of Vital Records and Statistics, Boston, MA. Births, 1874, Dracut, volume 260, page 93, record 29.

16   Between October 1887: Department of Veteran Affairs, Regional Office, Federal Building, Baltimore, MD 20201. VA File #XC-02-726-440. Veteran Records of Rear Admiral (Retired) Joseph Giles Eaton.

16   He was promoted to lieutenant commander: Pittsburgh Death Registrations, 1870-1905, volume 50, page 300. Carnegie Library of Pittsburgh, Pittsburgh, PA. Isabel died on June 17, 1888. The attending physician certified her death was caused by "sewer gas emitted from street…"

17   She was buried: "Funeral Services." *The Lowell Daily Courier*, June 20, 1988, 8.

17   The Navy promoted him to full commander: Department of Veteran Affairs, Regional Office, Federal Building, Baltimore, MD 20201. VA File #XC-02-726-440. Veteran Records of Rear Admiral (Retired) Joseph Giles Eaton.

18 In accordance with: Ibid.

18 …while on active duty: An Act to Reorganize and Increase the Efficiency of the Personnel of the Navy and Marine Corps of the United States (Navy Personnel Act) 30 Stat. at L. 1004, section 11, March 3, 1899.

18 He did, however: Department of Veteran Affairs, Regional Office, Federal Building, Baltimore, MD 20201. VA File #XC-02-726-440. Veteran Records of Rear Admiral (Retired) Joseph Giles Eaton.

CHAPTER 4

19 Fremont Smith brought in a specialist: "Doctor Who Attended Admiral's First Wife Gives Mrs. Eaton Praise." *The Washington Times* [Washington, DC], March 30, 1913, 10.

19 Fremont-Smith certified: State Center for Health Statistics, Vital Records Division, Washington, DC; Certificate of Death, 165524.

19 Annie, my wife, died: Dracut Historical Society, Dracut, MA. Joseph Giles Eaton file.

20 The Rev. Dr. Roland C. Smith: "Body of Mrs. A. V. Eaton Laid to Rest." *The Washington Post* [Washington, DC], February 8, 1906, 12.

20 On May 11, 1906: State Center for Health Statistics, Vital Records Division, Washington, DC; Certificate of Death, 165524, Disinterment Permit 5761.

20 A second funeral service: "Funerals." *Lowell Courier-Citizen*, May 24, 1906, 8.

20 Annie's remains: Massachusetts Registry of Vital Records and Statistics, Boston, MA. Deaths, 1906, Dracut, volume 32, page 503, record 30.

20 In her will, dated July 1, 1889: Middlesex County Probate Court, Cambridge, MA. Case No. 70729, filed March 20, 1906, allowed April 10, 1906; Will Book 687, page 108.

20 Jennie May (Harrison) Ainsworth was born: Frank P. Sibley, "Mrs. Eaton to Go On Stand; Defense Opens With Show of Great Assurance; Undertakes to Justify Wife's Oft-Repeated Charges; Clark of *Oregon* Fame a Witness in Laying Foundation For This." *The Boston Daily Globe*, October 24, 1913, 1.

20 Her father, a prosperous: Gilman Osgood, M.D., "The Admiral Eaton Case." *New England Journal of Medicine: Massachusetts Medico-Legal Society*. 112.3 (1934): 111-119.

21 In 1879, when the house: 1880 United States Federal Census: Census Place: Crawford's Quarry, Presque Isle, Michigan; roll: 601; page: 610D; enumeration district: 284.

21 There, he and his wife: "The Mystery of Mrs. Eaton's Childhood Unravelled [sic] by the Sunday Post." *Boston Sunday Post*, March 30, 1913, 1.

21 On September 24, 1881: Ibid.

21 All four drowned: Michigan Department of Community Health, ledger page 65, record 3, date of record: August 4, 1882.

21 She returned with her children: *Boston Sunday Post*, "The Mystery of Mrs.

Eaton's Childhood."

21 They courted for a short time: District of Columbia Marriages, 1811-1950. The couple married on July 2, 1891.

21 Jennie gave birth to Lucia June: District of Columbia, Births and Christenings, 1830-1955. June was born on June 21, 1892.

21 The Ainsworths welcomed: Frank P. Sibley, "Six Hours under Fire; Mrs. Eaton Calmly Baffles Prosecutor's Attacks; Remain on Stand When a Word Would Have Released Her; Exhaustive Cross-Examination Goes on Again Today." *The Boston Daily Globe*, October 28, 1913, 1. Dorothy's birth date has been reported in various sources as 1897, 1898, and 1901.

21 Evicted from place to place: *Boyd's Directory of the District of Columbia, 1894, Together with a Compendium of its Governments, Institutions and Trades, to which is added a Complete Business, Street and Congressional Directory,* (Washington, DC: William H. Boyd, Publisher, 1894), 167.

21 Anxious for a fresh start: "A Carpetbag. A Kansas Man Comes to the Guthrie Land Office." *The Daily Oklahoma State Capital* [Guthrie, OK], August 6, 1897, 4.

21 He arrived in Guthrie: "Personal." *The Daily Oklahoma State Capital* [Guthrie, OK], August 14, 1897, 4.

21 ...Jennie to join him: "Personal Mention." *The Guthrie Daily Leader*, September 14, 1897, 4.

22 Her husband had already accumulated: Frank P. Sibley, "Mrs. Eaton Confident as Own Story Goes to Jurors; Emphatic Denial That She Poisoned Admiral Comes as Climax to Five Hours of Testimony; Explains Words Which Might Carry Sinister Meaning; Full Day of Rest For Grilling by Prosecutor." *The Boston Daily Globe*, October 16, 1913, 1.

22 The family drifted: 1900 United States Federal Census: Census Place: Minneapolis Ward 4, Hennepin, Minnesota; roll: T623_767; page: 13A; enumeration district: 45.

22 Struggling to make ends meet: Sibley, "Mrs. Eaton to Go on Stand."

22 "Deciding at last": Ibid.

22 After their marriage: Massachusetts Registry of Vital Records and Statistics, Boston, MA. Marriages, 1906, Boston, volume 565, page 165, record 3787.

22 At summer's end: Sibley, "Mrs. Eaton Confident as Own Story Goes to Jurors."

CHAPTER 5

25 "I'd rather go to jail...": Frank P. Sibley, "Fails Absolutely to Trace Arsenic; Eaton Prosecution Rests Case with Testimony of Ralph P. Keyes, to Show Motive; Draft of the Defendant's Will Found on Typewriter March 11; Defense Opens at 2 p. m. Today." *The Boston Daily Globe*, October 23 1913, 1.

25 That afternoon, friends and neighbors: Brendan McNamara, McNamara-Sparrell Funeral Home, Norwell, MA – Record Book of 1913. The admiral was buried in a six-foot casket with three handles on each side. The casket had a crepe lining

and the U.S. Navy Seal displayed. A pine outer box was also supplied. The total cost for services was $185.80, which was paid in full on November 10, 1913 by G. W. Kelley, estate attorney.

25   "Oh my God," she groaned: *The Boston Daily Globe*, "Expect Inquiry as to Widow's Sanity."

26   ...Dorothy boarded in the front: Frank Cheney and Anthony Mitchell Sammarco, *Images of America: When Boston Rode the El*, (Charleston, SC: Arcadia Books, 2000), 57, 124. The Atlantic Avenue El operated between 1901 and 1938. It was dismantled in 1942.

27   June Ainsworth had married: Massachusetts Registry of Vital Records and Statistics, Boston, MA. Marriages, 1912, Boston, volume 613, page 298, record 6830.

27   ...on Commonwealth Avenue: "Miss Eaton Married to Ralph P. Keyes." *The Boston Daily Globe*, November 27, 1912, 9.

28   "If a request had been made...": "Eaton's Body May Be Exhumed; His Burial Will Not End the Investigation by State Authorities into Cause of Death." *The Lowell Sun*, March 13, 1913, 9.

29   "Don't say anything about that here": "Admiral Eaton's First Marriage a Happy One is Relative's Statement." *Lowell Courier-Citizen*, March 18, 1913, 9.

29   "...lowered into the grave": "Kearsarge Veteran's Marker Placed on Grave of Admiral Eaton." *Lowell Courier-Citizen*, March 22, 1913, 1.

29   "...you ought to let me alone": *The Boston Daily Globe*, "Expect Inquiry as to Widow's Sanity."

CHAPTER 6

30   Earl MacQuarrie Heartz was born: Massachusetts Registry of Vital Records and Statistics, Boston, MA. Births, 1909, Boston, volume 585, page 33, record 1465. Earl MacQuarrie Heartz was born on February 1, 1909 to Elizabeth Nettie Heartz and an unnamed father.

30   After a hearing: "Told Story of the Adoption; Statement by Wife of Admiral Eaton; Paternity of Infant Who Died Mysteriously; Charges against Husband Resented by Daughter; What the Court Records Show; Admiral Was Opposed." *The Boston Daily Globe*, August 27, 1909, 7.

30   The couple formally announced: "Births." *Rockland Standard and Plymouth County Advertiser*, April 16, 1909, 8.

31   After stopping at the pharmacy: "Seek Cause of Baby's Death; Harvard Medical Men to Determine; Mrs. Eaton Insists Son at Scituate Was Poisoned; Admiral Scouts Theory, Hints at Divorce." *The Boston Daily Globe*, August 25, 1909, 1.

31   ...he was dead: "Massachusetts Registry of Vital Records and Statistics, Boston, MA. Deaths, 1909, Scituate, volume 85, page 345, record 40.

31   ...Harvard Medical School the next day for analysis: "Will Analyze Baby's Stomach for Poison Sign." *The Boston Herald*, August 25, 1909, 1.

32 "…the baby was poisoned": "Believes Baby Was Poisoned; Autopsy Made after Demand by Admiral's Wife." *Boston Post*, August 25, 1913, 1.

32 "…experts for analysis": "Eaton Poisoning Charges; Rear Admiral Consults Lawyer; Wife Sticks to Her Story." *The New York Times,* August 26, 1909, 2.

32 "…the baby has suddenly died": Ibid.

32 "…'June has been poisoned'": "Eaton Family Row." *The Washington Post* [Washington, D.C.], August 25, 1909, 1.

33 "That would make almost…": Ibid.

33 "…soon she was alright": Ibid.

33 "…but if I thought such people": Ibid.

33 "…never witnesses them in real life": Ibid.

34 "…fed him and dressed him": Ibid.

34 "The story is ridiculous": *The New York Times*, "Eaton Poisoning Charges."

34 "His mother did not even wait…": "Poison, Says Baby's Mother." *The Sun* [New York, NY], August 25, 1909, 1.

35 "…unbounded satisfaction": *The Boston Daily Globe*, "Told Story of the Adoption."

35 "…the admiral's son in fact": Ibid.

35 "…as I would be afraid": Ibid.

35 "It is pitiful, pitiful": "Admiral Eaton's Grief; Had Planned Naval Career for Adopted Son, Now Dead." *The New York Times*, August 26, 1909, 4.

36 "…poison all of the time": "Eatons Still Apart; Chemist Will Examine Food of Baby That Died; She Lived in Alexandria." *The Washington Post* [Washington, D.C.], August 28, 1909, 14.

36 "…infancy to manhood": "Eaton Tells His Son's Identity." *Nevada State Journal* [Reno, NV], September 2, 1909, 2.

36 "…in the court records": Ibid.

36 …"good, healthy family": Ibid.

37 "…kept her own counsel": Ibid.

37 "…with full sympathy": Ibid.

37 "…empty as my hearth is": Ibid.

38 "…myself long ago": *The New York Times*, "Admiral Eaton's Grief."

38 "withdraw my promise": *The Washington Post*, "Eatons Still Apart."

38 "…thought me a widow": "Admiral's Widow in Cell as Slayer; Mrs. Eaton Leaves Home Thinking She is a Witness, and is Charged with Murder." *The New York Times*, March 21, 1913, 1.

CHAPTER 7

41 …*if it is possible*: "Said Admiral Eaton Poisoned 100 Men; Accused Widow's Strange Story Related by a Witness at Murder Trial; Queer Letter to Doctor; In it Prisoner Rebuked Him for Alleged Rudeness to Her; Prosecution Rests its Case." *The New York Times*, October 23, 1913.

41 …*saved the life of my dear little boy*: Ibid.

41 "…had already been said": "The Eatons Together Again; Rear Admiral's Wife and Daughters Go to House Where Boy Died." *The New York Times*, September 2, 1909, 1.

42 …*came here to Assinippi*: Frank P. Sibley, "Poison Taken in at Least Two Portions; State Medical Witnesses Fix First as Probably Thursday Evening, March 6; Mrs. Eaton's Counsel Forces Them to Ignore Earlier Illness of Admiral." *The Boston Daily Globe*, October 21, 1913, 1.

43 Whitney's analysis of these items: Massachusetts Registry of Vital Records and Statistics, Boston, MA. Deaths, 1909, Scituate, volume 85, page 345, record 40.

44 "…as innocent as you or I": "Favors Eaton; Mother of Admiral's Wife Blames Her Daughter; Calls Her Erratic; Writes Encouraging Letter to Retired Naval Officer; Mailed in Atlantic City." *The Washington Herald* [Washington, D.C.], August 31, 1909, 1.

44 …to study voice and piano: Maryalice Perrin-Mohr, New England Conservatory of Music, Boston, MA. "June Ainsworth Eaton." Message to John F. Gallagher, August 16, 2012. Email. School record attached. (June was a student from September 1909 to June 1911.)

44 During her first year: 1910 United States Federal Census; Census Place: Braintree, Norfolk, Massachusetts; roll: T624_607; page: 10A; enumeration district: 1082. (June was one of 6 boarders in the home of Mrs. Viola King, 16 Brookside Road. The census was taken on April 20, 1910).

45 June later left Braintree: Frank P. Sibley, "Evidence in Death Chamber of Either Murder or Suicide; Authorities Will Not Say to Which Theory Eaton Investigation Has Since Been Tending; Mrs. Harrison Gives a New Clew [*sic*]; Night Visit to Weymouth a Consequence." *The Boston Daily Globe*, March 18, 1913, 1.

45 …home of Mrs. Frank Floyd: 1910 United States Federal Census; Census Place: Weymouth Ward 3, Norfolk, Massachusetts; roll: T624_610; page: 20A; enumeration district: 1166. (Jennie boarded with Mr. and Mrs. Frank Floyd, 53 Commercial Street).

45 "…when I saw June": "Murder Hypothesis in Eaton Inquest; Police Scout Suicide Theory and Question Members of the Family Closely; Shadow His Stepdaughter; Mrs. Keyes Followed by a Detective; Mrs. Eaton Complained of Husband's Parsimony." *The New York Times*, March 19, 1913, 6.

46 *My Dear Mrs. Farrar*: Charles E. Parker, "Eaton Gave $30,000 to Wife Then Lost It in Stock Deal; Accused Poisoner of Husband, in Seven-Hour Ordeal Under Cross-Examination, Says She Was Puzzled as to Where Admiral Got the Money; Calm Under Attack of District Attorney; Married Naval Officer to Save His Life, She Tells District Attorney; Letter, in Which She Scored Women Gossips of Assinippi, Read in Court." *Boston Post*, October 28, 1913, 1.

CHAPTER 8

48 …meeting with Mrs. Eaton and Judge Kelley: "Barker Imposes Seal of Silence; Protracted Conference at the Eaton Home in Norwell; Widow of Rear Admiral and Her Mother Both Reported Ill." *The Boston Daily Globe,* March 14, 1913, 1.

49 "…what hour you will do it": Ibid.

49 "…my place was at her side": Frank P. Sibley, "Mrs. Eaton Demands Some Action Today; Widow of Rear Admiral Tires of Mystery and Delay of Authorities in Investigation; Assumes the Aggressive; Is Persecuted, She Declares; Unspoken Suspicion Must Cease; Report of Prof Whitney Is Probably in Hand; Judge Kelly Believed to Know Finding." *The Boston Daily Globe*, March 15, 1913, 1.

50 "…repeated in print": Ibid.

50 "…watched with care and fear": "Inquest to Learn How Admiral Died; Authorities Have Traced Sale of Chloral Said to Have Been Found in Stomach; Suspense Rasps Mrs. Eaton." *The New York Times*, March 5, 1913, 3.

50 "…smoked before breakfast": Sibley, "Mrs. Eaton Demands Some Action Today."

50 "…on members of the family": Ibid.

51 "…protest at their attitude": Sibley, "Mrs. Eaton Demands Some Action Today."

CHAPTER 9

52 …drove his Thomas automobile: *1913 Brockton and Bridgewaters Directory of the Inhabitants, Business Firms, Institutions, City Government, Manufacturing Establishments, Societies, Streets, with House Directory, Map, Etc.*, No. XXXI, (Boston: W.A. Greenough & Co., 1913), Auto Owners, 901.

52 …ushered the prosecutor inside: Sibley, "Evidence in Death Chamber of Either Murder or Suicide."

53 "…to be an investigation," she added: Sibley, "Traced Anew to Dr. Frame."

53 …for her duplicity: Ibid.

54 "…questions put to her": Sibley, "Evidence in Death Chamber of Either Murder or Suicide."

54 "…this matter is finished": "Begin Eaton Inquest; Secret Inquiry at Hingham; Transferred to Norwell." *Boston Evening Transcript*, March 17, 1913, 1.

54 "…toward suicide or murder": Sibley, "Evidence in Death Chamber of Either Murder or Suicide."

55 Kelley knew Geogan: "Francis J. Geogan." *Rockland Standard and Plymouth County Advertiser*, June 7, 1912, 27.

55 "…how far I shall go in the case": Sibley, "Evidence in Death Chamber of Either Murder or Suicide."

56 "…told not to talk": Frank P. Sibley, "Eaton Death Inquest So Far Barren of Results; Authorities, as Much in Dark as Public, Finding Nothing on Which to Base Even a Suspicion; 'No Mystery,' Says Stepdaughter; Further Hearing Goes

Over to Tomorrow." *The Boston Daily Globe*, March 19, 1913, 1.
56 "...she loved the admiral dearly": Ibid.

CHAPTER 10

58 "...when all are heard": Frank P. Sibley, "Frame's Delay New Mystery; Knowledge of Case Gained While Eaton Was Alive; Suspicions Not Voiced Till Early the Next Morning; Inquest Now Said to Point Closely to One Person." *The Boston Daily Globe*, March 20, 1913, 1.
58 "...fishing expedition of the authorities": Ibid.
59 ...took a sample of the powder with them: Ibid.
59 ...Navy officers and sailors": "Kearsarge Veterans Will Mark the Grave of Admiral Eaton." *Lowell Courier-Citizen*, March 20, 1913, 1.
60 "...Eaton, U.S. Navy": "Naval Flag for Grave." *The Boston Daily Globe*, March 20, 1913, 2.

CHAPTER 11

61 "...how I ever lived with him": Frank P. Sibley, "Mrs. Eaton Goes to Jail under Charge of Murder; Arrest at Hingham Without Warning; Mrs. Eaton, under Arrest, Starting for Plymouth Jail in Custody of State Detective Scott; Another Person May Be Taken Into Custody Later; No Purchase of Poison Traced, No Motive Established; Dist. Atty. Barker Secures Order For a Special Grand Jury; New Plymouth County Jail, Showing Room Assigned to Accused Woman." *The Boston Daily Globe*, March 21, 1913, 1.
62 ...on the second floor to await DA Barker: Ibid.
62 "...peace of the Commonwealth": "Mrs. Eaton in Jail." *Old Colony Memorial* [Plymouth, MA], March 22, 1913, 1.
63 "I will not go through": Sibley, "Mrs. Eaton Goes to Jail under Charge of Murder."
63 "...died from arsenical poisoning": Massachusetts Bureau of Vital Records and Statistics, Boston, MA. Deaths, Norwell, 1913, volume 79, page 376. The cause of death was certified by Dr. Gilman Osgood as "Arsenical Poisoning-Manner Unknown." Osgood did not file the certificate until November 21, 1913.
63 "...where the poison was procured": Sibley, "Mrs. Eaton Goes to Jail under Charge of Murder."
63 "...of striking appearance": *The New York Times*, "Admiral's Widow in Cell as Slayer."
63 ...saw tears in her eyes: Sibley, "Mrs. Eaton Goes to Jail under Charge of Murder."
64 ...with his umbrella: "Mrs. Eaton in Jail." *Old Colony Memorial* [Plymouth, MA], March 22, 1913, 1.
64 ...exclusively for female prisoners: Ibid.

65 "…second arrest may be possible": Sibley, "Mrs. Eaton Goes to Jail under Charge of Murder."

65 "…against another person": "Mrs. Eaton Cries from Prison Cell: 'I'll Soon Be Free;' Accused Woman Sure She Will Prove Innocence; Renew Search For Poison Sale As Missing Link in Eaton Death Case; Second Arrest is Hinted at by State Detectives at Work on Mystery." *Boston American*, March 21, 1913, 1, 10.

65 "…she were guilty of poisoning": Sibley, "Mrs. Eaton Goes to Jail under Charge of Murder."

65 …sitting of the grand jury on March 24: Ibid.

66 "…the cause of the rear admiral's death": "Another Woman to Be Arrested in Eaton Case; Police Believe She Obtained Poison Which Killed the Rear Admiral; William A. Morse as Widow's Counsel." *The New York Herald*, March 24, 1913, 7.

67 "…on the part of the defendant": Office of the Clerk of the Circuit Court of Cook County, Chicago, IL. Divorce Case File Copy: Ainsworth, Jennie and Daniel; Case #G271692.

67 …The *Globe* and the *New York Times* exposed the letter: "Wife's Fear of Eaton Voiced in March, 1911; Begged Counsel For Advice and Aid; Admiral Then Described as a 'Dangerous Maniac;' James Thom Says June Was Also in Terror of Stepfather; Accused Woman Writes Cheerful Letter to Her Household; Fascination For Strange Poisons." *The Boston Daily Globe*, March 22, 1913, 1.

68 "…the admiral leering at her": Ibid.

69 "…dependent for support": Frank P. Sibley, "Search for Poison Sale; State Said to Be Weak in Eaton Murder Case; 'Exclusive Opportunity' Is Charge Expected; June Keyes Tells of Injury to Head of Admiral in Big Gun Practice." *The Boston Daily Globe*, March 23, 1913, 1.

CHAPTER 12

70 …in a name they could link to her: "Seek Seller of Poison." *Boston Evening Transcript*, March 22, 1913, 2.

70 …required to record every sale: *Public Health Reports Issued Weekly by the United States Public Health Service Containing Information of the Current Prevalence of Disease, the Occurrence of Epidemics, Sanitary Legislations, and Related Subjects. Volume XXVIII, Part II, Numbers 27-52, July – December, 1913* (Washington: Government Printing Office, 1914) 2013.

70 "…also in Medford and Somerville": "A Special Jury for Mrs. Eaton." *The Sun* [New York, NY], March 22, 1913, 4.

71 "…something may be learned": Ibid.

73 "…detrimental to her character": "Basis of Frame's First Suspicion." *The Boston Daily Globe*, March 22, 1913, 1.

73 …her mother and the farm: Angela Morgan, "Accused Woman Marvels at Strange Fate in Poison Tragedy; Angela Morgan's Study of Admiral Eaton's Widow in her Cell at Plymouth County Jail." *Boston American*, Sunday Ed.,

March 23, 1913, 9L.

73 …a former Massachusetts state senator: Edwin Monroe Bacon, *The Book of Boston: Fifty Years' Recollections of the New England Metropolis.* (Boston: Book of Boston Co., 1916), 410.

74 "…who are now there alone": "Guard at Eaton Home to Protect the Women." *The Washington Post* [Washington, DC], March 23, 1913, 3.

74 "…money he had, long ago": Sibley, "Search for Poison Sale."

74 Hawley had graduated from the Naval Academy…: Hamersly, Lewis Randolph. *The Records of Living Officers of the U. S. Navy and Marine Corps, Compiled from Official Sources.* Fifth Edition. (Philadelphia: L. R. Hamersly and Company, 1894). 169, 189.

75 "…by the firing of big guns.": "Another Woman to Be Arrested in Eaton Case." *New York Herald* 24 March 1913, 7.

75 "…great nerve and quiet bravery": "Naval Men Deny Eaton Dabbled With Poisons." *Boston American*, April 1, 1913, 4.

75 "fraught with riddles and weird problems": Morgan, "Accused Woman Marvels at Strange Fate in Poison Tragedy."

76 "…anything happened to her": "Eaton Case Breaks Up Daughter's Home; Eldest Child of Woman Held on Murder Charge Leaves Husband for Sister." *The Washington Times* [Washington, DC], April 4, 1913, 1.

77 …granddaughter back to June in Dorchester: Frank P. Sibley, "State Probably Not to Call June Keyes; Contents Itself With the Story of the Birth of Her Baby in Washington in April, 1912; Defense in Eaton Trial Nears Its Opening Without Disclosing What Its Lines Will Be." *The Boston Daily Globe*, October 22, 1913, 1.

CHAPTER 13

78 "…I had to stop her": "Feared Admiral Would Poison Her, Mrs. Keyes Told Neighbor." *Boston Journal*, March 20, 1913, 2.

78 …Weyand Secret Service Bureau of Boston: "Mrs. Eaton Asked if Expert Could Detect Poisons After Death." *The Washington Times* [Washington, DC], March 23, 1913, 1.

79 "…dead when I get home": "Accused Wife, In Fear, Tried to Shadow Eaton; Told Nordstrom of Admiral's Queer Actions with Fatal Drugs in Sea Chest." *Boston American*, March 23, 1913, 8L.

79 …she asked the admiral: Sibley, "State Probably Not to Call June Keyes."

79 "…while shaking hands": *The Washington Times*, Mrs. Eaton Asked if Expert Could Detect."

80 …never heard from her again: *Boston American*, "Accused Wife, In Fear, Tried to Shadow Eaton."

80 "…from my list of patients": "Grand Jurors Warned; Must Not Talk of Eaton Case; Number of Witnesses Testify Before Them; Sanity Board Suggested for

Mrs. Eaton; Members and Acquaintances of Family at Court." *Boston Evening Transcript*, March 24, 1913, 1.

81 "...which was $300": "Wife Wished Eaton Put in an Asylum." *The New York Times*, March 22, 1913, 20.

81 ...the possibility of a second arrest: Frank P. Sibley, "Mrs. Keyes Not Heard By Grand Jury; Waits All Day for Call That Does Not Come; Husband Examined; Eaton Ill When June Arrived, March 5." *The Boston Daily Globe*, March 25, 1913, 1.

81 "...dangers removed from the patient": Sibley, "Frame's Delay New Mystery."

82 "knowing the circumstances": "Tell Grand Jury about Eaton's Death." *Meriden Morning Record*, March 25, 1913, 12.

82 "strained and worried look": Frank P. Sibley, "Mrs. Keyes Heard; Called to Testify, Following Long Ordeal for Younger Sister; Dorothy Ainsworth Examined for Four Hours at Plymouth." *The Boston Daily Globe*, March 26, 1913, 1.

83 ...safely at home a short time later: "Surrounded by Crowd; Restaurant Doors Locked While Mrs. Keyes and Dorothy Ainsworth are Served Supper in Rockland" *The Boston Daily Globe*, March 26, 1913, 2.

83 Judge George Kelley appeared: Plymouth County Registry of Deeds, Plymouth, MA, Land Records – Book 1149, Page 381.

85 "...only a matter of time": "Eaton Indictment is Expected Today." *Boston Journal*, March 27, 1913, 4.

86 "Oh, dear": Ibid.

86 "...no trouble within": "Mrs. Eaton Calm at Arraignment; Pleads Not Guilty to Murder Charge; Her Council May Attack Indictment Later; Dist. Atty. Barker Again Hints at Insanity." *The Boston Daily Globe*, March 29, 1913, 11.

87 "Not guilty" Jennie murmured: Ibid.

87 "...to jail without bail, is granted": Ibid.

87 "...will be very carefully examined": Ibid.

87 Reporters, hungry to explore: Ibid.

88 ...red iron bars. Morgan, "Accused Woman Marvels at Strange Fate."

88 ...after she was gone: *The New York Times*, "Admiral's Widow in Cell as Slayer."

89 "...defense of his country in war": *The Washington Times*, "Doctor Who Attended Admiral's First Wife Gives Mrs. Eaton Praise."

CHAPTER 14

90 Jennie's defense team filed: "Four Motions Made; Filed by Attorneys in Eaton Case on Wednesday." *Old Colony Memorial* [Plymouth, MA], April 12, 1913, 1.

90 On the same date, Judge Kelley sent his personal secretary: "Nearly All to Widow; Will of the Late Admiral J. G. Eaton Filed on Wednesday." *Old Colony Memorial* [Plymouth, MA], April 12, 1913, 1.

90 ...to his beloved stepdaughter, Dorothy: Plymouth County Registry of Probate,

Plymouth, MA. Last Will and Testament of Joseph Giles Eaton, Volume 245, Page 413; filed April 9, 1913.

90 Nearly two months after Jennie's arrest: "Four Jurors Quickly Chosen in Eaton Trial at Plymouth; Accused Widow, in Good Spirits, Poses for Photographers Before Case Is Called; Few Spectators Able to Enter Court Room." *Boston Traveler and Evening Herald*, October 14, 1913, 4.

91 …in 1913 was $800: IRS: Understanding Taxes. The Whys of Taxes, Theme 6; Understanding the IRS, Lesson 1: The IRS Yesterday and Today. http://apps.irs.gov/app/understandingTaxes/student/whys_thm06_les01.jsp#taxTrivia

91 …the bulk of his assets, some $30,000: ($30,000 is the equivalent of $717,000 today): Measuring Worth. www.measuringworth.com.

92 …characteristics of the paranoiac wife: Osgood, "The Admiral Eaton Case."

93 …the purchase of poison: *The Sun*, "A Special Jury for Mrs. Eaton."

94 Wright testified about a transaction: "No Poison Sold to Mrs. Eaton; Rockland Druggist Destroys a Clew [sic] to Supposed Purchase; One Mysterious Witness among the Seven Heard at Inquest." *The Boston Daily Globe*, May 17, 1913, 1.

94 Judge Aiken set a trial date: "Prosecution Won't Disclose Its Hand; Chief Justice Denies Motions of the Eaton Defense." *Fitchburg Daily Sentinel*, July 22, 1913, 11.

95 …to testify once more: "To Resume Eaton Inquest Today; Eight New Witnesses Said to Have Been Called; Trial of Widow Accused of Murder Set to Open October 14." *The Boston Daily Globe*, October 2, 1913, 1.

96 As to criminal responsibility: Sibley, "State Probably Not to Call June Keyes."

97 …thirty feet from the witness stand: "To Report Murder Trial; Sheriff Porter Makes Arrangements for Newspapermen at Trial of Mrs. Eaton." *Old Colony Memorial* [Plymouth, MA], October 5, 1913, 1.

98 …a fair and impartial trial until its conclusion: Frank P. Sibley, "Full Jury Named; Eaton Murder Trial at Plymouth Got Speedily Under Way; Defendant, in Good Spirits, Assists Her Counsel in Selection; Jury Chosen for the Eaton Trial." *The Boston Daily Globe*, October 15, 1913, 1.

CHAPTER 15

100 "…one day nearer home": Frank P. Sibley, "Ainsworth Girl a State Witness; Daughter of Mrs. Eaton Called to Plymouth by Dist. Atty. Barker; Court Day Occupied by Jury's View at the Home in Assinippi." *The Boston Daily Globe*, October 16, 1913, 1.

101 …darting nervously about the courtroom: "Eaton Jury Visits Home of Accused Widow." *The Meriden Daily Journal*, October 15, 1913, 9.

101 …waived her right to do so: "Eaton Murder Jury Visits Home of the Dead Admiral; Accused Widow Hears Reading of the Indictment and Barker's Opening Statement; Judge Orders Recess Till Tomorrow Morning." *Boston*

Traveler and Evening Herald, October 15, 1913, 1.

102 ...until called to take the stand: "Mrs. Eaton Hears Charges; Trial for Murder of Her Husband Is Now On; Daughter Is Star Witness." *Quincy Daily Ledger,* October 16, 1913, 2.

102 Four bailiffs bearing white staffs: Sibley, "Ainsworth Girl a State Witness."

104 "...maintained its contention": "Jealousy as Motive for Eaton Death." *The Brockton Times,* October 16, 1913, 1.

105 ...restlessly in her chair: "Says Jealousy Was Motive of Eaton Murder." *The Syracuse Herald,* October 16, 1913, 1.

105 ...agitated by Katzmann's allegations: Ibid.

106 "...repeated what June told her": Ibid.

106 "...herself, June, and Dorothy": Ibid.

106 "...to an insane asylum": Ibid.

107 "...first thing in the morning": Sibley, "Chided by Mother for Going to Father's Aid."

107 "I never studied them": Ibid.

107 "...a wealthy lover in the West": Ibid.

107 "...a sane or insane woman": "Eaton Murder Attributed to Quarrel over Stepdaughter; Assistant Prosecutor Declares June Keyes Came First in Mother's Affections; Says State Will Prove Wife Threatened Admiral." *Boston Traveler and Evening Herald,* October 16, 1913, 1.

109 ...the admiral smoked opium: Sibley, "Chided by Mother for Going to Father's Aid."

109 Barker next tried to draw: *The Brockton Times,* "Jealousy as Motive for Eaton Death."

110 "About three hours": "Eaton Murder Attributed to Quarrel Over Stepdaughter; Assistant Prosecutor Declares June Keyes Came First in Mother's Affections; Says State Will Prove Wife Threatened Admiral; Attributes Eaton Crime to Hatred." *Boston Traveler and Evening Herald,* October 16, 1913, 3.

110 "No," answered the doctor: Sibley, "Chided by Mother for Going to Father's Aid."

110 ...the aftereffects of alcohol: *The Brockton Times,* "Jealousy as Motive for Eaton Death."

111 "...without a poison effect," he said: Sibley, "Chided by Mother for Going to Father's Aid."

111 ...excused Wheatley and ordered a short recess: Ibid.

112 "I believe it does," Osgood replied: Ibid.

112 ...remarked on how attractive she was: Ibid.

CHAPTER 16

113 "...as if she was his own daughter": Sibley, "Chided by Mother for Going to Father's Aid."

115 "...perhaps mosquito bites": Ibid.

116 "...she was angry with father": Ibid.
119 "...she gave me one hour": Ibid.
122 "...I would telephone from Mrs. Simmons's": Ibid.

CHAPTER 17

125 "He couldn't bear him": Sibley, "Eaton Defense Scores Upon the State's Case."
127 Judge Aiken interrupted: Ibid.
129 Dorothy repeated her testimony: Ibid.
131 "...nothing she could do": Ibid.
132 "No, I never did," said Dorothy: Ibid.
132 ...remove Dorothy from the courtroom: *The New York Times*, "Mrs. Eaton Jealous, Says Her Daughter."

CHAPTER 18

136 Aiken called a recess when the conference ended: Sibley, "Eaton Defense Scores upon the State's Case."
137 "I have never heard her say that," Mrs. Harrison said: Ibid.
139 ...Mrs. Harrison to each question: Ibid.
140 "Yes, two or three times," replied the witness: Ibid.
140 The prosecutor turned to the inquest transcript: Ibid.
141...she had no recollection of it: Ibid.
144 "He did": Ibid.

CHAPTER 19

147 "...anything about the brain": Sibley, "Asked Aid of Girls."
150 "...no memory of her saying it": Ibid.
151 "...pass through the admiral's hand?" No": Ibid.
151 ...a nurse at St. Luke's Hospital: "Mrs. Eaton Asked Choir Singer to Accuse Aged Admiral of Flirting; Miss Grace B. Howard Tells of Letter Received on Which Words 'Old Hypocrite' Are Used; Wife Accused Husband of Using Drugs, Doctor Says." *Boston Traveler and Evening Herald*, October 18, 1913, 1.
152 ...*know of you in any way*: Ibid.
153 "...after receiving this letter": Sibley, "Asked Aid of Girls."
153 "...like that had happened": "Testified to Mrs. Eaton's Fear of Admiral." *Boston American*, October 19, 1913, 1.
153 ...bookkeeper for Rice and Hutchins: *Resident and Business Directory of Rockland and Abington, Massachusetts – 1916 – Containing a Complete Resident, Street and Business Directory, Town Officers, Schools, Societies, Churches, Post-Offices, Rates of Postage, and Other Useful Matter*, (Hopkinton, MA: A. E. Foss & Co.), 79.

153 "…reference to household affairs": *Boston Traveler and Evening Herald,* "Mrs. Eaton Asked Choir Singer."

154 "…should have said so," she replied: Sibley, "Asked Aid of Girls."

CHAPTER 20

157 "…letter would not reach me": Sibley, "Poison Taken in at Least Two Portions."

157 …a total of 16.67 grains (1.08 grams): Ibid.

158 …no evidence of alcoholism in any of the organs he had examined: Ibid.

158 "From two to three grains," the witness answered: Parker, "Heard Mrs. Eaton Wish Her Husband Was Dead."

158 "…mingled with solid food," the doctor offered: Sibley, "Poison Taken in at Least Two Portions."

159 "It could not," the doctor replied: Ibid.

160 Morse attacked Whitney's assertion: Ibid.

161 "…inconsistent with the assumption of only one initial dose?" Morse asked: Ibid.

161 "…as late as Thursday evening?" asked Barker. "Yes," the doctor answered: Ibid.

162 "…there was violent nausea," replied Balch: Ibid.

163 …throughout the circulatory system: Parker, "Heard Mrs. Eaton Wish Her Husband Was Dead."

163 …six to eight hours before death: Sibley, "Poison Taken in at Least Two Portions."

164 "At least two," the chemist said: Ibid.

165 …the amount of arsenic was small: Ibid.

165 "…thought of a cup of tea," Balch responded: Ibid.

166 "…the woman across the way," said the witness: Ibid.

166 "…you can come home now": Ibid.

166 …helped Dorothy with her school lessons: Parker, "Heard Mrs. Eaton Wish Her Husband Was Dead."

166 "…where the money went": Sibley, "Poison Taken in at Least Two Portions."

166 "…but I told her I couldn't": Parker, "Heard Mrs. Eaton Wish Her Husband Was Dead."

167 "…sending the boy to him for a talk": Sibley, "Poison Taken in at Least Two Portions."

168 "…consider that a threat," asked Cate: Ibid.

168 "…he had heard her say it more than once": Parker, "Heard Mrs. Eaton Wish Her Husband Was Dead."

168 …which he carried in his coat pocket: Sibley, "Poison Taken in at Least Two Portions."

169 …Griffith replied simply: Ibid.

170 …arm-in-arm on the grounds of their home: Ibid.

CHAPTER 21

171 ...on the most affectionate of terms: Sibley, "State Probably Not to Call June Keyes."

172 ...the witness stepped down: Ibid.

173 ...consistent with the testimony of others: Ibid.

173 "Nor was he of unsound mind: "State Won't Call June Keyes as Witness against Accused Mother; 'I'm Through with Her,' Says Barker; 'You'd Better See Defence [*sic*];' Neighbors on the Stand; Admiral 'Drug Fiend,' Wife Told Visitors." *Boston Traveler and Evening Herald*, October 21, 1913, 1.

174 ...always seemed happy together: Sibley, "State Probably Not to Call June Keyes."

175 ...never discussed it with the admiral: Ibid.

175 ...polite to her that day: Ibid.

175 ...had never flirted with her: Ibid.

176 ...whenever they visited the store: Ibid.

177 ...admiral under the influence of alcohol: Ibid.

178 ...appeared to be on friendly terms: Ibid.

179 ...his fledgling detective business: Ibid.

183 ..."letters from Assinippi were from her husband?": Ibid.

186 "No, not that," said the investigator: Ibid.

CHAPTER 22

187 "...we will summon her": "Mrs. Eaton Will Testify About Death." *Meriden Daily Journal*, October 23, 1913, 9.

187 ...the mystery of her husband's death: "Mrs. Eaton's Story is Told by Detective on the Witness Stand; Bought No Poison; State Cannot Find Any Record of Widow's Purchase." *Meriden Daily Journal*, October 22, 1913, 1.

188 "...hopping round the bars": Sibley, "Fails Absolutely to Trace Arsenic."

188 "...he was too weak": *Meriden Daily Journal*, "Mrs. Eaton's Story is Told."

188 ...arsenic mixed into the soda: Ibid.

188 ...testimony on October 17: Ibid.

188 ...stricken from the record: "State Fails to Trace Poison Sale to Accused Eaton Widow; Detectives Tell of Futile Search in Bay State, Alexandria, Va., and Georgetown, DC; Say Widow Drafted Will, Leaving Estate to June." *Boston Traveler and Evening Herald*, October 22, 1913, 1.

189 "It was horrible": Ibid.

189 "She did": Ibid.

190 ...admiral had placed poison in it: "Wife Accused the Admiral of Being a Poisoner, 'Twas Said." *Boston Traveler and Evening Herald*, October 23, 1913, 3.

190 "...his mind was all right": "Kin Claims Eaton Planned Murder; Son-in-Law

345

Testifies He Overheard Women Discuss Admiral's Plans; Death Came Soon After." *Daily Republican* [Cape Girardeau, MS], October 23, 1913, evening edition, 1.

190 ...*my dear, little boy*: "Said Admiral Eaton Poisoned 100 Men; Accused Widow's Strange Story Related by a Witness at Murder Trial; Queer Letter to Doctor; In it, Prisoner Rebuked Him for Alleged Rudeness to Her; Prosecution Rests its Case." *The New York Times*, October 23, 1913.

190 Ask your wife to speak: Sibley, "Six Hours under Fire."

191 ...so Aiken excused Colgate: Sibley "Fails Absolutely to Trace Arsenic."

192 ...a signature for receipt of the drug: Ibid.

193 "...five o'clock the next morning," Keyes recalled: Ibid.

194 ...affectionate in tone: Ibid.

195 "...daughter of Mr. Keyes is false.": "Mrs. Eaton's Daughter Says Mother Didn't Kill Admiral." *Syracuse Daily Journal*, October 21, 1913, 5.

195 In a new development: *Meriden Daily Journal*, "Mrs. Eaton Will Testify about Death."

CHAPTER 23

202 "...a fair, honest verdict": Sibley, "Mrs. Eaton to Go on Stand."

202 ...the force and logic of his address: Ibid

206 "...answer as well as you can": Ibid.

207 ...at Morse's urgent request: Ibid.

209 "...I did my whole duty": Ibid.

210 "...what he thought was right," Clark said: Ibid.

CHAPTER 24

211 "...know me perfectly well": Frank P. Sibley, "Steeling Mrs. Eaton for Today's Ordeal; Counsel Many Hours With Her at Jail, Preparatory to Her Taking the Stand This Morning; Story of Sale of Arsenic to Admiral Provokes Battle of the Day." *The Boston Daily Globe*, October 25, 1913, 1.

212 "...in general, spruce up": "Convict-Doctor Swears He Sold Adm'l Eaton 4600 Arsenic Tablets; Physician Also Declares Naval Officer Said Adopted Baby Ate Pill and Died; M'Nally Says Eaton Drank Heavily at Navy Yard." *Boston Traveler and Evening Herald*, October 24, 1913, 1.

212 ...might hinder his case: Sibley, "Steeling Mrs. Eaton for Today's Ordeal."

212 ...known the Eatons since 1907: Ibid.

213 ...bills in excess of $1700: *Boston Traveler*, "Convict-Doctor Swears He Sold Adm'l Eaton 4600 Arsenic Tablets."

214 "As a friend," Kelley replied: Sibley, "Steeling Mrs. Eaton for Today's Ordeal."

214 "...be helpful to her": *Boston Traveler*, "Convict-Doctor Swears He Sold Adm'l Eaton 4600 Arsenic Tablets."

215 ...so Kelley was excused: Sibley, "Steeling Mrs. Eaton for Today's Ordeal."

216 "I knew Joseph G. Eaton": *Boston Traveler*, "Convict-Doctor Swears He Sold Adm'l Eaton 4600 Arsenic Tablets."

216 "...heard of for his trouble": Sibley, "Steeling Mrs. Eaton for Today's Ordeal."

216 Bromide of gold mixed with arsenic: Frank L. James, PhD., M.D. and A. H. Ohmann-Dumesnil, A.M., M.D., editors, "Medical Progress-Therapeutics: Remarks upon Gold in Therapy." *St. Louis Medical and Surgical Journal.* Vol. 69, Jul-Dec (1895): 354.

217 "...dogs about the place": Sibley, "Steeling Mrs. Eaton for Today's Ordeal."

217 "I kept them two weeks": *Boston Traveler*, "Convict-Doctor Swears He Sold Adm'l Eaton 4600 Arsenic Tablets."

217 ...to Bridgewater due to illness: "C. F. King Dead; No Pardon; Red Tape Blocks Wish of Financier to Die a Free Man." *The New York Times*, July 22, 1913, 3.

217 King died at Bridgewater: Ibid.

219 ...instructed the jury to disregard it: Sibley, "Steeling Mrs. Eaton for Today's Ordeal."

220 "...nor anybody else": Ibid.

222 "...intoxicated on this occasion?" "Yes": Ibid.

222 "during the entire watch": Ibid.

222 "...it was a happy home": Ibid.

223 "...he didn't smell of liquor": Ibid.

224 "...two doctors to examine him": Ibid.

CHAPTER 25

225 "...for such an opportunity": "Doctor Sold Eaton Poison; Admiral Said Baby Took Pill and Died; Widow on Stand Today." *Fitchburg Daily Sentinel*, October 25, 1913, 12.

225 ...as the sole beneficiary: Sibley, "Mrs. Eaton Confident as Own Story Goes to Jurors."

226 "...for Dorothy's lameness": *Gould's St. Louis Directory for 1902 (for the year ending April, 1903). Being a Complete Index of the Residents of the Entire City, and a Classified Business Directory to which is added an Appendix Containing Useful Information of the Churches, Societies, Railroads, City, State and Other Miscellaneous Matter, Also Street and Avenue Directory.* (St. Louis, MO: Gould Directory Company, 1902), 108.

226 "...fully three years": Ibid.

227 ...six days before she died: Sibley, "Mrs. Eaton Confident as Own Story Goes to Jurors."

229 "...the admiral's financial condition": Ibid.

231 "...to be taunted," Jennie explained: Ibid.

231 *...not considered dangerous: Sidney Ringer, M.D., F.R.S. and Harrington Sainsbury, M.D., F.R.S., *A Handbook of Therapeutics, Thirteenth Edition.* (New York: William Wood and Company, 1897), 222-223.

232 "...examinations at the conservatory": Sibley, "Mrs. Eaton Confident as Own Story Goes to Jurors."

233 ...*with a warm kiss, Your Joe.*: "Mrs. Eaton Bares Tragedy of Life With Her Two 'Drunken Husbands;' Forced to Become Book Agent, Then Nurse, She Met Admiral at Wife's Deathbed; Declares Naval Officer Attacked Her Daughter." *Boston Traveler and Evening Herald*, October 25, 1913, 1.

233 ...from the stand to the anteroom: Sibley, "Mrs. Eaton Confident as Own Story Goes to Jurors."

CHAPTER 26

236 "...with my dressing things": Sibley, "Mrs. Eaton Confident as Own Story Goes to Jurors."

238 "...to get rid of him": Ibid.

239 ...*is now exacted*: Ibid.

240 "...the effect of the drug": Ibid.

243 "...never in my life!" she declared: Ibid.

243 "...fond of Admiral Eaton": Charles E. Parker, "Mrs. Eaton Denies Poisoning Admiral; Plymouth Prisoner, Cool and Smiling, Tells Life Story on Stand; Describes Two Attacks on June; Doctors Watch as She Testifies." *Boston Sunday Post*, October 26, 1913, 1.

244 "...I shall be at home": Sibley, "Mrs. Eaton Confident as Own Story Goes to Jurors."

244 "...not afraid of it": Frank P. Sibley, "No Fears of Today's Ordeal; Mrs. Eaton Ready for Cross-Examination; Holds It Necessary Part of Her Experience; Dist. Atty. Barker Gives No Hint of Probable Length." *The Boston Daily Globe*, October 27, 1913, 1.

CHAPTER 27

245 Once sworn, Jennie took her seat: "Mrs. Eaton Declares She Married Naval Officer to Save His Life; Accused Widow Asserts Admiral Was Drinking Himself to Death in Washington; Defendant Cool under Grilling by Prosecutor." *Boston Traveler and Evening Herald*, October 27, 1913, 1.

246 "Selling books two days a week" "...at thirty five dollars a pair": *Boston Traveler*, "Mrs. Eaton Declares She Married Naval Officer to Save His Life."

247 "...at the Washington Hospital and Nurse's Home": Sibley, "Six Hours under Fire."

247 "Before, I am sure": *Boston Traveler*, "Mrs. Eaton Declares She Married Naval Officer to Save His Life."

248 "...a course of treatment": Ibid.

248 ...keep his remarks to himself: Sibley, "Six Hours under Fire."

249 "...too ill to give it to him": *Boston Traveler*, "Mrs. Eaton Declares She Married Naval Officer to Save His Life."

250 "...liquor to do so": Ibid.

250 "It wouldn't make any difference": Sibley, "Six Hours under Fire."

250 "...he wasn't there," she said defiantly: *Boston Traveler*, "Mrs. Eaton Declares She Married Naval Officer to Save His Life."

251 "...fifteen at each meal": Ibid.

251 "That would be forty-five...": Sibley, "Six Hours under Fire."

251 "...He asked me to marry him": *Boston Traveler*, "Mrs. Eaton Declares She Married Naval Officer to Save His Life."

251" ...to save his life," Jennie said softly: Sibley, "Six Hours under Fire"

252 "Yes, I had": *Boston Traveler*, "Mrs. Eaton Declares She Married Naval Officer to Save His Life."

252 "...realize his situation," she replied: Sibley, "Six Hours under Fire."

252 "...shortly after to the admiral": *Boston Traveler*, "Mrs. Eaton Declares She Married Naval Officer to Save His Life."

252 purchased in her name: Parker, "Eaton Gave $30,000 to Wife Then Lost It in Stock Deal."

252 "Wasn't it because he had lost money": Sibley, "Six Hours under Fire."

253 "...he guessed he would": *Boston Traveler*, "Mrs. Eaton Declares She Married Naval Officer to Save His Life."

253 "...he did give me thirty thousand dollars": Ibid.

254 "During the time..." "No, he didn't.": *Boston Traveler*, "Mrs. Eaton Declares She Married Naval Officer to Save His Life."

CHAPTER 28

256 "He did act rudely": *Boston Traveler*, "Mrs. Eaton Declares She Married Naval Officer to Save His Life."

256 "...all my troubles myself: Ibid.

257 "...affected my ankle: Parker, "Eaton Gave $30,000 to Wife Then Lost It in Stock Deal."

258 ...lest she frighten her: *Boston Traveler*, "Mrs. Eaton Declares She Married Naval Officer to Save His Life."

258 Jennie told Barker: Parker, "Eaton Gave $30,000 to Wife Then Lost It in Stock Deal."

258 "...know what he was doing": *Boston Traveler*, "Mrs. Eaton Declares She Married Naval Officer to Save His Life."

259 ...was an opium user: Sibley, "Six Hours under Fire.

259 "I went to Boston": Ibid.

260 "...and pretty dresses": Ibid.

260 "...visit us every Tuesday": Parker, "Eaton Gave $30,000 to Wife Then Lost It in Stock Deal."

260 ...which was in cubes: Sibley, "Six Hours under Fire."

260 "...that I didn't keep it": Parker, "Eaton Gave $30,000 to Wife Then Lost It in

Stock Deal."
261 "...live in the hospital," she declared: Sibley, "Six Hours under Fire."
261 "...the admiral take a drug?" asked Barker: Parker, "Eaton Gave $30,000 to Wife Then Lost It in Stock Deal."
261 "Pretty cute, wasn't he": Sibley, "Six Hours under Fire."
262 ...as frightened as Howard: Ibid.
262 "I got some medicine": Parker, "Eaton Gave $30,000 to Wife Then Lost It in Stock Deal."
262 Barker asked if the medicine: Sibley, "Six Hours under Fire."
263 ...jurors would convict her: Frank P. Sibley, "Jury to Get Case Today; Eaton Murder Trial Comes to Argument Stage; Defendant Maintains Story to End of Examination; Verdict of Guilty Not Looked for By Plymouth Public; Verdict of Guilty Not Expected." *The Boston Daily Globe*, October 29, 1913, 1.
263 "She is the most wonderful": Ibid.

CHAPTER 29

265 ...Barker's derision: Sibley, "Jury to Get Case Today."
266 "...asylum would be horrible": "Doctors Watch Mrs. Eaton as She Again Describes Death of Husband; Denies She Intended to Put Admiral in Asylum; 'Wanted Only Hospital Treatment;' Prosecution Concludes Examination at 12:08." *Boston Traveler and Evening Herald*, October 28, 1913, 1.
266 ...*By the way*: Sibley, "Jury to Get Case Today."
267 "...I still think he was lucky": Ibid.
267 "...a delightful trip": *Boston Traveler*, "Doctors Watch Mrs. Eaton as She Again Describes Death of Husband."
268 "...needed somebody with him": Ibid.
272 "I don't admit it": Ibid.
274 "...breaking down of the tissue": Sibley, "Jury to Get Case Today."
274 "...in four or five years," the physician acknowledged: Ibid.
275 "Had you talked with her": Charles E. Parker, "Mrs. Eaton May Know Her Fate by Tonight; Jury Expected to Get Case This Afternoon; Attorneys to Make Final Please This Morning; Prisoner All Smiles as Case Closes; Witnesses Deny Story Told by Mrs. Eaton About Baby's Death; Letter About Dorothy Feature of the Last Day's Testimony." *Boston Post*, October 29, 1913, 1.
276 "...while you were there?" "No": Ibid.
276 "What a lovely woman": Sibley, "Jury to Get Case Today."

CHAPTER 30

282 "...no relative of his has come forward": "Morse Says State Failed to Show Motive for Eaton Crime; Picture's Admiral's Wife as Wonderful, Self-Sacrificing, and Much-Wronged Woman; Case Expected to be Given to Jury Tonight." *Boston Traveler and Evening Herald*, October 29, 1913, 1.

282 "I'm very glad": Frank P. Sibley, "Plymouth Jury Finds Mrs. Eaton Not Guilty; Verdict Reached at 5:10 This Morning; Court Remained in Session during the Night; Deliberations on Case Begun at 7:42 Last Evening; Last Day of the Trial Occupied by Arguments and Charge." *The Boston Daily Globe*, extra edition, October 30, 1913, 1.

282 "The day the admiral brought in": *Boston Traveler*, "Morse Says State Failed to Show Motive for Eaton Crime."

283 "As I listened to their testimony": Ibid.

283 "...the lover in Chicago": Ibid.

284 "...the last days of his life": Sibley, "Plymouth Jury Finds Mrs. Eaton Not Guilty."

284 "I said when I first opened": *Boston Traveler*, "Morse Says State Failed to Show Motive for Eaton Crime."

284 "...her duty to the admiral": Ibid

284 "I am not obliged": Sibley, "Plymouth Jury Finds Mrs. Eaton Not Guilty."

285 "...it is a strong motive": Ibid.

285 "that she can't act": Ibid.

285 ..."constructed with the art": Ibid.

CHAPTER 31

287 "Mr. Morse appealed": Sibley, "Plymouth Jury Finds Mrs. Eaton Not Guilty."

287 "...my sworn duty": Ibid.

288 "If we fail": Ibid.

290 "...was losing its money": Ibid.

290 "They didn't dare ask": Ibid.

290 "...out to the woman in pity": "Mrs. Eaton Sobbed When She Heard Verdict 'Not Guilty;' The First Time She Had Shown Any Emotion since Arrest; Jury Reported at 5:30 O'clock Thursday Morning, After Having Been Deliberating for Nearly Nine Hours; Statement Issued." *Lewiston Evening Journal*, October 30, 1913, 1, 2.

291 "...Is it a hallucination": Sibley, "Plymouth Jury Finds Mrs. Eaton Not Guilty."

291 "...four years after the baby's death": "Barker Makes Powerful Plea; Asks God's Help for Prosecutor in Like Position." *The Brockton Times*, October 30, 1913, 2.

291 "You know and I know": Sibley, "Plymouth Jury Finds Mrs. Eaton Not Guilty."

292 "...after the admiral's death?": Ibid.

293 "...could have done it": Ibid.

293 "...of the time he died": "Mrs. Eaton Not Guilty; Jury Acquits Her of Murder of the Admiral; She Was Charged with Administering Poison; Jury Out Eight and Three-Quarters Hours." *Boston Evening Transcript*, October 30, 1913, 10.

293 "...cloud your eyes with": "Eaton Jury Deadlocked After All Night Session; Rumors Fly Thick and Fast as Hour after Hour Passes With No Sign of Verdict; Guesses That Jury Stands 8 to 4 for Acquittal Are Made; Remarkable Closing

Argument of District Attorney Barker Makes Impression on Jury; Mrs. Eaton Appears Confident During Long Wait That She Will Be Freed." *Boston Post*, October 30, 1913, 1.

293 "...the whole of the defense": *Lewiston Evening Journal*, "Mrs. Eaton Sobbed When She Heard Verdict 'Not Guilty.'"

293 "...that was required of him": Sibley, "Plymouth Jury Finds Mrs. Eaton Not Guilty."

293 "more dangerous than a rattlesnake": *Boston Evening Transcript*, "Mrs. Eaton Not Guilty."

293 "...to a grave in Dracut": Ibid.

294 "Look at that fifteen grains": Sibley, "Plymouth Jury Finds Mrs. Eaton Not Guilty."

294 "May God help you": *The Brockton Times*, "Barker Makes Powerful Plea."

294 "...shouted and gestured wildly": Sibley, "Plymouth Jury Finds Mrs. Eaton Not Guilty."

294 "With fire flashing": Charles E. Parker, "Jury Gets Case; Deliberations Start at 7:41 p.m. after Day of Arguments." *Boston Post*, October 30, 1913, 1.

295 "It has been said": Sibley, "Plymouth Jury Finds Mrs. Eaton Not Guilty."

298 "...satisfactory to others": Ibid.

CHAPTER 32

302 "I told you so": "Mrs. Eaton Found 'Not Guilty;' 'I Told You So,' Widow Cries; Verdict Announced at Daybreak after All Night Debate in Plymouth Court House." *Boston Traveler and Evening Herald*, October 30, 1913, 1.

302 "You did it": Dick Sears, "Sears Tells of Drama as Verdict Came." *Boston American*, October 30, 1913, 10.

302 ...gently closed the door: *Boston Traveler*, "Mrs. Eaton Found 'Not Guilty.'"

303 "...sorrows of the one now gone": *Boston American*, "Sears Tells of Drama."

304 "...remain a mystery": "Jury Finds That Mrs. Eaton is Not Guilty of Murder." *Meriden Morning Record*, October 31, 1913, 10.

304 "...this woman was innocent": "'Never Had Any Doubt,' Says Morse." *Boston American*, October 30, 1913, 10.

304 "...care for Jennie": "'Two Promises Kept,' Says Judge Kelley; Significant Comment by Eaton Lawyer on Woman's Acquittal." *Boston American*, October 30, 1913, 10.

305 "...those I love and who love me": Solita Solano, "Mrs. Eaton Plans 'To Fight It Out;' 'I'm Going Home, Keep Chickens and Bees, Make Money and Try to Add to Others' Happiness,' She Declares." *Boston Traveler and Evening Herald*, October 30, 1913, 1.

305 "...I can add any more": "Prayer Answered, Says Mrs. Keyes; Daughter of Mrs. Eaton Told by Reporter of Mother's Acquittal." *Boston Traveler and Evening Herald*, October 30, 1913, 1.

305 ...surprised at the outcome: *Boston American*, "'Never Had Any Doubt.'"

306 "That is all": Ibid.

306 ...who surrounded them: *Boston Traveler*, "Mrs. Eaton Found 'Not Guilty.'"

307 "...forget this case entirely": *Boston Traveler*, "Mrs. Eaton Found 'Not Guilty.'"

307 ...the poison that killed the admiral: "Favored Woman on First Ballot." *Boston American*, October 30, 1913, 10.

307 ...comment further on the issue: "Three on Eaton Jury Fought to Convict; Secrets of Nine-Hour Session Leak Out; Declared Woman Is Sane Despite Judge Aiken's Instructions." *Boston Post*, October 31, 1913, 1.

307 ...in reaching their decision: *Boston American*, "Favored Woman."

308 "...in his widow's favor": "Juror Murphy Home; Was Convinced of Mrs. Eaton's Innocence, He Says." *The Brockton Times*, October 30, 1913, 2.

308 ...of the murder charge: *Boston Post*, "Three on Eaton Jury Fought to Convict."

308 "...received from the judge": "Says Charges of Judge Respected; Eaton Jurymen Deny Considering Insanity First." *The Brockton Times*, November 1, 1913, 9.

308 "I am very tired": "Happy Reunion at Assinippi; Jury's Verdict Brings Fourfold Joy; Mother's Fervent 'Thank God' Greets Mrs. Eaton; Dorothy and June Both at Homecoming." *The Boston Daily Globe*, October 31, 1913, 10.

309 "...glad it's all over": Ibid.

309 "...in their happiness": Ibid.

EPILOGUE

310 ...property back to her: Plymouth County Registry of Deeds, Plymouth, MA; Land Records, book 1282, page 256, November 13, 1913.

310 ...experts who had testified at trial: "Asks State to Reimburse Her." *Fitchburg Daily Sentinel*, December 6, 1913, 12.

310 "great and needless expense": Ibid.

310 "An Act to Authorize: "State Can't Pay Mrs. Eaton; Governor Foss So Informs Her on Request for Reimbursement for Expenses of Her Defense; She May Invoke New Law to Compensate Persons Unjustly Accused." *Boston Evening Transcript*, December 6, 1913, 8.

310 ...generally limited to $500: Ibid.

311 "The Vampire of the City," "Clothes or the Girl, Which?": *The Syracuse Herald*, "Rear Admiral Eaton Poisoned."

311 "Love of a Man": Osgood, "The Admiral Eaton Case."

311 ...affair with her husband: "How Will Mrs. Mohr Capitalize Her Publicity? Provided, of Course, the Jury Finds Her Innocent of the Murder for Which She Has Been Indicted." *The Washington Herald* [Washington, DC], October 24, 1915, Feature Section.

312 "...this relic of barbarism?": "'Literature' as First Aid to the White Light;' A New 'Tropical Idyl' Type of Romance Springs from Pen of Mrs. Jeanie [sic] Eaton, Sensational Murder Trial Heroine." *The Washington Herald* [Washington, DC], September 26, 1915, Feature Section.

312 In December 1913: "Eaton Family is Broken Up Again; Mother of Admiral's Widow Comes to Washington To Live with Another Daughter." *The Washington Times* [Washington, DC], December 7, 1913, 8.

313 She died at Gertrude's: Government of the District of Columbia, Department of Health, Certificate of Death #249656, Virginia Harrison, December 20, 1918.

313 In March 1914: "Mrs. Eaton Sails with Daughters for Norfolk; Woman Acquitted of Murder of Husband Goes South." *The Boston Herald*, March 23, 1914, 14.

313 ...a brief marriage ceremony: "District of Columbia Marriages, 1811-1950," D. Henry Ainsworth and Jannie [*sic*] M. Eaton, 1914.

313 "Won't you tell us": "Widow of Late Admiral Eaton Again Weds D. H. Ainsworth." *Olean Evening Herald*, June 4, 1914, 2.

313 ...returned to Assinippi: Ibid.

313 In late October 1914: "Sees Admiral's Ghost; Witness in Eaton Trial on Verge of Breakdown." *The Frederick Post*, October 26, 1914, 1.

314 ...on the steps of an abandoned grocery store: "Eatons Worried by June Keyes's Strange Actions." *Boston Sunday Herald*, October 25, 1914, 1.

314 ...filed for divorce from June: "Keyes Asks Divorce, Alleging Desertion." *The Boston Daily Globe*, May 4, 1916, 15. Also, "Asks Divorce From Daughter of Mrs. Eaton." *The Boston Herald*, May 4, 1916, 8. Also, Libel for Divorce, Number 10455, filed March 31, 1916, Middlesex Superior Court, Cambridge, MA.

314 ...leave the state and never return: "Husband Will Again Leave Mrs. Eaton." *The Boston Herald*, February 15, 1917, 8.

314 "I suppose I made": "Admiral Eaton's Widow to Seek another Divorce – Remarried to Ainsworth, She Will Sue to Recover Her Liberty Once More." *The Boston Herald*, April 21, 1917, 11.

314 Jennie filed for divorce: Ibid.

314 ...with his brother: *Boyd's Directory of the District of Columbia – 1920, Washington, DC*, R. L. Polk & Co., 1920, 10.

315 Copper Company in Arizona: "Dan Ainsworth, Pioneer Miner, Dies Suddenly." *The Arizona Republican* [Phoenix, AZ], November 23, 1922, page 5.

315 O'Connell dismissed his case: Criminal Docket of Plymouth Superior Court, 1917-1918, October Sitting, Appeal 6978 (Records in custody of Plymouth Superior Court Clerk Magistrate, Plymouth, MA).

315 ...specter of the admiral's face: "June Keyes, In Eaton Case, Now Insane – In House, Where Admiral Died, She Imagines She Sees Man Mother was Accused of Killing." *Boston Evening American*, February 11, 1917, 1.

315 She told Jennie: Osgood, "The Admiral Eaton Case."

315 Taunton State Hospital: "Daughter of Eaton's Widow Goes to Asylum; Mrs. June Ainsworth Keyes, Who Was Living with Mother Since Trial, Placed in Taunton State Hospital on Complaint of Parent, Who Declines to Be Responsible." *The Boston Herald*, February 11, 1917, 1.

315 In April, the *Herald*: "Admiral Eaton's Widow Takes June from Asylum; Moves Mrs. Keyes to Her Home, Fearing for Her Health." *The Boston Herald*, April 27, 1917.

315 ...Jennie sold the Assinippi farm: Plymouth County Registry of Deeds, Plymouth, MA; Land Records, book 1282, page 257.

315 ...under her maiden name, Harrison: Madison Town Clerk, Madison, CT, Land Records, volume 33, page 310 (Caroline Pfeiffer to Jennie M. Harrison, June 19, 1917).

315 Dorothy married: New York City Municipal Archives, State of New York, Certificate and Registration of Marriage #2775, June 30, 1917.

316 Dorchester neighborhood: 1920 United States Federal Census: Census Place: Boston Ward 20, Suffolk, Massachusetts; roll: T625_738; page: 33B; enumeration district: 498.

316 June's baby, a boy: "Infant Left on Doctor's Doorsteps; Typed Note Suggests Child Would Make Fine Lawyer; Brookline Physician Turns Baby Over to Officials." *The Boston Daily Globe*, September 14, 1917, 6.

316 ...unrelated to his abandonment: *The Syracuse Herald*, "Rear Admiral Eaton Poisoned."

317 "...face another scandal": "Governor Signs Extradition Papers; Mrs. Ainsworth to Go Back to Massachusetts; Wants to Save Dorothy." *The Hartford Courant*, January 17, 1918, 10.

317 "...do the same thing again": "Child Gave Clue That Led to Arrest of Mrs. Ainsworth; Baby Eleanor, Who Told Story Which Brought about Her Grandmother's Arrest; Little Girl Told of Disappearance of Baby Brother to Madison Folks and Abandonment of Insane Woman's Infant, Then Came Home to Family; Mrs. Ainsworth under Guard and Insane Daughter Locked in House While Other Crippled Daughter is under Arrest in Massachusetts; Tragedy Woven In All Their Lives." *The Hartford Courant*, January 16, 1918, 1.

318 ...on Dr. Bowditch's doorstep: Ibid.

318 ...case was ultimately dropped: "Plead Guilty of Abandoning Baby; Sentence of Mrs. Ainsworth and Daughter Deferred; Women Allowed to Return to June Keyes, Who is Reported Dying." *The Boston Daily Globe*, April 18, 1918, 11.

318 Jennie sold the Madison property: Madison Town Clerk, Madison, CT, Land Records, volume 38, page 30 (Jennie M. Harrison to Mabel Chittenden, August 22, 1919).

318 They reunited: *Boyd's Directory of the District of Columbia – 1920, Washington, DC*, R. L. Polk & Co., 1924, 237. (*U.S. City Directories, 1821-1989-Washington DC City Directory, 1924*).

318 ...on New Jersey Avenue: 1920 United States Federal Census: Census Place: Washington, Washington, District of Columbia; roll: T625_209; page: 9A; enumeration district: 133.

318 ...a Washington psychiatric facility: *The Syracuse Herald*, "Rear Admiral Eaton Poisoned."

318 ...second child, a daughter: Massachusetts Bureau of Vital Records and Statistics, Boston, MA. Births, Boston, 1921, volume 1, page 180.

318 The U. S. Customs Service appointed: "William B. McMahon, Immigration

Officer, Died Thursday." *Chateaugay Record and Franklin County Democrat*, 3 Apr 1958, 1.

318 In the early morning: "Wife of Immigration Inspector Killed in Crackup; Fails to Make Curve, Smashes into Pole, Tree." *Plattsburgh Press-Republican*, June 17, 1957, page 3.

319 Dorothy's husband died: *Chateaugay Record and Franklin County Democrat*, "William B. McMahon, Immigration Officer, Died Thursday."

319 buried in a family plot: Washington Street Cemetery, Norwell, MA. Cemetery records; Joseph Eaton plot, section A-7.

319 By 1937, Harry and Jennie: Department of Veteran Affairs, Regional Office, Federal Building, Baltimore, MD 20201. VA File #XC-02-726-440. Veteran Records of Rear Admiral (Retired) Joseph Giles Eaton.

319 Harry died of pneumonia: Government of the District of Columbia, Department of Health, Certificate of Death #389156, Daniel H. Ainsworth, October 28, 1937.

319 Jennie found herself destitute: Department of Veteran Affairs, Regional Office, Federal Building, Baltimore, MD 20201. VA File #XC-02-726-440. Veteran Records of Rear Admiral (Retired) Joseph Giles Eaton.

319 *My dear Mr. McIntyre*: Ibid

321 …rate permitted by law: Ibid.

322 …increases in her benefits during the next twenty years: Ibid.

322 On March 1, 1944: Ibid.

322 Legislation passed in January: Ibid.

322 …a total monthly income of $121.: ($121 was the equivalent of $300 in today's dollars): Measuring Worth. www.measuringworth.com.

322 Jennie fell while walking: Department of Veteran Affairs, Regional Office, Federal Building, Baltimore, MD 20201. VA File #XC-02-726 440. Veteran Records of Rear Admiral (Retired) Joseph Giles Eaton.

322 On January 27, 1959: Government of the District of Columbia, Department of Health, Certificate of Death #59-744, Jennie E. Ainsworth, January 27, 1959.

322 Following a funeral: "Died." *The Washington Post and Times Herald*, January 28, 1959.

322 Jennie's grave is not marked: Government of the District of Columbia, Department of Health, Certificate of Death #59-744, Jennie E. Ainsworth, January 27, 1959.

322 Dr. Gilman Osgood shared his opinion: Osgood, "The Admiral Eaton Case."

324 "…in criminal cases": Rogers, *Murder and the Death Penalty in Massachusetts*, 50-52.

324 Osgood praised the Briggs law: Osgood, "The Admiral Eaton Case."

JOHN F. GALLAGHER

Bibliography

Bacon, Edwin Monroe. *The Book of Boston: Fifty Years' Recollections of the New England Metropolis.* Boston: Book of Boston Co., 1916.

Barker, Barbara U., and Molyneaux, Leslie J. *Images of America: Hanover.* Charleston, SC: Arcadia Publishing, 2004.

Blum, Deborah. *The Poisoner's Handbook: Murder and the Birth of Forensic Medicine in Jazz Age New York.* New York: The Penguin Press, 2010.

Bridgman, A. M. *A Souvenir of Massachusetts Legislators, 1896,* Volume V. Stoughton, MA: A. M. Bridgman, 1896.

Cheney, Frank, and Sammarco, Anthony Mitchell. *Images of America: When Boston Rode the El.* Charleston, SC: Arcadia Books, 2000.

Dwelley, Jedediah, and Simmons, John F. *A History of the Town of Hanover, Massachusetts with Family Genealogies.* Hanover, MA: Town of Hanover, 1910.

Eaton, J. G., Captain. *The Last Exploit of Old Ironsides. The United Service: A Monthly Review of Military and Naval Affairs.* Volume 1, Third Series, 1902.

Eaton, J. Giles. *Perry's Victory on Lake Erie.* Boston: Houghton, Mifflin & Co., 1901. [Military Historical Society of Massachusetts. Papers, Volume 11, No. 7].

Eaton, J. Giles. *The Chesapeake and the Shannon.* Boston: Houghton, Mifflin & Co., 1901. [Military Historical Society of Massachusetts. Papers, Volume 11, No. 6].

Emsley, John. *The Elements of Murder: A History of Poison.* New York: Oxford University Press, 2005.

Green, Samuel Abbott. *Groton Historical Series: A Collection of Papers Relating to the History of the Town of Groton, Massachusetts.* Volume IV. Groton, MA: University Press, 1899.

Hamersly, Lewis Randolph. *The Records of Living Officers of the U. S. Navy and Marine Corps, Compiled from Official Sources.* 5th ed. Philadelphia: L. R. Hamersly and Co., 1894.

357

BIBLIOGRAPHY

Hanover Historical Society, under the direction of Fanny Hitchcock Phillips. *History of the Town of Hanover, Massachusetts, 1910-1977*. Hanover, MA: Hanover Historical Society, 1977.

Herold, Justin, A.M., M.D. *A Manual of Legal Medicine for the Use of Practitioners and Students of Medicine and Law*. Philadelphia: J. P. Lippincott Co., 1902.

James, Frank L., PhD., M.D., and Ohmann-Dumesnil, A. H., A.M., M.D. "Medical Progress-Therapeutics: Remarks upon Gold in Therapy." *St. Louis Medical and Surgical Journal*. Vol. 69. St. Louis: St. Louis Medical and Surgical Journal Publishing Company, 1895.

Kenny, Herbert A. *Newspaper Row: Journalism in the Pre-Television Era*. Chester, CT: The Globe Pequot Press, 1987.

Krafft-Ebing, Richard, M.D. *Textbook of Insanity – Based on Clinical Observations – For Practitioners and Students of Medicine*. Philadelphia: F. A. Davis Co., 1905.

Long, John D. *The New American Navy*. London: Grant Richards, 1904.

Marquis, Albert Nelson. *Who's Who in New England – A Biographical Dictionary of Leading Living Men and Women of the States of Maine, New Hampshire, Vermont, Massachusetts, Rhode Island and Connecticut*. 2nd ed. Chicago: A. N. Marquis & Co., 1916.

Marquis, Albert Nelson. *Who's Who in New England: A Biographical Dictionary of Leading Living Men and Women of the States of Maine, New Hampshire, Vermont, Massachusetts, Rhode Island and Connecticut*. 1st ed. Chicago: A. N. Marquis and Company, 1909.

McAdie, Alexander, and Pickering, Edward Charles. "Observations and Investigations Made at the Blue Hill Meteorological Observatory, in the Years 1911, 1912, 1913, and 1914, under the Direction of Alexander McAdie," *Annals of the Astronomical Observatory of Harvard College*, Volume 73, Part 2. Cambridge, MA: Published by the Observatory, 1915.

McCullough, David G. *The Path Between the Seas – The Creation of the Panama Canal 1870-1914*. New York: Simon & Schuster, 1977.

Morris, John E. *The Bontecou Genealogy: A Record of the Descendants of Pierre Bontecou, a Huguenot Refugee from France in the Lines of His Sons*. Hartford, CT: Press of Case, Lockwood, and Brainard Company, 1885.

Owen, Thomas McAdory, L.L.D. *History of Alabama and Dictionary of Alabama*

Biography. Vol. III. Chicago: S. J. Clarke Publishing Co., 1921.

Park, Benjamin. *The United States Naval Academy: Being the Yarn of the American Midshipman (Naval Cadet)*. New York: G. P. Putnam's Sons, 1900.

Peel, Robert. *Mary Baker Eddy: Year of Authority*. New York: Holt, Rinehart and Winston, 1977.

Pendergast, John. *Images of America: Dracut*. Charleston, SC: Arcadia Publishing Company, 1997.

Ringer, Sidney, M.D., F.R.S., and Sainsbury, Harrington, M.D., F.R.S. *A Handbook of Therapeutics*. 13th ed. New York: William Wood and Co., 1897.

Rogers, Alan. *Murder and the Death Penalty in Massachusetts*. Boston: University of Massachusetts Press, 2008.

Scott, Gini Graham. *American Murder: Homicide in the Early 20th Century*. Westport, CT: Praeger Publishers, 2007.

Sleeper, Rev. Frank Braman. "Fifty Years of Probation Work in Massachusetts." *The Massachusetts Magazine: Devoted to Massachusetts History, Genealogy, and Biography*, Volume 1, Number 4. Salem, MA: The Salem Press Company, 1908.

Titherington, Richard H. *A History of the Spanish-American War of 1898*. New York: D. Appleton and Company, 1900.

Varnum, John Marshall. *The Varnums of Dracutt (in Massachusetts), a History*. Boston: David Clapp & Sons, 1907.

Watson, Katherine. *Poisoned Lives: English Pioneers and their Victims*. London: Hambledon Continuum, 2004.

CPSIA information can be obtained at www.ICGtesting.com
Printed in the USA
LVOW05s1612081014

407869LV00019B/955/P

9 781937 588380